The Changing Legal Orders in Hong Kong and Mainland China

# The Changing Legal Orders in Hong Kong and Mainland China

## Essays on "One Country, Two Systems"

*Albert H.Y. Chen*

香港城市大學出版社
City University of Hong Kong Press

ISBN: 978-962-937-450-1

Published by
City University of Hong Kong Press
Tat Chee Avenue
Kowloon, Hong Kong
Website: www.cityu.edu.hk/upress
E-mail: upress@cityu.edu.hk

Printed in Hong Kong

*I dedicate this book to my wife, Vanessa,*
*without whose loving and unfailing support over the years*
*this work would not have been possible.*

# *Table of Contents*


*Preface* ..... ix
*About the Author* ..... xv
*Acronyms and Abbreviations* ..... xvii

*Part I* *The Practice of "One Country, Two Systems"*

Chapter 1 The Rule of Law under "One Country, Two Systems" ..... 3
Chapter 2 The Law and Politics of Constitutional Reform and Democratisation in Hong Kong ..... 31
Chapter 3 The Theory and Practice of Autonomy: The Case of Hong Kong ..... 57
Chapter 4 Social Movements and the Law in Post-Colonial Hong Kong ..... 87
Chapter 5 A Perfect Storm: Hong Kong-Mainland China Rendition of Fugitive Offenders ..... 117

*Part II* *Tradition and Modernity in Chinese Law*

Chapter 6 Confucian Legal Culture and its Modern Fate ..... 133
Chapter 7 Three Political Confucianisms and Half a Century ..... 167
Chapter 8 Chinese Cultural Tradition and Modern Human Rights ..... 193
Chapter 9 Legal Thought and Development in the People's Republic of China ..... 203
Chapter 10 Socialist Law, Civil Law, Common Law, and the Classification of Contemporary Chinese Law ..... 237
Chapter 11 The Law of Property and the Evolving System of Property Rights in China ..... 265
Chapter 12 Socio-legal Thought and Legal Modernisation in Contemporary China: A Case Study of the Jurisprudence of Zhu Suli ..... 303

*Part III* *Constitutionalism in Asia*

Chapter 13 Constitutions, Constitutional Practice, and Constitutionalism in East Asia 335

Chapter 14 Five Decades of Constitutional Change in Hong Kong and East Asia 363

*Epilogue* 385

*Selected Bibliography* 413

# *Preface*

The works selected for publication in this volume represent the three major dimensions of my academic inquiry since I began my teaching career at the Department of Law, University of Hong Kong in February 1984. Most of the selected works were previously published as chapters in various books edited by other scholars. As I have not previously published any English book that consolidates my writings on "One Country, Two Systems" (OCTS) and my study of public law in Hong Kong, mainland China, and Asia over the last 36 years, it is hoped that this volume will make the works concerned more easily accessible to both local and international audiences. This book is divided into three parts: (1) the practice of OCTS; (2) tradition and modernity in Chinese law; and (3) constitutionalism in Asia. These are the three major domains of my research since I began my academic career.

Part I of this volume includes five chapters related to the practice of OCTS. This is a field of research I embarked on when I first began my academic career in 1984. This was the same year in which the Sino-British Joint Declaration was signed. As the only local Chinese member of the academic staff of the Faculty of Law at that time (all other law teachers at the University of Hong Kong being expatriates), I considered it my mission to research the constitutional and legal issues faced by Hong Kong in its era of transition leading up to the handover in 1997, including concerns that arose during the drafting of the Basic Law of the Hong Kong Special Administrative Region (HKSAR) that would be established. Most of my writings in the 1980s were, therefore, focused on such issues.

Hong Kong constitutional law, the Basic Law, and the jurisprudence of OCTS continued to be a main area of my research in the 1990s and in the post-1997 era. In my writings (in both English and Chinese), I tried to document and provide commentary and analysis on major constitutional developments and leading constitutional law cases decided by the Hong Kong courts since the HKSAR was established in 1997. My research orientation is based on what I believe to be a balanced approach to the study of OCTS, taking into account both the "sovereignty" claims of the Central Government in Beijing and the "autonomy" and "democracy" aspirations of the people of Hong Kong, and aiming at an objective study of relevant legal developments.

**Chapter 1** of this volume introduces the constitutional and legal issues arising from the practice of OCTS in the HKSAR by reviewing key developments from the time of the establishment of the HKSAR in 1997 to the close of the first decade of the twenty-first century. It covers major episodes such as the "right of abode" controversy that led to the first ever interpretation of the Hong Kong Basic Law by the National People's Congress Standing Committee (NPCSC) and the failed attempt to implement article 23 of the Basic Law. **Chapter 2** reviews the development of Hong Kong's political system since colonial times and analyses the political, constitutional, and legal controversies that culminated in the "Occupy Central Movement" of 2014. The OCTS model was premised on the "high degree of autonomy" the HKSAR was promised by the Sino-British Joint Declaration of 1984. Thus, **Chapter 3** studies various aspects and elements of the autonomy enjoyed by the HKSAR under the Basic Law in the context of general theories and considerations of autonomy as an internationally prevalent constitutional arrangement. **Chapter 4** looks at the complex relationship between law and social movements both as a matter of general theory and in the context of the HKSAR. Finally, **Chapter 5** brings readers up-to-date by discussing the Anti-Extradition Bill Movement of 2019, which brought about the most serious challenge for OCTS to date.

Part II of this volume includes seven chapters focusing on tradition and modernity in Chinese law. The study of the mainland Chinese legal system and of Chinese legal modernisation from a comparative law perspective was a field of research I began to venture into in the early 1990s. My postgraduate study at Harvard Law School was in the discipline of comparative law, and I believed I was well-equipped to study Chinese law from a comparative law perspective. My research interest in Chinese law was partly an extension of my research interest in the Hong Kong Basic Law and the jurisprudence of OCTS. I came to understand that Hong Kong's reunification with China in 1997 meant that legal scholarship in Hong Kong, which traditionally had focused on Hong Kong and common law legal developments, should expand its horizons to look into the legal system in mainland China.

Since the era of "reform and opening" began in China in 1979, legal reforms were being introduced at a rapid pace. I believed that Hong Kong, being an English-speaking jurisdiction and well-linked to the international scholarly community, had a special role to play in developing and promoting the study of Chinese law from a comparative law perspective. Hong Kong could serve as a bridge for facilitating understanding of Chinese legal developments by the international community, on the one hand, and for introducing Western legal knowledge into China, on the other hand.

In the early 1990s, there was no book in English that provided a systematic and comprehensive description and analysis of the contemporary Chinese legal system. This was the research gap I intended to fill when I published my book on the Chinese legal system in 1992. The fifth edition of this book was published in 2018. Since the initial publication of the book, I have also published on major legal developments (including institutional and doctrinal developments) and trends of legal thinking and legal policy in contemporary China. As in the case of my work on OCTS, my scholarship in Chinese law is also based on a balanced approach that takes into account the significant progress that has been made in post-Mao Chinese legal reforms as well as the weaknesses, deficiencies, and limitations in the existing Chinese legal system from the perspectives of the Rule of Law and human rights.

I have also attempted to view developments in contemporary Chinese law from the perspective of Chinese legal modernisation, or the transition of Chinese law from traditional to modern. My work in this domain investigates the relationship between legal phenomena in contemporary China and the long history of traditional Chinese Confucian and Legalist thought. I believe that at this present stage of the development of the Chinese legal system, there is much which China can and should learn from Western philosophies of liberalism, Rule of Law, human rights, constitutionalism, and civil society. Thus, I have spent time in multiple Chinese publications discussing the relevance of Western legal and political philosophy to contemporary China and to its legal modernisation. I have also written in both Chinese and English about exploring Chinese cultural traditions (particularly the Confucian tradition) and how they relate to current issues of Chinese legal and political reforms. This work elaborates on how a synthesis of Confucianism, liberalism, and constitutionalism might be achievable and desirable.

A total of seven chapters have been selected to highlight the primary aspects of my exploration of tradition and modernity in Chinese law. These can be divided into two groups. The first group (Chapters 6, 7, and 8) studies the Chinese legal tradition and the challenge of modernity. **Chapter 6** introduces traditional Chinese legal thought and practice, including Confucianism and Legalism. **Chapter 7** discusses three strands of "political Confucianism" (Confucianism as applied to political philosophy) in twentieth century China and compares and contrasts the more liberal line of thought with strands that are more politically conservative (in terms of their affinity with one-party rule). **Chapter 8** explores the relationship between Chinese legal tradition and modern human rights thinking, and argues that this is not completely different from the relationship between Western legal tradition and modern human rights, in the sense that there co-exist elements in the tradition that are contrary to and compatible with human rights thinking.

The next group of chapters (Chapters 9–12) investigates the developing legal system of contemporary China from four different perspectives. **Chapter 9** adopts a historical approach and analyses the different periods of legal thought and legal practice in the history of the People's Republic of China (PRC). **Chapter 10** draws on the perspective of comparative law and considers the significant extent to which contemporary Chinese law has been shaped by the Soviet Socialist tradition and the Continental European tradition. **Chapter 11** studies the developing Chinese property law as an important system of legal protection of private property rights for the purpose of economic development. Finally, **Chapter 12** views the legal modernisation of China from a sociological perspective and comments on the work of Zhu Suli, a leading scholar of law and society in contemporary China.

In the mid-2000s, I decided to broaden my comparative law studies to include constitutional law and developments in Taiwan, East Asia, and Southeast Asia. This expansion of my focus was largely because I came to realise that the case of China, which I had been studying for two decades at this point, was merely one among many Asian countries in search of legal modernisation and the constitutionalisation of politics. To achieve a better understanding of the current stage of development of the Chinese legal system and its possible future, it became necessary (and useful) to take into account the constitutional and legal trajectories of China's neigbhours in East and Southeast Asia.

The two chapters in Part III of this volume exemplify my work in the domain of constitutionalism in Asia. **Chapter 13** provides a comparative study of constitutionalism and constitutional practice in East Asia and develops a four-fold typology. **Chapter 14** surveys, from a "macro-historical" perspective and using the "lens of constitutionalism", the far-reaching constitutional changes in five East Asian jurisdictions in the last five decades. The chapter is the text of a public lecture I delivered on 15 March 2019 as part of the lecture series organised by our law school to celebrate the 50th anniversary of its founding. It concludes with a certain degree of cautious optimism regarding the globalisation of constitutional values and the possibility of progress in human history.

Overall, this book integrates my work on three sectors — Hong Kong, mainland China, and Asia at large — to give a broad view of the changing legal orders across the region. While each chapter focuses on a particular aspect, when viewed together, the connection between sectors is discernible. In the Epilogue, I set out some concluding reflections on the main themes of this book. While the text of the original publication has been edited to enhance the flow, reduce repetition between chapters, and ensure consistent formatting, the use of pinyin or Chinese characters (as the case may be) is maintained as used in the original. I have also made minor revisions to update the information and footnote references as necessary.

According to Buddhist philosophy, everything that happens in this world is the outcome of the co-dependent arising of a particular set of conditions or circumstances. This book would not have been published but for the steadfast support and encouragement of Professor Zhu Guobin, Professor of Law and Director of the City University of Hong Kong Press, and the dedicated work of Dr Abby Manthey, Editor, and her colleagues at the Press. I am immensely grateful to them all. I also acknowledge with gratitude the permission of the relevant publishers to use previously published works of mine in this volume. These are indicated at the end of each respective chapter.

Albert H.Y. Chen
*Faculty of Law, The University of Hong Kong*
January 2021

# *About the Author*

Albert H.Y. Chen (陳弘毅) was born in and grew up in Hong Kong. He graduated from the Bachelor of Laws programme at the University of Hong Kong in 1980 and obtained a Postgraduate Certificate in Laws there in 1981. He then undertook postgraduate study in comparative law and theories of law and development at Harvard University and was awarded a Master of Laws degree in 1982. Between 1982 and 1984, he worked in a solicitors' firm in Hong Kong, and in 1984, he became qualified to practise as a solicitor.

In February 1984, Chen began his academic career as a Lecturer in Law at the University of Hong Kong. He served as Head of the Department of Law in 1993–1996 and as Dean of the Faculty of Law in 1996–2002. He is currently the Cheng Chan Lan Yue Professor in Constitutional Law in the Department of Law.

Professor Chen has, over the years, taught the subjects of legal system and legal method, constitutional law, administrative law, law and society, jurisprudence, the legal system of the People's Republic of China, Rule of Law in modern China, research methodology, and the use of Chinese in law. In addition to the present work and over 200 journal articles and book chapters in English and Chinese, he has written the following books: *Hong Kong's Legal System and the Basic Law* (1986) (in Chinese); *Human Rights and the Rule of Law: The Challenges of Hong Kong's Transition* (1987) (in Chinese, co-authored); *The Workers' Compensation System in Hong Kong* (1987) (co-authored); *Law and Politics in Hong Kong* (1990) (in Chinese); *The Rule of Law, Enlightenment and the Spirit of Modern Law* (1998) (in Chinese); *The World of Legal Theory* (2003) (in Chinese); *Hong Kong's Search for the Rule of Law under "One Country, Two Systems"* (2010) (in Chinese); and *The World of Constitutional Jurisprudence* (2014) (in Chinese). He is also a co-editor or editor of several books in English and Chinese, including *The Basic Law and Hong Kong's Future* (1988); *General Principles of Hong Kong Law* (3rd Edition, 2015) (in Chinese); *Administrative Law and Governance in Asia* (2009); *Legal Reforms in China and Vietnam* (2010); *Public Law in East Asia* (2013); *Constitutionalism in Asia in the Early Twenty-First Century* (2014); *Perspectives on the Hong Kong Basic Law* (2015) (in Chinese); and *Constitutional Courts in Asia* (2018).

Professor Chen is currently a member of the Hong Kong Basic Law Committee under China's National People's Congress Standing Committee (NPCSC) (a position which he has held since 1997) and a Justice of the Peace. He is an honorary professor at several universities in mainland China and a member of the Academic Advisory Committee of the Institute of Law of the Academia Sinica, Taipei. He is also Associate Editor of *Hong Kong Law Journal* and a member of the editorial or advisory boards of several other journals published in Hong Kong, mainland China, Taiwan, and overseas, including the *China Review*, *Journal of Comparative Law*, *Legal Studies*, *Transnational Legal Theory*, *Chinese Journal of Comparative Law*, *Asian Journal of Law and Society*, *Asian Journal of Comparative Law*, and *National Taiwan University Law Review*.

# *Acronyms and Abbreviations*

| | |
|---|---|
| BGB | *Bürgerliches Gesetzbuch* (German Civil Code) |
| BORO | Hong Kong Bill of Rights Ordinance |
| BPCL | Basic Principles of Civil Legislation |
| CCDI | Central Commission for Disciplinary Inspection |
| CCP | Chinese Communist Party |
| CFA | Court of Final Appeal |
| CGJ | Council of Grand Justices |
| CORL | *Chengbao* Operational Right in Land |
| ExCo | Hong Kong's Executive Council |
| FOO | Fugitive Offenders Ordinance |
| GL | Guarantee Law |
| GPCL | General Principles of Civil Law |
| HKSAR | Hong Kong Special Administrative Region |
| ICCPR | International Covenant on Civil and Political Rights |
| ICESCR | International Covenant on Economic, Social and Cultural Rights |
| KMT | Kuomintang |
| LAL | Land Administration Law |
| LAURE | Law on the Administration of Urban Real Estate |
| LegCo | Hong Kong's Legislative Council |
| LP | Law of Property |
| LRLC | Law of Rural Land Contracts |
| MLAO | Mutual Legal Assistance in Criminal Matters Ordinance |
| NPC | National People's Congress |
| NPCSC | National People's Congress Standing Committee |
| NSC | National Supervisory Commission |
| NSL | Law of the PRC on Safeguarding National Security in the HKSAR |
| OCTS | One Country, Two Systems |
| PLC | Provisional Legislative Council |
| ROC | Republic of China |
| PRC | People's Republic of China |
| PRCT | Provisional Regulations on the Grant and Transfer of the Right to Use State-owned Land in Cities and Towns |

| | |
|---|---|
| RSFSR | Russian Socialist Federal Soviet Republic |
| RUCL | Right to Use Construction Land |
| RUHS | Right to Use Land for House Sites |
| SAR | Special Administrative Region |
| SARS | severe acute respiratory syndrome, or atypical pneumonia |
| USSR | Union of Soviet Socialist Republics (the Soviet Union) |
| WTO | World Trade Organization |

# Part I

## The Practice of "One Country, Two Systems"

# 1

# The Rule of Law Under "One Country, Two Systems"

## INTRODUCTION

The transplant of English common law to, as well as the development of a set of legal institutions that supported the Rule of Law in, Hong Kong is one of the major legacies of British colonial rule in Hong Kong. When the Sino-British Joint Declaration was signed in 1984 and Hong Kong began to prepare itself for reunification with the motherland in 1997, there were concerns about the possible deterioration of standards of the Rule of Law and of civil liberties in Hong Kong after the handover. It was generally recognised that one of the crucial tests for whether the "One Country, Two Systems" (OCTS) model works would be whether the Rule of Law could be maintained in Hong Kong after 1997.

Paradoxically, the practice of OCTS is itself dependent on a particular kind of Rule of Law — that which is practiced with regard to the Basic Law of the Hong Kong Special Administrative Region (HKSAR) — the "mini-constitution" enacted by the National People's Congress (NPC) of the People's Republic of China (PRC) in 1990 that came into effect in 1997 as the constitutional instrument of the HKSAR of the PRC. Would the Basic Law, which embodies the grand promises made by the PRC Government in the text of the Joint Declaration regarding how the HKSAR would be administered, be faithfully implemented by the Chinese authorities? Would Hong Kong be able to practice autonomy (with "Hong Kong people ruling Hong Kong") while evolving a higher degree of democracy than ever before, and ensure the protection of human rights and property rights under the Rule of Law? Would the Rule of Law continue to contribute to Hong Kong's economic prosperity and continue to safeguard it as a free, pluralistic, and open society as well as an international city?

This chapter seeks to provide a basis for answering these questions by reviewing the legal and constitutional history of the HKSAR since its establishment in 1997. It focuses on what the author considers to be the most important events, cases, and developments, and divides the legal history of the HKSAR so far into four periods.

## 1997–1999: TRIAL AND ERROR, CONFRONTATION AND ADAPTATION

After the establishment of the HKSAR in July 1997, it was immediately plagued by two legal or constitutional problems regarding the interpretation of the Basic Law. The problems concerned the legality of the establishment of the

Provisional Legislative Council (PLC) in 1997, and the right of abode in Hong Kong of mainland-born children of Hong Kong residents. These issues were litigated all the way from the Court of First Instance to the Court of Appeal, and then finally to the Court of Final Appeal (CFA). On 29 January 1999, the CFA rendered its judgments in the cases of *Ng Ka Ling v Director of Immigration*[1] and *Chan Kam Nga v Director of Immigration*.[2] In retrospect, these were the most momentous decisions of the Hong Kong courts in the SAR's early history.

Both *Ng Ka Ling* and *Chan Kam Nga* were cases litigated against the government with the support of legal aid by seekers of the "right of abode" in Hong Kong. The applicants were children of Hong Kong permanent residents, but they were born in mainland China. The children (some of whom were adults already), who did not have any right of abode in Hong Kong under pre-1997 Hong Kong law, claimed the right of abode in Hong Kong under the Basic Law[3] which came into full force on 1 July 1997. They argued that the immigration legislation (passed by the PLC)[4] that defined who would be entitled to such right (thereby excluding some of them from such entitlement) and regulated the procedures for migration to Hong Kong for settlement was invalid because it contravened the Basic Law. Two controversies stemmed from the CFA's decisions in these two cases.

The first arose in the context of the CFA's handling of the issue of the legality of the PLC. In *Ng Ka Ling*, the CFA, like the Court of Appeal below it in *HKSAR v Ma Wai Kwan*,[5] had to deal with the question of the legality of the PLC, because it was argued that the immigration legislation passed by the PLC was invalid as the PLC itself was not lawfully established. The PLC was established by the Preparatory Committee for the HKSAR appointed by the NPC Standing Committee (NPCSC). It was argued that the PLC was not lawfully established as it was not provided for in the Basic Law. Since the Basic Law was enacted in 1990 on the assumption that there would be a political "through train" in the sense that the members of the pre-1997 legislature would

1. *Ng Ka Ling v Director of Immigration* [1999] 1 HKLRD 315 (CFA).
2. *Chan Kam Nga v Director of Immigration* [1999] 1 HKLRD 304 (CFA).
3. Art. 24(2)(3) of the Basic Law.
4. Immigration Ordinance No. 2, 3 (1997) (amended 1997).
5. *HKSAR v Ma Wai Kwan* [1997] HKLRD 761 (CA), [1997] HKC 315. The court judgments in the cases discussed in this chapter are all available at the website of the Hong Kong Judiciary: http://legalref.judiciary.gov.hk.

become members of the first legislature of the HKSAR,[6] there was indeed no provision for the establishment of the PLC (whose members were chosen by the 400-member Selection Committee for the first Chief Executive). The PLC was essentially a contingency measure to deal with the "derailing" of the through train as a result of political reforms introduced by Governor Chris Patten in the mid-1990's which Beijing considered to be contrary to the Basic Law and to the understanding reached between the Chinese and British Governments in 1990 when the Basic Law was enacted.

While the CFA reached the same conclusion as the Court of Appeal in affirming the legality of the PLC, it attempted in its judgment to overrule the Court of Appeal's ruling that Hong Kong courts had no jurisdiction to overturn acts of the NPC or NPCSC. The CFA stated in *Ng Ka Ling* that Hong Kong courts have the jurisdiction "to examine whether any legislative acts of the [NPC] or [NPCSC] are consistent with the Basic Law and to declare them to be invalid if found to be inconsistent".[7] This immediately provoked a strong reaction from the mainland Chinese side,[8] which led to the HKSAR Government's surprise and unprecedented application to the CFA on 26 February 1999 requesting it to "clarify" the relevant part of its judgment. The CFA acceded to the request and stated that (1) the Hong Kong courts' power to interpret the Basic Law is derived from the NPCSC under article 158 of the Basic Law; (2) any interpretation made by the NPCSC under article 158 would be binding on the Hong Kong courts; and (3) the judgment of 29 January did not question the authority of the

---

6. See the "Decision of the National People's Congress on the Method for the Formation of the First Government and the First Legislative Council of the Hong Kong Special Administrative Region", enacted at the same time as and published with the Basic Law on 4 April 1990. The Decision is reproduced in Yash Ghai, *Hong Kong's New Constitutional Order: The Resumption of Chinese Sovereignty and the Basic Law* (Hong Kong: Hong Kong University Press, 2nd edition, 1999) 568–569.
7. *Ng Ka Ling* (N1), at 377.
8. In a highly publicised seminar reported in Hong Kong and mainland Chinese media on 7 February 1999, four leading Chinese law professors, who were also former members of the Drafting Committee for the Basic Law and the Preparatory Committee for the establishment of the HKSAR, attacked the statement. They suggested that it had the effect of placing Hong Kong courts above the NPC, which is the supreme organ of State power under the Chinese Constitution, and of turning Hong Kong into an "independent political entity". After the HKSAR's Secretary for Justice Elsie Leung's visit to Beijing on 12–13 February 1999 to discuss the matter, it was reported that Chinese officials had criticised the statement as unconstitutional and called for its "rectification". See generally J.M.M. Chan, H.L. Fu, and Y. Ghai (eds.), *Hong Kong's Constitutional Debate: Conflict Over Interpretation* (Hong Kong: Hong Kong University Press, 2000) 73.

NPC or NPCSC "to do any act which is in accordance with the provisions of the Basic Law and the procedure therein".[9]

The practical significance of the "clarification",[10] which is also a consequence flowing directly from the Basic Law itself, is that the Hong Kong courts' power to interpret the Basic Law and to determine whether an act of any governmental authority is consistent with the Basic Law, albeit a real and important power, is nevertheless not an absolute one. It is not absolute because it is subject to the overriding power of the NPCSC. In the absence of an interpretation by the NPCSC, the Hong Kong courts have full authority to interpret the Basic Law on their own and to decide cases in accordance with their own interpretation, but once the NPCSC has spoken, the Hong Kong courts must comply. However, when can or will the NPCSC speak? This question was answered in the course of the second controversy flowing from the CFA's decisions of 29 January 1999.

This controversy stemmed from the CFA's interpretation of articles 24(2)(3) and 22(4) of the Basic Law, and its decision not to refer the latter to the NPCSC for interpretation even though it seems to be covered by under article 158(3) of the Basic Law.[11] The HKSAR Government estimated that the implementation of articles 24(2)(3) and 22(4) as interpreted by the CFA would mean that Hong Kong would need to absorb a migrant population from mainland China of 1.67 million in the coming decade.[12] In the government's opinion, Hong Kong need not bear this burden because the CFA's interpretation of the relevant Basic Law provisions was of dubious validity. On 21 May 1999, the

9. *Ng Ka Ling and Others v Director of Immigration* [1999] 1 HKLRD 577 (CFA).

10. Albert H.Y. Chen, "Constitutional Crisis in Hong Kong: Congressional Supremacy and Judicial Review" (1999) 33 *The International Lawyer* 1025; B. Ling, "Can Hong Kong Courts Review and Nullify Acts of the National People's Congress?" (1999) 29 *Hong Kong Law Journal* 8.

11. Art. 158(3) of the Basic Law requires the CFA to refer to the NPCSC for interpretation of relevant Basic Law provisions "concerning affairs which are the responsibility of the Central People's Government, or concerning the relationship between the Central Authorities and the Region". See Albert H.Y. Chen, "*Ng Ka-ling* and Article 158(3) of the Basic Law" (2002) 5 *Journal of Chinese and Comparative Law* 222.

12. This figure is the sum total of 690,000 (being the "first generation" consisting of children of current Hong Kong permanent residents) and 980,000 (being the "second generation" consisting of children already born of the "first generation" who will be entitled to the right of abode after their parents — as members of the "first generation" — have migrated to Hong Kong and resided there for 7 years). See generally Ho-lup Fung, "The 'Right of Abode' Issue: A Test Case of 'One Country, Two Systems'" in Y.C. Wong (ed.), *"One Country, Two Systems" in Crisis* (Lanham, Maryland: Lexington Books, 2004) 253–260; Anne S.Y. Cheung and Albert H.Y. Chen, "The Search for the Rule of Law in the Hong Kong Special Administrative Region, 1997–2003" in Y.C. Wong (*ibid.*) 61–96.

Chief Executive, Mr Tung Chee-hwa, despite strong opposition from certain sectors of the community, particularly the legal professional and pro-democracy politicians, requested the State Council to refer the relevant Basic Law provisions to the NPCSC for interpretation.[13] The request was acceded to, and the NPCSC issued an interpretation on 26 June 1999.[14] The NPCSC adopted the same interpretations as those adopted by the Court of Appeal before its decision was overturned by the CFA. The CFA's interpretations on these points were effectively overruled. In the text of its Decision, the NPCSC also pointed out that the litigation did involve Basic Law provisions concerning the Central Government's responsibility or the Central-HKSAR relationship that ought to have been referred to the NPCSC for interpretation by the CFA in accordance with article 158(3) of the Basic Law in the first place.

The reference to the NPCSC for interpretation was extremely controversial because there is nothing in the Basic Law which suggests that the executive branch of the HKSAR Government can request the NPCSC to interpret the Basic Law. Furthermore, the reference to the NPCSC was criticised as a self-inflicted blow to Hong Kong's autonomy, judicial authority, Rule of Law, and system for protecting individuals' rights.[15] With respect, most of these criticisms cannot be sustained. First, as was acknowledged by the CFA in December 1999 in *Lau Kong Yung v Director of Immigration*,[16] the NPCSC's power to interpret the Basic Law under article 158(1) of the Basic Law is a "free-standing" one, in the sense that it can be exercised at any time, even in the absence of a reference by the CFA in accordance with article 158(3) of the Basic Law. Any interpretation issued by the NPCSC, whether on its own initiative or upon

13. It should be noted that although art. 158(3) provides for reference by the CFA of a Basic Law provision to the NPCSC for interpretation in certain circumstances, art. 158 does not provide expressly that the HKSAR Government may request the NPCSC to interpret the Basic Law. Art. 158(1) does stipulate however that "[t]he power of interpretation of this Law shall be vested in" the NPCSC. See Albert H.Y. Chen, "The Interpretation of the Basic Law — Common Law and Mainland Chinese Perspectives" (2000) 30 *Hong Kong Law Journal* 380.
14. Government of the Hong Kong Special Administrative Region Gazette Extraordinary, Legal Supplement No. 2, 28 June 1999, p. 1577 (LN 167 of 1999).
15. See generally Chan, Fu, and Ghai (N8); Peter Wesley-Smith, "Hong Kong's First Post-1997 Constitutional Crisis" (1999) *LawAsia Journal* 24; Feng Ling, "The Constitutional Crisis in Hong Kong — Is It Over?" (2000) 9 *Pacific Rim Law and Policy Journal* 281; Yongping Xiao, "Comments on the Judgment on the Right of Abode by Hong Kong CFA" (2000) 48 *American Journal of Comparative Law* 471.
16. *Lau Kong Yung v Director of Immigration* [1999] 3 HKLRD 778 (CFA).

a reference by the CFA, is binding on the Hong Kong courts. Second, the CFA also acknowledged in *Lau Kong Yung* that since the preamble to the NPCSC interpretation of June 1999 suggests that a reference to the NPCSC for interpretation should have been made by the CFA in this case, it might be necessary for the CFA to re-visit in future the test (such as the "predominant provision" test) for determining when a reference should be made to the NPCSC. This means that the CFA implicitly conceded that it might have been a mistake for it to decide in *Ng Ka Ling* not to refer article 22(4) of the Basic Law to the NPCSC for interpretation. Third, it should be stressed that the parties to the litigation in the *Ng* and *Chan* cases were not affected by the NPCSC's interpretation.[17] This means that the interpretation only operates as a guide to Hong Kong courts on how to interpret the relevant Basic Law provisions in cases that come before the courts after the interpretation was made.

Although the 1999 NPCSC interpretation should not in itself, given the circumstances in which it was made, be regarded as a blow to Hong Kong's Rule of Law or autonomy, the concern is valid that if the NPCSC were to exercise its overriding power to interpret the Basic Law frequently, the autonomy and authority of the Hong Kong courts in deciding cases on their own (at least in cases that touch upon an interpretation of the Basic Law) would be severely hampered. Fortunately, this has not happened. The NPCSC has practised self-restraint in exercising its power of interpretation of the Basic Law. Since its interpretation of 1999, only two other interpretations have been issued in the first decade of the twenty-first century — one in 2004 on the issue of political reform and democratisation in Hong Kong and the Beijing authorities' role in the process,[18] and one in 2005 on the issue of the term of office of the successor (to be elected in Hong Kong and appointed by Beijing) to Chief Executive Tung Chee-hwa who resigned in March 2005 before completing his second term of office of 2002–2007.[19] The 2004 interpretation was issued on the NPCSC's own initiative in the absence of any litigation on

17. This is provided for in art. 158(3) of the Basic Law and is also reiterated in the text of the NPCSC's interpretation.

18. This chapter confines itself to the "Rule of Law issues" in post-1997 Hong Kong, while the issues of political reform, democratisation, and Beijing's interventions in the process of constitutional reform in post-1997 Hong Kong are outside its scope. On the latter issues, see Chapter 2 of this volume.

19. Albert H.Y. Chen, "The NPCSC's Interpretation in Spring 2005" (2005) 35 *Hong Kong Law Journal* 255.

the matter or any request for interpretation by the Hong Kong Government. The 2005 interpretation was issued at the request of the Hong Kong Government at a time when litigation (to challenge a bill introduced in the Hong Kong legislature on the Chief Executive's term of office) was pending but before a full trial in any court.

To conclude this section, it may be said that 1997–1999 was a period of initial trial operation for the Basic Law. The CFA's decisions on 29 January 1999 did precipitate two constitutional crises or "confrontations" between the legal orders of Hong Kong and of the PRC, one leading to the "clarification" by the CFA and the other leading to the June 1999 interpretation by the NPCSC. How the legal order of Hong Kong should position itself with regard to the power of the NPCSC was a fundamental problem raised by the 1997 handover. By the time of the CFA's decision in *Lau Kong Yung*, the Hong Kong courts led by the CFA had already adjusted themselves to this new constitutional order.

## 2000–2002: THE ELABORATION AND CONSOLIDATION OF THE REGIME OF RIGHTS

The CFA delivered its judgment in *Lau Kong Yung* on 3 December 1999. Later, on 15 December 1999, the same court rendered its decision in *HKSAR v Ng Kung Siu*,[20] which inaugurated what this author would classify as the second period of the legal history of the HKSAR. The developments in this period should be understood against the background of Hong Kong's pre-1997 regime of rights protection.

Hong Kong's pre-1997 constitution was contained in the Letters Patent issued by the British Crown.[21] Before its 1991 amendment, Letters Patent provided only a crude and rudimentary written constitution for the colony. In particular, it did not contain any guarantee of civil liberties and human rights. In 1991, in an attempt to restore confidence in Hong Kong's future which had been deeply shaken by the Tiananmen incident of 4 June 1989, the Hong

20. *HKSAR v Ng Kung Siu* [1999] 3 HKLRD 907 (CFA), (1999) 2 HKCFAR 442.

21. N. Miners, *The Government and Politics of Hong Kong* (Hong Kong: Oxford University Press, 5th edition, 1995) ch. 5; Peter Wesley-Smith, *Constitutional and Administrative Law in Hong Kong* (Hong Kong: Longman Asia, 1995) ch. 2.

Kong Government passed the Hong Kong Bill of Rights Ordinance (BORO),[22] incorporating into the domestic law of Hong Kong the provisions of the International Covenant on Civil and Political Rights (ICCPR) which had already been applied by the United Kingdom to Hong Kong on the level of international law since 1976. A corresponding amendment was made to the Letters Patent to give the ICCPR supremacy over laws enacted by Hong Kong's legislature. Since 1991, the courts of Hong Kong have on such constitutional basis exercised the power of judicial review of legislation (striking down any existing law which was considered to fail to meet the human rights norms embodied in the Bill of Rights and the ICCPR), and developed a solid body of case law on the protection of human rights.[23] The era of constitutional adjudication thus began in Hong Kong.

Upon the establishment of the HKSAR in July 1997, the colonial constitution embodied in the Letters Patent lost its force. Article 8 of the Basic Law provides for the continued validity of the laws previously in force in Hong Kong except for any law that contravenes the Basic Law and subject to any amendment by the HKSAR legislature. Under article 160 of the Basic Law, the NPCSC may declare which of Hong Kong's pre-existing laws contravene the Basic Law and cannot therefore survive the 1997 transition. Such a declaration was made by the NPCSC on 23 February 1997 in its "Decision on the Treatment of the Laws Previously in Force in Hong Kong".[24] The Decision declared the non-adoption, *inter alia*, of three interpretative

---

22. Cap. 383, L.H.K. See generally R. Wacks (ed.), *Hong Kong's Bill of Rights* (Hong Kong: Faculty of Law, University of Hong Kong, 1990); J.M.M. Chan and Y. Ghai (eds.), *The Hong Kong Bill of Rights: A Comparative Approach* (Hong Kong: Butterworths Asia, 1993); Peter Wesley-Smith, "Protecting Human Rights in Hong Kong" in R. Wacks (ed.), *Human Rights in Hong Kong* (Hong Kong: Oxford University Press, 1992) ch. 1; Johannes M.M. Chan, *The Annotated Ordinances of Hong Kong: Hong Kong Bill of Rights Ordinance* (Hong Kong: Butterworths Asia, 1999).
23. Y. Ghai, "Sentinels of Liberty or Sheep in Woolf's Clothing? Judicial Politics and the Hong Kong Bill of Rights" (1997) 60 *Modern Law Review* 459; Johannes M.M. Chan, "Hong Kong's Bill of Rights: Its Reception of and Contribution to International and Comparative Jurisprudence" (1998) 47 *International and Comparative Law Quarterly* 306; A. Byrnes, "And Some Have Bills of Rights Thrust Upon Them: The Experience of Hong Kong's Bill of Rights" in P. Alston (ed.), *Promoting Human Rights Through Bills of Rights: Comparative Perspectives* (Oxford: Oxford University Press, 2000).
24. For an English translation of this Decision, see Albert H.Y. Chen, "Legal Preparation for the Establishment of the Hong Kong SAR: Chronology and Selected Documents" (1997) 27 *Hong Kong Law Journal* 419.

provisions in the Hong Kong BORO,[25] apparently on the ground that they purported to give the Ordinance a superior status overriding other Hong Kong laws, which is inconsistent with the principle that only the Basic Law is superior to other Hong Kong laws. Does this mean that the pre-existing regime of legal protection of rights in Hong Kong before 1997 would be dismantled or weakened? A negative answer has been revealed by various major judicial decisions in the second period of the post-1997 legal history of the HKSAR.

The CFA's decision in *Ng Kung Siu* is probably the most theoretically significant constitutional case on civil liberties and human rights in the early history of the HKSAR. In this case, the defendants had participated in a demonstration in Hong Kong for democracy in China during which they displayed a defaced national flag (of the PRC) and a defaced regional flag (of the HKSAR). They were subsequently charged with violations of section 7 of the National Flag and National Emblem Ordinance[26] and section 7 of the Regional Flag and Regional Emblem Ordinance. The sections provide for the offences of desecration of the national and regional flags and emblems.

The defendants were convicted by the magistrate; they were neither fined or imprisoned, but bound over[27] to keep the peace on a recognisance of HK$2,000 for each of the two charges for 12 months. They successfully appealed against their conviction before the Court of Appeal.[28] The government appealed the case to the CFA, which rendered its judgment in December 1999.[29] The appeal was allowed by the CFA unanimously, and the impugned ordinances were upheld as constitutional and valid. The CFA pointed out that the national and regional flags are important and unique symbols of the nation and of the HKSAR, respectively. There are, therefore, societal and community interests in the protection of the flags. Such protection constitutes the objective behind the flag desecration laws. Such protection was held to fall within the concept of

25. The interpretative provisions concerned were sections 2(3), 3, and 4 of the BORO. For the effect of the non-adoption of these provisions, see Peter Wesley-Smith, "Maintenance of the Bill of Rights" (1997) 27 *Hong Kong Law Journal* 15; Johannes M.M. Chan, "The Status of the Bill of Rights in the Hong Kong Special Administrative Region" (1998) 28 *Hong Kong Law Journal* 152.
26. This section was largely reproduced from art. 19 of the PRC Law on the National Flag and art. 13 of the PRC Law on the National Emblem. Since 1 July 1997, these two PRC laws have been listed in Annex III to the Basic Law as mainland laws that are applicable to Hong Kong under art. 18 of the Basic Law.
27. For the practice of "binding over", see Wesley-Smith (N22) 26–27.
28. *HKSAR v Ng Kung Siu and Another* [1999] 1 HKLRD 783 (CA).
29. *HKSAR v Ng Kung Siu* [1999] 3 HKLRD 907, (1999) 2 HKCFAR 442.

"public order (*ordre public*)" as used in the ICCPR. It was held that the court below adopted too narrow a conception of "public order (*ordre public*)".[30]

The next questions for the CFA were whether the flag desecration laws impose restrictions on the freedom of expression, and, if so, whether such restrictions can be justified on the ground that they are necessary for the protection of "public order (*ordre public*)" and proportionate to the objective sought to be achieved (and thus not excessive). This is the application of the principles of rationality and proportionality well-established in human rights jurisprudence elsewhere and already introduced into Hong Kong since 1991. The CFA held that flag desecration is indeed "a form of non-verbal speech or expression",[31] and the impugned laws do constitute a restriction thereon. However, the court pointed out that the restriction is a limited one, because while one mode of expression is prohibited, the same message which the actor wants to express can still be freely expressed by other modes.[32] It was therefore concluded that the "necessity" and "proportionality" tests had been satisfied.[33]

Although the CFA's actual decision in *Ng Kung Siu* was to uphold the flag desecration law, the approach and mode of reasoning adopted by the CFA in this case have had far-reaching positive implications for the regime of rights protection in post-1997 Hong Kong. The case demonstrates that the operative force of the Bill of Rights and the ICCPR, and the Hong Kong courts' power to review the constitutionality of Hong Kong legislation on human rights grounds, and, if necessary, to strike down such legislation, have survived the non-adoption (by the NPCSC) of the relevant provisions in the Hong Kong BORO as mentioned above. In fact, the HKSAR courts may review whether any legislative or executive action in Hong Kong violates the human rights guaranteed by chapter III of the Basic Law or by the ICCPR (the applicable provisions of which have, as mentioned above, been reproduced in the BORO) which is given effect to by article 39 of the Basic Law. Article 39 has

30. Both the English and French expressions appear in the text of art. 19 of the ICCPR. In its judgment, the court below (the Court of Appeal) referred to two decisions of the American Supreme Court — *Texas v Johnson* 491 U.S. 397 (1989) and *United States v Eichman* 496 U.S. 310 (1990) — in which the criminalisation of flag desecration was found to violate the "free speech" clause in the U.S. Constitution and is, therefore, unconstitutional. Both cases were decided by a majority of 5 to 4 in the Supreme Court and were extremely controversial in the United States.

31. *HKSAR v Ng Kung Siu* (1999) 2 HKCFAR 442, at 455.

32. *Ibid.*, 456.

33. *Ibid.*, 460–461.

been interpreted to mean that the relevant provisions of the ICCPR have the same constitutional force as the Basic Law itself, thus overriding laws that are inconsistent with these provisions.

We now turn to two other cases decided in 2000–2002 that demonstrate the vitality of judicial protection of human rights in post-1997 Hong Kong. *Secretary for Justice v Chan Wah and Tse Kwan Sang*[34] concerns the system of local village elections in the New Territories. Some of the residents of the villages of the New Territories are known as "indigenous inhabitants" or "indigenous villagers",[35] defined as descendants through the male line of residents in 1898 of villages in the New Territories.[36] The rules governing the election of village representatives in most villages in the New Territories limited the right to vote and the right to stand as candidates to indigenous inhabitants. In the *Chan* case, Chan and Tse were non-indigenous inhabitants of the villages in which they lived. They challenged the electoral rules as discriminatory in denying them their right to take part in the conduct of public affairs under article 21(a) of the Bill of Rights (article 25 of the ICCPR).

In the final judgment delivered in December 2000, the CFA held that the impugned electoral rules in this case imposed unreasonable restrictions on Chan's and Tse's right to take part in the conduct of public affairs through freely chosen representatives. In response to this ruling, the government subsequently reformed the village election system by introducing legislation providing for a dual system in which each village would elect two village representatives, one serving only the indigenous inhabitants and the other all the villagers.[37]

The Chan case concerns discrimination on the basis of origin or status, while the next case concerns gender discrimination. In *Equal Opportunities Commission v Director of Education*,[38] the Equal Opportunities Commission challenged the Education Department's policy regarding the system of allocation of secondary school places to students completing primary school education. The effect of the operation of this system was that with regard to a

34. *Secretary for Justice v Chan Wah and Tse Kwan Sang* [2000] 3 HKLRD 641 (CFA), (2000) 3 HKCFAR 459.

35. See the Government Rent (Assessment and Collection) Ordinance, Cap. 515, L.H.K.

36. 1898 was the year in which the British colony of Hong Kong — then comprising Hong Kong Island and the Kowloon Peninsula — was expanded in size to include the New Territories north of Kowloon.

37. See the Village Representative Election Ordinance, Cap. 576, L.H.K. (Ordinance No. 2 of 2003).

38. *Equal Opportunities Commission v Director of Education* [2001] 2 HKLRD 690 (CFI).

boy and a girl who had equal academic merits (as measured by scores), the boy stood a better chance of being admitted to his preferred secondary school than the girl. The policy was based on findings that girls' academic achievements (as measured by scores) at the time of completion of primary education were, on average, higher than boys', presumably because of a faster pace of intellectual development at that age (though boys typically caught up later). The policy was designed to ensure a more balanced ratio between male and female students in the elite schools (i.e., schools to which admission is most competitive).

The Court of First Instance of the High Court[39] held that the Education Department's policy is discriminatory against female students and the discrimination fails to be justified by any of the reasons advanced by the Department. Referring to article 25 of the Basic Law, article 22 of the Hong Kong Bill of Rights, the Sex Discrimination Ordinance, and the Convention on the Elimination of All Forms of Discrimination Against Women which was extended to Hong Kong in 1996, the court stressed that the right to equal treatment free of sex discrimination in this case is an individual's fundamental right, and cannot be easily subordinated to considerations of "group fairness"[40] or the interest in achieving a better balance in schools between boys and girls. Any restriction of the girls' right in this case must pass the stringent standards of scrutiny of the "proportionality test"[41] in order to be justified. After examining the government's arguments and the evidence submitted by it, the court held that the impugned scheme of allocation of school places fails to pass this test. As a result, the Education Department changed its original policy.

Both the *Chan* case and *Equal Opportunities Commission* case concern matters of public policy; their ramifications extend far beyond the individual litigants or complainants in the cases. They demonstrate the increasingly significant role of the courts in Hong Kong in shaping social policy and in promoting social reform by employing jurisprudential concepts — in these two cases, the right to the equal protection of the law without discrimination.

The three cases above elucidate the structural components of the post-1997 regime of rights protection in Hong Kong, namely article 39 of the Basic Law, the ICCPR, and the BORO. However, the significance of rights-conferring provisions in the Basic Law other than article 39 should not be ignored. After

39. The case was not appealed to any higher court.

40. Para. 80 of the judgment.

41. Para. 121 of the judgment.

the Basic Law came into effect in 1997, the grounds on which legislative and executive actions may be challenged by way of judicial review have actually been broadened. After 1991 but before 1997, it was possible to launch such a challenge on the basis of the provisions of the BORO, which are identical to those provisions of the ICCPR that are applicable to Hong Kong. After 1997, a challenge may still be launched on this basis, but in addition a challenge may also be based on other provisions of the Basic Law, particularly those which confer rights that are not expressly or adequately provided for in the ICCPR, such as the right of abode or the freedom to travel.[42]

Indeed, 2000–2002 may be described as a period of elaboration and consolidation of the regime of rights in the HKSAR. The CFA's decision in *Director of Immigration v Chong Fung Yuen*,[43] another landmark case decided in this period, also marks such consolidation. In this case, the issue was whether, as a matter of interpretation of article 24(2)(1) of the Basic Law, the right of abode in Hong Kong vests in children born in Hong Kong to Chinese parents who are not Hong Kong residents but who are mainlanders visiting Hong Kong temporarily or illegally staying in Hong Kong. On a literal interpretation of article 24(2)(1), such children are Hong Kong permanent residents and enjoy the right of abode. However, the Preparatory Committee for the HKSAR in 1996 suggested otherwise when it issued an opinion on the implementation of article 24. In the NPCSC's interpretation of June 1999, it stated, *inter alia*, that the Preparatory Committee's 1996 opinion "reflected" the "legislative intent" behind article 24(2) of the Basic Law. The question for the CFA in *Chong Fung Yuen* was whether it should follow the views of the Preparatory Committee in this regard.

The CFA's judgment in this case was an emphatic statement that when Hong Kong courts interpret the Basic Law, they should adopt the common law approach to interpretation, and do not need to resort to or otherwise take

42. For example, in *Bahadur v Director of Immigration* (2002) 5 HKCFAR 480, which reached the CFA in July 2002, Bahadur, a citizen of Nepal living in Hong Kong as a non-permanent resident, successfully asserted his freedom to travel which was held by the CFA to include the right to re-enter Hong Kong after traveling. The CFA reiterated the approach it stated in previous cases that the rights and freedoms guaranteed by the Basic Law should be given a generous interpretation "whilst restrictions to them should be narrowly interpreted" and that "these rights and freedoms lie at the heart of Hong Kong's separate system" under OCTS. For a commentary on this case and its significance, see Simon N.M. Young, "Restricting Basic Law Rights in Hong Kong" (2004) 34 *Hong Kong Law Journal* 109.

43. *Director of Immigration v Chong Fung Yuen* [2001] 2 HKLRD 533 (CFA).

into account any principle or norm of the mainland legal system. Applying the common law approach to interpretation in this case, the CFA held that there was only one possible answer to the legal question raised: the child concerned was entitled to the right of abode in Hong Kong. The CFA did not attach any weight to the passage in the June 1999 interpretation by the NPCSC suggesting that the Preparatory Committee's opinion reflected the legislative intent behind article 24 of the Basic Law. The CFA stressed that the June 1999 interpretation was an interpretation only of articles 22(4) and 24(2)(3) of the Basic Law. It was not an interpretation of article 24(2)(1) of the Basic Law, which was the provision being interpreted in the *Chong Fung Yuen* case. In the absence of any binding interpretation by the NPCSC of article 24(2)(1), the CFA was free to interpret it on its own, applying the common law approach to interpretation.[44]

The case aroused public concerns about pregnant women from the mainland coming to Hong Kong to give birth to their babies. The concerns proved to be justified; in the next few years following the CFA's decision in the *Chong* case, increasing numbers of pregnant women from the mainland visited Hong Kong in order to give birth, thus constituting a great strain on Hong Kong's hospitals. In 2007, administrative measures were adopted to reduce the influx.

## 2003–2004: THE ARTICLE 23 SAGA

The next period of the HKSAR's legal history was dominated by ten months of drama which culminated in a march of an estimated half a million people in the streets of Hong Kong Island, one of the greatest events in the political, legal, and social history of Hong Kong which also changed the course of PRC policy towards the HKSAR. The drama had a specifically legal theme — namely, the implementation of article 23 of the Basic Law.[45]

44. In a very unusual manner not seen since the constitutional crisis of February 1999, Beijing reacted publicly to the decision. On 21 July 2001, the morning immediately following the day of the CFA's decision, a spokesman of the Legislative Affairs Commission of the NPCSC in a widely reported press statement pointed out that the CFA's decision in *Chong Fung Yuen* was "not consistent" with the NPCSC's interpretation and "expressed concern" about the matter. However, apart from this terse statement, no further action on the matter was taken by Beijing. In particular, no interpretation on the issue was issued by the NPCSC. See generally Albert H.Y. Chen, "Another Case of Conflict Between the CFA and the NPC Standing Committee?" (2001) 31 *Hong Kong Law Journal* 179.

45. H.L. Fu, C.J. Peterson, and S.N.M. Young (eds.), *National Security and Fundamental Freedoms: Hong Kong's Article 23 Under Scrutiny* (Hong Kong: Hong Kong University Press, 2005).

Article 23 of the Basic Law requires the HKSAR to "enact laws on its own to prohibit any act of treason, secession, sedition, subversion against the Central People's Government". It also deals with issues of State secrets and the activities of foreign political organisations in Hong Kong. Many of the issues raised by article 23 are considered to be politically sensitive. Ever since the Basic Law was enacted in 1990 and brought into effect in July 1997, there had been anxiety over the implementation of article 23.

It was therefore understandable that the publication of the Consultation Document on *Proposals to Implement Article 23 of the Basic Law*[46] by the HKSAR Government on 24 September 2002 caused much public anxiety as to whether the Hong Kong or Beijing Government had a sinister intention of curtailing human rights in Hong Kong and extending mainland standards regarding matters such as subversion or the theft of State secrets to Hong Kong. During the three-month consultation period for the legislative proposal, public opinion in Hong Kong was sharply divided. The debate was at times impassioned, and demonstrations were organised by both supporters and opponents of the proposal.

The consultation period ended in December after a demonstration of nearly 60,000 people against the legislative proposal on 15 December 2002. In response, the government amended the proposal by giving several major "concessions" on its substance,[47] but rejected the call for a White Bill — a bill published for public consultation but not yet introduced into the Hong Kong Legislative Council (LegCo). The National Security (Legislative Provisions) Bill, designed to implement article 23 of the Basic Law, was introduced into the legislature in February 2003.

In my opinion,[48] the proposed reforms in the bill regarding treason and sedition demonstrated that the article 23 exercise was not primarily intended to make Hong Kong's laws more draconian. Instead, it was an exercise intended to review and reform the existing law in light of the principles enshrined in article 23 of the Basic Law, and to remove repressive laws that Hong Kong

46. For further discussion of the issues by the author, see Albert H.Y. Chen, "Proposals A Credit to '1 Country, 2 Systems'" (7 October 2002) *China Daily (Hong Kong edition)* 3–4; Albert H.Y. Chen, "Will Our Civil Liberties Survive the Implementation of Article 23?" (November 2002) *Hong Kong Lawyer* 80–88.

47. On 28 January 2003, the government published the multi-volume *Compendium of Submissions* and announced nine sets of clarifications or modifications of the original proposal.

48. Albert. H.Y. Chen, "How Hong Kong Law Will Change When Article 23 of the Basic Law Is Implemented" (2003) 33 *Hong Kong Law Journal* 1.

had inherited from its colonial era which are now out-of-date and inconsistent with progressive notions of human rights. Regarding subversion and secession, the bill did not import the relevant mainland laws and standards to Hong Kong, and creatively designed legislative models for these two crimes that would be unique to the HKSAR. For State secrets, the proposed amendments to the Official Secrets Ordinance were not unreasonable and were basically consistent with the spirit of OCTS. The most controversial provisions in the bill related to "proscribed organisations". The bill proposed a set of amendments to the Societies Ordinance to the effect that in a situation where a local organisation (a) has the objective of engaging in or (b) has committed or is attempting to commit treason, secession, subversion, sedition, or spying, or (c) is "subordinate to" an organisation in mainland China which has been proscribed by the Central Authorities' open decree for reasons of national security, the HKSAR's Secretary for Security may proscribe the local organisation "if he reasonably believes that the proscription is necessary in the interests of national security and is proportionate for such purpose". Part (c) of the proposal aroused much public opposition.

After the bill was introduced into LegCo in February 2003, a Bills Committee under LegCo was set up to examine the bill. During the Bills Committee's deliberations, the government agreed to some amendments. However, critics said that the amendments were insufficient, and in any event the government's timetable of passing the bill in LegCo's week-long meeting beginning on 9 July did not allow sufficient time for deliberation. Meanwhile, the onslaught of severe acute respiratory syndrome, or atypical pneumonia (SARS) in March 2003 distracted public attention from the bill. There was therefore little understanding of the bill on the part of members of the public in Hong Kong. As Hong Kong began to recover from the SARS crisis in June, opponents of the bill woke members of the public up to the fact that the bill was to be pushed through LegCo in early July.

On 1 July 2003, a hot summer day which was also a public holiday marking the 6th anniversary of Hong Kong's return to China, half a million Hong Kong residents took to the streets to demonstrate against the article 23 legislative exercise and to express other grievances against the Tung Chee-hwa administration that had accumulated since the 1997 handover. Opponents of the bill immediately demanded that it be shelved and planned to organise a rally of tens of thousands surrounding the LegCo building on 9 July if proceedings on the bill were to go ahead on that day. The government finally decided to postpone the bill — the decision came 3 hours after the Liberal Party on the evening of 6 July withdrew from the "governing coalition" of political parties in protest against the Tung administration's original decision on 5 July to adhere to the 9 July deadline for the passage of the bill.[49] On 17 July 2003, Chief Executive Tung Chee-hwa announced that the government would re-open public consultation on the bill to ensure that its content would receive broad public support before it was passed into law. However, in an about-turn on 5 September 2003, Tung announced that the bill was to be withdrawn from LegCo. Since then, the implementation of article 23 has been shelved indefinitely.

In the circumstances, the government's decision to postpone the National Security Bill was to be welcomed.[50] It would be a flagrant violation of the democratic principle of law-making for a government or legislature to enact a controversial law hastily in the face of extremely strong public opposition. On the other hand, it should also be recognised that article 23 of the Basic Law does impose a legal obligation on the HKSAR Government to enact laws on the matters covered by the article. This constitutional duty cannot be abdicated indefinitely. Article 23 will therefore return one day to the agenda of the HKSAR Government.

## 2005–2010: ACTIVE EXERCISE OF JUDICIAL POWER

The fourth period of the HKSAR's legal history saw the further consolidation of the regime of rights that was elucidated in the second period as discussed above, as well as the further strengthening of the role of the courts as the guardians of constitutional rights in the HKSAR. The NPCSC's second and third interpretations of the Basic Law in 2004 and 2005 (on the mechanics of further democratisation and on the term of office of the Chief Executive as mentioned above) did not have an adverse impact on the position of the courts. Unlike the first interpretation, they were not targeted at any judicial decision in Hong Kong and did not detract from the authority of the Hong Kong courts. Indeed, the

49. On 5 July, the government also announced three major "concessions" on the content of the bill: deletion of the provision on the power to proscribe a local organisation that is subordinate to a mainland organisation proscribed on the mainland; introduction of a public interest defence in the State secrets law; and deletion of the provision on the police's power to search without a warrant.

50. Albert. H.Y. Chen, "Hong Kong's Political Crisis of July 2003" (2003) 33 *Hong Kong Law Journal* 265.

courts in this fourth period exercised their power as actively as, or even more so than, ever before. Four leading cases are discussed below as examples.

The first case is *Yeung May-wan v HKSAR,*[51] concerning the prosecution of Falun Gong protesters in 2002, in which the police resorted to the law of obstruction of public places[52] in dealing with demonstrators. The case arose from a small-scale demonstration staged by 16 Falun Gong activists[53] outside the entrance to the Liaison Office of the Central People's Government in Hong Kong on 14 March 2002. Since the number of demonstrators was small, there was no need under the Public Order Ordinance to notify the police in advance or to comply with procedural requirements which are only applicable to assemblies involving more than 50 persons or processions involving more than 30 persons. After the protesters refused to leave despite repeated police warnings, the police arrested them. There was some physical violence during and after the arrests. The protesters were charged with obstruction of a public place and of obstructing or assaulting police officers in the execution of their duty. After a 27-day trial in August 2002, the protesters were convicted by the magistrate who imposed fines ranging between HK$1,300 and HK$3,800 on them. They appealed to the Court of Appeal, which gave judgment in November 2004.[54] The appeal against conviction for obstruction of a public place was successful, although the appeal against conviction on the other charges failed. In an unanimous decision, the Court of Appeal held that due regard to the protection of the right of assembly should be given in applying the law of obstruction of public places. It overturned the conviction for obstruction on the ground that the magistrate failed to address sufficiently whether the manner in which the protesters exercised their right of assembly was so unreasonable as to constitute an unlawful obstruction. The defendants appealed further to the CFA against the conviction on the other charges.

The appeal was successful. On 5 May 2005, the CFA[55] unanimously held that the arrest of the defendants had been unlawful, since the police officers

51. The citations of the Court of Appeal's and the CFA's decisions in this case are provided below.
52. See the Summary Offences Ordinance, sections 4(28) and 4A.
53. For Falun Gong in Hong Kong, see Albert H.Y. Chen and Anne S.Y. Cheung, "Debating Rule of Law in the Hong Kong Special Administrative Region, 1997–2002" in R. Peerenboom (ed.), *Asian Discourses of Rule of Law: Theories and Implementation of Rule of Law in Twelve Asian Countries, France, and the U.S.* (London: Routledge, 2004) 261–262.
54. *HKSAR v Yeung May Wan* [2004] 3 HKLRD 797 (CA).
55. *Yeung May Wan v HKSAR* [2005] 2 HKLRD 212 (CFA).

who carried out the arrest were not able to satisfy the court that they had reasonable grounds for suspecting that the defendants had committed the offence of obstruction of a public place. The court stressed that the offence was not constituted by mere obstruction; the use of the public place or highway must be unreasonable, otherwise there could be a lawful excuse for the obstruction, in which case no offence had been committed. The court held that in determining what is unreasonable use of the pavement or lawful excuse, the defendants' right to peaceful assembly and demonstration should be given due weight. The court further held that the defendants in the present case could not be convicted for obstructing or assaulting police officers in the execution of their duty even though physical resistance was involved. Since the arrest was unlawful, the police officers were not actually acting in the due execution of their duty when they encountered resistance from the defendants. It was also pointed out that citizens have a right to use reasonable force to resist an unlawful arrest and detention. In this case and in the related case of *Leung Kwok Hung v HKSAR*,[56] the CFA stressed the importance of the constitutional right to freedom of peaceful assembly and demonstration which is guaranteed by the Basic Law, the Hong Kong Bill of Rights and the ICCPR. The decision in the Falun Gong case testifies to the equality of all before the law, so that Falun Gong members, though persecuted in the mainland, are accorded the right to demonstrate directly in front of the Liaison Office of the Central Government in Hong Kong. The landmark decision epitomises the vibrancy of the life of the law and the spirit of human rights in Hong Kong and reveal the deeper meaning of OCTS.

The second case, *Leung Kwok Hung and Koo Sze Yiu v Chief Executive of the HKSAR*,[57] is probably the most important constitutional law case in this fourth period of the HKSAR's legal history, because it led to a comprehensive legislative overhaul of the existing law on the relevant issues. The issues concern covert surveillance conducted by law enforcement officers on suspected criminals. Covert surveillance activities include wire-tapping of phones, interception of postal communications, and covert sound or video recording of people's conversations or activities. The legal basis for covert surveillance first came under critical scrutiny in two criminal cases in the District Court in 2005. It was pointed out that the existing practice

56. *Leung Kwok Hung v HKSAR* (2005) 8 HKCFAR 229.

57. The citations of the courts' decisions in this case are provided below.

was probably a violation of article 30 of the Basic Law, which protects the "freedom and privacy of communication" and permits interception of communication only if it is done "in accordance with legal procedures to meet the needs of public security or of investigation into criminal offences". Also relevant is article 17 of the ICCPR, which prohibits "arbitrary or unlawful interference with … privacy, family, home or correspondence". To plug the legal loophole, the Chief Executive in August 2005 promulgated the Law Enforcement (Covert Surveillance Procedure) Order ("the 2005 Order").[58]

Leung and Koo, two political activists who claimed that they had been targets of covert surveillance, brought an action before the court to challenge the constitutionality of the practice of covert surveillance. They were successful before the Court of First Instance, which delivered judgment on 9 February 2006.[59] The court held that both section 33 of the Telecommunications Ordinance (which dealt with wire-tapping) and the 2005 Order were unconstitutional: the former created a power of interception of communications without adequate legal safeguards against its abuse, and the latter failed to comply with the procedural requirements of article 30 of the Basic Law.

What is most interesting and significant about the court's decision is that the court did not declare (as the litigants requested) that the impugned legislative provision and order should be immediately regarded as invalid and void, which is what would normally be the case when a law is determined by the court to be unconstitutional. Instead, the court agreed to the request by the lawyers acting for the government[60] in this case to suspend the effectiveness of the declaration of invalidity for six months, and held that the impugned legislative provision and order may still be regarded as temporarily valid during this six-month period. The purpose of this arrangement was to give the government time to propose and enact new legislation to replace the defective laws challenged and held to be unconstitutional in this case. The court recognised that this arrangement was an exceptional course of action for the court, but declared that the court in exercise of its inherent jurisdiction had the power to make this arrangement. For if law enforcement agencies were to suddenly lose their powers of conducting covert surveillance, this would be tantamount to "an

58. The order was promulgated under art. 48(4) of the Basic Law.

59. *Leung Kwok Hung and Another v Chief Executive of the HKSAR*, HCAL 107/2005 (9 February 2006).

60. They relied strongly on the Canadian case of *Manitoba Language Rights* [1985] 1 SCR 721.

amnesty for conspirators"[61] and "would give rise to the probability of danger to Hong Kong residents, disorder by way of a threat to the Rule of Law and deprivation to Hong Kong residents generally".[62]

The decision of the Court of First Instance was affirmed on appeal to the Court of Appeal.[63] The further appeal to the CFA was also unsuccessful.[64] However, unlike the courts below it, the CFA drew a distinction between granting a declaration of temporary validity (for six months) with regard to the impugned laws and suspending (for six months) the declaration of invalidity of such laws. The CFA only agreed to grant the latter remedy in this case. In the event, the government did comply with the six-month deadline for introducing new legislation to regularise the practice of covert surveillance in Hong Kong. The Interception of Communications and Surveillance Ordinance was passed by LegCo at around 2 a.m. on 6 August 2005 after a 58-hour marathon debate which started on 2 August. More than 200 amendments proposed by the "democrats" were voted down by pro-government legislators, although some other amendments proposed by them had been incorporated into amendments proposed by the government and were adopted.

In the *Leung Kwok Hung* case, the courts refrained from immediately outlawing the practice of covert surveillance even though the existing legal basis for it was found to be defective, and gave the government and legislature a "grace period" of six months to rectify the legal situation. This seems to reflect an attitude of judicial restraint. However, insofar as the remedy granted by the court in this case is innovative, unprecedented in the legal and constitutional history of Hong Kong, and represents a breakthrough in the creative fashioning of judicial mechanisms to deal with novel situations, it may also be considered an example of judicial activism. Judicial activism is further demonstrated by the next two cases discussed.

In *Leung T C William Roy v Secretary for Justice*,[65] Leung, the applicant for judicial review, was a homosexual aged 20 at the time he brought this action before the court. He challenged the constitutionality of certain provisions in the existing criminal law on the grounds that they were discriminatory on the basis of sex or sexual orientation and violated the constitutional rights to equality and

---

61. Para. 159 of the judgment.

62. Para. 165 of the judgment.

63. *Leung Kwok Hung and Another v Chief Executive of the HKSAR*, CACV 73/2006 (10 May 2006).

64. *Koo Sze Yiu and Another v Chief Executive of the HKSAR* [2006] 3 HKLRD 455 (CFA).

65. *Leung T C William Roy v Secretary for Justice* [2006] 4 HKLRD 211 (CA).

privacy. The main provision that was controversial in this case was section 118C of the Crimes Ordinance, which provided that if two men committed buggery with each other and one or both of them were under the age of 21, then each of them was guilty of a criminal offence the maximum punishment for which would be life imprisonment. Both the Court of First Instance and the Court of Appeal held that this provision was unconstitutional and invalid, because it discriminated against male homosexuals and the government was not able to give good reasons to persuade the court that the discrimination or differential treatment was justified. The impugned provision was discriminatory against male homosexuals because under Hong Kong's existing law, in the case of consensual sexual intercourse between heterosexuals, no criminal liability exists so long as both parties are above the age of 16. Thus, homosexual males between the age of 16 and 21 were discriminated against.

This case has been controversial as it involved the judiciary stepping into the domain of social or sexual morality and overturning a law (made by the legislature) reflecting what was supposed to be the moral standards of the community. It may be questioned whether judges in Hong Kong may legitimately set the behavioural norms for the community in this regard. However, the court's decision may be defended on the ground that one of the legitimate functions of the constitutional review of laws by the courts is to protect the fundamental rights of minorities against oppressive or unjust laws enacted by a legislature that represents only the views or interests of the majority in society. In any event, the *William Roy Leung* case underscores the increasingly important role played by the courts in Hong Kong society during the fourth period of the SAR's legal history.

While the above case concerns homosexuals' rights, the next case concerns prisoners' rights. In *Chan Kin Sum v Secretary for Justice*,[66] the applicants applied for judicial review to challenge the constitutionality of provisions in the Legislative Council Ordinance which disenfranchised persons otherwise eligible to vote in the LegCo election who were in prison serving a sentence or who had been sentenced to imprisonment but had not yet served their sentence. The applicants based their arguments on provisions on the right to vote in the Basic Law and the Hong Kong Bill of Rights (which reproduces the relevant provisions in the ICCPR),[67] as well as case law in favour of prisoners'

66. *Chan Kin Sum v Secretary for Justice* [2009] 2 HKLRD 166 (CFI).

67. Art. 26 of the Basic Law; art. 21 of the Hong Kong Bill of Rights; art. 25 of the ICCPR.

right to vote from the Canadian Supreme Court, European Court of Human Rights, Australian High Court, and Constitutional Court of South Africa. The Court of First Instance of the High Court of Hong Kong held that while the right to vote is not an absolute right and may be subject to reasonable restrictions, such restrictions should be subjected to rigorous judicial scrutiny as the right to vote belongs to the category of rights "of high constitutional importance"[68] and "is without doubt the most important political right".[69] It was held in this case that the restrictions failed to pass the "proportionality test", and that the government was not able to provide convincing arguments and evidence to justify the "general, automatic and indiscriminate restrictions"[70] on prisoners' right to vote imposed by the impugned legislation. The relevant statutory provisions were therefore declared unconstitutional. Following the precedent established by the covert surveillance case mentioned above, the court granted a temporary suspension order regarding the declaration of unconstitutionality so as to give the government and the legislature time (until the end of October 2009) to amend the existing law.[71]

On 24 June 2009, the Hong Kong LegCo enacted the Voting by Imprisoned Persons Ordinance, which essentially removes all restrictions or disqualifications relating to prisoners' right to register as voters and to vote in all elections in Hong Kong — not only LegCo elections, but also elections for the District Councils and for village representatives. The new ordinance also goes beyond what was required by the court in the *Chan Kin Sum* case by removing the provisions in the existing law on the disenfranchisement of those convicted of election-related offences for three years after conviction. The *Chan Kin Sum* case is thus another illustration of the potency of constitutional judicial review in the HKSAR and the role of the judiciary in safeguarding minorities' rights. It also furnishes yet another example of how judges in Hong Kong have been receptive to international and comparative jurisprudence on civil and political rights, and have been ready and willing to bring Hong Kong's law in line with the more "progressive" jurisdictions overseas. As noted in a government document quoted in the judgment in the *Chan* case, a total

68. Para. 154 of the judgment.

69. Para. 164 of the judgment.

70. Para. 164 of the judgment.

71. For the judgment relating to the temporary suspension order, see *Chan Kin Sum v Secretary for Justice*, HCAL 79/2008 (11 March 2009) (CFI).

ban on voting by prisoners is still practiced in many states of the United States, Japan, Singapore, and Malaysia.[72]

## CONCLUSION

How should we understand this 13-year period of constitutional and legal history of the HKSAR? From the perspective of the Rule of Law, the following general observations may be made.

First, autonomy, the Rule of Law, human rights, and civil liberties have successfully been practiced in the HKSAR under the constitutional framework of OCTS and on the basis of the Basic Law. Both the people of Hong Kong and the international community would appreciate that the Central Government in Beijing has indeed respected the high degree of autonomy of the HKSAR, and has not interfered with the SAR Government's policy-making and policy-implementation activities.[73] The common law-based legal system, judicial independence, and the tradition of the Rule of Law have continued to flourish in post-1997 Hong Kong. As promised by the Sino-British Joint Declaration, the "lifestyle" of the people of Hong Kong has remained unchanged. The level of protection of human rights and civil liberties has not dropped as some had feared before 1997.

Second, the three interpretations of the Basic Law by the NPCSC and the legislative exercise to implement article 23 of the Basic Law were indeed among the most significant legal events in this period. They were highly controversial. The article 23 incident shook the whole of Hong Kong society. However, the power of the NPCSC to interpret the Basic Law is an integral part of the new legal order of post-1997 Hong Kong. It has been built into the structural design of the Basic Law itself. Each of the three interpretations has its own rationale and justification; none may be regarded as an arbitrary or irrational exercise of power by the NPCSC. The power of the Hong Kong courts to try and decide cases has been left intact. The government's intention

72. Para. 45 of the judgment.

73. I do not consider the interventions by the NPCSC in 2004 on the question of political reform and democratisation an interference with the autonomy of the HKSAR. The Basic Law establishes a particular political system in Hong Kong and authorises the government under this political system to exercise autonomy. The autonomy of Hong Kong is the autonomy of the government under this political system to govern Hong Kong. Such autonomy does not include the autonomy to change the political system itself.

with this exercise was not to curtail human rights and civil liberties in Hong Kong. However, the trauma of this legislative exercise was the result of the convergence of various circumstances, including the hasty legislative process, the lack of a White Bill for prior consultation, the failure of communication between the government and the people, the incidence of SARS, the economic downturn, and the accumulated social dissatisfaction with the Tung administration over the years.

Third, in the post-1997 era, the courts of Hong Kong have flourished as the guardians of the Rule of Law, constitutionalism, human rights, and civil liberties. Increasing numbers of major issues of social and public policy have been litigated in the courts, as members of the public become more aware of the possibilities of judicial review of governmental and legislative measures and more conscious of their rights. The discourse of the law has become more powerful than ever before in Hong Kong society. At the same time, the courts have been careful not to over-extend their jurisdiction in a manner that would upset the delicate balance of judicial, executive, and legislative powers in the HKSAR and the even more delicate power relationship between the HKSAR courts and the Central Authorities in Beijing. As I have written elsewhere:

> [C]onsidering the inevitable tensions that inhere in the constitutional experiment of [OCTS], the record of the Hong Kong courts in dealing with these challenges has thus far been positive. The judiciary, led by the [CFA], has chosen the middle path[74] or the "golden mean"[75] between confrontation with and subservience to Beijing, and between judicial activism and judicial restraint. In tackling their relationship with Beijing, the courts have adopted an approach that may be described — in a phrase translated from the Chinese — as "neither too proud nor too humble" (*bukang bubei*). In the domain of human rights, the tenor of the courts' decisions may be described as moderately liberal — neither radically liberal nor conservative … such a middle path is indeed appropriate in the context of Hong Kong under [OCTS].[76]

---

74. [footnote from the original text quoted here] In the language of Chinese philosophy, such a middle path may be called *zhongyong zhidao*. *Zhong Yong* (Book of the Mean) is one of the "Four Books" in the Confucian classics. See generally Yu-Lan Fung, *A Short History of Chinese Philosophy* (New York: The Free Press, 1966).
75. [footnote from the original text quoted here] As discussed in Aristotle's philosophy.
76. Albert H.Y. Chen, "Constitutional Adjudication in Post-1997 Hong Kong" (2006) 15 *Pacific Rim Law and Policy Journal* 629–630.

Fourth, more than a decade after the handover, the linkage between the legal systems of Hong Kong and mainland China has remained weak and loose. The level of judicial cooperation between the two jurisdictions is still lower than that between Hong Kong and many other jurisdictions overseas, particularly common law jurisdictions. This is because of the huge differences between the two legal systems and the political sensitivity of some issues of judicial assistance, such as extradition or rendition. In this regard, what I wrote on the fifth anniversary of the HKSAR remains true even today:

> The constitutional and legal design of [OCTS] is such that the points of contact and interface between the two systems are few, and in the overwhelming majority of cases and circumstances, the two systems operate autonomously without any interaction with one another. ... The looseness of the connection between the two systems (at least from the legal point of view) is exemplified by the fact that despite the long negotiations between the [HK]SAR Government and Beijing on a possible rendition agreement on fugitive offenders, no agreement has yet been reached, and neither side sees the matter as a pressing one.[77]

There are some signs in recent years of increasing cooperation between the two legal systems, although such developments have not expanded significantly the interface between the two legal systems which is still kept to a minimum. July 2006 saw the conclusion between the two sides of a judicial cooperation agreement known as the "Arrangement on Reciprocal Recognition and Enforcement of Judgments in Civil and Commercial Matters by the Courts of the Mainland and of Hong Kong SAR Pursuant to the Choice of the Court Agreement between Parties Concerned".[78] In October 2006, the NPCSC passed a Decision authorising the HKSAR authorities to exercise jurisdiction in a port control zone located in a spot in Shenzhen where there would be "co-location" of immigration and customs officers of both the mainland and Hong Kong sides to facilitate travel between Hong Kong and Shenzhen on the

---

77. Albert H.Y. Chen, "The Constitution and the Rule of Law" in S.K. Lau (ed.), *The First Tung Chee-hwa Administration: The First Five Years of the Hong Kong Special Administrative Region* (Hong Kong: Chinese University Press, 2002) 85–86.

78. The Arrangement was implemented in Hong Kong by the Mainland Judgments (Reciprocal Enforcement) Ordinance (Ordinance No. 9 of 2008, Government of the Hong Kong Special Administrative Region Gazette).

new Shenzhen-Hong Kong Western Corridor.[79] On the basis of the NPCSC's Decision, legislation to implement the co-location scheme was enacted by LegCo in Hong Kong in April 2007.[80]

As mentioned in the introduction to this chapter, the successful practice of OCTS actually depends on the practice of a kind of Rule of Law relating to the Basic Law of the HKSAR. Given the low level of the Rule of Law in the PRC as of 1984, to have faith then in the successful implementation of OCTS after 1997 was to take a leap in the dark. Even thirteen years ago, it was still unknown whether the OCTS model would work from a legal and constitutional perspective. The past thirteen years have been a learning experience for all who have a stake in the success of the model. By trial and error, episode by episode, sometimes painful, sometimes joyful, we have gradually mastered the legal art of the practice of OCTS. Tuition fees have been paid; lessons have been learned; history has been written. It is a history that the people of Hong Kong have participated in making; a history that we can justifiably feel proud of; and a history that inspires confidence about ourselves, faith in our partners, and hope for the future.

## Acknowledgement

This chapter was first published as "The Rule of Law under 'One Country, Two Systems': The Case of Hong Kong 1997–2010" (2011) 6:1 *National Taiwan University Law Review* 269–299.

79. Gazette of the Standing Committee of the National People's Congress of the PRC [*Zhonghua renmin gongheguo quanguo renmin daibiao dahui changwu weiyuanhui gongbao*], No. 8, p. 697 (2006).

80. Shenzhen Bay Port Hong Kong Port Area Ordinance (Ordinance No. 4 of 2007, Government of the Hong Kong Special Administrative Region Gazette).

# 2

# The Law and Politics of Constitutional Reform and Democratisation in Hong Kong

## INTRODUCTION

Shortly after China's National People's Congress Standing Committee (NPCSC) promulgated its 31 August 2014 Decision on the model for the election by universal suffrage of Hong Kong's Chief Executive in 2017, the Occupy Central Movement (also known as the Umbrella Movement) engulfed several key government and business districts in Hong Kong. As in the case of the "Sunflower" Movement in Taipei earlier the same year, students played a very important role in the Hong Kong-based movement. Whereas the movement in Taipei was in protest against the ruling regime's policy of economic cooperation with Beijing, the movement in Hong Kong was a protest against Beijing's policy towards, or restrictions on, democratisation in Hong Kong.

Beijing's policy on Hong Kong's democratisation was purportedly based on the provisions of the Basic Law of the Hong Kong Special Administrative Region (HKSAR), which was enacted by the National People's Congress (NPC) in 1990 and came into force when Hong Kong's status changed from that of a British colony to a Special Administrative Region (SAR) of the People's Republic of China (PRC) on 1 July 1997. Ironically, so were the demands of the protesters, who alleged that the NPCSC Decision of 31 August 2014 constituted a breach of Beijing's promise to the people of Hong Kong that the democratic election of the Chief Executive of the HKSAR by universal suffrage would be introduced — a promise enshrined in the text of the Basic Law itself.[1] In this sense, the Occupy Central Movement in Hong Kong can be considered a social movement that drew on legal norms as an important component of its strategy of mass mobilisation. How then could both the legitimacy of the NPCSC's 31 August 2014 Decision and the claims of the protesters be simultaneously based on the Basic Law? This chapter seeks to answer this question by reviewing the evolution of Hong Kong's political system and investigating the different interpretations of the Basic Law from the perspective of the Chinese regime and that of democracy activists in Hong Kong.

## THE DEVELOPMENT OF HONG KONG'S POLITICAL SYSTEM

The British Empire acquired the colony of Hong Kong from China in three stages: the cession of Hong Kong Island by the Qing Emperor in 1842 after

1. Art. 45 of the Basic Law.

the First Opium War; the cession of Kowloon Peninsula (to the north of Hong Kong Island) by the Qing to Britain in 1860 after the Anglo-French forces invaded Peking; and the 99-year lease of the "New Territories" (north of Kowloon) by the Qing to Britain in the midst of the foreign powers' "scramble for concessions in China" in 1898.[2]

Although the British transplanted its common law and its tradition of the Rule of Law to colonial Hong Kong, it did not introduce the British style of parliamentary democracy or the "Westminster-style" of government. Instead the colonial government ruled Hong Kong by means of a kind of "soft authoritarianism".[3] Power was concentrated in the hands of the Governor (appointed directly by the British Crown) and senior expatriate officials appointed by the Governor, who formed the top tier of a civil service bureaucracy which at its lower levels was recruited largely from the local Chinese populace. The legislature — known as the Legislative Council (LegCo) — consisted of senior government officials and "unofficial members" chosen by the Governor from the local British and Hong Kong business and professional elite.[4] The system was described as "administrative absorption of politics".[5] Since the 1950s, Hong Kong enjoyed rapid economic growth as one of the "Four Little Dragons" of East Asia (together with Taiwan, Singapore, and South Korea). Hong Kong's population consisted largely of migrants from the Chinese mainland and their descendants, particularly those who fled to Hong Kong during the communist revolution in the mainland in the late 1940s.[6] They were willing to accept colonial rule in Hong Kong, and did not engage in struggles for democratisation and decolonisation that might provoke the PRC Government (established in 1949 after the defeat of the Nationalist Party Government by the Chinese communists).

---

2. See generally Peter Wesley-Smith, *Constitutional and Administrative Law* (Hong Kong: China and Hong Kong Law Studies, 2nd edition, 1994) 23–30.
3. For a thorough description of the political system of colonial Hong Kong, see generally N.J. Miners, *The Government and Politics of Hong Kong* (Hong Kong: Oxford University Press, 3rd edition, second impression, 1982).
4. See generally Kathleen Cheek-Milby, *A Legislature Comes of Age: Hong Kong's Search for Influence and Identity* (Hong Kong: Oxford University Press, 1995).
5. Ambrose Y.C. King, "Administrative Absorption of Politics in Hong Kong: Emphasis on the Grassroots Level" in A.Y.C. King and R.P.L. Lee (eds.), *Social Life and Development in Hong Kong* (Hong Kong: Chinese University Press, 1981) ch. 7.
6. See generally Albert H.Y. Chen, "The Development of Immigration Law and Policy: The Hong Kong Experience" (1988) 33 *McGill Law Journal* 631.

As the British "lease" over Hong Kong's New Territories would expire in 1997, British Prime Minister Margaret Thatcher visited Beijing in 1982 and initiated negotiations with the PRC Government on Hong Kong's constitutional future. The result was the Sino-British Joint Declaration, which was signed at the end of 1984.[7] The Joint Declaration provided for Hong Kong's return to China in 1997. The PRC undertook to allow Hong Kong to practise a high degree of autonomy. There would be "Hong Kong people ruling Hong Kong" instead of the PRC Government sending its Chinese Communist Party (CCP) cadres to rule the HKSAR.[8] Hong Kong would be permitted to retain its existing economic, social, and legal systems (including capitalism, private property, the English common law, and existing provisions for the protection of human rights and civil liberties) in accordance with Deng Xiaoping's concept of "One Country, Two Systems" (OCTS), in which Hong Kong would become an integral part of the "one country" of China, but the Chinese mainland and Hong Kong would practice different "systems" — "socialism" and "capitalism", respectively.[9]

The Joint Declaration contains detailed provisions on the systems and policies to be practised by the HKSAR. It is a treaty that binds the Chinese and British Governments in international law, but the PRC would need to translate its provisions into domestic law so as to provide a legal basis for the operation of the HKSAR. The drafting of such a domestic law began in 1985 and was completed in 1990, when the NPC enacted the Basic Law — the product of nearly five years of work, including two public consultation exercises in 1988 and 1989. This Basic Law would serve as a "mini-constitution" for Hong Kong after 1997. It provides for the constitutional relationship between the HKSAR Government and the Central Government in Beijing; it defines the structure, mode of formation, and powers of the HKSAR Government; it guarantees the rights and liberties of the Hong Kong people; and it sets out the social and economic policies and systems to be practised in the HKSAR.

---

7. See generally Yash Ghai, *Hong Kong's New Constitutional Order* (Hong Kong: Hong Kong University Press, 2nd edition, 1999) ch. 2.
8. Para. 3(4) of the Joint Declaration provides that "[t]he Government of the Hong Kong Special Administrative Region will be composed of local inhabitants". See also the 3rd para. of section 1 of Annex I to the Joint Declaration.
9. Section 1 of Annex I to the Joint Declaration provides that "after the establishment of the Hong Kong Special Administrative Region the socialist system and socialist policies shall not be practised in the Hong Kong Special Administrative Region" and "Hong Kong's previous capitalist system and life-style shall remain unchanged for 50 years".

Regarding Hong Kong's political system, the Joint Declaration only provided for it briefly, while the Basic Law provides the details. One of the main areas of controversy during the drafting of the Basic Law[10] was the extent to which the political system of the HKSAR should be democratic, given that the colonial political system at the time the Joint Declaration was signed in 1984 was not (neither the executive nor the legislature was elected by the people of Hong Kong). On the mode of selection of the Chief Executive of the HKSAR — who would replace the colonial Governor as the head of the Hong Kong Government — the Joint Declaration states that they "shall be selected by election or through consultations held locally and be appointed by the Central People's Government".[11] For the legislature, which was an entirely appointed body at the time, the Joint Declaration provided that the members "shall be constituted by elections", but did not elaborate further on the precise mode of election.[12] Regarding the relationship between the executive and the legislature, the Joint Declaration provided that the executive "shall be accountable to the legislature".[13]

The Basic Law is also specific with regard to provisions on the political system of the HKSAR. For instance, the Basic Law declares that the "ultimate aim"[14] of the political evolution of the HKSAR is the election of both the Chief Executive and all members of LegCo by universal suffrage. However, it also specifies that such political evolution depends on "the actual situation in the HKSAR" and "the principle of gradual and orderly progress".[15] The Basic Law provides for a progressive increase in the number of directly elected members (i.e., members elected by universal suffrage in geographical constituencies in different parts of Hong Kong, as distinguished from members elected by the "functional constituencies" discussed below) of LegCo from 20 (out of a total membership of 60) in the first-term LegCo of

10. See generally Peter Wesley-Smith and Albert Chen (eds.), *The Basic Law and Hong Kong's Future* (Hong Kong: Butterworths, 1988).
11. This is provided for in the 3rd para. of section 1 of Annex I to the Joint Declaration and in para. 3(4) of the Joint Declaration itself.
12. This is provided for in the 3rd para. of section 1 of Annex I to the Joint Declaration.
13. *Ibid*.
14. Arts. 45 and 68 of the Basic Law.
15. *Ibid*.

the HKSAR to 24 in the second LegCo, and then to 30 in the third LegCo.[16] Regarding selection, it is provided that the first Chief Executive would be chosen by a Selection Committee of 400 members, and the second and third Chief Executives elected by an Election Committee of 800 members largely elected from four sectors of Hong Kong society. Given that the Joint Declaration provided that the Chief Executive may be chosen either by election or consultation, and did not make it clear that the elections to LegCo must be by direct election rather indirect election or election by "functional constituencies", many citizens recognise these as gains for democracy.[17]

A noteworthy feature of the political system prescribed by the Basic Law is that it is not a static one but an evolving one, and the logic and mechanism of its evolution is provided for in the Basic Law itself. The ultimate aim of universal suffrage — the principle of gradual and orderly progress and the phased increase in the number of directly elected legislators — has been mentioned above. Another important characteristic of the political system established by the Basic Law is its openness to change after 2007. Annexes I and II to the Basic Law expressly provide that the methods for electing the Chief Executive and LegCo may change after 2007. They also expressly provide for the procedure for such constitutional change, which involves the support of a two-thirds majority in LegCo, the Chief Executive's consent, and the approval of (in the case of a change in the electoral method for the Chief Executive) or "reporting for the record" to (in the case of a change in the electoral method for LegCo) the NPCSC.

The Basic Law, though already enacted in 1990, only fully came into effect in 1997 upon the establishment of the HKSAR. In the "transition period" between 1984 (the year the Joint Declaration was signed) and 1997, the British colonial government continued to govern Hong Kong. It introduced a series of measures for Hong Kong's democratisation in preparation for the handover. Some of these measures were contested by the PRC Government, which

---

16. See Annex II to the Basic Law, and the Decision of the NPC on the Method for the Formation of the First Government and the First Legislative Council of the HKSAR. In the first and second LegCos, 10 and 6 members were to be elected by an Election Committee, respectively. In the first, second, and third LegCos, 30 members were elected by functional constituencies.

17. It is noteworthy in this regard that in the Basic Law of the Macao SAR, which is in most respects almost identical to the Hong Kong Basic Law, there is no mention whatsoever of the direction of political evolution or any eventual destination of universal suffrage for the election of the Chief Executive and all members of the legislature. This testifies to the relative strength of the democracy movement in Hong Kong in the 1980s.

argued that constitutional reforms in Hong Kong during the transition period must "converge" with the model of the HKSAR political system prescribed by the Basic Law.[18] However, not all of the political reforms introduced by the colonial government were objected to by Beijing. In fact, some of the political institutions created by the colonial government in the transition period were recognised by and incorporated into the Basic Law itself. The most important of such institutions was that of "functional constituencies".

Functional constituencies were introduced in 1985 as part of the first major step taken by the colonial government towards Hong Kong's democratisation.[19] This included the creation of 24 elected seats in LegCo. Twelve of these seats were elected by electoral colleges comprising the District Boards, the Urban Council, and the Regional Council, which were largely consultative bodies at local levels. The other twelve were elected by "functional constituencies" consisting of business and professional groups, such as chambers of commerce, industrialists' federations, and trade unions, as well as members of various professions, such as lawyers, doctors, engineers, and teachers. The original logic of functional constituencies,[20] as explained by the colonial government, was that they represented sectors of society from which appointed unofficial members of LegCo were formerly drawn, and in the course of democratisation, it was appropriate that the corporate bodies or individual members of these sectors would elect their own representatives into LegCo. These two modes of electing LegCo members were incorporated into the Basic Law when it was enacted in 1990. Thus, the first LegCo of the HKSAR would consist of 20 members elected by universal suffrage, 30 members elected by functional constituencies, and 10 members elected by an electoral college. The number of members elected by universal suffrage would then increase to 30 in the third LegCo.

Functional constituencies also have a role to play in picking the members of the Election Committee for the Chief Executive. As prescribed in Annex I to the Basic Law, the Election Committee would consist of persons from four sectors, with equal numbers of members from each sector. The sectors

18. See generally Albert H.Y. Chen, "From Colony to Special Administrative Region: Hong Kong's Constitutional Journey" in Raymond Wacks (ed.), *The Future of the Law in Hong Kong* (Hong Kong: Oxford University Press, 1989) 76–126.

19. White Paper, *The Further Development of Representative Government in Hong Kong* (Government Printer, November 1984).

20. See generally Christine Loh and Civic Exchange (eds.), *Functional Constituencies: A Unique Feature of the Hong Kong Legislative Council* (Hong Kong: Hong Kong University Press, 2006).

are (a) business (comprising mainly corporate voters in various commercial, financial, and industrial fields), (b) professional bodies, (c) labour and other social sectors, and (d) the political sector (including legislators, Hong Kong deputies to the NPC, and Hong Kong members of the Chinese People's Political Consultative Conference, etc.). Thus, in the Election Committee of 800 members, there were 200 members from each of the four sectors. Annex I to the Basic Law was subsequently amended in 2010, increasing the size of the Election Committee to 1,200 members, including 300 members from each of the four sectors.[21]

## POST-1997 MOVEMENTS TOWARDS DEMOCRATISATION[22]

In the first few years after the handover, elections of the Chief Executive conducted by the Election Committee and elections of LegCo members by both universal suffrage and functional constituencies took place in accordance with the relevant provisions of the Basic Law. A major turning point in the post-1997 history of Hong Kong was the Hong Kong Government's attempt to enact the National Security Bill in 2003 for the purpose of implementing article 23 of the Basic Law, which requires the HKSAR to enact laws on treason, secession, sedition, subversion, and protection of State secrets. This legislative exercise was aborted after a march of an estimated half a million people on 1 July 2003 in opposition to the bill.[23] The bill was supported by the "pro-China" camp (also known as the "pro-establishment" camp) in Hong Kong politics but opposed by the "pro-democracy" camp (also known as the "pan-democrats"),[24] which

21. The political reform of 2010 is discussed below.

22. This section and the following section draw on my chapter, "Development of Representative Government" in Johannes Chan and C.L. Lim (eds.), *Law of the Hong Kong Constitution* (Hong Kong: Sweet & Maxwell, 2nd edition, 2015) ch. 8.

23. See generally Fu Hualing, Carole J. Petersen, and Simon N.M.Young (eds.), *National Security and Fundamental Freedoms: Hong Kong's Article 23 Under Scrutiny* (Hong Kong: Hong Kong University Press, 2005); Ngok Ma, "Civil Society in Self-Defense: The Struggle Against National Security Legislation in Hong Kong" (2005) 14 *Journal of Contemporary China* 465.

24. The basic cleavage in the politics of the HKSAR has been the division between the "pro-China" camp and the "pro-democracy" camp. The former supports the policies of the PRC Government towards Hong Kong, including its cautious and gradualist approach to its democratisation. The camp also supports one-party rule in mainland China and does not criticise its human rights record. The pan-democrats advocate Western-style liberal democracy for Hong Kong, and are critical of authoritarian one-party rule in China and its human rights record.

led the social movement against the bill. With their prestige bolstered by their success in opposing the National Security Bill, the pro-democracy camp launched a movement to demand the speedy democratisation of the HKSAR.[25] In late 2003 and early 2004, a number of pro-democracy assemblies and demonstrations were held and were attended by tens of thousands of people. Pro-democracy politicians found a powerful source of legitimacy for their demands in the Basic Law. As mentioned above, the provisions of the Basic Law allow changes to the existing "undemocratic" system for the election of the third-term Chief Executive in 2007 and the fourth-term LegCo in 2008. Thus, the pan-democrats' slogan was "double universal suffrage": the introduction of universal suffrage for the election of the Chief Executive in 2007 and full universal suffrage for the election of all legislators in 2008.

In early 2004, Beijing decided to respond to the democracy movement in Hong Kong. Departing from its normal practice of holding one session of meetings once every two months, the NPCSC held two successive sessions in April 2004. At the end of the first session on 6 April, the NPCSC issued an Interpretation of the Basic Law.[26] It elaborated upon Annexes I and II to the Basic Law by stipulating a procedure for initiating changes to the relevant electoral methods: the Chief Executive should first submit a report to the NPCSC on whether there is a need to introduce electoral reform, whereupon the NPCSC will decide the matter in accordance with articles 45 and 68 of the Basic Law. After this interpretation was promulgated, Chief Executive Tung Chee-hwa submitted a relevant report to the NPCSC on 15 April 2004.[27] Another session of the NPCSC was immediately convened to consider the report, and on 26 April the NPCSC promulgated its Decision on the matter.

---

25. See generally Ming Sing, "Public Support for Democracy in Hong Kong" (2005) 12:2 *Democratization* 244 (explaining the upsurge in public support for democracy in Hong Kong since the 1 July 2003 rally).

26. This was the second interpretation of the Basic Law issued by the NPCSC. For the first interpretation, see Johannes M.M. Chan, H.L. Fu, and Yash Ghai (eds.), *Hong Kong's Constitutional Debate: Conflict Over Interpretation* (Hong Kong: Hong Kong University Press, 2000).

27. *Report by the Chief Executive of the Hong Kong Special Administrative Region to the Standing Committee of the National People's Congress on Whether There is a Need to Amend the Methods for Selecting the Chief Executive of the Hong Kong Special Administrative Region in 2007 and for Forming the Legislative Council of the Hong Kong Special Administrative Region in 2008* (Hong Kong: Hong Kong Government, 2004); the *Second Report of the Constitutional Development Task Force: Issues of Principle in the Basic Law Relating to Constitutional Development* (Hong Kong: Hong Kong Government, 2004).

The Decision ruled out the introduction of universal suffrage for the Chief Executive and all legislators in 2007 and 2008, respectively, but would permit political reforms in 2007 and 2008 within certain parameters (e.g., the proportion of directly elected legislators to those elected by functional constituencies would remain unchanged).[28]

After the NPCSC Decision, the Constitutional Development Task Force of the Hong Kong Government conducted public consultations on political reform for 2007–2008, leading to the publication of its Fifth Report in October 2005.[29] This was a major initiative on the part of Donald Tsang, who succeeded Tung Chee-hwa as Chief Executive following the latter's resignation from office in spring 2005. The Fifth Report proposed the election of the Chief Executive in 2007 by an Election Committee of 1,600 persons, which would include, *inter alia*, all members of the District Councils (formerly known as District Boards), and the expansion of LegCo in 2008 from 60 members to 70 members (including five new seats to be directly elected by universal suffrage and five new seats elected by District Councillors). Under Annexes I and II to the Basic Law, the adoption of the proposed reform would require the support of a two-thirds majority in LegCo. On 21 December 2005, the proposal was defeated by 24 "pan-democrats" in LegCo voting against it, mainly on the grounds that it was not democratic enough (e.g., the District Councillors entitled to vote under the proposed system included not only elected Councillors but also appointed Councillors, who comprised approximately one-fifth of all District Councillors), and that the government had failed to provide a timetable for the introduction of universal suffrage.[30]

After the defeat of the political reform proposal in December 2005, discussion on political development continued to be carried out in the Committee on Governance and Political Development of the Commission on Strategic Development of the Hong Kong Government. The Committee was established by Tsang in late 2005 partly in response to criticisms that the

28. See generally Albert H.Y. Chen, "The Constitutional Controversy of Spring 2004" (2004) 34 *Hong Kong Law Journal* 215; Johannes Chan and Lison Harris (eds.), *Hong Kong's Constitutional Debates* (Hong Kong: Hong Kong Law Journal Limited, 2005).

29. *The Fifth Report of the Constitutional Development Task Force: Package of Proposals for the Methods for Selecting the Chief Executive in 2007 and for Forming the Legislative Council in 2008* (Hong Kong: Hong Kong Government, 2005).

30. See generally Albert H.Y. Chen, "The Fate of the Constitutional Reform Proposal of October 2005" (2005) 35 *Hong Kong Law Journal* 537.

government was not able to provide any timetable for the introduction of universal suffrage. It was on the basis of the deliberations in this Committee that the Green Paper on Constitutional Development[31] was published on 11 July 2007, initiating a three-month consultation on the subject.

On 12 December 2007, the government published its "Report on Public Consultation on the Green Paper on Constitutional Development".[32] At the same time, Chief Executive Donald Tsang submitted his report to the NPCSC on "the Public Consultation on Constitutional Development and on whether there is a need to amend the methods for selecting the Chief Executive of the HKSAR and for forming the Legislative Council of the HKSAR in 2012".[33] On 29 December 2007, the NPCSC enacted its "Decision on Issues Relating to the Methods for Selecting the Chief Executive of the HKSAR and for Forming the Legislative Council of the HKSAR in the Year 2012 and on Issues Relating to Universal Suffrage".[34] The most significant provisions were:

(a) In 2012, neither the Chief Executive nor all legislators may be elected by universal suffrage. In 2012, the ratio (50:50) of legislators elected by universal suffrage to those elected by functional constituencies will remain unchanged. Subject to these parameters, the electoral arrangements for the Chief Executive and LegCo in 2012 may be amended in accordance with the "principle of gradual and orderly progress" as provided for in the Basic Law.

(b) At its meeting, the NPCSC was "of the view" that "the election of the fifth [Chief Executive] of the HKSAR in the year 2017 may be implemented by the method of universal suffrage; that after the [Chief Executive] is selected by universal suffrage, the election of the LegCo of the HKSAR may be implemented by the method of electing all the members by universal suffrage".

---

31. Hong Kong: Government Logistics Department, 2007.

32. Hong Kong: Government Logistics Department, 2007. The Green Paper on Constitutional Development was published on 11 July 2007, and the consultation period for the Green Paper ended on 10 October 2007.

33. Hong Kong: Government Logistics Department, 2007.

34. *Gazette of the HKSAR Government*, Special Supplement No. 5 to Gazette Extraordinary No. 48/2007 (31 December 2007) pp. E48 (Chinese version), E49 (English version). For a commentary on the Decision, see Albert H.Y. Chen, "A New Era in Hong Kong's Constitutional History" (2008) 38 *Hong Kong Law Journal* 1.

(c) "At an appropriate time prior to" the election of the Chief Executive or of all legislators by universal suffrage, the five-step procedure prescribed in Annexes I and II to the Basic Law and the NPCSC Interpretation of 6 April 2004 should be followed: (1) the Chief Executive must make a report to the NPCSC, (2) the NPCSC then renders a decision thereon, (3) a government bill for electoral reform would have to be passed by a two-thirds majority in LegCo, (4) the Chief Executive would then consent to the bill, and (5) the bill would be reported to the NPCSC for approval or for the record.

(d) At its meeting the NPCSC was "of the view that" the nominating committee (referred to in the Basic Law) for candidates for election of the Chief Executive by universal suffrage "may be formed with reference to the current provisions regarding the Election Committee in Annex I to the Hong Kong Basic Law". The nominating committee shall in accordance with democratic procedures[35] "nominate a certain number of candidates for the office of the [Chief Executive], who is to be elected through universal suffrage by all registered electors of the HKSAR, and to be appointed by the Central People's Government".

On the basis of the 2007 Decision of the NPCSC, Donald Tsang introduced the political reform exercise of 2009–2010, which was designed to revise the models for the election of the Chief Executive and LegCo in 2012. This exercise began with the publication in November 2009 of the government's "Consultation Document on Methods for Selecting the Chief Executive

35. The reference to "democratic procedures" is not new but exists in art. 45 of the Basic Law (which provides for "the selection of the Chief Executive by universal suffrage upon nomination by a broadly representative nominating committee in accordance with democratic procedures"). The meaning of this phrase has been a major source of controversy in the context of the debate on universal suffrage for the election of the Chief Executive in Hong Kong. According to one school of thought, the phrase means that all members of the nominating committee should vote for the purpose of selecting a number of candidates who may then participate in the election of the Chief Executive by universal suffrage. Under Annex I, art. 4 of the Basic Law and the Chief Executive Election Ordinance (as it stood at the time of the 2007 NPCSC Decision), nomination by not less than 100 members of the 800-member Election Committee was sufficient to enable a person to become a candidate in the election of the Chief Executive.

and for Forming the Legislative Council in 2012",[36] which put forward proposals ("the 2009 Proposal") for electoral reforms in 2012 largely similar to, but designed to be an improved version of, the reform proposal ("the 2005 Proposal") contained in the Fifth Report of the Constitutional Development Task Force that was vetoed by the pan-democrats in LegCo in December 2005.

The 2009 Proposal was similar to the 2005 Proposal in at least three ways: (1) the proposed expansion of the size of the Election Committee for the Chief Executive; (2) the proposed increase in the total number of seats in LegCo from 60 to 70; and (3) the prominent role proposed for District Councillors in the election of LegCo and in the Election Committee. There were however two main differences between the two proposals. First, the expanded Election Committee under the 2009 Proposal would have 1,200 members instead of 1,600 members. Second, under this proposal the District Councillors who would participate in the election of the five additional seats in LegCo and of relevant additional seats in the Election Committee would only include elected members of District Councils and exclude the appointed members.

More precisely, the expanded Election Committee in the 2009 Proposal would be elected by four sectors of society, each of which originally elected 200 members of the Election Committee under the existing system. However, under the 2009 Proposal, each of these sectors would elect 300 members. Regarding the additional 100 seats allocated to the fourth sector (the "political sector"), the 2009 Proposal suggested that most of them be elected by the elected members of the District Councils. On the issue of the "nomination threshold" for candidates for Chief Executive, it was proposed that it would remain at one-eighth of the total number of members of the Election Committee (i.e., 150 among the 1,200-member committee, as compared to the existing rule of 100 among the 800-member committee).

On 14 April 2010, after considering the views of members of the public collected during the three-month consultation period for the Consultation Document, the government formally announced its "Package of Proposals for the Methods for Selecting the Chief Executive and for Forming the Legislative Council in 2012" — a constitutional reform proposal ("the Reform Package") that was basically the same as that proposed in the Consultation Document.

36. The document was published on 18 November 2009 and was available in both hard copy and electronically.

The motions for the relevant amendments to Annexes I and II of the Basic Law for the purpose of implementing the Reform Package were formally submitted to LegCo on 7 June 2010 for debate and voting before the end of June 2010.

After the publication of the Consultation Document, the pan-democrats publicly stated their opposition to the Reform Package on the ground that it was not democratic enough. Thus, it was expected that they would veto the motion for the Reform Package — a repetition of what happened in December 2005. To the surprise of most observers, the situation suddenly changed on 14 June 2010, when Henry Tang, Chief Secretary of the HKSAR Government, met with Albert Ho, Chairman of the Democratic Party — one of the pan-democratic political parties, and asked him whether the Democratic Party would support the government's LegCo motion for constitutional reform if the government were to modify the Reform Package and accept the Democratic Party's counter-proposal regarding the five additional District Councils functional constituency seats being elected (after each of the candidates from the District Councils was jointly nominated by several elected District Councillors) by all voters in Hong Kong who did not already have the right to vote in any existing functional constituency.[37] In light of the affirmative answer given by Mr Ho, Chief Executive Donald Tsang announced on 21 June the government's acceptance of the Democratic Party's counter-proposal as a modification to its original Reform Package. Although not all the pan-democrats in LegCo supported the modified Reform Package, the government with the support of the Democratic Party secured the necessary two-thirds majority in LegCo for the modified Reform Package to be passed by LegCo on 24–25 June 2010.[38]

## THE STRUGGLE FOR "GENUINE" UNIVERSAL SUFFRAGE

To the pan-democrats, the political reform of 2010 was only of limited significance, since Hong Kong's political system was still far away from

37. Approximately 200,000 persons had the right to vote in existing functional constituencies. According to the Democratic Party's proposal, more than three million registered voters would be enfranchised with regard to the five newly created LegCo functional constituency seats, and all voters in Hong Kong would have two votes — one in a geographical constituency, and one in a functional constituency.

38. See generally Albert H.Y. Chen, "An Unexpected Breakthrough in Hong Kong's Constitutional Reform" (2010) 40 *Hong Kong Law Journal* 259.

achieving the goals of what they called "double universal suffrage" — the election of the Chief Executive and of all members of LegCo by universal suffrage. As the NPCSC in its 2007 Decision had set the target date for the implementation of universal suffrage for the election of the Chief Executive as 2017, a third exercise in political reform (following the first two exercises in 2005 and 2010, respectively) would need to be conducted in 2013–2015 to work out the precise model for such elections. Pro-democracy political activists in Hong Kong started in early 2013 to prepare for this exercise.

On 16 January 2013, associate professor Benny Tai of the Law School at the University of Hong Kong published a newspaper article[39] in which he put forward the idea of an "Occupy Central" campaign to pressure the Central and Hong Kong Governments to introduce a model for universal suffrage that is consistent with international standards of democratic elections. The idea was widely circulated on the Internet and received much media attention, snowballing into a real Occupy Central Movement,[40] supported by many civil society groups in addition to the pro-democracy politicians in Hong Kong. "Occupy Central" in this context referred to demonstrators practising civil disobedience and occupying the Central District — the central business district of Hong Kong — to paralyse it if the government failed to come up with a model for universal suffrage that complies with international standards on free and fair elections.[41] On 6 May 2014, after months of deliberation, the Occupy Central Movement proposed three models for election of the Chief Executive by universal suffrage for public consideration, all including the element of civic nomination (also known as "public nominations" or "citizens' nominations", which are translations of the original Chinese term *gongmin timing*), that is, nomination of candidates by prescribed numbers of citizens. In the week of 22 June 2014, the Occupy Central Movement held a "referendum" at which people could vote by mobile phone, on the Internet, or at voting

39. The article was in Chinese and titled "公民抗命的最大殺傷力武器" ["The Most Powerful Weapon of Civil Disobedience"], and was published in the newspaper《信報》[*Hong Kong Economic Journal*].

40. See the website of this movement (the full English name of which is "Occupy Central with Love and Peace"), available at: www.oclp.hk/.

41. For such international standards, see generally Michael C. Davis, "The Basic Law, Universal Suffrage and the Rule of Law in Hong Kong" (2015) 38 *Hastings International and Comparative Law Review* 275; Alvin Y.H. Cheung, "Road to Nowhere: Hong Kong's Democratization and China's Obligations under Public International Law" (2015) 40 *Brooklyn Journal of International Law* 465.

booths to indicate whether they supported any of the three proposed models, and whether they believed that LegCo should reject any model introduced by the government which was inconsistent with international standards of universal suffrage. More than 700,000 people in Hong Kong participated in the "referendum" and indicated their support for the demands put forward by the Occupy Central Movement.

Another major development in the struggle for democracy was the formation of the Alliance for True Democracy on 21 March 2013.[42] The Alliance consisted of all the pan-democrats in LegCo, all the "pro-democracy" political parties, and some civil society organisations. Their objective was to promote the realisation of "genuine" universal suffrage in Hong Kong. Then, on 8 January 2014, after months of deliberation, the Alliance proposed a "three-track" model for the election of the Chief Executive by universal suffrage — the three tracks being nominations by citizens ("civic nominations"), by political parties, and by the nominating committee, respectively.

Earlier, on 17 October 2013, C.Y. Leung, the Chief Executive of the HKSAR at that time, had announced the establishment of a three-person "Task Force on Constitutional Development", led by Chief Secretary Carrie Lam, which would launch a public consultation exercise on the electoral reforms for LegCo members and the Chief Executive to be elected in 2016 and 2017, respectively. The exercise formally commenced on 4 December 2013 with the publication of the Consultation Document titled "Let's talk and achieve universal suffrage", initiating a five-month consultation period which ended on 3 May 2014.[43] During the consultation period, many political parties and civil society groups, including those that were considered "pro-China" and those that were considered "pro-democracy", put forward their proposed electoral models.[44] On 15 July 2014, the government released its report on the outcomes of the consultation exercise. On the same day, Chief Executive C.Y. Leung submitted his "Report on whether there is a need to amend the

42. See its website, available at: www.atd.hk/.

43. For official documents relating to this consultation exercise and subsequent developments relating to the introduction of universal suffrage for the Chief Executive election in 2017, see the government's websites, available at: www.2017.gov.hk/en/home/index.html (English version); www.2017.gov.hk/tc/home/index.html (Chinese version).

44. For information on various models that were proposed, see the government's report on the consultation exercise published on 15 July 2014, titled the "Report on the Public Consultation on the Methods for Selecting the Chief Executive in 2017 and for Forming the Legislative Council in 2016" (N43).

methods for selecting the Chief Executive of the HKSAR in 2017 and for forming the Legislative Council of the HKSAR on 2016" to the NPCSC,[45] recommending the introduction of universal suffrage for the Chief Executive election in 2017 as well as suggesting that no constitutional change should be made regarding the electoral arrangements for LegCo in 2016.

On 31 August 2014, the NPCSC rendered its Decision on political reform in the HKSAR.[46] It accepted the Chief Executive's recommendation that no constitutional change regarding the election of LegCo members was called for in 2016. On the question of the election of the Chief Executive by universal suffrage, the following points in the Decision are particularly noteworthy:

(1) "Since the long-term prosperity and stability of Hong Kong and the sovereignty, security and development interests of the country are at stake, there is a need to proceed in a prudent and steady manner."

(2) "The formulation of the method for selecting the Chief Executive by universal suffrage must strictly comply with the relevant provisions of the Hong Kong Basic Law, accord with the principle of 'one country, two systems', and befit the legal status of the HKSAR. It must meet the interests of different sectors of the society, achieve balanced participation, be conducive to the development of the capitalist economy, and make gradual and orderly progress in developing a democratic system that suits the actual situation in Hong Kong."

(3) "Since the Chief Executive of the HKSAR shall be accountable to both the HKSAR and the Central People's Government in accordance with the provisions of the Hong Kong Basic Law, the principle that *the Chief Executive has to be a person who loves the country and loves Hong Kong* must be upheld. This is a basic requirement of the policy of 'one country, two systems'. It is determined by the legal status as well as important functions and duties of the Chief Executive, and is called for by the actual need to maintain long-term prosperity and stability of Hong Kong and uphold the sovereignty, security and development interests of the

45. See the websites mentioned in N43.

46. The "Decision of the NPCSC on Issues Relating to the Selection of the Chief Executive of the HKSAR by Universal Suffrage and on the Method for Forming the Legislative Council of the HKSAR in the year 2016" (31 August 2014) (N43).

country. *The method for selecting the Chief Executive by universal suffrage must provide corresponding institutional safeguards for this purpose*." (emphasis added)

(4) The Chief Executive of the HKSAR may be elected by universal suffrage "starting from 2017".

(5) Regarding the "number of members, composition and formation method" of the "broadly representative nominating committee" that nominates candidates for the Chief Executive, provisions "shall be made in *accordance with* the number of members, composition and formation method of the Election Committee for the Fourth Chief Executive". (emphasis added)

(6) "The nominating committee shall nominate *two to three candidates* for the office of the Chief Executive in accordance with democratic procedures. Each candidate must have *the endorsement of more than half of all the members of the nominating committee*." (emphasis added)

On 1 September 2014 — the day following the NPCSC Decision — several senior Chinese officials visited Hong Kong and made important speeches to explain the Decision to members of the public and to Hong Kong Government officials.[47] They pointed out that the model for universal suffrage prescribed by the Decision provides the institutional guarantee that the Chief Executive elected by universal suffrage in future would be someone who is both trusted by the Central Government and supported by the people of Hong Kong, and that non-patriots or those confrontational towards the Central Government could not become the Chief Executive. It was also said that the question of the model for universal suffrage in Hong Kong involves "a struggle for the power to govern the HKSAR". It further notes that some people in Hong Kong are

> unwilling to accept the fact that the PRC has resumed the exercise of sovereignty over Hong Kong, and are unwilling to accept the governing power of the central authority over Hong Kong; they adopt an "alternative interpretation" of [OCTS] and the provisions of the Basic Law; they make use of foreign forces, continuously stir up political disputes, pointing their fingers at the central government, and

47. See various Hong Kong newspapers published on 2 September 2014, such as *Ta Kung Pao* and *Wen Wei Po*.

> attempt to turn Hong Kong into an independent political entity. On the issue of universal suffrage, their views and demands may be summarized in one sentence: let their representative become the Chief Executive. This, of course, cannot be permitted. If they are allowed to become the Chief Executive, this would necessarily prejudice the central government's governing power over the HKSAR, prejudice our country's sovereignty, security and developmental interests, and damage the stability and prosperity of Hong Kong ... If we understand the political nature of the question of universal suffrage, we can see that the question involves matters of fundamental principles on which there can be no compromise. ... Those who insist in being confrontational towards the central government cannot be the Chief Executive, whether in the past, present or future.[48]

The Decision of the NPCSC was met by strong protest from pro-democracy forces in Hong Kong, which condemned the electoral model as "fake universal suffrage", and accused Beijing of acting in breach of its promise of universal suffrage in the Basic Law. They launched the Occupy Central Movement that started in late September and continued until mid-December 2014, resulting in the occupation of central business and government districts in Admiralty, Causeway Bay, and Mong Kok. On 7 January 2015, after the occupation came to an end, the government launched the "second round consultation" on political reform and published the consultation document, titled "2017 Seize the Opportunity: Method for Selecting the Chief Executive by Universal Suffrage Consultation Document",[49] for the purpose of consulting the public on the model for electing the Chief Executive in 2017, which was to be formulated on the basis of the NPCSC's Decision. The pan-democrats boycotted the consultation exercise, stating that they would reject any electoral model that conformed to the parameters set by the NPCSC Decision.

On 22 April 2015, the government published a policy document titled "2017 Make It Happen! Method for Selecting the Chief Executive by Universal Suffrage: Consultation Report and Proposals",[50] proposing a concrete model for nominating candidates for and electing the Chief Executive in 2017. The proposed model was subsequently introduced in LegCo and put to a vote on 18 June 2015. With 28 (including 27 "pan-democrats") of the 70 members

---

48. Extract from Li Fei's speech translated by the author. The original Chinese version is available at: http://news.takungpao.com.hk/paper/q/2014/0902/2707720.html. See also his other speech in Chinese on the same day, available at: www.fmcoprc.gov.hk/chn/xwdt/zt/rdjd/t1187495.htm.
49. Chen (N38).
50. *Ibid*.

of the Council voting against the proposal, it failed to secure the requisite two-thirds majority for amendment of Annex I to the Basic Law.[51] The veto meant that the existing system of the election of the Chief Executive by a 1,200-member Election Committee would continue for the foreseeable future.

## CONTRADICTIONS AND TENSIONS INHERENT IN THE "ONE COUNTRY, TWO SYSTEMS" POLICY

In the struggle over the model of universal suffrage to be introduced in Hong Kong in 2017, the key players were the Central Government, on the one hand, and the pan-democrats and their supporters (including the Occupy Central Movement), on the other hand. The HKSAR Government and the pro-China political forces in Hong Kong largely followed the line taken by the Central Government. The most crucial issues in the debate on the model of universal suffrage for the election of the Chief Executive concerned the "nomination threshold" or "screening of candidates" in the operation of the nominating committee and the "civic nomination" proposed by the pro-democracy forces.

The Central Government in Beijing naturally wants to ensure that the candidates for election by universal suffrage to the office of the Chief Executive are all acceptable, trustworthy, and appointable, in the sense that they are not "confrontational" towards the Central Government or ideologically opposed to the "socialist political system" in mainland China. The nomination system for candidates by a nominating committee as provided for in article 45 of the Basic Law enables this objective to be achieved if the majority of the members of the nominating committee are "pro-China" or "patriots", and if the nominations the committee makes are "institutional nominations" expressing the majority

51. Actually, the government's motion was rejected by a vote of 8 (for the motion) to 28 (against). Just before the voting took place, 31 pro-government legislators walked out of the chamber, intending to precipitate an insufficient quorum so that the voting could be delayed until one absent pro-government legislator (Lau Wong-fat) could come back to vote with the others. Due to failure in coordination and communication, 9 pro-government legislators did not join the walkout, hence the quorum (half of the membership of LegCo) was still satisfied and the voting in the chamber was completed. In the confusion, one of the pro-government legislators in the chamber failed to press the voting button in time, hence only 8 votes in support of the government's motion were recorded. Jasper Tsang, President of LegCo, followed the convention of the President not voting. See the reports in Hong Kong newspapers on 19 June 2015; for example, "Reform Package Fails, as Does Walkout" (19 June 2015) *South China Morning Post*.

will of members of the committee.[52] Thus, the 2014 Decision of the NPCSC required the size and composition of the nominating committee to follow that of the pre-existing Election Committee for the Chief Executive. The political reality since the handover in 1997 has been that with the four-sector composition of the Election Committee and its members being largely elected by functional constituencies in these sectors, the majority of the committee's members were indeed "pro-China", "pro-Establishment", or "patriots", and those who were pan-democrats or sympathetic to them only constituted a minority (slightly more than one-eighth) of the Election Committee.[53]

On the other hand, the pan-democrats were firmly opposed to any "screening" to be performed by the nominating committee for the purpose of preventing persons (such as leading members of the pan-democrats) who have considerable public support among Hong Kong voters but are not "patriots" in Beijing's eyes from becoming candidates for election by universal suffrage to the office of the Chief Executive. In their view, this would be "fake" universal suffrage and inconsistent with international standards of democracy and elections, which prohibit unreasonable restrictions on the right to be a candidate in an election (such as restrictions or discrimination based on a person's political opinion).[54] "Genuine" universal suffrage, in their view, requires a truly competitive election in which candidates with different platforms and political opinions (including opinions critical of Beijing and its policies towards Hong Kong or the mainland itself) may freely and fairly compete for votes. Ever since direct election by universal suffrage was introduced for a portion of LegCo seats in 1991, the pan-democrats had in every election obtained a majority of the popular votes for those LegCo seats that were elected by universal suffrage (as

52. The concept of "institutional nomination" (*jigou timing*) was first mentioned by Qiao Xiaoyang, Chairman of the Law Committee of the NPC, in his speech in Shenzhen to "pro-establishment" Hong Kong legislators on 24 March 2013. See various Hong Kong newspapers on 25 March 2013, such as *Ta Kung Pao* and *Wen Wei Po*.

53. In the existing system for election of the Chief Executive by the Election Committee under Annex I to the Basic Law, a candidate may be nominated jointly by at least one-eighth of the members of the Election Committee, followed by election by members of the Election Committee. In the Chief Executive elections of 2007 and 2012, persons supporting or sympathetic to the pan-democrats won more than one-eighth of the seats in the elections to the Election Committee, and thus Alan Leong (of the Civic Party) and Albert Ho (of the Democratic Party) were nominated as one of the two candidates in the 2007 election and one of the three candidates in the 2012 election, respectively.

54. Davis (N41); Cheung (N41).

distinguished from seats elected by functional constituencies).[55] Thus, they felt justified in believing that any nomination system for the election of the Chief Executive by universal suffrage which makes it impossible for their leaders to be nominated as candidates would not be genuine universal suffrage. The pan-democrats and their supporters, therefore, condemned the model for universal suffrage stipulated in the NPCSC Decision and boycotted the government's "second round" of consultation regarding more detailed arrangements for universal suffrage. They eventually vetoed the government's electoral proposal which was based on the model stipulated by the NPCSC.

During the debate in 2013–2014 on the nomination system for election of the Chief Executive by universal suffrage in 2017, the principal demand of the pan-democrats and the Occupy Central Movement was civic nomination, although there were proposals from pro-democracy scholars considered to be "moderate", and also a proposal from Ronny Tong,[56] a legislator and member of the Civic Party, that did not insist on civic nomination but advocated a relatively low threshold for nomination by a nomination committee (such as one-eighth of its members being able to nominate a candidate)[57] which, according to these proposals, should be more democratically constituted than the existing Election Committee. The pan-democrats and other democracy activists in Hong Kong considered civic nomination to be more consistent with democracy and free election than nominations by a nominating committee that is not elected by universal suffrage, as civic nomination would allow everyone who has the requisite degree of popular support (say tens of thousands of eligible voters) to participate as a candidate in the election. They argued that civic nomination is not necessarily inconsistent with article 45 of the Basic Law, as in their view it leaves open the possibility of allowing the nominating committee to endorse the candidates nominated by the requisite number of citizens, in addition to members of the nominating committee making their own nominations of candidates. However, in the eyes of Beijing, civic nomination was out of the question as it was plainly inconsistent with the Basic Law.

55. The pan-democrats have consistently won approximately 55–60 percent of the popular votes in each election and the pro-China camp approximately 40–45 percent of the popular votes. Such distribution has hardly changed in 20 years.

56. Tong's proposal was first publicised at a press conference on 15 October 2013. See http://designdemocracy.hk/ronny-tong-proposal/?lang=tw and http://specials.mingpao.com/cfm/Category.cfm?SpecialsID=137&Page=1&CategoryID=4660.

57. This was the existing threshold for nomination of candidates for election of the Chief Executive by the Election Committee as prescribed in Annex I to the Basic Law.

The Decision of the NPCSC in August 2014 might be understood as the outcome of a cost-benefit analysis conducted by Beijing regarding the introduction of elections of the Chief Executive by universal suffrage in Hong Kong. The benefit would be that they would be seen as honouring the promise of universal suffrage made in the 2007 Decision of the NPCSC and in the Basic Law, and would win the support of Hong Kong people who aspire towards democracy. Furthermore, some believed that the government would become more effective if its Chief Executive was elected by universal suffrage and thus have a popular mandate and greater legitimacy to govern. On the other hand, an electoral model acceptable to the pan-democrats would only be one in which the pan-democrats would have a reasonable chance of getting their leaders nominated by the nominating committee as candidates. For Beijing, agreeing to such an electoral model would have meant they accept that there is a chance that a pan-democrat would be elected as Chief Executive. Beijing would have assessed the likelihood of this scenario materialising, and considered how to deal with this should it occur. Would the pan-democrat be appointed as Chief Executive? Or would the appointment be declined — a power which it has under the Basic Law[58] — and another election held? What would be the nature and magnitude of the political crisis in Hong Kong should this happen? How would such a crisis (taking into account its likelihood and its magnitude) compare with the crisis that would be precipitated by the electoral model favoured by Beijing being unacceptable to the pro-democracy forces in Hong Kong? These were likely the factors Beijing considered before reaching the Decision in August 2014 on the model for universal suffrage for the Hong Kong Chief Executive in 2017. The Decision implies that according to Beijing's analysis, the risk and negative consequences of a non-patriot winning an election by universal suffrage and of a crisis precipitated by Beijing refusing to appoint them as Chief Executive are more serious than the risk and negative consequences of "Occupy Central" materialising or of any discontent or unrest flowing from Beijing's model for universal suffrage being rejected by the pro-democracy forces in Hong Kong.

Interestingly, a cost-benefit analysis may also be used to explain why the pan-democrats in LegCo vetoed the model of universal suffrage for the election

58. Art. 15 of the Basic Law provides that "[t]he Central People's Government shall appoint the Chief Executive and the principal officials of the executive authorities of the Hong Kong Special Administrative Region in accordance with the provisions of Chapter IV of this Law". Ch. IV, art. 45(1) provides that "[t]he Chief Executive of the Hong Kong Special Administrative Region shall be selected by election or through consultations held locally and be appointed by the Central People's Government".

of the Chief Executive proposed by the HKSAR Government on the basis of the NPCSC Decision of August 2014. As the composition of the Nominating Committee and the high nomination threshold specified by the Decision effectively rules out the possibility of the pan-democrats being nominated as candidates, the adoption of the electoral model proposed by the government would effectively mean that the election by universal suffrage in 2017 would be a competition among two or three "pro-China" candidates considered to be "patriots" by a majority of the members of the Nominating Committee. The candidate eventually elected can then claim a popular mandate and political legitimacy greater than that of any pan-democratic leader. This would work against the interests of the pan-democrats, because their claim that they represent the majority of Hong Kong voters would be weakened — a claim which they have been able to make so far because the majority of Hong Kong voters voted for the pan-democrats rather than pro-China or pro-Establishment candidates in LegCo elections from 1991 to 2012. For the pan-democrats, therefore, there was little to be gained, but much to lose, from the introduction of universal suffrage for the election of the Chief Executive in 2017 in accordance with the nomination model prescribed by the NPCSC Decision of August 2014. This, then, explains why they vetoed the electoral package in LegCo, despite the fact that opinion polls showed that members of the public who supported electoral reform outnumbered those opposed to it.[59]

Neither the considerations which Beijing probably took into account in conducting the cost-benefit analysis discussed above, nor those which probably led to the pan-democrats vetoing the electoral reform as discussed in the preceding paragraph, were the publicly stated reasons for the respective decisions. Beijing insisted that the NPCSC Decision was made in accordance with the text of article 45 of the Basic Law. Pan-democrats condemned the Decision and accused Beijing of breaching its promise of universal suffrage — which for the pan-democrats meant "genuine universal suffrage" — for Hong Kong people under the Basic Law and the timetable for

59. The LegCo vote on the electoral reform proposal took place on 18 June 2015. According to the "Survey on 2017 Chief Executive Election Proposal" conducted by the University of Hong Kong's Public Opinion Programme, among those polled on 5–14 June 2015, 51 percent supported the proposal, while 37 percent were opposed; see www.hkupop.hku.hk/english/report/superSurvey2015/index.html. According to the "Joint-University Rolling Survey on 2017 Chief Executive Election Proposal" on 12–16 June 2015, 47 percent supported the electoral reform proposal, while 38 percent were opposed; see www.hkupop.hku.hk/english/features/jointUrollingSurvey/.

democratisation stipulated in the NPCSC Decision of 2007. Yet what the Basic Law and the NPCSC Decision of 2007 promised was no more than a system of appointment of the Chief Executive by the Central People's Government after an election by "universal suffrage upon nomination by a broadly representative nominating committee in accordance with democratic procedures".[60] Control or pre-selection — or what the pan-democrats objected to as the "screening" — of candidates by a nominating committee had thus been written into the Basic Law as enacted in 1990.

In inaugurating the grand experiment of the OCTS model, the Hong Kong Basic Law has not only provided for the co-existence of two economic systems — one socialist and the other capitalist — within the PRC, but it has also envisioned a process of democratisation in Hong Kong towards eventual election of the Chief Executive and of all legislators by universal suffrage, thus moving the political systems of Hong Kong and of mainland China further apart over time (unless the latter also democratises). The Basic Law has thus nourished the aspirations of many people in Hong Kong towards a full liberal democracy. However, are these aspirations consistent with, and realisable within, the concept and structure of the OCTS model, under which the "one country" adheres to the supremacy of the CCP, which must resist Western-style liberal democracy in order to survive? The story of the debate on and struggle for universal suffrage in Hong Kong thus reveals such underlying tensions behind, and the contradictions inherent in, the very concept and practice of OCTS.

It is unlikely that these tensions and contradictions will be resolved in the foreseeable future. The most likely scenario is that the existing "semi-democratic" political system in Hong Kong[61] will be maintained without further democratisation or a move towards election of the Chief Executive by universal suffrage, and the confrontation and stalemate between the pro-China camp and pan-democratic camp in the politics of the HKSAR will

60. Art. 45 of the Basic Law.

61. The existing political system of the HKSAR has been described as a semi-democracy; see, for example, William H. Overholt, "Hong Kong: The Perils of Semidemocracy" (2001) 12:4 *Journal of Democracy* 5; Ming Sing, "Origins of Anti-Partyism in Hong Kong" (2004) 21:3 *East Asia* 37; Ma Ngok, *Political Development in Hong Kong* (Hong Kong: Hong Kong University Press, 2007) 226. See also Sonny Shiu-hing Lo, *Hong Kong's Indigenous Democracy* (New York: Palgrave Macmillan, 2015).

continue to plague it and make it difficult to govern.[62] There thus seems to be an inexorable logic that the political costs, and ultimately the economic and social costs, of OCTS are rising as a result of the clash between Hong Kong people's aspirations towards Western-style democracy and the Chinese Party-State's insistence that the HKSAR Government must be led by "patriots" loyal to the Central Government. Whether such costs can be contained, and whether social stability and economic prosperity can continue to be maintained in Hong Kong, will be a challenge for the people of Hong Kong and the PRC Government in the years to come.

## Acknowledgement

This chapter was first published as "The Law and Politics of Constitutional Reform and Democratization in Hong Kong" in Brian Christopher Jones (ed.), *Law and Politics of the Taiwan Sunflower and Hong Kong Umbrella Movements* (2017), chapter 4, pp. 65–82. This edited version is reprinted with permission from the publisher, Routledge.

62. The difficulties of Hong Kong's governance have been exacerbated by the filibuster in LegCo by radical pan-democrats, which has steadily increased in scale since 2012 and resulted in partial paralysis of the LegCo's functions of law-making and financial approval.

# 3

# The Theory and Practice of Autonomy: The Case of Hong Kong

## INTRODUCTION

This chapter considers the case of Hong Kong's autonomy in terms of the general theory and practice of autonomy as an important political and constitutional phenomenon in the contemporary world. Part I introduces the general considerations and usual features of arrangements of autonomy in federal and unitary states. Part II considers the "One Country, Two Systems" (OCTS) constitutional framework in the Hong Kong Special Administrative Region (HKSAR) from the perspective of autonomy. The historical origins of OCTS, its constitutional design and its practice since 1997 will be discussed, and the strengths and limitations of the autonomy of the HKSAR will be identified. Part III explores some distinctive features of Hong Kong's autonomy under OCTS, particularly the political divide between the pro-China and pro-democracy forces in Hong Kong's politics as well as the informal role played by Beijing within Hong Kong's political system. The chapter finishes with a reflection on Hong Kong's experience in the practice of autonomy and speculates about its future.

## THE CONCEPT OF AUTONOMY

It has been said that "'autonomy' is not a term of art in international or constitutional law".[1] The word "autonomy" can be used in a broad sense, which includes (a) territorial autonomy, often on an asymmetrical basis (in the sense that not all territories or regions of the state enjoy the same degree of territorial autonomy), within a unitary state;[2] and (b) the autonomy enjoyed by constituent units of a federal state.[3] In the discussion below, the word "autonomy" will be used in its broad sense, unless otherwise indicated,

---

1. Hannum Hurst, *Autonomy, Sovereignty and Self-Determination: The Accommodation of Conflicting Rights* (Philadelphia: University of Pennsylvania Press, Revised edition, 1996) 4; Markku Suksi, *Sub-State Governance through Territorial Autonomy: A Comparative Study in Constitutional Law of Powers, Procedures and Institutions* (Berlin: Springer, 2011) 101.
2. Y. Dinstein (ed.), *Models of Autonomy* (New Brunswick: Transaction Books, 1981); M. Weller and K. Nobbs (eds.), *Asymmetric Autonomy and the Settlement of Ethnic Conflicts* (Philadelphia: University of Pennsylvania Press, 2010); Suksi (N1); Y. Ghai and S. Woodman (eds.), *Practising Self-Government: A Comparative Study of Autonomous Regions* (Cambridge: Cambridge University Press, 2013).
3. K.C. Wheare, *Federal Government* (London: Oxford University Press, 4th edition, 1963).

expressly or by the context. "Autonomy" in the narrow sense refers to territorial autonomy within a unitary state in situation (a) above.[4]

The concept of autonomy refers to a particular form of distribution of governmental power within a sovereign state. It may be explained as follows. Suppose there is a sovereign state X, and a part of the territory of X is Y. The people of Y can be said to exercise a power of autonomy within the state X if they — usually through their representatives — are empowered to govern themselves in respect of certain affairs, for instance housing, education, transport, social welfare, environmental hygiene, medical services, taxation, etc. The more extensive the kinds of affairs over which they are self-governing, the higher the degree of autonomy. The idea of autonomy, however, presupposes that there are at least some governmental affairs over which the people of Y have no ultimate control. For if the people of Y, through their representatives, have complete control over every aspect of their existence and operation as a community, then they are not merely autonomous but constitute an independent sovereign state.

In the above example, there are at least two levels of government in state X. The first is the national or central government of state X, representing, exercising power on behalf of, and having authority over all the citizens of X. Second, there is the local government, or autonomous government, of area Y, representing, exercising power on behalf of, and having authority over the people of Y. Of course, insofar as the people of Y are also citizens of X, they can also participate in the formation and operation of the national government. However, is likely that the local government of Y will be able to represent their interests more directly and effectively than the national government, at least where the "autonomous affairs" (i.e., affairs specified as the local autonomous government's responsibilities) are involved. For otherwise the people of Y will not derive any substantial benefit from the arrangement of autonomy.

The above analysis illustrates another possible way of defining the concept of autonomy: the people of Y are said to be exercising autonomy within

---

4. In addition to "territorial autonomy", there also exists the concept of "cultural autonomy"; see A. Eide, "Cultural Autonomy: Concept, Content, History, and Role in the World Order" in M. Suksi (ed.), *Autonomy: Applications and Implications* (The Hague: Kluwer, 1998) 251–276. Furthermore, "[a]utonomy usually takes territorial forms, but some sort of autonomy can also be exercised through cultural councils or other limited forms of self-government, such as the regimes of personal laws"; see Yash Ghai, "Introduction: Nature and Origins of Autonomy" in Ghai and Woodman (N2), 6.

state X (Y being part of X) if there exists a division of governmental powers between the local or regional government of Y and the central or national government of X. This division is based on the classification of governmental affairs into different types, and the allocation of power over certain types of affairs to one government, while power over other types of affairs is allocated to the other government. Under this arrangement, the local government will exercise various powers, such as policy-making powers, legislative powers, and judicial powers, over certain designated types of affairs, and the national government will exercise governmental powers over other affairs. The more extensive the powers of the local government, the higher the degree of autonomy, and vice versa.

If the concept of autonomy is understood as explained above, then it follows that autonomy is in fact a fairly widespread phenomenon in the nations of the contemporary world. Every regional or provincial government, every city council or local authority, exercises some powers of autonomy. The difference among them lies mainly in the degree of autonomy. If a particular local authority has autonomous power only over relatively trivial affairs in a small area, then according to the ordinary usage of language, it can hardly deserve the title "autonomous government", although in theory the general concept of autonomy may still be applicable and relevant to it.

The scope of autonomy which is desirable or appropriate in any particular context usually depends on a complex of political, economic, social, cultural, and even racial, linguistic, and religious factors. Where the population in a particular area of a nation-state is sharply distinguishable from those in other areas by reason of some of these factors, they might demand a high degree of autonomy for the purpose of protecting certain basic interests or values against encroachment by the nation-state. Even where no such considerations are involved, some lower degrees of autonomy may be advantageous in the operation of certain levels of local government to stimulate local initiative, interest, and participation, and thus to promote efficiency and democracy.

Although the policy to be adopted in any historical situation[5] regarding whether and what degree of autonomy for an area within a state should exist is almost always determined by extra-legal considerations, technical constitutional devices do need to be examined in the process of the creative design of autonomous arrangements in any given set of circumstances. In particular, the

5. For historical perspectives on autonomy, see Susan J. Henders, *Territoriality, Asymmetry, and Autonomy: Catalonia, Corsica, Hong Kong, and Tibet* (New York: Palgrave Macmillan, 2010) 6–11; Ghai (N4) 7.

following issues are likely to command the attention of constitutional and legal experts advising politicians on the construction of models of autonomy:

(1) *Method by which the local government is to be formed.* Advocates of local autonomy would seek to ensure that the government of the autonomous region will truly represent and govern in the interests of the people of that region.

(2) *Division of powers in the legislative, executive, and judicial spheres between the central government and the local government.* The challenge here is to draw a line between the domain of the local government and that of the central government, a line which is rational and reasonable in theory and practicable in reality.

(3) *Mechanisms for rectification of errors and resolution of disputes.* What institutional devices are to be established to ensure, on the one hand, that the local government will not exceed the scope of its autonomy, and, on the other hand, that the central government will not infringe upon the scope of such autonomy? Where such errors have indeed occurred, how are they to be rectified? Where conflicts of opinion regarding these matters arise between the two sides, how are they to be resolved?

We consider below the salient features of federal and non-federal models of autonomy, respectively. A federal state is formed by the union of more than one member state or province, each of which usually enjoys the same degree of autonomy (in what can be called a "symmetrical" manner) vis-à-vis the federal state.[6] There is a division of power between the federal government and the state (or provincial) governments. Thus, the former will have exclusive jurisdiction over certain affairs; each of the state governments will have exclusive jurisdiction over other affairs within its territory; and over some affairs, the federal and state governments will have "concurrent powers". Concurrent powers exist where, for example, both the federal legislature and a state legislature may be able to make law on a particular matter, but if there is a conflict between a relevant federal law and a state law, the former will prevail.

The division of power between the federal government and the state governments in a federal state is almost invariably set out in a written

6. Wheare (N3).

constitution which forms the constitutional and legal foundation of the federal state. In some federal states, the state governments possess "residuary powers" (or "residual powers"),[7] which means that any power which has not been expressly assigned to the federal government by the constitution remains vested in the state government. This principle may be regarded as a reflection of the fact that each member state of the federal state had originally been a full sovereign state, or at least a separately governed entity, before the federation was formed. However, the reservation of residuary powers by the states is by no means a necessary feature of a federal state. It is perfectly possible and proper for the federal constitution to allocate such residuary powers to the federal government.

A fundamental legal characteristic of the federal state is that the federal constitution, in which the division of powers is set out, is binding not only on the state governments but also on the federal government. The supremacy of this constitutional division of powers over the federal government means that the latter may not unilaterally upset the original division of powers by expanding its actions and activities beyond their constitutional limit, thus infringing the autonomy of the member states. This original division of powers may only be altered by amendment of the constitution, which usually requires the overwhelming support not only of the federal legislature but also of the legislatures of most of the states, or even of the people of the states themselves voting in a referendum.

Since the federal constitution limits the power of both the federal government and state governments, it is necessary to provide in its design a mechanism for interpreting and enforcing these constitutional limits on power and for imposing legal sanctions where such limits have been exceeded. In many federal states, this mechanism takes the form of either a constitutional court or a supreme court at the apex of a system of ordinary courts. The court may, for example, declare as invalid federal laws touching upon a matter within the exclusive jurisdiction of a state and thus trespassing upon the state's autonomy, or conversely, a state law which deals with a matter within the exclusive jurisdiction of the federal government. Thus, conflicts or disputes between the federal and state governments arising from the constitutional division of power are resolved in this judicial forum.

The autonomy of a member state of a federation is, however, not the sole model of autonomy. Even in a unitary state, it is possible to have within

7. Suksi (N1) 126–127, 131, 139.

it one or more autonomous areas or regions each practising territorial autonomy (i.e., autonomy within the territory of the region). It is also possible for such an autonomous region to exercise a degree of autonomy higher than that of a member state of a federation. As explained above, the degree of autonomy depends primarily on the range of subject matters presided over by the local autonomous government, and not on whether the arrangement is federal or not. What, then, are the differences between autonomy in a federation and that in a unitary state?

First, a federation usually consists of constituent units or member states that have equal status within the federal state and equal powers of autonomy distributed among them in a symmetrical manner. Furthermore, the member states are usually equally represented in the upper house of a bicameral legislature of the federal state,[8] such as the Senate of the U.S. Congress. By contrast, arrangements of territorial autonomy within a unitary state are usually asymmetrical arrangements under which one or some — but not all — regions of the state are granted high degrees of autonomy.

Second, the power of a local government in an autonomous region forming part of a unitary state is often, though not invariably, derived not from the constitution of the unitary state but from a law enacted by the legislature of the state. While a constitution is both supreme over and binding on the national legislature, a law enacted by it is not. Thus, whereas in a federal state the autonomy of each member state is constitutionally guaranteed by the provisions regarding division of power in the federal constitution, the territorial autonomy of an autonomous region within a unitary state is not necessarily directly protected by the constitution. Where territorial autonomy is derived from ordinary national legislation, it may, at least in constitutional theory, be withdrawn by legislative amendment without the need for constitutional amendment. Thus, from the point of view of the constitutional theorist, the autonomy of a local government in a unitary state may (unless it is constitutionally entrenched) be less securely guaranteed or entrenched than the autonomy of a member state in a federation.

Third, whereas in a federal state the federal government and state governments are usually considered "independent" and "coordinate",[9] with each government having exclusive jurisdiction over certain matters that is

8. *Ibid.*, 126, 130–131, 139.

9. *Ibid.*, 86, 117, 126–127.

constitutionally protected, in a unitary state the relationship between the national government and the regional government to which autonomous powers have been devolved may be described as that between a "superior" and an "inferior" or "subordinate" organ of government.[10] The powers of autonomy within the region enjoyed by the "inferior" organ of government have been granted and transferred to it by the "superior" organ (i.e., the national legislature), which may at least in theory resume or override such powers.

The difference between federalism and territorial autonomy within a unitary state can also be highlighted by analysing the delegation of governmental power from historical and logical points of view. In the formation of a federal state, sovereign powers which were originally vested in the states are usually relinquished, subject to the condition of having a fundamental constitutional guarantee of the division of power securing certain powers for the member states. On the other hand, the autonomy enjoyed by the people of an autonomous region of a unitary state does not logically exist prior to, but is usually the direct result of, a voluntary delegation or devolution of power by the national authority. In this situation, the grant of autonomy or the transfer of autonomous governmental powers to the region may be regarded as a concession made by the fully sovereign nation-state. This may be contrasted with the federal situation, where the autonomy of the member state is often a reserved right of a community which once possessed sovereignty but voluntarily decided to transfer it to a new federal state subject to the reservation of rights and division of powers set out in the new federal constitution.

Examples of federal states in the contemporary world include the United States, Canada, Australia, India, and Germany. It is noteworthy that in these countries, the ultimate forum for settling disputes regarding the interpretation and enforcement of the constitutional division of power between national and state authorities is the federal supreme court (or the Federal Constitutional Court in the case of Germany). Examples of autonomy within a unitary state include the case of Greenland under the sovereignty of Denmark, the devolution to Scotland in the case of the United Kingdom, and the case of Hong Kong and Macau in China under the constitutional framework of OCTS, to which we now turn.

10. *Ibid.*, 114–117, 121.

## HONG KONG'S AUTONOMY UNDER "ONE COUNTRY, TWO SYSTEMS"

The People's Republic of China (PRC) has always insisted that it is a unitary state and cannot accept a federal structure.[11] The concept of a special administrative region (SAR) within the PRC with a high degree of autonomy, and the related concept of OCTS, represent a substantial modification of the original model of a highly centralised unitary state, although they do not go so far as to move China into federalism.

The Chinese Government's concept of OCTS was originally developed as a new cornerstone of its policy towards Taiwan, although the full elaboration of the concept took place during the Sino-British negotiations in 1982–1984 on the status of the British colony of Hong Kong after 1997. The origins of the concept can be traced back to the late 1970s, when a fundamental shift in the PRC's Taiwan policy occurred.[12] The original position before the policy change was that the "liberation of Taiwan" should be pursued. "Liberation" refers, of course, to liberation from the evils of capitalism and imperialism, and the revolutionary introduction of communism.

The new Taiwan policy was revealed in several official statements published after 1979, the most important of which was the nine-point proposal of Ye Jianying, then Chairman of the PRC National People Congress Standing Committee (NPCSC), published in September 1981. The proposal envisaged the peaceful reunification of China, with Taiwan being given the status of an SAR of the PRC. As such it would retain its existing social and economic systems after unification. It would enjoy a high degree of autonomy; it could enter into external economic and cultural relations with other countries, and even maintain its own armed forces. Shortly afterwards, in January 1982, elder statesman Deng Xiaoping coined the expression "One Country, Two Systems", and said that this was the essence of Ye Jianying's statement. There was to be one China, but two systems — the socialist system on the mainland and the capitalist system in Taiwan. In December 1982, a new Constitution of the PRC was enacted. It contains a new article which contemplates the establishment

11. Shuwen Wang (ed.), *Introduction to the Basic Law of the Hong Kong Special Administrative Region* (Beijing: Law Press, 2000) 57–62, 67.
12. Ying-jeou Ma, "Policy Towards the Chinese Mainland: Taipei's View" in S. Tsang (ed.), *In the Shadow of China: Political Developments in Taiwan Since 1949* (Hong Kong: Hong Kong University Press, 1993), 193–211.

of SARs of the PRC which may practise social systems different from those in other parts of China.[13] In a speech delivered in July 1983, Deng elaborated the idea further, pointing out that the Chinese Government would not send any civilian or military officials to Taiwan after reunification under the OCTS scheme, the government and armed forces in Taiwan would be entirely managed by local people, and at the same time, Taiwan representatives would be able to serve in leading positions in the Central Government of the PRC.

Although the Taipei Government showed no interest in the OCTS model of reunification, the PRC was soon to be given the opportunity to show to the world that the concept of OCTS was sound in theory and workable in practice. In September 1982, British Prime Minister Margaret Thatcher visited Beijing, seeking a solution to the question of Hong Kong's constitutional status after 1997. High-level negotiations between the two governments started after her visit. Two years of hard bargaining and strenuous work finally produced the "Sino-British Joint Declaration on the Question of Hong Kong" in September 1984 in which the OCTS concept was enshrined and applied to post-1997 Hong Kong. The model has also been applied subsequently to the recovery of Macau, a Portuguese colony adjacent to Hong Kong. The wording of the Sino-Portuguese Joint Declaration in 1987 is largely similar to the Sino-British Joint Declaration of 1984.[14]

The OCTS model may be usefully compared with the federal model of autonomy described above. After the reunification of Hong Kong and Macau with China, the structure of the PRC consists of a national or central government, and, at the level directly below it, 27 provincial governments (including the governments of five autonomous regions, excluding Taiwan), four municipality governments directly under the central government, and two SAR governments (Hong Kong and Macau). It is not a federal system; there is nothing in the national constitution which provides for a formal division of power between the national government and the provincial, municipal, and SAR governments. There is no constitutional (as distinguished from legal) limitation on the capacity of the national government to exercise power with regard to any matter within any province, city, or SAR of the PRC.

13. Art. 31 of the 1982 Constitution provides: "The State may establish special administrative regions when necessary. The systems to be instituted in special administrative regions shall be prescribed by law enacted by the National People's Congress in the light of specific conditions."
14. Paulo Cardinal, "Macau: Transformations of An Historic Autonomy" in Ghai and Woodman (N2) 383–411.

From a legal perspective, the basis of the HKSAR's autonomy under OCTS is the Basic Law of the HKSAR, which is a law enacted in 1990 by the national legislature, the National People's Congress (NPC), in pursuance of article 31 of the PRC Constitution and the Sino-British Joint Declaration.[15] The Basic Law

(a) provides for the modes of formation and operation of the government of the SAR,

(b) identifies the sources of law in the SAR,

(c) guarantees the human rights of its residents,

(d) stipulates the social and economic systems and policies to be practised in the SAR, and

(e) defines its relationship with the Central Government and the scope of its autonomous powers.

Generally speaking, the Basic Law establishes political, legal, social, and economic systems in the HKSAR that are very different from those in force in mainland China; hence the expression "One Country, Two Systems". However, the model comes with various strengths and limitations in terms of autonomy.

The greatest strength of the OCTS model as enshrined in the Basic Law of Hong Kong is the very wide scope of autonomy it confers on the HKSAR in terms of the subject matters over which the executive, legislative, and judicial branches of the HKSAR Government have jurisdiction. The scope of autonomy enjoyed by the HKSAR is much larger than that enjoyed by members of federal states.[16] Basically, all governmental affairs in the HKSAR other than defence, foreign affairs, and constitutional change in the electoral system are within the jurisdiction of the HKSAR Government. Aspects of this high degree of autonomy include, but are not limited to, the following:

(1) More than 95 percent of the laws enacted by the national legislature (the NPC and NPCSC) are not applicable to the HKSAR, in which the pre-existing common law system is preserved. The only

15. P.Y. Lo, *The Hong Kong Basic Law* (Hong Kong: LexisNexis, 2011).

16. Hannum (N1) 137–149; Yash Ghai, "Hong Kong's Autonomy: Dialects of Powers and Institutions" in Ghai and Woodman (N2) 335–336.

national laws that apply to Hong Kong are listed in Annex III to the Basic Law. There are 14 such laws at the moment, including the Nationality Law, National Flag Law, National Anthem Law, Law on the Territorial Sea, Law on the Garrisoning of the HKSAR, Law on Safeguarding National Security in the HKSAR, etc.[17]

(2) Cases litigated before the Hong Kong courts are dealt with entirely within the Hong Kong court system, with the Hong Kong Court of Final Appeal (CFA) being the highest appellate court. No appeal lies from a Hong Kong court to any court or institution in mainland China. The Basic Law requires the CFA to refer relevant provisions of the Basic Law to the NPCSC for interpretation in certain circumstances.[18] However, interpretations made by the NPCSC cannot have the effect of overturning a court judgment previously rendered, in the sense that litigants in the case that the court has already decided would not be affected by a subsequent NPCSC interpretation.[19]

(3) Hong Kong residents do not have to pay any tax to the Central Government, and the tax which they pay to the HKSAR Government will be used for the HKSAR exclusively — no part of it has to be handed over to the Central Government.

(4) The HKSAR can continue to have and issue its own currency, the Hong Kong dollar.

(5) The HKSAR can control and regulate entry and exit of persons into and out of the HKSAR.

17. See art. 18 of the Basic Law. Annex III has been amended four times after the Basic Law was enacted in 1990. On 1 July 1997, the NPCSC added to it five new laws enacted between 1990 and 1997: the Law on the Garrisoning of the HKSAR, the National Flag Law, the National Emblem Law, and two other laws on the territorial sea and consular privileges. After 1 July 1997, only four laws have been added: the Law on the Exclusive Economic Zone and the Continental Shelf was added to Annex III in December 1998; the Law on Judicial Immunity from Compulsory Measures Concerning the Property of Foreign Central Banks was added in October 2005; the National Anthem Law was added in November 2017; the National Security Law (NSL) was added in June 2020. For the "co-location" controversy regarding the application of mainland Chinese law in the "port control zone" of the West Kowloon express railway station, see *Leung Chung Hang v President of Legislative Council* [2018] HKCFI 2657.

18. The circumstances are specified in art. 158(3) of the Basic Law.

19. See art. 158(3) of the Basic Law.

(6) The HKSAR is a customs territory separate from other parts of China.

(7) The HKSAR, using the name of "Hong Kong, China", can enter into economic and cultural relations with other countries and participate in some international organisations (such as the World Trade Organization or WTO) whose membership is not restricted to sovereign states.[20] The Basic Law authorises the HKSAR Government to handle certain "external affairs" even though, generally speaking, "foreign affairs" are within the power of the Central Government.[21]

The degree of autonomy which the HKSAR has enjoyed since 1997 is certainly not less than what it had under British colonial rule. Indeed, whereas Hong Kong's autonomy in the colonial era was largely a product of unwritten practices and constitutional conventions, the HKSAR's autonomy in many domains is now expressly guaranteed by the Basic Law.[22] This, then, is the strength of the OCTS model of autonomy.

On the other hand, there are at least two principal limitations or weaknesses of the OCTS model in Hong Kong. One is that the constitutional and legal guarantees for autonomy are less secure than they are in federalism. The other relates to the limited extent of democratisation in the HKSAR.

As discussed above, in federalism the division of power between the federal and state governments is written into the constitution which cannot be easily amended, and when jurisdictional disputes arise, the federal supreme court or constitutional court is the final arbiter. In the OCTS model, the division of power between the Central Government and the HKSAR Government is provided for in a Basic Law enacted by the NPC. In the extreme and highly unlikely scenario of the NPCSC acting unilaterally in changing the Basic Law to curtail the HKSAR's autonomy, there is no legal or judicial remedy.[23] Moreover,

---

20. Roda Mushkat, *One Country, Two International Legal Personalities: The Case of Hong Kong* (Hong Kong: Hong Kong University Press, 1997); Roda Mushkat, "Hong Kong's Exercise of External Autonomy: A Multi-faceted Appraisal" (2006) 55 *International and Comparative Law Quarterly* 945–962.

21. See art. 13 of the Basic Law.

22. Albert H.Y. Chen, "From Colony to Special Administrative Region: Hong Kong's Constitutional Journey" in R. Wacks (ed.), *The Future of the Law in Hong Kong* (Hong Kong: Oxford University Press, 1989) 112–115.

23. Albert H.Y. Chen, "Constitutional Crisis in Hong Kong: Congressional Supremacy and Judicial Review" (1999) 33 *Hong Kong Lawyer* 1025–1040.

there is no independent judicial forum for the determination of jurisdictional disputes between the Central Government and the HKSAR. Under articles 17 and 158 of the Basic Law, it is not a court but the NPCSC, acting in consultation with the Basic Law Committee,[24] which has the power to determine whether an HKSAR law is *ultra vires*, and to issue an interpretation of the Basic Law.

What is the difference between having a federal supreme court or constitutional court and having the NPCSC to resolve jurisdictional disputes arising from the practice of autonomy within a sovereign state? The question is ultimately a question of trust. If Hong Kong people have as much confidence in the NPCSC as Americans have in the U.S. Supreme Court, then the weakness in the OCTS system discussed here would disappear. Unfortunately, the sad reality is that the NPCSC is not able to command sufficient respect from the Hong Kong community as an impartial arbiter of constitutional disputes.[25]

There are however two ways in which the practical implications of this weakness in the system can be and have been minimised. One relates to the broad scope of autonomy of the HKSAR which we have identified as a strength of the system. In federal systems like those in the United States, Canada, and Australia, the constitution stipulates a complicated formula for dividing up power between the federal and state governments. Both levels of government exercise power over a wide range of governmental affairs, and many grey areas exist. The complexity of the formula gives rise to demarcation problems and frequent jurisdictional disputes. By contrast, the formula for division of power in the OCTS model is relatively simple. The HKSAR has jurisdiction over almost all matters other than defence, foreign affairs, and changes in the Basic Law. The scope of autonomy of the HKSAR is so large that few demarcation problems or jurisdictional disputes of the kind that are frequent in federal

24. The Basic Law Committee was formed in pursuance of a Decision of the NPC made on 4 April 1990, the same day as the date of the enactment of the Basic Law. According to the Decision, the Basic Law Committee shall consist of 12 members, including 6 mainland members and 6 Hong Kong members, each appointed for a five-year term. The Hong Kong members are to be appointed by the NPCSC on the basis of joint nominations made by the Chief Executive of the HKSAR, the Chief Justice of the CFA of the HKSAR, and the President of the Legislative Council of the HKSAR. For a commentary on the role of the Basic Law Committee, see Eric C. Ip, "Prototype Constitutional Supervision in China: The Lessons of the Hong Kong Basic Law Committee" (2015) 10:2 *Asian Journal of Comparative Law* 323–342.

25. Yash Ghai, "The Intersection of Chinese Law and the Common Law in the Hong Kong Special Administrative Region: Question of Technique or Politics?" (2007) 37:2 *Hong Kong Law Journal* 363–405.

systems have occurred in Hong Kong since the OCTS framework was put into practice in 1997.

Furthermore, although in theory the powers which the Central Government has under articles 17, 18, 158, and 159 of the Basic Law are quite substantial and may be exercised in such a way as to threaten the HKSAR's autonomy, a practice or unwritten norm seems to have been developed whereby the Central Government exercises self-restraint to minimise its interventions and to maximise the HKSAR's autonomy.[26] For example, under article 17, the NPCSC has the power to nullify HKSAR laws that exceed the scope of the HKSAR's autonomy. However, since the HKSAR was established in 1997 and up to the time of writing (summer 2016), the Central Government has never exercised this power to nullify an HKSAR law. Under article 18, national laws may be applied to the HKSAR, but after 1 July 1997, only four national laws have been applied in this way.[27] Furthermore, the NPCSC's power to amend the Basic Law has never been exercised.[28]

Under article 158 of the Basic Law, the NPCSC may issue an interpretation of the Basic Law. In the last two decades, a total of five interpretations have been issued, showing a considerable degree of self-restraint on the part of the Central Government.[29] The first interpretation was in 1999, which was issued on articles 22 and 24 of the Basic Law relating to the right of abode in the HKSAR of children born in the mainland to Hong Kong permanent residents. This interpretation was issued because the HKSAR Government submitted a request for interpretation to the Central Government after the CFA rendered its decisions in early 1999 in the cases of *Ng Ka Ling*[30] and *Chan Kam Nga*.[31] The government estimated that the CFA's interpretation of the relevant Basic Law provisions would result in 1.67 million mainland residents being entitled

26. Johannes M.M. Chan, "Asymmetry in the Face of Heavily Disproportionate Power Relations: Hong Kong" in Weller and Nobbs (N2) 140.

27. See the commentary about these in N17.

28. The amendment of the Basic Law is governed by art. 159 of the Basic Law. The amendment of Annex I and Annex II of the Basic Law is separately provided for in these Annexes, and involves, among other steps, an act of the Legislative Council of the HKSAR. The Annexes were amended once in 2010.

29. Sir Anthony Mason, "The Rule of Law in the Shadow of the Giant: The Hong Kong Experience" (2011) 33 *Sydney Law Review* 623–644.

30. (1999) 2 HKCFAR 4.

31. (1999) 2 HKCFAR 82. See generally Johannes M.M. Chan, H.L. Fu, and Yash Ghai (eds.), *Hong Kong's Constitutional Debate* (Hong Kong: Hong Kong University Press, 2000).

to migrate to Hong Kong in the next ten years. Responding to the Chief Executive's request for interpretation, the NPCSC issued its interpretation in June 1999, overruling the CFA's decision. Under article 158 of the Basic Law, the NPCSC's interpretation did not have the effect of reversing the CFA's judgments and orders concerning the litigants in the *Ng* and *Chan* cases; it only meant that Hong Kong courts in future cases must follow the NPCSC's interpretation instead of the CFA's interpretation of the relevant Basic Law provisions. In *Lau Kong Yung*,[32] the CFA considered the effect of the NPCSC interpretation and recognised its binding force.

After 1999, the NPCSC has exercised the power of Basic Law interpretation on four other occasions. In 2004, acting on its own initiative (instead of at the request of the Chief Executive), the NPCSC issued an interpretation of the Basic Law provisions relating to electoral reform.[33] In 2005, upon the request of the Acting Chief Executive, the NPCSC issued an interpretation to clarify the term of office of a Chief Executive who succeeds one who resigns before completing his term of office.[34] In the *Congo* case in 2011,[35] the CFA used the reference procedure in article 158(3) of the Basic Law for the first time to refer certain Basic Law provisions relating to foreign affairs and "acts of State" to the NPCSC for interpretation.[36] This *Congo* case concerned whether the applicable law of foreign sovereign immunity in the HKSAR was the same as that in the mainland. In November 2016, the NPCSC, again acting on its own initiative, issued an interpretation of article 104 of the Basic Law, which relates to the oath-taking requirements applicable to officials, judges, and members of the Legislative and Executive Councils (LegCo and ExCo). This interpretation was particularly controversial as it was issued three days after Hong Kong's High Court heard a case on oath-taking and before the court delivered judgment in that case. In this case,[37] the government argued that two pro-Hong Kong

---

32. (1999) 2 HKCFAR 300.
33. Albert H.Y. Chen, "The Constitutional Controversy of Spring 2004" (2004) 34 *Hong Kong Law Journal* 215–225.
34. Albert H.Y. Chen, "The NPCSC's Interpretation in Spring 2005" (2005) 35 *Hong Kong Law Journal* 255–264.
35. (2011) 14 HKCFAR 95, 395.
36. Albert H.Y. Chen, "The Congo Case" (2011) 41 *Hong Kong Law Journal* 369–376.
37. *Chief Executive of the HKSAR v President of the Legislative Council and Leung Chung Hang Sixtus*, HCAL 185/2016 (CFI, 15 November 2016; CA, 30 November 2016). The two Legislative Councillors were disqualified.

independence Legislative Councillors had been disqualified by reason of their failure to comply with the oath-taking requirements stipulated in article 104 of the Basic Law and other Hong Kong legislations. The increased role of the NPCSC interpretations creates additional grey area in the guarantees for autonomy in the OCTS model.

The second limitation or weakness of the OCTS model as practised in Hong Kong relates to whether the autonomous regional government can really represent and govern in the interests of the people of the autonomous unit.[38] A major factor to consider is the nature of the domestic political system of the autonomous unit, and, in particular, whether it is sufficiently democratic.

Here it must be pointed out that the domestic political system of the HKSAR falls short of international or Western standards of liberal democracy.[39] The first Chief Executive of the HKSAR was elected by a 400-member Selection Committee which was elected (on the basis of business, occupational, and community groupings in various social sectors) by the HKSAR Preparatory Committee appointed by Beijing. The second-term Chief Executive and his successor were elected by an 800-member Election Committee itself elected by groups from business, professional, and other social sectors. In 2012 and 2017, the fourth-term and fifth-term Chief Executives were respectively elected by an Election Committee of 1,200 members constituted by the same social sectors. After each election, the elected candidate is not yet Chief Executive until and unless the Central Government exercises the power to appoint them.[40]

Regarding the legislature, in each of the first four terms of office of the Legislative Council (LegCo) of the HKSAR (other than the Provisional Legislative Council of 1997–1998), not more than half of the members were directly elected by universal suffrage, the others being elected mainly or wholly by "functional constituencies" based on business, professional and other social groupings.[41] In 2012, the number of LegCo members was increased from 60 to 70, half of whom are elected by universal suffrage, and half by functional

38. Albert H.Y. Chen, "Some Reflections on Hong Kong's Autonomy" (1994) 24 *Hong Kong Law Journal* 173–180.

39. Y. Ghai, "Hong Kong's Autonomy" in Ghai and Woodman (N2) 315–348.

40. See art. 45 of the Basic Law.

41. See Annex II to the Basic Law and the Legislative Council Ordinance.

constituencies, including five District Councillors elected by "quasi" universal suffrage in the "super District Councils" functional constituency.[42]

The Basic Law has made provisions for the possibility of further democratisation of the HKSAR. Regarding LegCo, article 68 stipulates that the "ultimate aim" is the election of all legislators by universal suffrage. For the Chief Executive, article 45 also stipulates that the "ultimate aim" is the selection of the Chief Executive by universal suffrage "upon nomination by a broadly representative nominating committee". The installation of a nominating committee effectively introduces a "screening" stage in the process of producing candidates for the Chief Executive election, which can be used to reject persons not acceptable to Beijing. This, together with the reservation to the Central Government of the power to appoint the Chief Executive, was apparently intended to ensure that the HKSAR will not be governed by anyone who is not trustworthy and acceptable from the Central Government's point of view. The rejection in 2015 by more than one-third of the Legislative Councillors from the "pan-democratic" camp via this "screening" mechanism led to the failure of the HKSAR Government's attempt to introduce universal suffrage for the election of the Chief Executive in 2017 (which, because it involves an amendment of Annex I to the Basic Law, can only be introduced with the support of a two-thirds majority in LegCo).[43]

Paradoxically, there might be a connection between the limited democracy within the HKSAR's political system and the huge scope of its autonomy.[44] Precisely because the HKSAR's degree of autonomy is so high, the Central Government apparently cannot afford to let the HKSAR be governed by someone who may be ideologically opposed to or otherwise unable or unwilling to adopt a cooperative attitude towards the Central Government. This, then, is another difference between the OCTS model and federal systems or other arrangements for territorial autonomy in liberal-democratic states.

---

42. Albert H.Y. Chen, "An Unexpected Breakthrough in Hong Kong's Constitutional Reform" (2010) 40 *Hong Kong Law Journal* 259–270; Ngok Ma, "Negotiating Democracy and 'High Autonomy': The 2010 Political Reform" in R. Yep (ed.), *Negotiating Autonomy in Greater China: Hong Kong and its Sovereign before and after 1997* (Copenhagen: Nordic Institute of Asian Studies Press, 2013) 242–268.

43. Albert H.Y. Chen, "The Law and Politics of the Struggle for Universal Suffrage in Hong Kong, 2013–15" (2016) 3 *Asian Journal of Law and Society* 189–207.

44. Hannum comments that "the extensive grants of autonomous powers to the Hong Kong SAR make a certain degree of informal or indirect control by the central government almost inevitable"; see Hannum (N1) 149.

## SOME DISTINCTIVE FEATURES OF THE PRACTICE OF AUTONOMY IN THE HKSAR

In a federal system like the United States, each member state of the federation practises autonomy in the sense that people in the state freely elect their own governor and members of their legislature. The limits of the state's autonomous powers are defined by the Constitution, but within these limits the people of the state may practise full democracy in determining who will be their governor and legislators.[45] Similarly, the non-federal arrangement of devolution of power to Scotland (as provided for in the Scotland Act 1998) in the United Kingdom enables the people of Scotland to practise full democratic self-government in freely electing the Scottish Parliament, which in turn nominates the First Minister of Scotland. However, this is apparently not how autonomy is understood in contemporary Chinese political culture.

In the context of the PRC, autonomy does not imply full political self-determination within the constitutional and legal limits of autonomy. Beijing's understanding of Hong Kong's autonomy under OCTS seems to be that of Hong Kong people ruling Hong Kong (instead of mainland officials doing so), but the Hong Kong people who hold key governmental posts in Hong Kong must be people whom Beijing considers acceptable and trustworthy for this purpose.[46] Hence, Beijing has reserved the power to appoint the Chief Executive (after an election held in Hong Kong) and other principal officials of the HKSAR under the Basic Law. However, this limitation on autonomy is not unique to the HKSAR under OCTS. In some autonomous arrangements elsewhere, the national or central government participates (e.g., by giving its

45. As pointed out by Hannum and Lillich: "In the context of federal States, both local responsibility for and local selection of the chief executive official are common. ... [I]n none of the federal examples examined was there direct national influence over the selection of the local governor or other chief executive official." See Hurst Hannum and Richard Lillich, "The Concept of Autonomy in International Law" in Dinstein (N2) 219.

46. Thus, Wang Guangya, Director of the Hong Kong and Macau Affairs Office of the State Council, pointed out a few months before the Chief Executive election in March 2017 that the Chief Executive should meet four criteria: loving the nation and loving Hong Kong; being trusted by the Central Government; being capable of governing Hong Kong; and enjoying the support of Hong Kong people. See "Beijing Not Ready to Show Its Hand on Hong Kong Chief Executive Preference, Top Official Hints" (31 December 2016) *South China Morning Post*; "Crucial for Next Hong Kong Leader to Have Central Government's Trust, According to Beijing Official" (17 February 2017) *South China Morning Post*.

approval or consent) in the selection of the Chief Executive or top officials of the autonomous region.[47] Indeed, it is not unusual for territorial autonomy in other states to involve "cooperation, coordination, and consultation between the central authorities and the autonomous entity".[48]

Hong Kong's political forces have been divided between pro-China forces and pro-democracy forces.[49] The pro-China camp supports the policies of the PRC Government towards Hong Kong, including its cautious and gradualist approach to Hong Kong's democratisation. The camp also supports, or at least does not question, one-party rule in mainland China, and generally refrains from criticising its human rights record. On the other hand, the pan-democrats advocate Western-style liberal democracy for Hong Kong, and are critical of authoritarian one-party rule in China and its human rights record.

The cleavage in Hong Kong politics between the "pro-China" and "pro-democracy" camps can be traced back to the 1980s, when the question of Hong Kong's future first arose.[50] The division has been intensified by the different positions they have adopted towards major political events, such as the Beijing student movement in 1989, Governor Patten's political reform in the 1990s, the establishment of the Provisional Legislative Council (PLC) in 1997,[51] the

---

47. Lapidoth points out that in arrangements for autonomy, "coordination is often needed between the center and the autonomous authorities regarding the appointment of one or more high-ranking officials (for example, the representative of the central government in the autonomous region or the head of the local administration). In most cases, the official is appointed either jointly, or by the local authorities with the consent of the center, or vice versa". See Ruth Lapidoth, *Autonomy: Flexible Solutions to Ethnic Conflicts* (Washington D.C.: United States Institute of Peace Press, 1997) 35. According to Hannum and Lillich, "[i]n non-federal States [where arrangements for autonomy exist], it is difficult to perceive a consistent pattern in selection of the chief executive or his or her responsibilities. ... There are several examples in which the chief executive of the autonomous territory or region is appointed by political authorities outside the territory, either by the central government or an international organisation. In some instances, this outside appointment requires either formal or *de facto* local consent". See Hannum and Lillich (N45) 221.
48. Lapidoth (N47) 34.
49. Ngok Ma, "The Rise of 'Anti-China' Sentiments in Hong Kong and the 2012 Legislative Council Elections" (2015) 15:1 *China Review* 39–66; Jinhyeok Jiang, "Competing Political Visions in the Legislative Council of Hong Kong" (2016) 21 *Journal of Chinese Political Science* 89–102.
50. Siu-kai Lau and Hsin-chi Kuan, "Partial Democratization, 'Foundation Moment' and Political Parties in Hong Kong" (2000) 163 *The China Quarterly* 705–720; Ngok Ma, *Political Development in Hong Kong* (Hong Kong: Hong Kong University Press, 2007).
51. Albert H.Y. Chen, "The Provisional Legislative Council of the SAR" (1997) 27 *Hong Kong Law Journal* 1–11.

"right of abode" saga leading to the first interpretation of the Basic Law by the NPCSC in 1999, the article 23 saga in 2003 leading to the abortion of the National Security Bill,[52] the 2004 Interpretation by the NPCSC on political reform in Hong Kong, the 2005 Interpretation by the NPCSC on the term of office of the Chief Executive, the defeat of Chief Executive Donald Tsang's political reform proposal in December 2005,[53] the 2007 NPCSC Decision on political development in Hong Kong,[54] the 2014 NPCSC Decision on the mode of nomination and election of the Chief Executive by universal suffrage, and the 2016 NPCSC Interpretation on oath-taking.

In each of these events, Hong Kong's pro-democracy politicians opposed the Chinese Government's position. The pro-democracy camp has been labelled "the opposition camp" by pro-China commentators in Hong Kong.[55] They are considered to have consistently opposed the policies of the Chinese Government towards Hong Kong (particularly with regard to the pace and mode of Hong Kong's democratisation), and to have been unduly critical towards and unreasonably uncooperative with the Tung Chee-hwa administration, the Donald Tsang administration, the C.Y. Leung administration, and the Carrie Lam administration. Some of them are considered hostile towards the Chinese Communist Party (CCP)-led political system in China. Some are leaders of the Hong Kong Alliance in Support of Patriotic Democratic Movements of China, which was founded in 1989 and has continued to operate in Hong Kong after 1997, organising annual vigils and protests demanding the rehabilitation of the Beijing student movement of 1989 and the end of one-party rule in China. Some of them attended the ceremony in Norway for the award to Liu Xiaobo — a leading dissident in China — of the Nobel Peace Prize in 2010, a ceremony which China urged

---

52. H.L. Fu, C.J. Peterson, and S.N.M. Young (eds.), *National Security and Fundamental Freedoms: Hong Kong's Article 23 under Scrutiny* (Hong Kong: Hong Kong University Press, 2005).

53. Albert H.Y. Chen, "The Fate of the Constitutional Reform Proposal of October 2005" (2005) 35 *Hong Kong Law Journal* 537–543.

54. Albert H.Y. Chen, "A New Era in Hong Kong's Constitutional History" (2008) 38 *Hong Kong Law Journal* 1–13.

55. The term "opposition camp" or "opposition faction" (反對派) was first used by Chief Executive Donald Tsang to refer to the pro-democracy camp when the latter vetoed Tsang's political reform proposal in December 2005. The term was popularised among pro-China commentators after the publication of a lengthy article in the pro-China newspaper *Wen Wei Po*: "香港「民主派」實為反對派" [The Hong Kong 'Democracy Camp' is Actually the Opposition Camp] (29 December 2005) *Wen Wei Po* A8–A9.

all governments friendly to it to boycott. Some of them are suspected of having close relationships with foreign governments or foreign non-governmental organisations with "anti-China" views and interests. Some of them have been denied the issue of a *huixiang zheng*, a passport-like document which Hong Kong permanent residents who are Chinese nationals need to produce in order to enter mainland China, although a policy change to liberalise the grant of the "huixiang zheng" to pan-democrats was announced in November 2016 by Zhang Dejiang, Chairman of the NPCSC.[56]

Since the pro-democracy camp came into existence in the 1980s, it has consistently enjoyed significant support from civil society and the electorate in Hong Kong. It is noteworthy that since direct election by universal suffrage to a portion of LegCo seats was introduced in Hong Kong in 1991, the pro-democracy politicians have consistently succeeded in capturing approximately 55 to 60 percent of the popular votes for that portion of LegCo seats.[57] It is believed that Beijing has been concerned that if entirely free and unrestricted elections by universal suffrage were introduced in Hong Kong, the office of the Chief Executive and the majority of LegCo seats would be captured by members of the pro-democratic camp.

There seems to be a fundamental difference in the understanding of "autonomy" and of the relationship between "autonomy" and "democracy" on the part of the Chinese Government, on the one hand, and on the part of pro-democracy political parties, politicians, and civil society in Hong Kong, on the other hand. The pro-democracy camp's understanding of the autonomy of Hong Kong may be termed a Western liberal-democratic understanding of autonomy. It is believed that as in the case of, say, the people in a state of the United States who can freely elect their state legislature and state governor (or the case of Scotland), the people of Hong Kong should be able to freely elect their Chief Executive and all members of their legislature by universal

56. "Beijing Expected to Grant Permanent Home-return Permits to Current and Former Hong Kong Pan-democrats" (30 November 2016) *South China Morning Post*; "Central Opens Green Light, Pan-democrats may get *huixiang zheng*" (30 November 2016) *Ming Pao* (in Chinese); "Opposition Camp may get *huixiang zheng*, SAR Government Notified" (1 December 2016) *Wen Wei Po* (in Chinese). In April 2017, the radical pan-democrat legislator Leung Kwok-hung, nicknamed "Long Hair", together with five other pan-democrat legislators, were granted the home-return permits to visit mainland China as members of a LegCo delegation; see "Hong Kong Lawmaker 'Long Hair' Leung Kwok-hung Enters Mainland China for First Time in 10 years" (14 April 2017) *South China Morning Post*.

57. Ma (N50) 154, 223; Ma (N49) 58, 62.

suffrage. They believe there is no legitimate reason why Beijing should oppose full democratisation in Hong Kong and that the appointment of the Chief Executive by the Central Government after their being elected by the people of Hong Kong should be no more than a formality.

Beijing's understanding of autonomy is different. It has always been stressed that the power of appointment of the Chief Executive, who is accountable both to the Central Government and the HKSAR,[58] is a substantive power and not merely formal or ceremonial.[59] Since the 1990s, it has also been stressed that Hong Kong's system of government is an "executive-led" system and must not be allowed to become a "legislative-led" one.[60] The emphasis on executive-led government may be understood in light of the fact that it is the executive (including the Chief Executive and principal officials) and not LegCo that is appointed by Beijing and enjoys the confidence and trust of the NPCSC, and derives powers and authority from it. As is evident in Deng Xiaoping's speeches on OCTS in Hong Kong (which were re-published[61] in 2004 during the campaign[62] to stress the idea of "patriots ruling Hong Kong") and the White Paper of June 2014,[63] China's understanding of Hong Kong's autonomy is that of "Hong Kong people ruling Hong Kong", with the majority of those Hong Kong people exercising the power to rule Hong Kong being patriots to the Chinese Government. This kind of thinking may be understood in the context of the CCP's long tradition of "united front work",[64]

58. This is provided for in art. 43 of the Basic Law.

59. Wang (N11) 364–365; Ray Yep, "'One Country, Two Systems' and Special Administrative Region: The Case of Hong Kong'" in J.H. Chung and T.C. Lam (eds.), *China's Local Administration: Traditions and Changes in the Sub-national Hierarchy* (London: Routledge, 2010) 98.

60. Wang (N59) 346–369; Pang-Kwong Li, "The Executive" in W.M. Lam, P.L.T. Lui, and W. Wong (eds.), *Contemporary Hong Kong Government and Politics* (Hong Kong: Hong Kong University Press, 2nd edition, 2012).

61. Xiaoping Deng, *Deng Xiaoping On "One Country, Two Systems"* (Hong Kong: Joint Publishing, 2004). This is the English translation of 《鄧小平論「一國兩制」》 published by the same publisher. See particularly the speeches at pp. 13, 23, and 67 in the English version.

62. Ming Pao Editorial Department (eds.), 《愛國論爭》 [*The Debate on Patriotism*] (Hong Kong: Ming Pao Press, 2004).

63. Information Office of the State Council, the People's Republic of China, *The Practice of the "One Country, Two Systems" Policy in the Hong Kong Special Administrative Region* (Beijing: Foreign Languages Press, 10 June 2014).

64. Lyman P. Van Slyke, *Enemies and Friends: The United Front in Chinese Communist History* (Stanford: Stanford University Press, 1967).

in which friendly political relations are cultivated between the CCP and non-communists whom the Party considers to be trustworthy and reliable for the purpose of forming a political alliance to achieve a common goal. Such united front work has been actively undertaken in Hong Kong by the Chinese authorities both before and after the 1997 handover.[65]

It is noteworthy that Deng Xiaoping said in the context of "patriots ruling Hong Kong" that "direct elections" may not necessarily produce the right people for this purpose.[66] Thus, democracy in the sense of direct elections by universal suffrage is not an ultimate value or goal in itself. The goal is to choose the right people to rule Hong Kong. From the Chinese Government's perspective, Hong Kong already enjoys full autonomy in the sense of "Hong Kong people ruling Hong Kong" (i.e., not Communist cadres ruling Hong Kong), and the Central Government not interfering with the administration, policy-making, and law-making of Hong Kong. Hong Kong already enjoys a significant degree of democracy (including the Rule of Law, civil liberties, judicial independence, multi-party competition for and direct elections to the legislature, functional constituency elections, etc.). Hong Kong's further democratisation is viewed as being subject to the condition that the Chief Executive must be a "patriot", and probably also the condition that the majority of LegCo members should be patriots as well.

Since the establishment of the HKSAR, the effectiveness of the "executive-led" government in Hong Kong has depended on a loose coalition of pro-China political parties and independent legislators, which occupied the majority of seats in LegCo.[67] Even so, there has never been a ruling party in the HKSAR. No single political party has ever occupied the majority of, or any number close to half of, the seats in LegCo. The Chief Executive is elected independently of LegCo by an Election Committee, which has also never been dominated by a political party but is generally considered to be "pro-China" rather than supportive of the pan-democrats. Members of the pro-China camp in LegCo are generally supportive of the Chief Executive and their administration, although such support cannot be guaranteed in every instance of policy, bill,

---

65. Christine Loh, *Underground Front: The Chinese Communist Party in Hong Kong* (Hong Kong: Hong Kong University Press, 2010); Sonny S.H. Lo, Steven C.F. Hung, and Jeff H.C. Loo, *China's New United Front Work in Hong Kong* (Palgrave Macmillan, 2019); Eliza Lee, "United Front, Clientelism, and Indirect Rule: Theorizing the Role of the Liaison Office in Hong Kong" (2020) 29 *Journal of Contemporary China* 763–775.

66. Deng (N61) 75–76.

67. Percy Luen-tim Lui, "The Legislature" in Lam, Lui, and Wong (N60) 45–65.

or item of financial expenditure, because these elected legislators have to be answerable to their own constituencies. One of the distinctive features of the autonomy of the HKSAR under OCTS relates to the role — informal rather than constitutional — of the Central Government in promoting, coordinating among, and supporting this pro-China camp of politicians in Hong Kong.

The organ of the Central Government that performs this function in the HKSAR is the Liaison Office of the Central People's Government.[68] Various scholars and commentators have pointed out that this office has over the years played a significant role in coordinating among politicians of the pro-China camp in running for elections to the District Councils,[69] LegCo, and the Election Committee (for the Chief Executive), helping to mobilise support for them during elections among pro-China social organisations in Hong Kong, and, after they have been successfully elected into office, lobbying them occasionally for support for the Hong Kong Government on crucial issues of policy.[70] In the case of the Election Committee, it is believed that Beijing actually engaged in lobbying members of the committee for support for C.Y. Leung and Carrie Lam during the Chief Executive elections in 2012[71] and 2016,[72] respectively.

---

68. Yep (N59) 100.

69. Ming Sing, "Hong Kong's Democrats Hold Their Own" (2009) 20:1 *Journal of Democracy* 107–111; Sonny Shiu-Hing Lo, *The Dynamics of Beijing-Hong Kong Relations* (Hong Kong: Hong Kong University Press, 2008) 10–11, 18–19; Peter T.Y. Cheung, "The Changing Relations between Hong Kong and the Mainland since 2003" in Lam, Lui, and Wong (N60) 329; Ma (N49) 52; Brian C.H. Fong, "One Country, Two Nationalisms: Center-Periphery Relations between Mainland China and Hong Kong, 1997–2006" (2017) 43:5 *Modern China* 523–556.

70. On 10 March 2014, Shiu Sin-por, Head of the Central Policy Unit of the HKSAR Government, disclosed to the media that the Liaison Office has occasionally lobbied LegCo members for support for the HKSAR Government's policies. In response, Chief Executive C.Y. Leung said that it is the HKSAR Government's responsibility to lobby LegCo members for support for the government's position regarding autonomy. See various Hong Kong newspapers from 11–12 March 2014; for instance, *Ming Pao* and *Sing Tao Daily*.

71. Ray Yep, "Understanding the Autonomy of Hong Kong: Looking beyond Formal Institutions" in Yep (N42) 4; Ma (N49) 52–53.

72. Jeffie Lam, "Hong Kong Chief Executive Election was a 'Farce', Aide to Regina Ip Claims in Letter" (2 April 2017) *South China Morning Post*; Mark Pinkstone, "The Role of Beijing's 'Invisible Hand' in the Chief Executive Elections" (2 April 2017) *Hong Kong Free Press*, available at: www.hongkongfp.com/2017/04/02/role-beijings-invisible-hand-chief-executive-elections, last visited 10 April 2017; Chi-keung Choy, "剖析'陣前換馬'和'棄曾取林'的前因後果" [Analysis of the Causes and Consequences of "Changing the Horse before the Race" and "Abandoning Tsang for Lam"] (6 April 2017) *Ming Pao*.

As the tasks of governance have become more difficult for the executive branch of the HKSAR Government, in part because of the declining legitimacy of the HKSAR Government and the increasingly vocal opposition in LegCo and in civil society, the Liaison Office has stepped up its efforts to consolidate the pro-China camp of politicians and to persuade them to give necessary support for the Chief Executive and their administration. The HKSAR Government has thus become increasingly dependent on the support of the Central Government.[73] A kind of "patron-client politics"[74] has evolved, in which Beijing is a powerful patron that can effectively reward its clients by offering them benefits or advantages in return for their support for Beijing's policies towards Hong Kong. The Chief Executive and the administration is also a patron in this system. Examples of benefits that can be offered by Beijing and the HKSAR Government include appointment as members of the Chinese People's Political Consultative Conference,[75] membership in the NPC,[76] appointment to various positions in the Hong Kong Government (including the ExCo, advisory committees, and statutory bodies) being conferred honours and awards, or other positions of honour, etc. The increasing degree of integration between the economies of Hong Kong and the mainland (partly as a result of arrangements such as the Closer Economic Partnership Arrangement introduced in 2003 and gradually expanded), and the increasing dependence of the Hong Kong economy on the mainland, has also facilitated Beijing's "united front" work of co-option of Hong Kong's business elites.[77]

73. Yash Ghai, "The Legal Foundations of Hong Kong's Autonomy: Building on Sand" (2007) 29:1 *Asian Pacific Journal of Public Administration* 25.

74. Lo (N69) 3; Cheung (N69) 329.

75. Cheung (N69) 334–336.

76. Hualing Fu and D.W. Choy, "Of Iron or Rubber? People's Deputies of Hong Kong to the National People's Congress" in H.L. Fu, L. Harris, and S.N.M. Young (eds.), *Interpreting Hong Kong's Basic Law: The Struggle for Coherence* (New York: Palgrave Macmillan, 2007) 201–227.

77. On the other hand, it has been argued that Hong Kong's economic contribution to China is so significant that the Chinese Government has a strong incentive to maintain the HKSAR's autonomy as a "partially independent political entity", including its civil liberties, Rule of Law, judicial autonomy, and free press, which are seen as prerequisites for Hong Kong's economic success; see David A. Rezvani, "Dead Autonomy, A Thousand Cuts or Partial Independence? The Autonomous Status of Hong Kong" (2012) 42:1 *Journal of Democracy* 93–122. See also Yep (N59) 101–103; Cheung (N69) 329, 336–337, 339; Samson Yuen, "Under the Shadow of China: Beijing's Policy towards Hong Kong and Taiwan in Comparative Perspective" (2014) 2014:2 *China Perspectives* 69–76.

Thus, a distinctive feature of Hong Kong's autonomy is that although legally the Hong Kong Government system is separate and distinct from the Central Government, in the sense that the Chief Executive is elected by a locally constituted Election Committee (followed by appointment by Beijing), and LegCo is locally elected, the Central Government through its Liaison Office in Hong Kong participates in Hong Kong politics and seeks to ensure that (a) the Chief Executive elected by the Election Committee is someone whom Beijing considers to be suitable and appointable as Chief Executive; and (b) the majority of LegCo members and of members of the Election Committee (for the Chief Executive) are from the pro-China camp rather than the opposition. Furthermore, the Central Government renders support for the Chief Executive and his administration by mobilising pro-China politicians in Hong Kong to support the HKSAR Government. Ironically, the Central Government is politically compelled to play this role because of the inherent weakness of the "executive-led" government in the HKSAR — there is no ruling party, the Chief Executive lacks popular mandate and legitimacy, and there is no guaranteed, secure, or stable support in the fragmented legislature for the executive government. In these circumstances, the Central Government plays a crucial role of coordination among the pro-China camp of politicians in Hong Kong, securing where necessary the support that the HKSAR Government needs for effective governance of the territory. Taken together, these distinct features and conflicting views of OCTS in Hong Kong distinguish the autonomy of the HKSAR from that of a federalist system.

## CONCLUSION

The OCTS model as practised in the HKSAR should be understood not only in the light of the internationally accepted concept of territorial autonomy within unitary states, but also as an outgrowth of the political and legal culture of the PRC. While it may be considered deficient if we evaluate it by notions of autonomy in Western liberal-democratic states, the implementation of OCTS in the HKSAR since 1997 already represents a significant break from the CCP-led political and legal system in mainland China. Even though it falls short of the democratic ideal, it has delivered civil liberties, economic freedoms, open society, pluralistic culture, and free lifestyle to the people of Hong Kong.

The political system of the HKSAR is vested with powers which it can exercise in an autonomous manner over a wide range of governmental affairs, including domestic affairs as well as some foreign affairs that are labelled "external affairs" in the Basic Law. This political system may be said to be a "hybrid" system — neither authoritarian nor fully democratic — that practises constitutionalism but only partial democracy.[78] The hallmark of constitutional government is the existence of checks and balance within the political system. Such checks and balance can be found in the HKSAR, because of the existence of the Rule of Law, civil liberties, a free press, a vibrant civil society, and multiple political parties with opposing ideologies which compete vigorously in elections to the legislature and District Councils.[79]

OCTS was a pragmatic compromise enacted in the early 1980s by the CCP led by Deng Xiaoping, insofar as it allows a capitalist system with significant elements of Western-style liberal democracy to exist in Hong Kong as an SAR of the PRC. The project of OCTS has faced major challenges since it was fully put into practice in 1997. It has been rightly pointed out[80] that a dynamic "crisis-transformation perspective" should be adopted so as to understand the evolution of Chinese policies towards the HKSAR as various events — such as the march of half a million demonstrators on 1 July 2003 or the Occupy Central Movement of 2014 — unfolded in a manner not previously envisaged. The 2012 LegCo election witnessed a rise in anti-Chinese sentiments,[81] and since then there has been a "localist" turn in Hong Kong politics,[82] with the emergence of radical "localists" who are dissatisfied with the traditional thinking and strategy of the mainstream pan-democrats. The "localists" advocate self-determination or even independence for Hong Kong. Some of them were barred from

---

78. Political scientist Sonny Lo argues that the HKSAR "is already a democracy with home-grown characteristics, such as the rule of law, judicial independence, a strong civil society and above all horizontal accountability"; see Sonny Shiu-Hing Lo, *Hong Kong's Indigenous Democracy: Origins, Evolution and Contentions* (New York: Palgrave Macmillan, 2015) 33. Political sociologist Lau Siu-kai suggests that the "new political order" of the HKSAR is still under construction; see Siu-kai Lau, "In Search of A New Political Order" in Y.M. Yeung (ed.), *The First Decade: The Hong Kong SAR in Retrospective and Introspective Perspectives* (Hong Kong: Chinese University Press) 139–159.

79. Mathew Y.H. Wong, "Party Models in A Hybrid Regime: Hong Kong 2007–2012" (2015) 15:1 *China Review* 67–94.

80. Alvin Y. So, "'One Country, Two Systems' and Hong Kong-China National Integration: A Crisis-Transformation Perspective" (2011) 41:1 *Journal of Contemporary Asia* 99–116.

81. Ma (N49).

82. Joseph Y.S. Cheng (ed.), *New Trends of Political Participation in Hong Kong* (Hong Kong: City University of Hong Kong Press, 2014).

participating in the LegCo election in September 2016[83] — a controversial move which revealed the limits of Beijing's toleration of autonomy in the HKSAR. Despite this move, a total of six "localists" were elected into LegCo in this election, collectively capturing 19 percent of the popular votes.[84]

The practice of territorial autonomy of people within a region of a state can be a double-edged sword. On the one hand, autonomy can strike a good balance between the recognition of regional diversity and the promotion of national unity, and be mutually beneficial for the people of the autonomous region and the people of the state as a whole. On the other hand, the institutions of autonomy might foster or strengthen the sense of collective identity of the people in the autonomous region,[85] which may stand in tension with the original concept of the sovereign state with a fixed, sacred, and inalienable territory, a single citizenship and a single allegiance of all to one nation.[86] From the perspective of the government of the sovereign state, the worst case scenario is one in which the people of the autonomous region become dissatisfied with autonomy and begin to clamour for independence.

In the case of the HKSAR, the practice of autonomy under OCTS has been premised on a spirit of mutual accommodation and respect, in which Beijing tolerates a capitalist and semi-democratic enclave within the PRC, and the people of Hong Kong accept the exercise of sovereignty by the PRC over Hong Kong and do not challenge the existing political system in mainland China. The continued success of Hong Kong's practice of autonomy under OCTS depends on continual self-restraint on the part of both Beijing and the people

83. See Hong Kong newspapers of 3 August 2016; "Protests Shut Down Electoral Commission Briefing as Hong Kong Indigenous' Edward Leung Disqualified from Legco Elections" (2 August 2016) *South China Morning Post* (online edition); "Hong Kong's Returning Officers' Power to Dismiss Potential Legco Candidates Called into Question" (2 August 2016) *South China Morning Post* (online edition).

84. See "Localists and Self-determination Activists Capture 6 Seats, LegCo Divided into 3 Factions" and "Localist Self-determination Politicians Capture 400,000 Votes" (6 September 2016) *Ming Pao* (in Chinese). Some of the localists were subsequently disqualified by the court on the ground of their failure to comply with the oath-taking requirement in the Basic Law and other legislation. Chi-keung Choy and Jun-man Chan, "立法會選舉結果初步評析" [A Preliminary Analysis of the Outcome of the Legislative Council Election] (6 September 2016) *Ming Pao*.

85. For the legal and institutional basis of the identity of "Hongkongers", see Ng T.M. Simon, "The Legal Foundation of Hongkonger Identity" (2015) 6 *Hong Kong Journal of Catholic Studies* 111–147.

86. Susan J. Henders, *Territoriality, Asymmetry, and Autonomy: Catalonia, Corsica, Hong Kong, and Tibet* (New York: Palgrave Macmillan, 2010) 14, 19–22.

of Hong Kong in adhering to such mutual accommodation and respect, and on the rising level of "localism" or "peripheral nationalism" in Hong Kong being contained and reversed.[87]

## Acknowledgement

This chapter was first published as "The Autonomy of Hong Kong under 'One Country, Two Systems'" in Tai-lok Lui, Stephen W.K. Chiu, and Ray Yep (eds.), *Routledge Handbook of Contemporary Hong Kong* (2019), chapter 1, pp. 33–51. This edited version is reprinted with permission from the publisher, Routledge.

87. Fong (N69).

# 4

# Social Movements and the Law in Post-colonial Hong Kong

## INTRODUCTION

The relationship between social movements and the law in the Western world has been well studied. With regard to social movements in the United States, it has been pointed out that "legal norms, discourses, and practices in each case were an important constitutive element of evolving movement understandings, aspirations, and strategic action".[1] In Hong Kong, particularly since the handover in 1997, social movements have flourished, and the law has become an increasingly prominent arena of social and political conflict. What is the relationship between social movements and the law in post-colonial Hong Kong? Are theories developed in the West useful in understanding social movements and the law in Hong Kong? It is the purpose of this chapter to explore these questions.

## SOCIAL MOVEMENTS AND THE LAW

### What are social movements?

Social movements are a form of contentious politics that first emerged in Western Europe and North America in the late eighteenth and early nineteenth centuries.[2] According to Tilly, a social movement consists of a distinctive combination of three elements: (a) campaign, (b) repertoire, and (c) WUNC displays (WUNC being an abbreviation for worthiness, unity, numbers, and commitment). A campaign is "a sustained, organized public effort making collective claims on target authorities", whilst the repertoire of a social movement refers to the "employment of combinations from among the following forms of political action: creation of special-purpose associations and coalitions, public meetings, solemn processions, vigils, rallies, demonstrations, petition drives, statements to and in public media, and pamphleteering".[3] Finally, WUNC displays are public representations by the participants in the social movement on the part of themselves or their constituencies.[4]

---

1. Michael W. McCann, "How Does Law Matter for Social Movements?" in Bryant G. Garth and Austin Sarat (eds.), *How Does Law Matter?* (Evanston: Northwestern University Press, 1998) 76–108, at 84.
2. Charles Tilly, *Social Movements 1768–2004* (Boulder: Paradigm Publishers, 2004).
3. *Ibid.*, 3.
4. *Ibid.*, 4.

Another way to understand social movements is to consider concrete examples of phenomena that are generally regarded as social movements by scholars and writers. From this perspective, one of the earliest and important social movements is the labour movement.[5] Other classic examples of social movements in modern history include the anti-slavery movement in nineteenth-century America, the movement for women's suffrage, the U.S. civil rights movement in the 1960s, and the student movement of the late 1960s. Social movements that have emerged in the Western world since the 1960s include the feminist movement, environmental movement, and peace movement, which are collectively described as constituting "the irreducible core of social movement activity".[6] Other movements often discussed include the gay rights movement, consumer movement, animal rights movement, anti-psychiatry movement, pro- and anti-abortion movements, the solidarity movement in Poland, and, most recently, the anti-globalisation movement. It seems that the mass demonstrations in 1989 that led to the collapse of Communism in Eastern Europe may also be regarded as social movements.[7] Sometimes even nationalism, Nazism, and Fascism are also described as social movements.

In the contemporary world, social movements have become a popular and well-established form of political participation outside the formal institutional channels of electoral politics. They represent the vital forces of civil society at work, particularly as they seek to challenge the ruling elites, the establishment, and the existing social, economic, and political order in a particular country or in the global system as a whole. They symbolise politics from below or the grassroots as contrasted with the top-down mode of societal management. As various waves of democratisation swept the world in the late twentieth century, social movements and democratisation have mutually supported and reinforced each other in many countries in their transition from authoritarianism to democracy.

## Theoretical perspectives on social movements and the law

Let us now consider the general theoretical framework developed by Western scholars to understand the relationship between social movements and the law. What Doug McAdam called the "classical model" of social movements was premised on theories of collective behaviour and "mass society" that emphasise

5. *Ibid.*, 6.

6. Paul Byrne, *Social Movements in Britain* (London: Routledge, 1997) 12.

7. Tilly (N2) 78.

the structural strains in a society and the social psychology of its inhabitants.[8] Such theories throw light on the rise of Nazism and Fascism in Europe before the Second World War. With the civil rights movements in the United States in the 1960s and student activism in the United States and Europe in 1968, as well as "new social movements" of the kind mentioned above, social movements began to be perceived in a positive light. New perspectives were developed by European scholars who investigated how such movements respond to the crises of post-modern or post-industrial society in advanced Western nations.[9] In the United States, the paradigms for the study of social movements have been shaped by resource mobilisation theory and political process theory. It is these two approaches that seem most relevant to the study of law and social movements.

The insight contributed by resource mobilisation theory is that, whereas structural strains and grievances exist in almost every society, they do not necessarily lead to social movements. The formation and development of any social movement depends on the effective organisation and mobilisation of resources. Given the existence of a particular socio-political environment and certain resources at their disposal, the leaders and participants of a social movement must act rationally and strategically in order to maximise their influence and achieve their goals. There are at least four ways in which resource mobilisation theory can throw light on the relationship between law and social movements. First, depending on whether the legal system is repressive or respectful of civil liberties, that system may either constrain or facilitate mobilisation for a social movement:

> [P]olitical freedoms, and the extent of repression by agents of social control … may affect the costs for any individual or organization allocating resources to the SMS [social movement sector], [and] serve as constraints on or facilitators of the use of resources for social movement purposes.[10]

---

8. Doug McAdam, *Political Process and the Development of Black Insurgency 1930–1970* (Chicago: University of Chicago Press, 2nd edition,1999).
9. Alain Touraine, *The Voice and the Eye: An Analysis of Social Movements*, translated by Alan Duff (Cambridge: Cambridge University Press, 1981).
10. John D. McCarthy and Mayer N. Zald, "Resource Mobilization and Social Movements: A Partial Theory" in Mayer N. Zald and John D McCarthy (eds.), *Social Movements in an Organizational Society* (New Brunswick: Transaction Publishers, 1987) 15–42, at 26.

Second, litigation may be used as one of the strategies of a social movement, as in the initial phase of the U.S. civil rights movement.[11] Third, insofar as resource mobilisation theory points to the use of the media by a social movement as a significant factor,[12] litigation or other law-related strategies may generate media attention, and thus attention by members of the public, to the issues raised by the movement. Finally, resource mobilisation theory recognises that resources include "legitimacy, money, facilities, and labor"[13] as well as both "material and symbolic resources".[14] Hence, the expression of a social movement's demands in legal discourse (particularly the discourse of rights) or victories in court battles may be quite effective in conferring legitimacy on the movement and constitute an important symbolic resource for it.

Political process theory stresses that social movements are essentially political phenomena, and may therefore be examined in ways similar to those applicable to other political phenomena such as "institutionalized political processes".[15] What needs to be studied therefore includes the interaction and alignment of different political actors within the system and their response to the social movement. The theory not only recognises the importance of the internal dynamics of a social movement's development, but it also pays particular attention to the external political environment in which the movement finds itself, or what it calls the "political opportunities" and "political opportunity structures".[16] Changes in that structure may have a significant impact on the social movement, and may even be able to account for its rise and fall. For example, such changes may result in a sudden opening up of the political system that is either intentional or unintentional,[17] and may undermine its stability or otherwise improve the bargaining position or political leverage of the movement's constituents.[18]

11. See David A. Locher, *Collective Behavior* (Upper Saddle River: Prentice Hall, 2002) 273–279; Ron Eyerman and Andrew Jamison, *Social Movements: A Cognitive Approach* (Cambridge: Polity Press, 1991) 122, 125.

12. McCarthy and Zald (N10) 15, 31.

13. *Ibid.*, 22.

14. Donatella Della Porta and Mario Dini, *Social Movements: An Introduction* (Oxford: Blackwell, 1999) 8.

15. McAdam (N8) 36.

16. *Ibid.*, viii, xi, xiv.

17. Roberta Garner, *Contemporary Movements and Ideologies* (New York: McGraw-Hill, 1996) 50.

18. McAdam (N8) 42–43.

Like resource mobilisation theory, political process theory demonstrates that a legal system — as part of the structure of political opportunities for a social movement — that is repressive increases the "risks associated with movement participation",[19] and thus constrains the movement's development. In addition to this observation, political process theory also contributes at least two other insights into the relationship between law and social movements. First, the theory posits that the law-related aspects of the structure of political opportunities to be studied include not only "the state's capacity for and tendency toward repression",[20] but also "the relative weight and independence of judicial, legislative, and executive branches in governments".[21] Thus, the constitutional role of the courts in a particular legal system, and, in particular, whether the judiciary is independent, activist, and willing to develop new legal doctrines to meet the demands of particular social movements, may become highly relevant to the development of a social movement. In countries such as the United States where the judiciary is indeed powerful and activist, social movements are more likely to resort to litigation as a means for social reform.

Second, political process theory points out that an important factor in the formation of a social movement is "cognitive liberation"[22] or "the subjective transformation of consciousness" into an "insurgent consciousness".[23] When this insight is combined with discourse theory, which demonstrates that the language and discourse that people use shape their interpretation of their life experience and perception of the meaning of events and construct the social reality in which they live,[24] it is possible to understand how legal discourse matters for social movements. This point has been further elaborated by McCann's work on law and social movements to which we now turn.

Drawing upon various studies by scholars of law and social movements and his own empirical research on the movement for gender-based wage equity in the United States, McCann has developed a fairly comprehensive

19. *Ibid.*, 43.
20. Locher (N11) 267.
21. Garner (N17) 52.
22. McAdam (N8) 48.
23. *Ibid.*, 38, 40.
24. Garner (N17) 15–16.

theory of the relationship between law and social movements.[25] He describes his theory as one of "legal mobilization"[26] that "merges a dynamic dispute-oriented, interpretivist understanding of legal practice with insights from social movement theorizing about collective action based on 'political process'", also noting that the "law is mobilized when a desire or want is translated into an assertion of right or lawful claim".[27]

McCann points out that both legal discourse and litigation may be turned into a positive resource by a social movement that is striving to change the status quo. In particular, litigation may be used as a strategy that supplements the use of such non-institutional channels of mass protest as marches and demonstrations. Moreover, legal norms and rights discourse may be used by social movements as positive resources in mobilising support and making gains in struggles against the existing system. Thus, the law is itself a medium and arena of social struggle. Legal norms may be able to "play a role in shaping and expressing the terms of resistance, aspiration, and tactical struggle for institutional transformation"; "[w]e must, in Michel de Certeau's words, analyze law's 'manipulation by users who are not its makers'".[28] McCann notes, for example, that legal discourse may be drawn upon "to name and to challenge existing social wrongs or injustices" or to forge a "sense of collective aspiration and identity" among movement participants.[29] Legal norms contributed significantly in framing movement demands and shaping movement identity in the U.S. civil rights movement, as well as in the early U.S. labour movement and the movements for women's rights, welfare rights, animal rights, and gay and lesbian rights.[30] McCann also analyses the multi-fold functions of litigation as a possible strategy of social movements, particularly as "a source of institutional and symbolic leverage against opponents".[31]

---

25. McCann (N1); Michael W. McCann, "Social Movements and the Mobilization of Law" in Anne N. Costain and Andrew S. McFarland (eds.), *Social Movements and American Political Institutions* (Lanham: Rowman & Littlefield, 1998) 201–215; Michael McCann, "Law and Social Movements" in Austin Sarat (ed.), *The Blackwell Companion to Law and Society* (Oxford: Blackwell, 2004) 506–522.
26. McCann, "Law and Social Movements" (N25) 506.
27. *Ibid.*, 508.
28. McCann (N1) 84.
29. *Ibid.*, 83.
30. *Ibid.*, 84.
31. McCann, "Law and Social Movements" (N25) 513.

## SOCIAL MOVEMENTS IN HONG KONG

A dominant paradigm in socio-political studies of Hong Kong is premised on the view that post-War Hong Kong has been characterised by a high degree of political stability,[32] and thus has been spared the turmoil and civil disturbances that often accompany modernisation in the developing world.[33] Hong Kong's political stability has in turn been explained by the political apathy, "utilitarian familism", and "refugee mentality" that characterised Hong Kong[34] — a society that originally consisted largely of migrants from mainland China who came to Hong Kong in different periods of modern Chinese history to escape wars, political instability, or economic difficulties.[35]

However, this does not mean that there is no tradition of collective action and social protest in Hong Kong, where there have been "diverse forms of protests and resistance at the grass roots" level.[36] The government's expanded role in the provision of social service from the mid-1970s resulted in the increased frequency of social conflict and protest actions in areas such as housing, transport, the environment, and education.[37] Moreover, "the rising trend of social conflict was also a consequence of the increasing organizational and mobilizing capacity of … protest participants".[38] A leading work on social movements in Hong Kong states that:

> waves after waves of collective actions — from student activism to urban protests and organized actions of civil service unions — have been witnessed … since

32. H.C. Kuan, "Political Stability and Change in Hong Kong" in T.B. Lin, R.P. Lee, and U. Simonis (eds.), *Hong Kong: Economic, Social and Political Studies in Development* (New York: M.E. Sharpe, 1979) 127–146.
33. Benjamin K.P. Leung, *Perspectives on Hong Kong Society* (Hong Kong: Oxford University Press, 1996) 159.
34. Siu-kai Lau, *Society and Politics in Hong Kong* (Hong Kong: Chinese University Press, 1982).
35. Albert H.Y. Chen, "The Development of Immigration Law and Policy: The Hong Kong Experience" (1988) 33 *McGill Law Journal* 631–675.
36. Tai Lok Lui and Stephen Wing Kai Chiu, "Changing Political Opportunities and the Shaping of Collective Action: Social Movement in Hong Kong" in Stephen Wing Kai Chiu and Tai Lok Lui (eds.), *The Dynamics of Social Movement in Hong Kong* (Hong Kong: Hong Kong University Press, 2000) 1–19, at 6.
37. Leung (N33) 148–149.
38. *Ibid.*, 149.

> the 1970s … [T]he emergence of collective actions in the 1960s and 1970s was largely an outcome of social and political changes within Hong Kong society.[39]

The 1970s have been described as the "Golden Age" of social movements in Hong Kong.[40] At that time, the colonial government was largely insulated from society, with the political system closed to popular participation from below. Hence, dissatisfied groups resorted to non-institutional channels to express their grievances and demands.[41] The protest participants shared an anti-colonial administration mentality, and the conflict mode of collective action was used to attract media attention and mobilise the support of public opinion, and thus to strengthen the bargaining position of the protesters vis-à-vis the government.[42] The most significant social movements of the 1970s were the student movement,[43] the housing movement (a movement launched by the residents of public housing estates to improve their living conditions),[44] and the public sector labour movement.[45]

The signing of the Sino-British Joint Declaration in 1984 and the colonial government's policy in the 1980s of developing representative government in Hong Kong by opening up the political system to electoral politics resulted in a changed structure of political opportunities (in the language of political

39. Lui and Chiu (N36) 3, 5.

40. Linda Butenhoff, *Social Movements and Political Reform in Hong Kong* (Westport: Praeger, 1999) 25.

41. Lui and Chiu (N36) 8.

42. Tai Lok Lui (呂大樂), "迷失於急劇轉變政治環境中的香港民眾運動" [Hong Kong's Popular Movements: Lost in a Rapidly Changing Political Environment] (1994) 4 *Xianggang shehuikexue xuebao* [*Hong Kong Journal of Social Sciences*] 67–78.

43. See Benjamin K.P. Leung, "Social Movement as Cognitive Praxis: The Case of the Student and Labour Movements in Hong Kong", *Occasional Paper* 9 (Hong Kong: Social Sciences Research Centre and Department of Sociology, University of Hong Kong, 1992); Leung (N33) 155–158.

44. See Tai Lok Lui and J.K.S. Kung, *Chengshi zongheng: Xianggang jumin yundong ji chengshi zhengzhi yanjiu* [*City Unlimited: Housing Protests and Urban Politics in Hong Kong*] (Hong Kong: Wide Angle Press, 1985); Denny Kwok Leung Ho, "The Rise and Fall of Community Mobilization: The Housing Movement in Hong Kong" in Chiu and Lui (N36) 185–208.

45. See Benjamin Leung and Stephen Chiu, "A Social History of Industrial Strikes and the Labour Movement in Hong Kong, 1946–1989", *Occasional Paper* 3 (Hong Kong: Social Sciences Research Centre and Department of Sociology, University of Hong Kong, 1991); David A. Levin and Stephen Wing Kai Chiu, "Bureaucratic Insurgency: The Public Sector Labour Movement" in Chiu and Lui (N36) 139–183.

process theory) for social movements in Hong Kong.[46] Many social movement organisations "switched to the political participation mode",[47] in the sense of participating in electoral politics and trying to pursue their agendas through institutional channels such as the District Boards and Legislative Council (LegCo). Lui commented that "the 1997 question has pushed almost all active participants in politics to concentrate on political matters, especially those concerning China-Hong Kong relations. Issues which are most relevant to grassroots mobilisation have not been successfully articulated in the 1997 agenda".[48]

The anti-colonial consensus that had united protest groups, pressure groups, and social movement organisations in the 1970s gradually collapsed, with no new identity being established to replace it.[49] There was a "decline of grass roots protest groups" and "a 'hollowing out' of political organization at the grass roots level".[50]

In 1989, the student movement in Beijing and its suppression on 4 June provoked a series of demonstrations of a scale unprecedented in Hong Kong's history. However, this pro-Chinese democracy movement was not able to sustain itself in the 1990s despite well-attended annual vigils in memory of the victims of Tiananmen Square.[51] At the same time, the constitutional reforms and drafting of the Basic Law in the 1980s had stimulated the development of a pro-democracy movement in Hong Kong.[52] However, this pro-democracy movement was also unable to sustain itself in the 1990s.[53] The 1980s and 1990s saw the decline of the student movement as well,[54] although the environmental

46. Lui (N42) 75.

47. *Ibid.*, 76.

48. Tai Lok Lui, "The Development of Social Movements in Contemporary Hong Kong" in Sophia Woodman (ed.), *Hong Kong's Social Movements: Forces from the Margins* (Hong Kong: July 1 Link and Hong Kong Women Christian Council, 1997) 133–141, at 140.

49. Lui (N42) 77–78.

50. Lui and Chiu (N36) 12.

51. *Ibid.*, 12–13; see also Pik Wan Wong, "The Pro-Chinese Democracy Movement in Hong Kong", in Chiu and Lui (N36) 55–90.

52. Butenhoff (N40).

53. Lui and Chiu (N36) 13; Ming Sing, "Mobilization for Political Change — The Pro-democracy Movement in Hong Kong (1980s–1994)" in Chiu and Lui (N36) 21–53.

54. Benjamin K.P. Leung, "The Student Movement in Hong Kong: Transition to a Democratizing Society" in Chiu and Lui (N36) 209–225.

movement[55] and feminist movement[56] began to assert themselves in Hong Kong in that decade. Overall, however, social movements had only a limited role to play in the transition to 1997, and the demands articulated by the social movements of the 1960s and 1970s fell by the wayside.[57] Social movements remained at the periphery of the political system, albeit occasionally producing some disruptive effects.[58]

After 1997, the economic downturn and growing dissatisfaction with the Tung Chee-hwa administration gave rise to an increasing number of demonstrations and an "explosion of social protests" in Hong Kong,[59] culminating in the march of half a million people on 1 July 2003. The march was provoked by the impending passage of the National Security (Legislative Provisions) Bill for the purpose of implementing article 23 of the Basic Law, and was followed by assemblies and marches demanding the introduction of universal suffrage for the election of the Chief Executive in 2007 and for the election of all LegCo members in 2008. This pro-democracy movement subsided temporarily after the National People's Congress Standing Committee (NPCSC) rejected the democratic camp's demands in April 2004, but was resurrected and reached an unprecedented climax in the Occupy Central Movement (also referred to as the Umbrella Movement) of autumn 2014.

Post-colonial Hong Kong has been described as a "city of protests".[60] In the 1997–2007 period, there were an average of 2,200 public meetings and processions every year involving protests or policy demands.[61] Table 4.1,

55. Lui and Chiu (N36) 13; On Kwok Lai, "Greening of Hong Kong? — Forms of Manifestation of Environmental Movements" in Chiu and Lui (N36) 259–295.

56. Lui and Chiu (N36) 13; Ching Kwan Lee, "Public Discourses and Collective Identities: Emergence of Women as a Collective Actor in the Women's Movement in Hong Kong" in Chiu and Lui (N36) 227–257.

57. Lui (N48) 140–141.

58. Lui (N42) 78.

59. Lui and Chiu (N36) 14–16; Alvin Y. So, "Social Protests, Legitimacy Crisis, and the Impetus Toward Soft Authoritarianism in the Hong Kong SAR" in Siu-kai Lau (ed.), *The First Tung Chee-hwa Administration* (Hong Kong: Chinese University Press, 2002) 399–418, at 407.

60. Daniel Garrett and Wing-chung Ho, "Hong Kong at the Brink: Emerging Forms of Political Participation in the New Social Movement" in Joseph Y.S. Cheng (ed.), *New Trends of Political Participation in Hong Kong* (Hong Kong: City University of Hong Kong Press, 2014) 347–383, at 347.

61. Ngok Ma, "Social Movements and State-Society Relationship in Hong Kong" in Khun Eng Kuah-Pearce and Gilles Guiheux (eds.), *Social Movements in China and Hong Kong* (Amsterdam: Amsterdam University Press, 2009), 45–63 at 52–53.

compiled by Cheng,[62] reports the number of legal processions in the 2004–2014 period, as well as the number of prosecutions relating to such processions. "Legal processions" are public meetings of more than 50 people or public processions of more than 30 people that are approved by the police under the Public Order Ordinance.[63] Cheng points out that "[t]here were 51,915 approved applications, out of a total of 51,946, between July 1997 and September 2012, or an average of ten protests of that scale each day".[64]

Among the many protests and demonstrations, the best-known include the annual candlelight vigils in Victoria Park, organised by the Hong Kong Alliance in Support of Patriotic Democratic Movements in China, in memory of the victims of the Tiananmen incident on 4 June 1989, and the annual marches on Hong Kong Island on 1 July (the public holiday to commemorate Hong Kong's reunification with China) organised by the Civil Human Rights Front every year since 1 July 2003. These two annual events always attract tens of thousands of participants from all walks of life and are widely reported and broadcast in Hong Kong's mass media.

The march of hundreds of thousands of demonstrators on 1 July 2003 was not only the "largest indigenous social movement" in Hong Kong to date,[65] but also inaugurated a "post-modern mode of social movements"[66] characterised by loose organisational structures, open and diversified participation, and spontaneous mobilisation by the media, social media, and other information technology tools. "While the 1 July 2003 rally is widely considered to be a critical juncture that cast the strength of local civil society, the data suggest that 2006–2007 was another point when the number of collective actions increased rapidly."[67] The campaigns launched by the social movement organisation Local Action in 2006 and 2007 to resist the demolition of the Star Ferry Terminal and Queen's Pier, respectively, for the sake of preserving

62. Edmund W. Cheng, "Street Politics in a Hybrid Regime: The Diffusion of Political Activism in Post-colonial Hong Kong" (2016) 226 *China Quarterly* 383–406, at 389.

63. *Ibid.*, 389.

64. *Ibid.*

65. Alvin Y. So, "Social Conflict in Hong Kong after 1997: The Emergence of a Post-modern Mode of Social Movements?" in Ming K. Chan (ed.), *China's Hong Kong Transformed: Retrospect and Prospects Beyond the First Decade* (Hong Kong: City University of Hong Kong Press, 2008) 233–251, at 240; Ma (N61) 56.

66. So (N65) 240, 249.

67. Cheng (N62) 389.

**Table 4.1: Demonstrations in Hong Kong, 2004–2014**

| Year | Number of legal processions | Number of people prosecuted for unlawful assembly | Number of people prosecuted for assaulting a police officer |
|---|---|---|---|
| 2004 | 1,974 | 52 | 236 |
| 2005 | 1,900 | 65 | 266 |
| 2006 | 2,228 | 83 | 274 |
| 2007 | 3,824 | 55 | 326 |
| 2008 | 4,278 | 89 | 232 |
| 2009 | 4,222 | 45 | 202 |
| 2010 | 5,656 | 93 | 268 |
| 2011 | 6,878 | 30 | 470 |
| 2012 | 7,529 | 112 | 498 |
| 2013 | 6,166 | 35 | 467 |
| 2014 | 6,818 | 20 | 461 |

**Source: Cheng (N62).**

local cultural heritage and places invoking the collective memory of the Hong Kong people, marked a "localist" turn in Hong Kong's social movements, with increasing numbers of young activists of the "post-1980s" generation (those born in or after the 1980s) engaging in social actions to assert their identity as Hongkongers and to resist the integration of Hong Kong with the mainland.[68]

The movements to preserve the terminal and pier were followed by several other major movements of larger scale, which paved the way for the Occupy Central Movement of 2014.[69] These included the campaign in 2009–2010 to oppose LegCo's approval of funding to construct a high-speed railway connecting Hong Kong with the mainland, which included a movement to resist the demolition of Choi Yuen Village in the process of the railway's construction; the protests in 2012–2014 against the government's plan to develop the North East New Territories; the 2012 campaign against the introduction of a "moral and national education" curriculum in schools (which, unlike the other campaigns, actually succeeded in pressurising the government to abandon its original plan) and the 2013 protest against the government's decision not to issue a television licence to Ricky Wong's

68. So (N65); Garrett and Ho (N60).
69. Cheng (N62).

company, Hong Kong Television Network. Whereas only a few hundred protesters participated in the pro-pier events in 2006–2007, thousands participated in the protest against the construction of the express rail,[70] which resulted in a siege of the LegCo building, and tens of thousands protested against the national education curriculum (a campaign that persisted for weeks and involved many large-scale assemblies outside Government Headquarters) and the rejection of Wong's television licence application.[71]

Then came autumn 2014, when Hong Kong found itself in the international spotlight as another social movement as powerful and spectacular as the 1 July 2003 march of half a million people engulfed the city. This was the world-famous Occupy Central Movement. The unprecedented occupation, completely unlawful from a legal point of view, by thousands of demonstrators of key governmental and business districts in Admiralty, Mong Kok, and Causeway Bay for more than two months, with occasional gatherings of tens of thousands of protesters, was largely a spontaneous and self-mobilised social movement with a decentralised organisational structure. It went far beyond the original "script" or plan of the Occupy Central Campaign,[72] as conceived by the "Occupy trio" led by University of Hong Kong law professor Benny Tai. The original campaign promoted by Tai threatened the Beijing and Hong Kong Governments with the mass occupation of the Central District by protesters practising civil disobedience, so as to paralyse the city's main business district in the event that the two governments failed to put forward a proposal for election of the Chief Executive by universal suffrage in 2017 that complied with internationally accepted standards of democratic elections and universal suffrage. As observers and scholars have rightly pointed out,[73] this original campaign, which did not have a strong social base, was transformed by relatively contingent events into a resilient occupation of public space in the heart of the city by protesters too numerous for the police to evict. Those contingent events included (a) the storming of Civic Square, where

70. Chor-yung Cheung, "Hong Kong's Systemic Crisis of Governance and the Revolt of the 'Post-80s' Youths: The Anti-Express Rail Campaign" in Cheng (N60) 417–447.

71. Cheng (N62).

72. See the movement's website, the full English name of which is "Occupy Central with Love and Peace", available at: www.oclp.hk/, last accessed 2 August 2016.

73. Edmund W. Cheng and Wai-yin Chan, "Explaining Spontaneous Occupation: Antecedents and Contingencies in the Making of the Umbrella Movement" (2017) 16:2 *Social Movement Studies* 222–239.

demonstrations were originally prohibited, by a number of students on the evening of 26 September (leading to the students' arrest and a search of the home of student leader Joshua Wong Chi-fung) after several days of peaceful and lawful sit-in protests in Tamar Park and (b) the police's use of large amounts of tear gas in an attempt to disperse swelling crowds of demonstrators at Admiralty on the evening of 28 September. Both events, which were widely reported in the media and televised, provoked a public outcry and mobilised large numbers of citizens to participate in the social movement. The ensuing occupation led to top government officials engaging in a televised dialogue with student leaders on 21 October, but ultimately failed to secure any substantive concessions from the authorities on the proposed model for the election of the Chief Executive by universal suffrage, which was finally vetoed by Hong Kong's LegCo on 18 June 2015.[74]

## SOCIAL MOVEMENTS AND THE LAW IN HONG KONG

### The development of Hong Kong's legal system

In the colonial era, the British legal model and English common law were transplanted to Hong Kong. The British tradition of Rule of Law and the independence of the judiciary provided a strong foundation for Hong Kong's legal system.[75] However, for most of the time during Hong Kong's history as a colony, the people of Hong Kong did not enjoy the full extent of civil liberties enjoyed by the British people themselves.[76] As in other ceded colonies in the British Empire, the nature of colonial rule was authoritarian,[77] with a high degree of concentration of power in the hands of a governor appointed by London.[78] Laws on sedition, assembly, and association were draconian,

74. Albert H.Y. Chen, "The Law and Politics of the Struggle for Universal Suffrage in Hong Kong, 2013–15" (2016) 3 *Asian Journal of Law and Society* 189–207.
75. Steve Tsang (ed.), *Judicial Independence and the Rule of Law in Hong Kong* (Hong Kong: Hong Kong University Press, 2001).
76. Raymond Wacks (ed.), *Civil Liberties in Hong Kong* (Hong Kong: Oxford University Press, 1988).
77. Norman Miners, *The Government and Politics of Hong Kong* (Hong Kong: Oxford University Press, 4th edition, 1986).
78. Peter Wesley-Smith, *Constitutional and Administrative Law in Hong Kong* (Hong Kong: Longman Asia, 1995).

although they were not always strictly enforced.[79] Furthermore, the operation of the legislative and judicial systems in the English language made local inhabitants feel that the legal system was alien and imposed on them.[80]

The 1980s, however, saw a fundamental change in Hong Kong's legal culture, particularly in public attitudes towards issues related to the Rule of Law. The signing of the Sino-British Joint Declaration in 1984 and the prospects of reunification with China alerted the people of Hong Kong to the fact that the Rule of Law and protection of individual rights were much weaker in mainland China than in Hong Kong, and thus that there was a real danger that the human rights situation in Hong Kong would deteriorate upon its return to China. The people of Hong Kong therefore began to treasure the legal system they had inherited from the British colonisers, and to make efforts to safeguard and strengthen it in preparation for the challenges of 1997. There was a legal awakening in Hong Kong, a rise in rights consciousness. Law-related current affairs attracted increasing media and public attention.[81] A number of legal controversies in the 1980s testified to the increasing vigilance of members of the public with regard to human rights and fundamental freedoms.[82]

In 1989, the 4 June suppression of the student movement in Beijing brought about an unprecedented crisis of confidence in Hong Kong. One of the measures taken by the British colonial government to alleviate the difficult situation was the enactment of the Hong Kong Bill of Rights Ordinance (BORO) in 1991, which incorporated the human rights guarantees in the International Covenant on Civil and Political Rights (ICCPR) into the domestic law of Hong Kong. Under this new legal regime of the constitutional

---

79. Albert H.Y. Chen, "Civil Liberties in Hong Kong: Freedoms of Expression and Association" (1989) 19 *Hong Kong Law Journal* 4–9; Albert H.Y. Chen, "The Legal System" in Richard Y. C. Wong and Joseph Y. S. Cheng (eds.), *The Other Hong Kong Report 1990* (Hong Kong: Chinese University Press, 1990) 65–86.

80. Albert H.Y. Chen, "Law in a Foreign Language: The Case of Hong Kong" in Kathleen Cheek-Milby and Miron Mushkat (eds.), *Hong Kong: The Challenge of Transformation* (Hong Kong: Centre of Asian Studies, University of Hong Kong, 1989) 212–238.

81. Albert H.Y. Chen and Johannes M.M. Chan, *Renquan yu fazhi: Xianggang guoduqi de tiaozhan* [*Human Rights and the Rule of Law: The Challenges of Hong Kong's Transition*] (Hong Kong: Wide Angle Press, 1987); Albert H.Y. Chen, *Xianggang falü yu Xianggang zhengzhi* [*Law and Politics in Hong Kong*] ( Hong Kong: Wide Angle Press, 1990).

82. Albert H.Y. Chen, "Civil Liberties in Hong Kong: Recent Controversies, Evolving Consciousness and Future Legal Protection" (1988) 2 *Journal of Chinese Law* 137–151; Johannes M.M. Chan, *Renquan zai Xianggang* [*Human Rights in Hong Kong*] (Hong Kong: Wide Angle Press, 1990).

protection of human rights, the courts of Hong Kong acquired and began to exercise the power to review the validity of local legislation on the ground of its inconsistency with international standards of human rights.[83] As in other jurisdictions, the opportunity for constitutional review rendered the courts of Hong Kong more assertive and activist in ensuring that the law struck the proper balance between the rights and liberties of individuals, on the one hand, and the collective interest of society, on the other. A body of jurisprudence and principles of constitutional interpretation were gradually built up through the accumulation of case law.[84] At the same time, the government conducted a thorough review of existing legislation with regard to its compliance with the Bill of Rights and introduced relevant amendments to liberalise the law. In retrospect, the most significant amendments were those made to the Societies Ordinance and Public Order Ordinance, which Beijing found to be objectionable, with the result that the amendments were partially reversed at the time of the handover in 1997.[85]

The Basic Law — the constitutional instrument of the Hong Kong Special Administrative Region (HKSAR) — restricts the right of individual LegCo members to introduce private members' bills relating to government policy.[86] In the last weeks before it came into effect in July 1997, LegCo members, which had been elected in 1995 in a fairly democratic manner pursuant to the political reforms introduced by Governor Chris Patten, rushed through a number of private members' bills that turned out to be significant in the post-1997 era. One example is the amendment of the Housing Ordinance for the

83. Albert H.Y. Chen, "The Interpretation of the Basic Law — Common Law and Mainland Chinese Perspectives" (2000) 30 *Hong Kong Law Journal* 380–431, at 418–420.

84. See Yash Ghai, "Sentinels of Liberty or Sheep in Woolf's Clothing? Judicial Politics and the Hong Kong Bill of Rights" (1997) 60 *Modern Law Review* 459–480; Johannes M.M. Chan, "Hong Kong's Bill of Rights: Its Reception of and Contribution to International and Comparative Jurisprudence" (1998) 47 *International and Comparative Law Quarterly* 306–336; Andrew Byrnes, "And Some Have Bills of Rights Thrust Upon Them: The Experience of Hong Kong's Bill of Rights" in Philip Alston (ed.), *Promoting Human Rights Through Bills of Rights: Comparative Perspectives* (Oxford: Oxford University Press, 2000), 318–391.

85. Albert H.Y. Chen, "Hong Kong's Legal System in the New Constitutional Order: The Experience of 1997–2000" in Jianfu Chen, Yuwen Li, and Jan Michiel Otto (eds.), *Implementation of Law in the People's Republic of China* (The Hague: Kluwer Law International, 2002) 213–245, at 216.

86. See art. 74 of the Basic Law. For a comparison with the pre-1997 position, see Albert H.Y. Chen, "From Colony to Special Administrative Region: Hong Kong's Constitutional Journey" in Raymond Wacks (ed.), *The Future of the Law in Hong Kong* (Hong Kong: Oxford University Press, 1989) 76–126, at 118.

purpose of ensuring that the rent payable by tenants of public housing estates remained affordable for them. Another is the enactment of the Protection of the Harbour Ordinance, which declares Victoria Harbour to be a "special public asset and a natural heritage of Hong Kong people" and discourages land reclamation within the Harbour. Laws like these, when enforced by the courts, have enabled the courts to play a major role in shaping social policies in Hong Kong in the post-1997 era. They reinforce the already enhanced role of the courts resulting from the aforementioned constitutional review of laws on human rights grounds and from the protection afforded by the Basic Law to various interests and its entrenchment of various policies.[87] Generally speaking, Hong Kong courts in the post-1997 era have addressed difficult issues of public policy more often than ever before.[88] Opportunities for social movements to challenge the existing order or existing policies by means of litigation have also become greater than ever before.

The interaction between social movements and the law in the post-1997 history of Hong Kong can be broken down into four main topics: (1) the legal space for social movements; (2) the law as a resource used by social movements; (3) the law as an arena of struggle for social movements; and (4) the multiple legal dimensions of the Occupy Central Movement.

## The legal space for social movements

As discussed above, the law may constrain the space for social movements by limiting the freedoms of speech, press, assembly, procession, and association without which social movements could not mobilise mass support. In both colonial and post-colonial Hong Kong, the space for social movements was constrained by the Public Order Ordinance and Societies Ordinance, which regulate the freedoms of assembly, procession, and association. As noted above, the colonial laws in these areas were originally strict, but were liberalised in the 1990s as part of the exercise to ensure that all existing Hong Kong laws were consistent with the newly enacted Bill of Rights. However, on the eve of Hong Kong's reunification with China, the NPCSC, exercising its power under the Basic Law of Hong Kong to determine which existing Hong Kong laws would

87. See, for example, arts. 40 and 99–103 in chs. 5 and 6 of the Basic Law.

88. Anthony Cheung and Max Wong, "Judicial Review and Policy Making in Hong Kong: Changing Interface Between the Legal and the Political" (2006) 28 *Asia Pacific Journal of Public Administration* 117–141.

survive the handover,[89] decided not to adopt the major amendments made to the Societies Ordinance and Public Order Ordinance in July 1992 and July 1995, respectively. At the same time, the HKSAR Government was given the freedom to devise new versions of societies and public order legislation for the SAR. Rising to the challenge, the Office of the HKSAR Chief Executive-designate published a Consultative Document titled "Civil Liberties and Social Order" on 9 April 1997 proposing new versions of the laws governing the freedoms of association, assembly, and procession. After consultation, respective bills were drafted and finally enacted by the Provisional Legislative Council (PLC) on 14 June 1997 in the form of the Societies (Amendment) Ordinance 1997 and Public Order (Amendment) Ordinance 1997. The amended laws largely preserved the improvements and liberalisations made in 1992 and 1995, and did not remove any significant substantive rights enjoyed under the existing laws.

Under the Public Order Ordinance (as amended), organisers of public meetings of more than 50 persons or public processions of more than 30 persons are obliged to give the police notice of the event at least seven days in advance (as a general rule, although the seven-day period may be shortened), and the police may impose conditions on the demonstration. In practice, some demonstrators do not comply with this advance notification requirement. For example, 126 protests were organised in 1998 and 183 in 1999 without complying with the requirement,[90] and the government did not prosecute any of the organisers. The organisers of other demonstrations have complied with the legal requirements, with 1,388 and 1,283 protests being approved in 1998 and 1999, respectively.[91] Cheung and Chen report that "between July 1997 and March 2002, about one in seven public rallies were in fact held without notifying the police in advance".[92] From 1998 to 2007, a total of 25,108 public meetings and processions were held, 679 in circumstances in which the law

89. Yash Ghai, "The Continuity of Laws and Legal Rights and Obligations in the SAR" (1997) 27 *Hong Kong Law Journal* 136–151; Yash Ghai, *Hong Kong's New Constitutional Order: The Resumption of Chinese Sovereignty and the Basic Law* (Hong Kong: Hong Kong University Press, 2nd edition, 1999) 379–386.

90. So (N59) 405.

91. *Ibid.*

92. Anne S.Y. Cheung and Albert H.Y. Chen, "The Search for the Rule of Law in the Hong Kong Special Administrative Region, 1997–2003" in Yiu-chung Wong (ed.), *"One Country, Two Systems" in Crisis: Hong Kong's Transformation Since the Handover* (Lanham: Lexington Books, 2004) 61–93, at 79.

required prior notification to the police but no such notification was given.[93] In the same period, the total number of persons arrested, prosecuted, and convicted for offences relating to demonstrations was 1,346 (of which 1,158 arrests took place in 2005),[94] 102 and 56, respectively.[95] In 1997–2004, the total number of demonstrations that failed to receive approval after prior notification was 21.[96]

The general picture that seems to emerge from these statistics and from the Department of Justice's Prosecution Code and its Prosecutions Division's Yearly Review documents is that "the Department of Justice has adopted a diversionary approach to public order cases", so that "[o]nly serious cases warrant prosecution".[97] Serious cases usually involve disorderly conduct, some degree of violence, and physical conflict with the police. The organisers of and participants in "unauthorised" assemblies and processions (i.e., those that fail to comply with the legal requirement of prior notification to the police) are often not prosecuted even though organising and participating in unauthorised demonstrations constitute criminal offences under the Public Order Ordinance. With regard to the period prior to the Occupy Central Movement, it has been pointed out that "[f]rom September 2003 to June 2014, there were 5,529 public order events and, as of 8 September 2014, only 16 protesters [have been] prosecuted".[98] Thus, it seems that legal restrictions on demonstrations have not always been strictly enforced in the HKSAR, leaving considerable physical and legal space for protests associated with social movements.

## Law as a resource used by social movements

Under some circumstances litigation may be an effective strategy for social movements, particularly when accompanied by other tactics such as demonstrations and other forms of expression of popular support for the cause of such movement. In other words, the law of the state may be relied upon as a useful resource, and turned into a weapon in the battle against existing laws

93. Ma (N61).
94. The abnormally high number of arrests in 2005 was probably attributable to the anti-globalisation protests in December 2005 during a World Trade Organization (WTO) meeting in Hong Kong.
95. Ma (N61).
96. *Ibid*.
97. Simon Young, "Prosecution Response to Occupy Central?" (11 November 2014) *HKU Legal Scholarship Blog*, available at: http://researchblog.law.hku.hk/2014/11/prosecution-response-to-occupy-central.html, last accessed 2 August 2016.
98. *Ibid*.; the cases relating to Occupy Central are discussed below.

and policies, or changes therein, for example by launching public interest litigation to challenge a law or policy or demand policy changes. As Tam notes, "[l]egal mobilization in post-colonial Hong Kong (and elsewhere) can be regarded as a social movement tactic".[99]

"Legal mobilisation" in this context has been defined as individuals invoking their legal rights in litigation relating to human rights and public policies.[100] Empirical studies of cases litigated in Hong Kong courts have shown that "[t]he number of human rights and policy-oriented cases on the judiciary's agenda has increased substantially since the early 1990s and particularly after July 1997".[101] The litigation in the majority of these cases has been funded by the government's Legal Aid Department and launched by litigants with the support of social movement organisations, rights advocacy organisations, and "cause lawyers" (lawyers active in human rights and public policy litigation).[102] Whereas social movement organisations and rights advocacy groups "rarely used litigation" to promote their causes in the 1970s and 1980s, and instead relied on "protests, petitions, or mass mobilization as their major strategies", since the 1990s they have "devoted an increasing share of their efforts to legal mobilization"; hence, "legal mobilization [has] intensified", particularly since 1997.[103] Social movement organisations[104] play an important role in public interest litigation by using their social networks "to gain access to potential sources of cases" and to search "for promising issues and cases for ligation".[105] They also help litigants in relevant cases to apply for legal aid and to recruit activist lawyers to represent them in court.

In his book-length study of legal mobilisation under authoritarianism in post-colonial Hong Kong, Tam[106] attributes the rise of such mobilisation since the 1990s to the interaction of several factors, including the "critical antecedents"

99. Waikeung Tam, *Legal Mobilization under Authoritarianism: The Case of Post Colonial Hong Kong* (New York: Cambridge University Press, 2013) 5.

100. *Ibid.*, 4.

101. *Ibid.*, 2, 30.

102. *Ibid.*, 21–22, 152.

103. *Ibid.*, 153.

104. Examples include the Society for Community Organization and the Neighbourhood and Workers' Service Centre (both are devoted to grassroots interests) as well as Green Sense (an environmental protection group), Society for the Protection of the Harbour, and Civil Rights for Sexual Diversities.

105. Tam (N99) 158–159.

106. Tam (N99).

or "historical legacies" of the existence of a well-developed institutional legal complex (consisting of courts, the legal profession, and the legal aid system), the "critical junctures" of the enactment of the Hong Kong Bill of Rights, the coming into force of the Basic Law and the establishment of a new Court of Final Appeal (CFA), the availability in Hong Kong of what Epp[107] calls a rights "support structure" comprising rights advocacy organisations and activist lawyers who play the role of "transformative agents",[108] and a shifting structure of legal and political opportunities after 1997 when it apparently became more difficult for social movement organisations to advance their cause in the political arena.[109]

The following are some examples of cases involving rights and public policies litigated in post-colonial Hong Kong in which social movement organisations participated by supporting the litigants or launching the litigation themselves:

(1) cases litigated with the support of the Neighbourhood and Workers' Service Centre and other groups

   (a) on public housing rental policy,[110]
   (b) against the privatisation of the shopping and car park facilities in public housing estates,[111] and
   (c) on a minimum wage for employees in Hong Kong;[112]

(2) cases litigated with the support of the Society for Community Organization on

   (a) issues of the right of abode in Hong Kong of persons with cross-border (mainland-Hong Kong) family relationships,[113]

---

107. Charles Epp, *The Rights Revolution: Lawyers, Activities and Supreme Courts in Comparative* Perspective (Chicago: University of Chicago Press, 1998).

108. Tam (N99) 23.

109. *Ibid.*, 153.

110. *Ho Choi Wan v Hong Kong Housing Authority* [2005] 4 HKLRD 706.

111. *Lo Siu Lan v Hong Kong Housing Authority* [2005] 3 HKLRD 257.

112. *Chan Noi Heung v Chief Executive in Council* [2008] HKEC 780, [2009] 3 HKLRD 362. See Tam (N99) 22.

113. There were many such cases, the best-known of which include *Ng Ka Ling v Director of Immigration* [1999] 1 HKLRD 315; *Chan Kam Nga v Director of Immigration* [1999] 1 HKLRD 304; *Lau Kong Yung v Director of Immigration* [1999] 3 HKLRD 778; *Tam Nga Yin v Director of Immigration* [2001] 2 HKLRD 644; *Director of Immigration v Chong Fung-yuen* [2001] 2 HKLRD 533.

  (b) social security assistance entitlements for new migrants and others,[114] and
  (c) prisoners' right to vote;[115]

(3) cases litigated by the Society for the Protection of the Harbour challenging the reclamation of Victoria Harbour;[116]

(4) a case brought by a Local Action activist against the demolition of Queen's Pier;[117]

(5) cases brought by environmental groups on
  (a) height restrictions on construction on the waterfront,[118]
  (b) air pollution and the right to life and health,[119]
  (c) the environmental impact of the construction of the Hong Kong-Zhuhai-Macau Bridge,[120] and
  (d) the environmental impact of the construction of an incinerator;[121] and

(6) a case on homosexuals' criminal liability litigated with the support of the LGBT group Civil Rights for Sexual Diversities[122] and a case on a transsexual's right to marriage.[123]

---

114. *Yao Man Fai George v Director of Social Welfare*, CACV 153/2010 (17 February 2012, CA); *Kong Yunming v Director of Social Welfare* (2013) 16 HKCFAR 950.

115. *Chan Kin Sum v Secretary for Justice* [2009] 2 HKLRD 166. See Tam (N99) 22, 159–162.

116. There were several cases, the most famous of which was *Town Planning Board v Society for the Protection of the Harbour Ltd* [2004] 1 HKLRD 396 (CFA), in which the Society won the lawsuit against the government. See also *Society for Protection of the Harbour Ltd v Chief Executive-in-Council* (No. 2) [2004] 2 HKLRD 902; *Society for Protection of the Harbour Ltd v Secretary for Justice* [2008] 4 HKLRD 417; Karen Kong, "Public Interest Litigation in Hong Kong: A New Hope for Social Transformation?" (2009) 28:3 *Civil Justice Quarterly* 327–343, at 338–340.

117. *Chu Hoi Dick v Secretary for Home Affairs*, HCAL 87/2007 (10 August 2007, 6 September 2007, CFI).

118. *Ng Ngau Chai v Town Planning Board* [2007] HKEC 1207 (CFI).

119. *Clean Air Foundation Ltd v Government of the HKSAR* [2007] HKEC 1356 (CFI).

120. *Chu Yee Wah v Director of Environmental Protection* [2011] 5 HKLRD 469 (CA).

121. *Leung Hon Wai* [2014] HKEC 1459 (CA). See Karen Kong, "The Uphill Battle for Sustainable Development: Can the Use of Public Interest Litigation Protect the Natural Environment in Hong Kong?" (2015) 23:1 *Asia Pacific Law Review* 7–29.

122. *Secretary for Justice v Yau Yuk Lung Zigo* [2007] 3 HKLRD 903. See Tam (N99) 163–166.

123. *W v Registrar of Marriages*, FACV 4/2012 (CFA, 16 July 2013).

## Law as an arena of struggle for social movements

Social movements are often about trying to change the law for the better, but they may also be launched to oppose a change in the law. In both cases, the law becomes an arena of struggle. The two largest and most internationally famous social movements in post-colonial Hong Kong are undoubtedly the movement against the National Security Bill to implement article 23 of the Basic Law in mid-2003 and the Occupy Central Movement in autumn 2014. In both cases, the law constituted an arena of struggle for a social movement. In this section, we consider the former case, in which the movement's aim was to oppose a change in the law, in contrast to the latter (considered in the following section), in which the aim was to protest against a legal decision imposed by Beijing on Hong Kong.

Article 23 requires the HKSAR to "enact laws on its own to prohibit any act of treason, secession, sedition, [or] subversion against the Central People's Government". It also addresses the protection of State secrets and the activities of foreign political organisations in Hong Kong. Many of the issues raised by article 23 are considered politically sensitive. Ever since the Basic Law was enacted in 1990 and brought into effect in July 1997, there has been anxiety over the implementation of article 23.

The publication on 24 September 2002 of the government's "Consultation Document on Proposals to Implement Article 23 of the Basic Law" opened a three-month consultation exercise on the legislative proposal. On 28 January 2003, the government published the results of the consultation, and announced nine sets of clarifications or modifications of the original legislative proposal. This was followed by the publication of the National Security Bill on 13 February 2003 and its first reading in LegCo on 26 February 2003. During the Bills Committee's deliberations on the bill, the government agreed to some amendments. However, critics said that these amendments were insufficient,[124] and in any event the government's timetable for passing the bill in LegCo's week-long meeting beginning on 9 July did not allow sufficient time for deliberation.

On 1 July 2003, a hot summer public holiday marking the anniversary of Hong Kong's return to China, an estimated half a million Hong Kong

---

124. Hualing Fu, Carole J. Petersen, and Simon N. M. Young (eds.), *National Security and Fundamental Freedoms: Hong Kong's Article 23 Under Scrutiny* (Hong Kong: Hong Kong University Press, 2005).

residents took to the streets to demonstrate against the article 23 legislative exercise and to express other grievances against the Tung Chee-hwa administration. The demonstration had the effect of tilting the balance in LegCo between legislators who supported the bill and those who opposed it: the Liberal Party, which had hitherto supported the bill, now advocated its postponement and opposed the Tung administration's decision on 5 July to adhere to the original 9 July deadline for its passage. Not having enough votes in the legislature to pass the bill, the government decided to postpone it.[125] On 17 July 2003, Tung announced that the government would re-open public consultations on the bill. However, in an about-turn on 5 September 2003, he announced that the bill was to be withdrawn. Since then, the implementation of article 23 of the Basic Law has been shelved indefinitely.

This episode is a paradigmatic case of a social movement with massive popular support succeeding in resisting a change in the law that movement participants consider a change for the worse. It has been suggested that it is also a case of "popular constitutionalism" at work in Hong Kong,[126] with citizens rising up to defend the liberal values and human rights enshrined in the Basic Law — the constitutional instrument of the HKSAR — against encroachment by legislative action. By the same token, supporters of the National Security Bill could of course point out that the implementation of article 23 is itself a constitutional obligation for the HKSAR under the Basic Law. Thus, the contest was over the meaning and implications of the relevant provisions of the Basic Law, particularly those on human rights and national security. The movement against the National Security Bill was therefore also about how the constitution should be understood and implemented.

## The multiple legal dimensions of the Occupy Central Movement

From the perspective of law and social movements, the Occupy Central Movement provides a most interesting case study. There are at least eight law-related dimensions or features, each of which is considered below.

---

125. Albert Chen, "A Defining Moment In Hong Kong's History" (4 July 2003) *South China Morning Post*; Albert Chen, "How the Liberals Stopped a Constitutional Crisis" (8 July 2003) *South China Morning Post*.

126. Eric Ip, "The High Court of the People: Popular Constitutionalism in Hong Kong under Chinese Sovereignty" (2014) 36:3 *Law and Policy* 314–338.

First, as in the case of the struggle against the bill to implement article 23, the law was an arena of struggle in the Occupy Central Movement, which originally justified its demands in legal and constitutional terms, thereby using the law as a symbolic and moral resource.[127] The Occupy trio led by Benny Tai pointed out that as article 45 of the Basic Law provides for the eventual introduction of the election of the Chief Executive by universal suffrage, and the NPCSC in its Decision of December 2007 had stipulated that such universal suffrage might be introduced in 2017, the main question that remained was the precise electoral model. They demanded that the model adopted should be consistent with international standards of democratic elections and genuine universal suffrage, as enshrined in the ICCPR (itself referred to in article 39 of the Basic Law and incorporated by it into Hong Kong law) and the related jurisprudence, which include the principle that there should be no unreasonable restrictions on the right to participate in the election as a candidate. Accordingly, they opposed any system of nomination that was so restrictive that only "pro-China" or "patriotic" politicians would have a chance of being nominated, such as the nomination model eventually adopted by the NPCSC in its Decision of 31 August 2014.[128]

Second, although the Occupy Central Campaign drew on legal norms as a source of legitimacy for its demands, it also amounted to a challenge to the law—particularly Hong Kong's public order law—in advocating civil disobedience via occupation of Central District by demonstrators so numerous as to be able to paralyse traffic.[129] It has been argued that such disobedience of the law by peaceful demonstrators (who are willing to endure arrests and legal sanctions) is not inconsistent with the Rule of Law, and can be justified by the movement's goals of democracy and justice, which are higher values inherent in the concept of the Rule of Law.[130] Opponents, in contrast, argue that the

127. See generally Michael C. Davis, "The Basic Law, Universal Suffrage and the Rule of Law in Hong Kong" (2015) 38 *Hastings International and Comparative Law Review* 275–298; Alvin Y.H. Cheung, "Road to Nowhere: Hong Kong's Democratization and China's Obligations under Public International Law" (2015) 40 *Brooklyn Journal of International Law* 465–545.

128. Chen (N74).

129. Jermain T.M. Lam, "The Occupy Central Movement and Political Reform in Hong Kong" in Cheng (N60) 449–481.

130. See Benny Tai, "Civil Disobedience and the Rule of Law" in Michael H.K. Ng and John D. Wong (eds.), *Civil Unrest and Governance in Hong Kong: Law and Order from Historical and Cultural Perspectives* (London: Routledge, 2017) ch. 8, 141–162.

unlawful occupation of the city's Central District could not be justified in the circumstances and undermined the Rule of Law in Hong Kong.

Third, as noted above, the Occupy Central Campaign as conceived by Benny Tai was transformed into the mass-scale occupation of Admiralty and two other districts as a result of public indignation aroused by police actions against student activists on the evening of 26 September and the police force's use of large quantities of tear gas against the gathering crowds on the evening of 28 September. Although the behaviour of the student activists (who stormed Civic Square) and the crowds (who engaged in an "unauthorised assembly") was technically unlawful,[131] the police actions to enforce the law were widely perceived as disproportionate and unjust.[132] After the occupation had initially succeeded, the police simply gave up any attempt to enforce the public order law and disperse the demonstrators, whose occupation of the roads continued for weeks. The legal constraints on assembly and demonstrations thus became totally ineffective, as protesters persisted in their defiance of the public order law.

Fourth, another noteworthy feature of the movement was that constitutional and legal arguments figured prominently in the televised dialogue between student leaders and senior government officials on 21 October.[133] Students argued that their demands for the introduction of an electoral model consistent with internationally accepted standards of democracy and genuine universal suffrage were perfectly consistent with the Basic Law, and that there were good legal grounds to challenge the validity of the NPCSC Decision of 31 August 2014, which they argued should be rescinded.

Fifth, and this is closely related to the fourth point above, two cases were brought before the court (including one brought by Yvonne Leung, one

---

131. Because of their storming of Civic Square on the evening of 26 September 2014, Joshua Wong and two other student activists were convicted by a magistrate on 15 August 2016 for unlawful assembly and sentenced to community service or suspended sentence of imprisonment; see "No Jail for Occupy Leaders Joshua Wong and Nathan Law" and "Clear to Run: Nathan Law, Joshua Wong and Alex Chow are Spared Jail in Time for Legco Elections" (16 August 2016) *South China Morning Post*. The case was appealed up to the CFA (see *Secretary for Justice v Wong Chi Fung* [2018] HKCFA 4), which affirmed the magistrate's decision.

132. There was further public outcry when video footage of seven policemen beating up a demonstrator (Ken Tsang, a social worker and member of the Civic Party) in a dark corner of the demonstration area after his arrest was broadcast on TV news programmes on 15 October 2014.

133. Sebastian Veg, "Legalistic and Utopian: Hong Kong's Umbrella Movement" (2015) 92 *New Left Review* 55–73.

of the student leaders who participated in the dialogue on 21 October) to challenge (a) the Chief Executive's report to the NPCSC that had paved the way for the NPCSC's Decision[134] and (b) the HKSAR Government's consultation document and report on the electoral model that had followed that Decision.[135] The legal arguments used in these judicial review cases were largely similar to those put forward in the televised dialogue, but the court was not persuaded.

Sixth, as the occupation continued for weeks, the protesters carved out in the heart of the city their own "nomosphere",[136] an enclave in which the ordinary legal norms of Hong Kong apparently lost their force, and "semi-permanent, self-sufficient communities ... *lived out* an alternative form of community in the heart of the city".[137] The city's "existing spatio-normative constructions were subverted", and a "new public space" was created in which an "alternative form of life" was imagined and lived out[138] in an "atmospheric glass house",[139] "providing opportunities for slowness and feeling, sharing and solidarity in a city that is otherwise predisposed".[140] A "performative mode of resistance" was enacted, which in retrospect serves "as a reminder of a democratic spirit that lies so closely behind the city's otherwise uncompromising edifices".[141]

Seventh, the prolonged occupation produced a stalemate, with both the protesters and the government seemingly at a loss as to what the exit strategy should be.[142] Eventually, it was the court injunctions to evict the protesters obtained by private parties such as the operators of buses and taxis and property owners that served as a focal point to coordinate the actions taken by the authorities,[143] with minimal physical resistance by the protesters, to end the two-month occupation. It is ironic that the timing of the Occupy Central

---

134. *Kwok Cheuk Kin v Chief Executive of the HKSAR*, HCAL 103/2014 (CFI, 25 June 2015).

135. *Leung Lai Kwok Yvonne v Chief Secretary for Administration*, HCAL 31/2015 (CFI, 5 June 2015).

136. Daniel Matthews, "Narrative Space and Atmosphere: A Nomospheric Inquiry into Hong Kong's Pro-democracy 'Umbrella Movement'" (2016) 26:1 *Social & Legal Studies* 25–46.

137. *Ibid.*, 12 (emphasis in the original).

138. *Ibid.*, 13–14.

139. *Ibid.*, 17.

140. *Ibid.*, 14.

141. *Ibid.*, 17.

142. Veg (N133) 61.

143. Eric Ip, "Constitutional Conflict in Hong Kong Under Chinese Sovereignty" (2016) 8 *Hague Journal on the Rule of Law* 75–99.

Movement's end was ultimately determined not by the police enforcing the public order law, but by private companies invoking their legal right not to be further subjected to the business losses caused by the occupation, which amounted in law to a nuisance and justified the granting of the injunctions.

The legal aftermath of the movement is also noteworthy. The government has continued to employ the "diversionary approach to public order cases",[144] although most of the participants in "unauthorised" assemblies who were not involved in acts of violence, disorderly behaviour, or clashes with the police have not been prosecuted. After some delay, the seven policemen filmed assaulting Ken Tsang were prosecuted. They were convicted in February 2018 and sentenced to two years' imprisonment, but two of them successfully appealed against their conviction.[145] Ken Tsang himself was also prosecuted and convicted.[146] The "Occupy trio", who had turned themselves in at a police station on 3 December 2014, were charged in March 2017 together with six others. In April 2019, they were convicted for inciting "public nuisance", and two of them (professors Benny Tai and Chan Kin-man) were sentenced to imprisonment for 16 months.[147] Of the 1,003 protesters arrested for illegal actions related to the movement, only 5 percent had been prosecuted as of June 2015, and just 34 percent of those had been found guilty.[148] As of 7 May 2015, only 21 of the 67 movement-related cases prosecuted had resulted in a conviction, with 13 cases resulting in an acquittal and 22 withdrawn from prosecution. Among the 21 "successful" cases of prosecution, there were 11 in which the accused had pleaded guilty.[149]

---

144. Young (N97).

145. The case was tried at first instance by the District Court; see "Hong Kong Court Rules Ken Tsang Arrest Footage Admissible as Evidence in Assault Trial" (29 June 2016) *South China Morning Post*; "Seven Policemen Guilty of Assaulting Occupy Activist" (15 February 2017) *South China Morning Post*; "Police Condemn Jail Terms for Ken Tsang Assault" (17 February 2017) *South China Morning Post*. For the Court of Appeal's decision, see *HKSAR v Wong Cho Shing* [2019] HKCA 839 (26 July 2019).

146. In May 2016, Tsang was convicted by a magistrate of assault and resisting arrest, and sentenced to five weeks' imprisonment; see "Activist Ken Tsang Convicted of Assaulting Police during Occupy Protests" (27 May 2016) *South China Morning Post*; "Activist Ken Tsang Gets Five Weeks in Jail for Assaulting Police and Resisting Arrest during Occupy Protest" (31 May 2016) *South China Morning Post*.

147. *HKSAR v Tai Yiu Ting and others* [2019] HKDC 450.

148. Cheng (N62) 400.

149. Adrian Pok-yin Chow, "Police-related Statements during the Umbrella Movement in Hong Kong" (2015) 16:3 *Inter-Asia Cultural Studies* 470–487, at 477.

## CONCLUSION

Although many social movements in Hong Kong are of small scale and limited duration, post-colonial Hong Kong has seen some extraordinary movements, most notably the Anti-National Security Bill Movement of 2003 and the Occupy Central Movement of 2014. As this chapter shows, Hong Kong provides an interesting case study of the relationship between the law and social movements. Theories of that relationship developed by scholars on the basis of Western experience are by no means irrelevant to Hong Kong. Indeed, cases and events in Hong Kong furnish plenty of examples of the law being used as a means to constrain the space for social movements, as a resource by social movements and as an arena of struggle for those movements. The Occupy Central Movement of 2014 demonstrates that there can be a close, complex, and ambivalent relationship between the law and social movements that is deserving of multi-dimensional analysis.

The transition in 1997 to Chinese sovereignty has not weakened the vitality of the law in Hong Kong. On the contrary, the life of the law and the policy-making role of the courts have been strengthened by enforcement of the Basic Law, and social movement organisations have been more active than ever in using litigation strategically to challenge government policies or at least make their claims visible to members of the public. As in the West, the law in Hong Kong has served in some instances as a symbolic and moral resource for social movements. The legal boundary of the free space for social movements has been contested, and those movements have generated debates surrounding the Rule of Law and civil disobedience. The future is unknown, but it is certain that the story of Hong Kong law and the story of Hong Kong social movements will continue to be intertwined as Hong Kong marches towards its uncertain future under "One Country, Two Systems" (OCTS).

## Acknowledgement

This chapter was first published as "Social Movements and the Law: The Case of Hong Kong" in Michael H.K. Ng and John D. Wong (eds.), *Civil Unrest and Governance in Hong Kong: Law and Order from Historical and Cultural Perspectives* (2017), chapter 7, pp. 117–140. This edited version is reprinted with permission from the publisher, Routledge.

# 5

# A Perfect Storm: Hong Kong-Mainland China Rendition of Fugitive Offenders, 2019

## INTRODUCTION

On 9 June 2019, Hong Kong became the focus of international attention as hundreds of thousands of demonstrators marched on Hong Kong Island to oppose the imminent enactment of the Fugitive Offenders and Mutual Legal Assistance in Criminal Matters Legislation (Amendment) Bill, or the Extradition Bill.[1] The bill would introduce a rendition arrangement as between Hong Kong and other parts of China (including mainland China, Taiwan and Macau), as well as new extradition arrangements between the Hong Kong Special Administrative Region (HKSAR) and over 170 entities with which the HKSAR had not yet entered into extradition treaties.[2] This bill not only led to the largest protests in Hong Kong's history, it also brought about the most serious crisis of governance.

Hong Kong politicians and civil society have been highly polarised since the introduction of the bill in March 2019, with the "pro-China camp" supporting the bill and the pro-democracy camp strongly opposed to the bill. Several foreign governments, including the United States, Canada, Britain, Germany, and Australia, as well as the European Union, publicly expressed concerns about the bill.[3] On the other hand, the Chinese Central Government in Beijing publicly expressed support for the bill in May 2019,[4] and criticised foreign interventions in China's domestic affairs.[5]

Despite the fact that the demonstration against the bill on 9 June was the largest demonstration in the history of post-colonial Hong Kong since the demonstrations against the National Security Bill in 2003 (which led to the bill

1. Full text available at: www.legco.gov.hk/yr18-19/english/bills/b201903291.pdf.
2. For the author's previously published commentary on the bill, see http://researchblog.law.hku.hk/search?q=commentary+fugitive+offenders.
3. See, for example, Mary Hui, "Why Foreign Governments Are So Worried About Hong Kong's Extradition Law" (14 June 2019) *Quartz*, available at: https://qz.com/1643858/foreign-governments-are-worried-about-hong-kongs-extradition-law/.
4. See, for instance, "Beijing Declares Full Support for Hong Kong Leader Carrie Lam over Controversial Extradition Bill" (21 May 2019) *South China Morning Post*, available at: www.scmp.com/news/hong-kong/politics/article/3011155/beijing-steps-support-hong-kong-leader-carrie-lam-over.
5. See, for example, "China Summons US Envoy in Protest over Washington's Condemnation of Hong Kong Extradition Bill" (14 June 2019) *South China Morning Post*, available at: www.scmp.com/news/china/diplomacy/article/3014573/china-summons-us-envoy-protest-over-hong-kong-extradition-bill.

being withdrawn) and during the pro-democracy Occupy Central (or Umbrella) Movement in autumn 2014, the HKSAR Government decided to press ahead with the final stage of the legislative process that was scheduled to begin with the commencement of the Legislative Council (LegCo) debate on the bill on 12 June.[6] On the morning of that day, Hong Kong's downtown area and streets surrounding the LegCo building were occupied by tens of thousands of demonstrators. In the afternoon, the protest escalated into what the Hong Kong police called a "riot" (a label which opponents of the bill strongly contested),[7] to which the police responded with large volumes of tear gas, pepper balls, baton rounds, and even rubber bullets and bean bag shots. The President of LegCo decided that the circumstances were such that it was impossible for the Council to begin the series of meetings and debates on the bill that were originally scheduled for 12–20 June, ending with the bill being put to a vote on the final day. Then, on 15 June, HKSAR Chief Executive Carrie Lam announced that the legislative process on the bill would be immediately suspended, and the issues raised by the bill would only be dealt with again after further consultation for which there would be no time table.[8]

This chapter seeks to introduce the legal and political background of the bill, and to explain the nature of the controversy in the context of the tensions and contradictions generated by China's policy of "One Country, Two Systems" (OCTS) which has been applied to Hong Kong since the 1997 handover. OCTS, as embodied in the Sino-British Joint Declaration on the Question of Hong Kong in 1984, refers to the retention of Hong Kong's existing economic and legal systems after its reunification with China in 1997, with the HKSAR enjoying a high degree of autonomy as part of the People's Republic of China (PRC) under the Basic Law.

6. See the Chief Executive's speech at her press conference on 10 June: www.info.gov.hk/gia/general/201906/10/P2019061000615.htm.

7. Subsequently, the Commissioner of Police at a press conference on 17 June clarified that the use of the term "riot" only referred to the behaviour of some violent protesters and not to all or most of the participants in the protest on 12 June; see www.news.gov.hk/eng/2019/06/20190617/20190617_224726_031.html.

8. For the full text of the Chief Executive's statement, see www.info.gov.hk/gia/general/201906/15/P2019061500707.htm. The government subsequently explained that all work on the bill had been stopped, and stated that it would accept that the bill would lapse upon the expiration of LegCo's current term in summer 2020. However, opponents were not satisfied and insisted that the bill must be "withdrawn". On 4 September 2020, the Chief Executive finally undertook to withdraw the bill, which was formally withdrawn on 23 October 2020.

## A SHORT HISTORY OF HONG KONG'S EXTRADITION LAWS

Before the handover on 1 July 1997, colonial Hong Kong's extradition policy consisted largely of British Acts of Parliament and Orders in Council made applicable to Hong Kong. Extradition was mainly practised between Hong Kong and other Commonwealth jurisdictions, while no extradition was practised between Hong Kong and mainland China.[9] Shortly before the handover, as part of the exercise to localise British laws that were applicable to Hong Kong, the Fugitive Offenders Ordinance (FOO) was enacted and came into force in April 1997. This Ordinance enabled extradition to be practised as between Hong Kong and foreign governments or states with which the HKSAR has entered into extradition treaties — which the HKSAR is authorised by the Basic Law to do. The provisions of the FOO largely followed the British extradition policy and incorporated many principles in the United Nations Model Treaty on Extradition and London Scheme on Extradition Within the Commonwealth. For example, there would be no extradition with regard to political offences, persons prosecuted by reason of their political opinion, religion, race, or nationality, or whose fair trial may be prejudiced for any of these reasons, and persons at risk of torture if extradited. Since 1997, the HKSAR has entered into extradition treaties with 20 countries,[10] and more than 100 persons — largely foreign nationals — have been surrendered by Hong Kong pursuant to these treaties, with the United States being the destination of the largest number of surrenders.[11]

A significant feature of the FOO and the related Mutual Legal Assistance in Criminal Matters Ordinance (MLAO) is that neither of these ordinances is applicable to other parts of China (including mainland China, Taiwan, and Macau). Apparently, at the time of enactment of these laws, it was considered that given the vast differences between Hong Kong's common-law-based legal system and the socialist legal system in mainland China, Hong Kong was not yet ready to enter into rendition arrangements with the mainland — a matter which would have to be dealt with at a future point in time.

9. In the nineteenth century, there did exist Hong Kong ordinances on Chinese extradition, but these laws subsequently fell into disuse. See Janice M. Brabyn, "Extradition and the Hong Kong Special Administrative Region" (1988) 20 *Case Western Reserve Journal of International Law* 169–194, at 183–184.

10. See www.doj.gov.hk/eng/laws/table4ti.html.

11. See generally Glenville Cross, "Fugitive Surrender: Rights and Responsibilities" (12 June 2019) *China Daily*, available at: www.chinadailyhk.com/articles/186/73/64/1560307116859.html.

## THE CASE THAT STARTED IT ALL

In March 2018, Chan Tong-kai, a 20-year old Hong Kong resident travelling with his girlfriend to Taiwan on holiday, was suspected of having murdered her, after which he fled to Hong Kong. He was subsequently arrested in Hong Kong and prosecuted for money laundering. Taiwan authorities requested Chan's extradition to Taiwan. In any event, under the existing law, Hong Kong courts have no jurisdiction to try a murder case where the murder has been committed outside Hong Kong.[12] It seems therefore that justice would require Chan's extradition to Taiwan for trial.

However, given the exclusion of "other parts of the PRC" from the application of the FOO (Taiwan being considered part of China under this law), the Hong Kong Government found that there was no legal basis for Chan's extradition to Taiwan. Chief Executive Carrie Lam decided to embark on a legislative exercise to introduce into the FOO a mechanism of making ad-hoc extradition arrangements on a case-by-case basis (in the absence of extradition treaties) with any foreign jurisdiction — including more than 170 entities with which Hong Kong has not entered into any extradition treaty, as well as mainland China, Taiwan, and Macau. It was also proposed to remove the exclusion of "other parts of the PRC" from the application of the MLAO. These legislative proposals, if adopted, would not only provide the legal basis for extradition of fugitive offenders (like Chan) to Taiwan but would also facilitate extradition between Hong Kong and other jurisdictions on an ad-hoc case-by-case basis in the absence of an extradition treaty. It would introduce for the first time a rendition scheme applicable between Hong Kong and mainland China — even though the two sides have not yet been able to enter into a long-term rendition agreement despite years of negotiation after 1997.

The original version of these proposals was first published on 13 February and discussed in LegCo's Panel on Security on 15 February 2019.[13] After some

12. Under Hong Kong's existing law, the courts have extraterritorial jurisdiction over a number of criminal offences, but they do not include murder; see *Archbold Hong Kong 2019* (Hong Kong: Sweet & Maxwell, 2018), sections 2-111–2-155F. The provisions on homicide in Hong Kong's Offences Against the Person Ordinance were largely modelled on the provisions on homicide in the UK's Offences Against the Person Act 1861. However, section 9 (on the extraterritorial jurisdiction of the British courts over murder or manslaughter committed abroad by a British subject) of the 1861 Act does not have any counterpart in the Hong Kong Ordinance. I am indebted to Dr P.Y. Lo for his drawing my attention to this point.

13. See www.legco.gov.hk/yr18-19/english/panels/se/papers/se20190215cb2-767-3-e.pdf.

consultation and taking into account the concerns of the business community regarding rendition to mainland for business-related offences which they may have committed in the past, the proposal was refined; the bill was gazetted on 29 March and introduced into LegCo on 3 April.[14]

## GROWING PROTESTS, EXPEDITED LEGISLATION,[15] AND PUBLIC CONCERN

The momentum of protests against the bill built up gradually, with the first demonstration against it on 31 March, followed by another demonstration of a larger size on 28 April (with 130,000 participants as estimated by the organisers and 22,800 estimated by the police). LegCo formed a Bills Committee to study the bill which met for the first time on 17 April.[16] However, the Committee failed to operate because the pan-Democrats filibustered at its first two meetings leading to its failure to elect a Chairman, and the pro-China legislators then convened further meetings of the Committee whose legality and validity were contested by the pan-democrats.[17] On 20 May, the government decided to by-pass the Bills Committee and to commence the final stage of the legislative process on 12 June. To compensate for the lack of deliberations on the bill in the Bills Committee, the LegCo Panel on Security was convened to discuss the bill on 31 May–5 June.[18] A slightly revised package had been announced by the government on 30 May to narrow down the

14. See the government's press release of 26 March 2019, available at: www.info.gov.hk/gia/general/201903/26/P2019032600708.htm. For the LegCo Brief, see www.legco.gov.hk/yr18-19/english/bills/brief/b201903291_brf.pdf.
15. For further comments on the procedural aspects of this legislative exercise, see Margaret Ng's speech at the conference on the National Secutiry Bill at The University of Hong Kong on 11 June 2019, video recording available at: https://video.law.hku.hk/extradition-law-and-human-rights-does-the-hong-kong-governments-bill-provide-sufficient-safeguard-for-our-rights/.
16. See www.legco.gov.hk/yr18-19/english/rescindedbc/b201903291/general/b201903291.htm.
17. After the first two meetings of the Bills Committee, the "pro-China" camp of legislators secured a direction from LegCo's House Committee to replace the (temporary) chairman of the Bills Committee (who belonged to the pan-Democrat camp) by a LegCo member from the pro-China camp. Then both the pan-Democrats and the pro-China camp purported to convene their own Bills Committee meetings twice.
18. See www.legco.gov.hk/yr18-19/english/rescindedbc/b201903291/papers/b201903291_ppr.htm.

offences covered by the proposed extradition arrangement and to improve the safeguards for the rights of the accused.[19]

Apart from concerns expressed by foreign governments and in a joint statement issued by 67 international institutions,[20] the Taiwan authorities in a series of statements issued since 9 May indicated that they would not cooperate on Chan's surrender to Taiwan if it was to be conducted on the basis of the bill (which implied that Taiwan was part of the PRC). Taiwan authorities also expressed sympathy for the public opposition to the bill in Hong Kong. President Tsai Ing-wen stated categorically on 13 June that Taiwan would not request Chan's surrender even if the bill were to be passed.[21]

A main justification provided by the government when it initiated the legislative exercise was the need to extradite Chan to Taiwan. The government also argued that there was urgency in the bill being passed as Chan was to be released from prison in October 2019 after serving his sentence for money laundering, and that if the extradition arrangement were not in place by that time, he would simply go free. The negative reaction of the Taiwan authorities to the bill undercut the government's justification for the bill and its urgency.

Many members of the public in Hong Kong doubted whether the Chan case was no more than a pretext for the introduction of a legislative scheme that was principally designed to achieve the rendition of people in Hong Kong to face trial in mainland China. Many politicians and members of the legal community[22] opposed the bill on the ground that it would put the people of Hong Kong at risk of being extradited to face trial in the mainland. The Chinese Communist

---

19. See the press releases dated 30 May, available at: www.info.gov.hk/gia/general/201905/30/P2019053000811.htm (Secretary for Security's speech in Chinese); www.info.gov.hk/gia/general/201905/30/P2019053000960.htm (replies to questions in English).

20. See www.tadc.ca/global-rally-against-extradition-to-china/.

21. See www.mac.gov.tw/cp.aspx?n=9CA780D737FE8017 (in Chinese).

22. See, for example, Hong Kong Bar Association, "Observations of the Hong Kong Bar Association on the Fugitive Offenders and Mutual legal Assistance in Criminal Matters Legislation (Amendment) Bill 2019" (2 April 2019), available at www.hkba.org/events-publication/submission-position-papers; Law Society of Hong Kong, "Fugitive Offenders and Mutual Legal Assistance in Criminal Matters Legislation (Amendment) Bill 2019, Submission" (5 June 2019), available at http://video3.mingpao.com/typeset/stb/inews/20190605/20190605law.pdf; "Withdraw the Fugitive Offenders Bill", joint statement of all members of the Election Committee Subsector Election (Legal) (8 April 2019), www.change.org/p/全體法律界選委-撤回逃犯條例草案-withdraw-the-fugitive-offenders-bill. On 6 June 2019, more than a thousand lawyers joined a "silent march" against the bill; see "'Record 3,000' Hong Kong Lawyers in Silent March Against Controversial Extradition Bill" (6 June 2019) *South China Morning Post*.

Party (CCP)-led legal system in the mainland is not trusted by many Hong Kong people, who doubt whether it would provide a fair trial for the accused. There were also concerns that once the rendition process is initiated in a case by the Chief Executive at the request of Beijing, there is little the Hong Kong courts can do to reject the request. This is because the existing law on extradition only requires the requesting state to provide written evidence that would constitute a prima facie case against the accused, and the accused cannot adduce evidence or call witnesses to prove their innocence.

Furthermore, many people who opposed the bill did not understand the scope of its application and were fearful that they could be extradited to mainland China even if the alleged crimes were committed in Hong Kong rather than in the mainland.[23] Others worried that they might be framed and falsely accused for the purpose of extradition. In fact, when the bill was shelved, even the Chief Executive admitted that the government had failed to explain the bill adequately to the people of Hong Kong, which presumably includes failure to explain why their fears were unfounded and why the bill would not put them at risk.

The concerns on the part of Hong Kong people about the inadequacies of the mainland Chinese legal system are understandable. Few Western countries have established extradition treaties with China.[24] Australia signed such a treaty in 2007 but did not ratify it because of internal opposition based on concerns about the Chinese legal system.[25] On the day before the bill was scheduled

23. An article published in the left-wing *Wen Wei Po* on 23 May 2019, quoting from an "authoritative source", seems to suggest that rendition to the mainland may be applicable to certain crimes committed by people outside mainland China; see "權威人士解讀韓正講話精神" [An Authoritative Source Explains the Spirit of Mr Han Zheng's Speech] (23 May 2019) *Wen Wei Po*.

24. Those which have done so include France, Spain, Portugal, and Italy. See Cross (N11). For a list of relevant extradition treaties, see https://baike.baidu.com/item/引渡條約 (in Chinese). It is noteworthy that in 2009, the PRC and Taiwan entered into a Cross-Strait Joint Crime-fighting and Judicial Mutual Assistance Agreement [海峽兩岸共同打擊犯罪及司法互助協議], which includes a rendition arrangement; see https://law.moj.gov.tw/LawClass/LawAll.aspx?PCODE=Q0070013.

25. See generally Nigel Stobbs, "The Law and Policy Context of Extradition from Australia to the People's Republic of China" (2017) 7 *Victoria University Law and Justice Journal* 32; Matthew Bloom, "A Comparative Analysis of the United States' Response to Extradition Requests from China" (2008) 33 *Yale Journal of International Law* 177; Anna MacCormack, "United States, China, and Extradition: Ready for the Next Step" (2009) 12 *NYU Journal of Legislation and Public Policy* 445; Sabrina Choo, "Circumventing the China Extradition Conundrum: Relying on Deportation to Return Chinese Fugitives" (2018) 50 *NYU Journal of Legislation and Public Policy* 1361; Huang Feng (黃風) (ed.), 中國境外追逃追贓 [*Fugitive Repatriation and Stolen Asset Recovery*] (Beijing: Zhongguo zhengfa daxue chubanshe, 2016).

to be debated in LegCo, a New Zealand court decided against extradition of a suspected murderer to China mainly because of concerns about the Chinese judicial system.[26]

In designing the bill, the government had not only under-estimated the magnitude of public opposition to the bill, but apparently failed to appreciate its far-reaching consequences from a legal point of view. Actually, there exists a fundamental practical difference between the introduction of the proposed ad-hoc case-by-case extradition arrangement vis-à-vis entities or states with which Hong Kong has not entered into extradition treaties, on the one hand, and the application of the same scheme to mainland China, on the other hand.

In the former situations, even if an extradition request from a state concerned satisfies all the criteria stipulated in the FOO and the bill, the HKSAR Government has an absolute discretion not to entertain the request at all, after taking into account, for example, the circumstances of the legal and judicial system of the state concerned. The HKSAR Government does not even need to give a reason for rejecting the request. This is because under public international law, a state is only under a duty to deal with an extradition request from another state if the request is made in accordance with an extradition treaty between them. In the absence of such a treaty, no such duty exists.

On the other hand, the relationship between the HKSAR Government and the Central Government in Beijing is regulated, not by public international law, but by the Basic Law of the HKSAR. Under the Basic Law, the HKSAR Government is appointed by and constitutionally subordinate to Beijing. The Chief Executive is accountable to both the Central People's Government and the HKSAR.[27] Thus, it is difficult to see how the HKSAR Government can reject any rendition request from Beijing that complies with the requirements of the FOO and the bill. As far as mainland China is concerned, there is, at least in practice, no difference between the adoption of the ad-hoc rendition scheme in the bill and the conclusion of a long-term rendition agreement of general application. Given the well-known difficulties in negotiating such a

26. *Kyung Yup Kim v Minister of Justice of New Zealand* [2019] NZCA 209 (11 June 2019). It is also noteworthy that on 18 June 2019, the Supreme Court of Sweden made a preliminary decision against the extradition to China of Qiao Jianjun, "one of Beijing's most wanted corruption suspects"; see "Chinese Ex-official Qiao Jianjun Arrested Again in Sweden — This Time at Request of US" (24 June, 2019) *South China Morning Post*.

27. See art. 43 of the Basic Law.

long-term agreement which still has not been established,[28] it is unrealistic to expect that the rendition scheme proposed in the bill would have gained public acceptance, even less so after the government tried to rush the bill through the legislative process.

In retrospect, the attempt to introduce a rendition arrangement between Hong Kong and the mainland, though well-intentioned for the purpose of facilitating inter-regional judicial cooperation in crime control, proved to be totally counter-productive. Politically it generated a "perfect storm" in Hong Kong that could have been avoided in the sense that unlike the introduction of national security legislation in Hong Kong to implement article 23 of the Basic Law, the HKSAR Government is not legally obliged to establish any rendition arrangement as between Hong Kong and the mainland.[29]

---

28. See, for example, Chau Pak-kwan and Stephen Lam, *Research Study on the Agreement between Hong Kong and the Mainland concerning Surrender of Fugitive Offenders* (Legislative Council Secretariat, 2001), available at: www.legco.gov.hk/yr00-01/english/library/erp05.pdf. For mainland scholars' views of rendition between mainland and the HKSAR, see, for instance, Zhao Bingzhi (趙秉志) and He Chaoming (何超明) (eds.), 中國區際刑事司法協助探索 [*A Study of Chinese Regional Criminal Judicial Cooperation*] (Beijing: Zhongguo renmin gong'an daxue chubanshe, 2003); Gao Mingxuan (高銘暄) and Ma Zhengnan (馬正楠), "論香港與內地移交逃犯的先例模式" [A Precedential Model for Rendition between Hong Kong and Mainland] (2011) 1 法學家 [*The Jurist*] 19. Mainland scholars almost unanimously argue that principles governing international extradition (e.g., non-extradition for political offences or non-imposition of the death penalty) are not applicable to inter-regional rendition as between the HKSAR and the mainland.

29. It is noteworthy that the Macau SAR adopted a Law on the Protection of National Security (in accordance with art. 23 of the Macau Basic Law) in 2009, and in August 2018 established a National Security Committee; see "Macau Moves on National Security" (28 August 2018) *The Standard*, available at: www.thestandard.com.hk/section-news.php?id=199521&sid=11. On the other hand, no rendition arrangement has yet been entered into between Macau and mainland China. In Macau, the Law on Criminal Judicial Assistance (刑事司法互助法) is not applicable to criminal judicial assistance between Macau and mainland. In December 2015, a bill for an Inter-regional Criminal Judicial Assistance Law (區際刑事司法協助法) was introduced (which was intended to regulate criminal judicial assistance, including rendition, as between Macau and mainland China, Hong Kong, and Taiwan), but was withdrawn by the government in June 2016. Apparently most principles governing international extradition (e.g., non-extradition for political offences or in prosecutions motivated by considerations of political opinion, religion, etc.) were absent from this bill, except the non-imposition of the death penalty. I am grateful to Dr Wang Rongguo (王榮國) of the University for Macau for providing the information on the Macau bill on inter-regional criminal judicial assistance.

## A SEMI-DEMOCRATIC SYSTEM PRACTISING SOFT AUTHORITARIANISM

Even after the suspension of the bill, half a million or more Hong Kong people took to the streets again on 16 June to demand the complete withdrawal of the bill and to protest against the police's use of excessive force against demonstrators on 12 June.[30] In response, Chief Executive Carrie Lam publicly apologised on 18 June for "deficiencies in the work of the HKSAR Government" on the legislative amendment exercise, which "has led to controversies, disputes and anxieties in society".[31] She acknowledged that

> [d]uring large-scale public processions over the past two Sundays, people have expressed in a peaceful and rational manner their concerns about the [FOO] and their dissatisfaction and disappointment with the Government — especially me. I have heard you loud and clear, and have reflected deeply on all that has transpired. ... During the several processions, we saw many people who love Hong Kong taking to the streets to make their views known to the Government. Parents took part for the sake of the next generation. Some who usually remain silent, and many young people, felt the need to express their opinions. I understand these feelings.[32]

The complex legislative package originally prompted by the need for justice following a murder committed by a Hongkonger in Taiwan led to one

---

30. The number of people who participated in the marches is difficult to estimate and has been a contested issue in Hong Kong. Regarding the number of participants in the 9 June march, the estimated numbers include 1.03 million (estimate by the organisers of the march — the Civil Human Rights Front (CHRF)), between 810,000 and 1.08 million (by Professor HUI Shu Yuen Ron), 240,000 (by the police), and 199,000 (by Professor Francis T. Lui). The estimated numbers for the 16 June march are 2 million (CHRF), 1.5 million (Professor Hui), 400,000 (Professor Lui), and 338,000 (the police). For comparison, the estimated numbers at the annual 1 July march in 2019 are 550,000 (CHRF), 265,000 (Professor Paul S.F. Yip and Professor Edwin T. Chow), 215,000 (Professor Lui), and 190,000 (the police). The figures here appear in *Ming Pao* and other Hong Kong newspapers on the relevant dates.
31. See www.info.gov.hk/gia/general/201906/18/P2019061800812.htm; and www.info.gov.hk/gia/general/201906/18/P2019061800950.htm.
32. *Ibid*.

of the greatest crises of governance in post-1997 Hong Kong.[33] The incident illustrates the peculiar and possibly unique feature of Hong Kong's semi-democratic political system,[34] in which civil liberties (particularly freedoms of speech, press, association, and assembly) and civil society flourish, and yet the executive branch of government is not democratically elected and accountable to the people of Hong Kong.

In authoritarian states, no demonstrations of any considerable size would be allowed, and the kind of protests that have taken place in Hong Kong recently against the bill would have been inconceivable. On the other hand, in liberal democracies, protests of the scale that took place in Hong Kong against the bill on 9 June — showing that "the people have spoken" — would probably have forced the government to defer to public opinion and to halt the legislative process immediately.

In Hong Kong, there was a peaceful march of hundreds of thousands of people on 9 June, and yet the government was unmoved. It was only when an estimated 40,000 people (outnumbering the total size of the Hong Kong police force) surrounded the legislature on the day of the proceedings on the bill and violence broke out, that the government decided to shelve the bill. The incident seems to suggest that the HKSAR Government is a "soft authoritarian" one, in the sense that it would restrain itself from resorting to massive physical force against the protests of civil society.

As civil society is vibrant and strong in Hong Kong, it may prevail over the government from time to time. The march of an estimated half a million people on 1 July 2003 prompted one of the pro-China political parties in the legislature to change course, and the Hong Kong Government was forced to shelve the National Security Bill. In June 2019, an even greater number of demonstrators initiated the dynamics that finally pressured the government to shelve the rendition bill. It has been fortunate that in this latest test of the challenging

33. Civil unrest continued in Hong Kong even after legislative proceedings on the bill had been shelved. For example, crowds of protesters laid siege to the Police Headquarters in Wan Chai on 21 and 26 June 2019. On 1 July 2019, they stormed the LegCo building and severely damaged its facilities to such an extent that the legislature would not be able to meet in the next few months.

34. Professor Lau Siu-kai characterises this system as a "liberal authoritarian" political system. See Lau Siu-kai (劉兆佳), 回歸後香港的獨特政治形態：一個自由威權政體的個案 [*The Unique Political System of Post-handover Hong Kong: A Case of Liberal Authoritarianism*] (Hong Kong: Commercial Press, 2017).

project of OCTS, the HKSAR and Beijing Governments ultimately chose to submit to the logic of reason rather than the logic of coercion, as the voice of the people of Hong Kong was heard throughout the world.[35]

## Acknowledgement

This chapter was first published as "A Perfect Storm: Hong Kong-Mainland Rendition of Fugitive Offenders" (2019) 49 *Hong Kong Law Journal* 419–430.

35. For the author's comment on the social movement against the rendition bill, see Albert H.Y. Chen, "Hong Kong's Internal Contradiction of 'One Country, Two Systems' " (11 October 2019) *The Economist*, available at: www.economist.com/open-future/2019/10/11/hong-kongs-internal-contradiction-of-one-country-two-systems.

# Part II

## Tradition and Modernity in Chinese Law

# 6

# Confucian Legal Culture and its Modern Fate

## INTRODUCTION

One of the paradoxical phenomena of post-modernity is that while the economic and technological forces of globalisation are increasingly welding the world into a single global village, many people, nations, ethnic, and religious communities in different parts of the world are re-discovering the importance of their cultural heritage and identity. The Enlightenment's prediction and hope that the development of science and the disappearance of religious "superstitions" would lead to the recognition by all human beings of values based on a universal rationality have not yet materialised even as the world approaches a new millennium. Instead, some of the most powerful social and political forces in the late twentieth century world are nationalism, traditionalism, religious fundamentalism, and ethnic aspirations for cultural and political autonomy.

Recently, the importance of culture as a factor to be reckoned with in economic, sociological, and political studies has been increasingly recognised. For example, the so-called East Asian economic miracle has spawned a culture-based thesis — parallel to Max Weber's thesis on Protestantism and the rise of capitalism — that traditional Confucian values in East Asian societies such as Japan, South Korea, Taiwan, Hong Kong, and Singapore make a positive contribution to the economic success of these territories.[1] In a 1993 essay which attracted worldwide attention, Samuel Huntington argued that with the global decline of communism, the world's major political conflicts in future will be between different cultural blocks or civilisations, and Confucian civilisation based in China is among them.[2]

Cultural factors have also become prominent in the arena of ideological struggles. For example, the human rights movement in the international and transnational domain has met resistance from certain Asian governments on the ground that Asian cultural values warrant a modification of human rights

1. See, for example, Peter L. Berger, "An East Asian Development Model?" in Peter L. Berger and H.H.M. Hsiao, *In Search of an East Asian Development Model* (New Brunswick: Transaction Publishers, 1988) ch. 1; Ezra F. Vogel, *The Four Little Dragons: The Spread of Industrialization in East Asia* (Cambridge, Mass: Harvard University Press, 1991).
2. Samuel P. Huntington, "The Clash of Civilisations?" (1993) 72:3 *Foreign Affairs* 22. This essay has subsequently been expanded into a book: Samuel P. Huntington, *The Clash of Civilisations and the Remaking of World Order* (New York: Simon and Schuster, 1996).

norms as originally developed in the West.[3] Some observers associate the Singaporean Government's previous efforts to promote Confucian learning in schools with its attempt to maintain an authoritarian style of governance. In recent decades, some Chinese thinkers have argued that a kind of "neo-authoritarianism" is appropriate for China's present stage of political and economic development, and culture is one of the considerations that loom behind this view.[4] There is also a movement among some Chinese philosophers outside the People's Republic of China (PRC) to revive Confucianism as a source of vitality for the renewal and modernising transformation of traditional Chinese culture, but these philosophers are at the same time committed to democracy and human rights.[5]

In view of the above, scholars of contemporary Chinese law cannot ignore the question of traditional Chinese legal culture, particularly its philosophy, basic concepts, attitudes, mentality, mode of thought, and values. Although there existed a clear discontinuity in China's legal history at the beginning of the twentieth century when China, like Japan before it, embarked on a kind of wholesale Westernisation of its legal doctrines and institutions, the survival of traditional perceptions of and attitudes towards law and legal institutions is evident from subsequent developments. Even today, many scholars studying the PRC admit in their contemporary writings that many "feudal" phenomena, such as denial of citizens' rights, "worship" of official power, and the arbitrary

3. See, for example, Joanne Bauer and Daniel Bell (eds.), *The East Asian Challenge to Human Rights* (Cambridge: Cambridge University Press, 1998); Yash Ghai, *Human Rights and Governance: The Asia Debate* (San Francisco: The Asia Foundation, 1994); Yash Ghai, "Human Rights and Asian Values" (1998) 9:3 *Public Law Review* 168; Michael C. Davis, "Constitutionalism and Political Culture: The Debate Over Human Rights and Asian Values" (1998) 11 *Harvard Human Rights Journal* 109.

4. See, for example, Qi Mo (ed.), *Xinquanwei zhuyi* [*Neo-authoritarianism*] (Taipei: Tangshan Chubanshe, 1991).

5. See, for example, Tu Wei-ming, *Ruxue disanqi fazhande qianjing wenti* [*The Prospects of Confucianism's Third Stage of Development]* (Taipei: Lianjing Chuban, 1989).

exercise of powers by officials, still persist in the socialist legal system.[6] On the more positive side, there is also the possibility that some elements of China's legal heritage may make a valuable contribution to the future jurisprudence of China and the world.

This chapter will first explore the history, nature, and characteristics of traditional Chinese legal culture, which may be characterised as Confucian legal culture. It will then analyse the work of contemporary Chinese scholars concerning the value and drawbacks of this heritage. Finally, the future fate of Confucian legal culture will be considered.

---

6. Such works include: Chinese Confucianism and Legal Culture Research Society (ed.), *Ruxue yu falü wenhua* [*Confucianism and Legal Culture*] (Shanghai: Xinhua shudian, 1992); Hao Tiechuan, *Rujia sixiang yu dangdai Zhongguo fazhi* [*Confucian Thought and the Rule of Law in Contemporary China*] (Kaifeng: Henan daxue chubanshe, 1994); Yu Ronggen, *Rujia fa sixiang tonglun* [*Confucian Legal Thought*] (Nanning: Guangxi renmin chubanshe, 1992); Gong Pixiang, *Zhongguo fazhi xiandaihua de jincheng* [*The Progress of the Modernisation of the Chinese Legal System*] (Beijing: Zhongguo renmin gong'an daxue chubanshe, 1991); Zhang Guohua, "An Evaluation of Traditional Chinese Legal Culture" (1990) 1 *Zhongwai faxue* [*Peking University Law Journal*] 3 (in Chinese); Zhang Jinfan and Lin Zhong, "Ancient Chinese Legal Culture" (1991) 5 *Zhengfa luntan* [*Political and Legal Forum*] 57 (in Chinese); Zhang Jinfan, "A Comparative Study of Chinese and Foreign Legal History (Part I)" (1988) 6 *Zhengfa luntan* [*Political and Legal Forum*] 1, 4 (in Chinese); Zhang Jinfan, "The Comparative Study of Chinese and Foreign Legal History (Part II)" (1989) 1 *Zhengfa luntan* [*Political and Legal Forum*] 1 (in Chinese); Duan Qiuguan, "An Analysis of Ancient Chinese Law and its Concept of Law" (1989) 5 *Zhongguo shehui kexue* [*Chinese Social Science*] 3, 10–12 (in Chinese); Duan Qiuguan, "The Existence in Contemporary Reality and Influence of Traditional Legal Concepts" (1989) 4 *Falü kexue* [*Legal Science*] 3 (in Chinese); Yu Ronggen, "Traditional Chinese Legal Culture and its Contemporary Role" (1986) 4 *Xinan shifan daxue xuebao* [*Southwestern Normal University Journal*] 7, 9 (in Chinese); Chen Jingliang, "The Internal Difference Between the Chinese and Western Legal Cultural Traditions and their Historical Significance" (1992) 4 *Faxue pinglun* [*Law Review*] 61 (in Chinese); Geng Yun, "A Critique of Confucian Ethical Law" (1990) 5 *Zhongguo faxue* [*Chinese Legal Science*] 109 (in Chinese); Ma Nan, "An Inquiry into the Ancient Chinese Legal Heritage" (1986) 12 *Faxue* [*Jurisprudence*] 39 (in Chinese); Ma Nan, "Reflections on the Critical Inheritance of the Legal Heritage of Ancient China" (1987) 5 *Zhengzhou daxue xuebao,* zhexue shehui kexue ban [*Zhengzhou University Journal*, Philosophy and Social Science section] 98 (in Chinese); Liu Quande, "A Comparative Study of Confucian Jurisprudence and Traditional Western Jurisprudence" (1990) 3 *Zhengfa luntan* [*Political and Legal Forum*] 54 (in Chinese); Li Bensen, "Order, Liberty and Morality: Reflections on Confucian Thought and Modern Law" (1994) 2 *Faxue* [*Jurisprudence*] 46 (in Chinese).

# CONFUCIAN LEGAL CULTURE

## An outline of China's legal history[7]

When the Qing dynasty fell in China in 1911, the Imperial Chinese State was the longest surviving political unit in the history of civilisation. For more than a millennium, it was also (and China still is) the most populous state in the world. The most striking contrast between the legal history of China and that of the West is that whereas the highly developed Roman law collapsed as a functioning legal system in Western Europe after the fall of the Western Roman Empire in the fifth century AD and thereafter no unified secular legal system has been in existence in Europe (although Roman jurisprudence did shape the development of the legal systems of the modern nation-states that emerged at the end of the Middle Ages), China's legal tradition ran continuously from the Tang dynasty (618–907 AD) until the fall of the Qing as an effective system of law and order administered by a unified and centralised bureaucratic empire. There was a remarkable degree of similarity and continuity between the major law codes of the Tang, Song (960–1279), Yuan (1271–1368), Ming (1368–1644), and Qing (1644–1911) dynasties, while the Tang codes can be traced back through a clear and continuing line of dynastic codes to the laws of the Qin (221–207 BC) and Han (206 BC–220 AD) dynasties. For the purpose of a general overview, the legal history of China may be divided into five periods.

## From prehistoric times to the end of the Western Zhou

The Western Zhou dynasty (circa 1027–770 BC) was established after the fall of the Shang dynasty, and the kings of the Zhou ruled by delegating authority to feudal vassals (mainly kin of the king's family) in different principalities. This was the formative period of Chinese culture; it was in this period that some of the key concepts of Chinese civilisation, such as the idea that the

7. See generally Chen Guyuan, *Zhongguo wenhua yu Zhongguo faxi* [*Chinese Culture and the Chinese Legal Family*] (Taipei: Sanmin shuju, 3rd edition, 1977); Xu Daolin, *Zhonguo fazhishi lunlüe* [*An Outline of Chinese Legal History*] (Taipei: Zhengzhong shuju, 7th impression, 1990); Zhang Jinfan, *Zhonguo gudai falü zhidu* [*The Legal System of Ancient China*] (Beijing: Zhongguo guangbo dianshi chubanshe, 1992). There is no English book on Chinese legal history as a whole, although several English books on Chinese law in certain dynastic periods have been published.

ruler ruled by virtue of a Mandate of Heaven and the doctrine of governing society in accordance with the *li*, were established. *Li* in its broad sense embraces all religious, political, and social institutions. In its narrower sense, it refers to the norms and rules governing religious, social, diplomatic, and military ceremonies, rituals, and rites (e.g. funeral rituals, wedding ceremonies, the capping ceremony for youths who reached the age of majority, rites for ancestral worship, and religious sacrificial rites), as well as rules and norms regarding proper behaviour, etiquette, manners, clothing, etc. for persons in different social classes or standings in particular familial or social relationships towards other persons.

In the study of Chinese legal history and culture, the dichotomy of the *li* (translated as "rites and norms of propriety") and the *fa* (usually translated as "law") is probably the most crucial concept to be understood.[8] *Fa* is not a direct counterpart of the concept of "law" in Western legal tradition, and is narrower in meaning. *Fa* refers to penal sanctions (*xing*), or norms the violation of which would lead to penal sanctions. *Fa* therefore corresponds to criminal law rather than to law in the broad and general sense.

Many norms, principles, and rules governing issues which have been regulated by law in the Western legal tradition were, in the case of traditional China, part of the *li*. The relationship between the *li* and the concepts of ethics, morality, and "natural law" (in the Western sense) is highly problematic. To deal with this briefly, it might be said that the *li* reflected and was based on ethical and moral standards; it is however doubtful whether these standards constitute a kind of natural law in the Western sense, since the ancient Chinese did not perceive a clear distance, strong tension, or sharp contrast between the moral requirements of nature and those prevailing in their society. On the contrary, it was believed that the *li* was established by the sages of antiquity, who were wise and virtuous enough to comprehend the requirements of heaven.[9]

The dichotomy of the *li* and the *fa* originally operated as follows. The *li* was applicable to members of the aristocratic ruling class, while the *fa* was applicable to subjects and slaves (mainly captives from conquered tribes). Legend had it that the cruel methods of punishment provided for in the *fa* were

---

8. See, for example, Benjamin I. Schwartz, "On Attitudes Toward Law in China" in M. Katz (ed.), *Government Under Law and the Individual* (Washington DC: American Council of Learned Societies, 1957) 27.
9. D. Bodde and C. Morris, *Law in Imperial China* (Cambridge, Mass: Harvard University Press, 1967) 20–21; Duan, "An Analysis of Ancient Chinese Law" (N6).

first invented by an alien tribe (the Miao), and such methods were originally used by the Chinese to deal with transgressors among defeated enemies. It was only later that the application of the *fa* was also extended to other subjects.

## The Spring and Autumn Period, the Warring States Period, and the Qin Dynasty

Starting in the eighth century BC, there was a steady decline in the power and authority of the Zhou kingship. The period from 770 BC to 256 BC was known as Eastern Zhou. The vassal principalities established themselves as independent kingdoms. At first there were over 140 states (at the beginning of what is known as the Spring and Autumn Period, 770–476 BC), but after many wars and fierce struggles for survival, only seven kingdoms were left at the beginning of the Warring States Period (475–221 BC).

It was in these periods that China transitioned from a phase of unpublicised and largely unwritten legal norms administered by the ruling class to a phase of publicised and written legal norms. In ancient Greece and Rome, such transitions also occurred, and they were often the result of struggle by the lower class against the monopolised administration of "secret" (in the sense that they were not made known to the subjects) legal norms by the upper class. In China's case, most historians do not interpret the appearance of publicised written laws as a result of class struggles.[10] Instead, the phenomenon was largely associated with the States' efforts to develop a more effective mode of governance for the purpose of enhancing their strength and of achieving success in power contests against competing states.

According to legal historians, the first states to promulgate written legal codes were the Zheng and the Jin in the Spring and Autumn Period. The Zheng State inscribed its Books of Punishment (*Xingshu*) on a set of bronze tripod vessels in 536 BC[11] (an event of comparable significance in legal history to the compilation of the Code of the Twelve Tables of Rome in 450 BC), and the Jin laws were inscribed in 512 BC.[12] However, from the point of view of subsequent legal developments, the most influential codification was the six books of the Canons of Law (*Fajing*) compiled in 407 BC by Li Kui, prime minister of the Wei State in the Warring States Period. When Shang Yang, a

10. Zhang, "A Comparative Study of Chinese and Foreign Legal History (Part I)" (N6).

11. Bodde and Morris (N9) 16.

12. Chen (N7) 10.

leading thinker of the Legalist school of philosophy, became prime minister of the Qin State, he adapted these Canons of Law for use in Qin. By the middle of the third century BC, the word *lü* came to be widely used in China in lieu of the word *fa* and other related words to refer to legislative codes, and this new usage was also adopted by the Qin. (In modern Chinese, the direct equivalent of the word "law" is *falü*, formed by combining the characters *fa* and *lü*.) Subsequently, the Qin conquered the whole of China and established a highly centralised bureaucratic empire governing the country according to Legalist philosophy.

The Spring and Autumn Period and the Warring States Period were times of great social, economic, and political upheavals, as well as the blossoming of many burgeoning schools of Chinese philosophy. The emergence of new legal systems spawned a heated debate among the Confucian and Legalist schools about the desirability of publicising legal norms and attaching physical penal sanctions to them. The Legalists advocated a kind of State-centred behavioural engineering by means of legal norms which would punish subjects for behaviour that the State considered to be undesirable, and reward them for desirable behaviour. These legal norms should be clear, precise, publicised, and equally applicable to all subjects irrespective of social rank, status, or nobility of birth.

The Confucians, on the other hand, argued that it was both morally preferable and, in the long run, more practically efficacious to solve the ills of the time — social chaos and political disorder — by moral regeneration and the reconstruction of a social order infused with the *li*. Rulers should first cultivate their own moral character and virtues, and behave in an exemplary manner. They should educate their subjects, inculcate them the *li*, and instil in them a sense of right and wrong, encourage them to act in accordance with their moral conscience and to have a sense of shame regarding improper conduct. The Confucians therefore criticised the Legalists' emphasis on legal coercion. They also believed that the publication of detailed legal rules would have the undesirable consequence of inducing people to be argumentative and contentious, to be concerned only with finding legal loopholes, and to lose the moral sense of propriety embodied in the *li*.[13]

The military victory of the Qin, which whole-heartedly followed the Legalists' advice, meant a total defeat for the Confucians. The powerful and extensive

13. A good account in English of the debate between the Confucians and the Legalists is provided in Bodde and Morris (N9) 17–27.

legal framework established by the Qin dynasty was a fundamental shaping force for the whole of China's subsequent legal history. However, Confucianism's defeat was only temporary; it was soon to be resurrected and used as the official ideology of one of the world's most long-lasting and extensive empires.

## From the Han to the end of the Southern and Northern Dynasties

The Han dynasty (206 BC–220 AD) which replaced the short-lived Qin dynasty took the historically decisive step of adopting Confucianism as the orthodoxy and rejected the many other schools of thought which had flourished before the Qin unification (it should, however, be noted that the State-established Confucianism of the Han, developed mainly by Dong Zhongshu, was not identical with primitive Confucianism, and is often described as an eclectic mixture of Confucianism and the Yin-yang school of cosmogony). Yet it continued to make considerable use of the system of codes of law and legal institutions established by the Qin. The more draconian Legalist provisions of the Qin were dropped — several cruel modes of punishment involving mutilation of the body were abolished — but the legal machinery and structures themselves were preserved.

Legal historians describe the development of Chinese law from the times of the Han to the Sui, which reunified China after the period of the Southern and Northern dynasties, as a process of the "Confucianisation of law" or "legalisation of Confucianism".[14] This means that Confucian values influenced the administration of the law and that the content of the *li* gradually found its way into formal legal provisions. Thus, Chen Guyuan, a leading Chinese legal historian, wrote:

> If we consider the formation of the Chinese legal tradition from the point of view of its systemic construction, then we can say that its body was created by the Legalists, whereas its soul was given to it by the Confucians.[15]

14. See generally Bodde and Morris (N9) 27–29; Schwartz (N8) 36; Herbert H.P. Ma, "Law and Morality: Some Reflections on the Chinese Experience Past and Present" (1971) 21:4 *Philosophy East and West* 458; John C.H. Wu, "The Status of the Individual in the Political and Legal Traditions of Old and New China" in Charles A Moore (ed.), *The Chinese Mind* (Honolulu: University of Hawaii Press, 1967) 340, 343; T'ung-tsu Ch'u, *Law and Society in Traditional China* (The Hague: Mouton and Co, 1965) 267–279. For a different view, see Hao Tiechuan, *Zhonghua faxi yanjiu [A Study of the Chinese Legal Family]* (Shanghai: Fudan University Press, 1997).
15. My own translation of a passage in Chen (N7) 41.

From the Han dynasty onwards, Confucian scholars participated in the drafting of laws, and a kind of legal scholarship (*lüxue*) in analysing and producing commentaries on legal provisions developed (yet due to the domination of Confucianism, the kind of wide-ranging theoretical and philosophical debates on the nature and functions of law which flourished in the pre-Qin period were never to be heard again in Chinese history until modern times). In the Jin dynasty (265–420), scholars compiled legal commentaries by applying the principles of the *li*. In the code of the Northern Qi (550–577), we find the prototype of what was later called the "ten abominations" (*shi'e*), which reflected Confucian perspectives on the gravest violations of the moral order. Throughout the period from the Han to the end of the Southern and Northern dynasties (420–589), the practice of deciding cases in accordance with Confucian classics rather than by applying legal provisions prevailed. This practice, however, came to an end in the Tang dynasty, when the gradual process of the Confucianisation of the law reached its completion, with the Tang Code representing an almost perfect expression of the legal recognition of Confucian morality and the *li*.

## From the Sui and Tang Dynasties to the end of the nineteenth century

In 581, the long period of disunity that began when the Han fell in 220 came to an end with the Sui unification of China. The fate of the Sui was similar to that of the Qin: its life was short (581–618) and its reign remembered in history as brutal. The Tang dynasty (618–907), which followed the Sui, saw the culmination of the development of Confucian legal culture in China and the crowning summation of imperial China's legal achievement in the famous Tang Code (*Tanglü*) (653 AD), which became a model law adapted for use in the "Confucian cultural sphere" of Japan, Korea, and Vietnam.[16] It was also during the Tang dynasty that legal scholarship in the form of *lüxue* produced its finest product — the *Tanglü Shuyi* (the Tang Code with Annotations), containing commentaries on every article of the Code, the commentaries themselves being considered an integral part of the Code and having legal force. Moreover, the Tang produced a famous set of six books of administrative

16. On the Tang Code, see *The Tang Code*, translated by Wallace Johnson (Princeton: Princeton University Press, 1979).

law ("liudian") which some scholars have described as the most sophisticated legislation on government and administration the world had ever seen.[17]

In the introductory commentary to Book I of the Tang Code, we find the best summary of the final synthesis of Confucianism and Legalism, of the *li* and the *fa*, and of morality and law:

> Virtue and morals are the foundation of government and education, while laws and punishments are the operative agencies of government and education. The former and the latter are necessary complements to each other, just as it takes morning and evening to form a whole day, or spring and autumn to form a whole year.[18]

The Tang Code represented a climax in the development of law and legal scholarship in traditional China. The codes of all subsequent dynasties followed the Tang Code in both substance and spirit. No significant departures from it or major innovations in legal thought and doctrine occurred until China belatedly embarked upon fundamental legal reforms in the late Qing after decades of contact and confrontation with the West. Thus, in contrast to the rapid development of law and jurisprudential thought in the West since the late eleventh century, China experienced a relative stagnation in legal development which lasted for twelve centuries (from the eighth to the nineteenth centuries).

## The twentieth century[19]

For China, the twentieth century was not only an age of political, social, and intellectual revolutions, but also one of the total disintegration of the traditional legal system, including its basic concepts, values, doctrines, institutions, procedures, and codes. While Chinese philosophers and intellectuals in the humanities debated the merits and feasibility of wholesale Westernisation and how to view the cultural heritage of China's ancient civilisation, the legal system quietly underwent wholesale Westernisation in the two decades that followed the fall of the Qing dynasty in 1911. Republican China's new legal system was no longer recognisable as having a unique identity and belonging to a legal tradition distinct from the West's, in the sense of Islamic law, Hindu

17. Chen (N7) 27.

18. Wu (N14) 361, specifically note 36 thereof.

19. See generally Albert H.Y. Chen, *An Introduction to the Chinese Legal System* (Hong Kong: LexisNexis, 5th edition, 2019) ch. 3.

law, or traditional Chinese law constituting distinct and unique legal traditions. Instead, China (at least before the Communist Revolution) found its way into the Continental European (or Roman-Germanic) family of legal systems, with codes and institutions bearing a close resemblance to their counterparts in Germany, France, and Japan.

After the Communist Revolution, and before the deterioration of relations with the Soviet Union, the new PRC, having completely abandoned the laws and legal institutions of its predecessor, attempted to construct a "socialist legality" modelled closely on Soviet legal texts and structures. However, the enthusiasm for socialist legality was soon replaced by the Maoist revolutionary utopianism of constructing an ideal communist society by moral mobilisation (in a way reminiscent of Confucian moral teachings) through mass campaigns without reference to legal norms and procedures, culminating in the hysteria of the Cultural Revolution. The failure of Maoism gave birth to the present era of economic reform and legal system reconstruction. The declining capacity of Marxism-Leninism-Mao Zedong thought (set up as the orthodoxy by the PRC Constitution in a way reminiscent of the Confucian orthodoxy of imperial times) to legitimise the regime and its laws, in conjunction with large-scale social and economic transformations sweeping across China's vast territory, provided fertile soil for soul-searching, particularly with regard to the cultural heritage of China's long and, at many points in the past, highly successful civilisation. The meaning, value, and significance of China's legal history thus rise to the horizon as live issues for reflection.

## BASIC CONFUCIAN CONCEPTS

The preceding section introduced the legal history of China, traced the process of the "Confucianisation of the law", and emphasised the remarkable stability of the dynastic codes and legal institutions since the Tang dynasty. The next section will discuss the key characteristics of Confucian legal culture. Before proceeding, it is necessary to explain some of the basic concepts of Confucianism.

### "*Ren*": the core concept in the *Analects*

Confucius (551–479 BC) was the founder of Confucianism, and the collection of his sayings in the *Analects* is a kind of bible in Confucianism. In the *Analects*, the word *ren* appears 109 times, and *li* appears 75 times. Thus, both *ren* and *li* are central concepts in Confucianism. The word *ren* may be translated as benevolence, and refers to feelings of humanity, sympathy, and empathy among human beings. Thus, on one occasion, Confucius said that *ren* means "love your fellow men".[20] It is also reflected in Confucius's golden rule: "Do not impose on others what you yourself do not desire."[21] There is a close relationship between the practice of *ren* and observance of the *li*: "To return to the observance of the rites through overcoming the self constitutes benevolence."[22]

The significance of *ren* as the ultimate or highest moral principle is shown by the fact that Confucius believed that it is worth laying down one's life for "Gentlemen of purpose and men of benevolence while it is inconceivable that they should seek to stay alive at the expense of benevolence, it may happen that they have to accept death in order to have benevolence accomplished".[23]

## The "five relationships": family-based ethics

For the Confucians, life is above all a moral practice of ethical values such as *ren* and *li*, and the family is the first and most basic locus for such practice. The feelings of love and sympathy on which ethical conduct rest should first be developed with respect to relatives closest to oneself, and then extend outward to the outside world. It may be said that the whole edifice of Confucian ethics is based on and derived from familial relationships. In contrast to the universal love preached by Christianity, Confucianism privileges the "five human-ethical relationships" which were systematically formulated by Mencius, regarded by posterity as the second most authoritative figure in Confucian thought.

The five relationships are those between (i) father and son, (ii) ruler and subject, (iii) husband and wife, (iv) old and young (or elder brother and younger brother), and (v) friend and friend. Each of these relationships is governed by mutuality and entails reciprocal moral obligations for each party. There was a deep recognition that individuals do not live in isolation and are not existentially self-sufficient; each lives amidst a network of human social relationships, and the full realisation of their nature, self, and destiny is a

20. Confucius, *The Analects*, translated by D.C. Lau (Hong Kong: Chinese University Press, 2nd edition, 1992) 17 (Book XII, section 22).
21. *Ibid.*, 109 (Book XII, section 2).
22. *Ibid.*, 109 (Book XII, section 1).
23. *Ibid.*, 151 (Book XV, section 9).

function of the fulfilment of the moral obligations associated with the social roles defined by these relationships.

Although the five relationships as conceived by the first Confucians involved reciprocal obligations, they were subsequently transformed into the concept of the "three bonds" (*sangang*) which were used for over two millennia to secure the absolute authority of a dominant party over a subordinate party in a rigidly hierarchical social and political order. On the positive side, it may also be said that the three bonds made a major contribution to Chinese civilisation by ensuring the maintenance of a relatively stable social and political order for two millennia. These three bonds were first formulated in the Han dynasty by leading statesman and philosopher Dong Zhongshu, who combined the Yin-yang philosophy with Confucian conceptions: "The ruler is the subject's bond, the father is the son's bond, and the husband is the wife's bond" (because the ruler, the father, and the husband belong to the *yang*, the subject, the son, and the wife belong to the *yin*, and it is a principle of nature or heaven that *yang* is superior and *yin* inferior).[24] Subsequently, in the "neo-Confucian" philosophy of the Song and Ming, the status of the three bonds was further elevated to that of the "heavenly principles" (*tianli*) governing the cosmic order of the universe. The first two bonds gave rise to the cardinal virtues and absolute duties (or what one contemporary scholar calls "the duties par excellence in traditional China")[25] of *zhong* (loyalty to the emperor) and *xiao* (filial piety), the violation of which constituted the cardinal sins and gravest crimes in traditional China.

## Internal moral self-cultivation and social participation

The Confucians preached the priority of internal moral self-cultivation as the aim and duty of being human. Generally speaking, they were optimistic about human nature, believing that moral goodness is inherent in each human being, that all people have the potential of moral growth to the level of sagehood. Unlike the sage in some religious traditions, the Confucian sage is both in

24. Lim Chee Then, "The Confucian Tradition and its Future in Singapore: Historical, Cultural and Educational Perspectives" in Yong Mun Cheong (ed.), *Asian Traditions and Modernisation* (Singapore: Times Academic Press, 1992) 204, 227. On the five primary human relationships and the "three bonds", see also Tu Wei-ming, "Confucianism" in Arvind Sharma (ed.), *Our Religions* (San Francisco: Harper Collins, 1993) 139, 186–194.

25. Wang Gungwu, "Powers, Rights, and Duties in Chinese History" in his book, *The Chineseness of China* (Hong Kong: Oxford University Press, 1991) 165, 169.

the world and of the world, actively participating in its moral and political construction. One of the most famous passages in *The Great Learning (Daxue)*, one of the greatest Confucian classics, reads:

> The ancients who wished to spread the knowledge of Bright Virtue to the world, first ordered well their own states. Wishing to order well their own states, they regulated their families. Wishing to regulate their families, they first cultivated their persons. Wishing to cultivate their persons, they first rectified their hearts. Wishing to rectify their hearts, they first sought to be sincere in their thoughts. Wishing to be sincere in their thoughts, they sought after true knowledge. The attainment of knowledge depends upon the investigation of the nature of things and relationships.[26]

Thus, internal self-cultivation, having an orderly family, participating in government of the State, and finally bringing peace and enlightenment to the world, are seen as successive stages in the unfolding of the possibilities of a life that is truly and fully lived. The whole process may also be seen as "a continuous harmonious movement from the innermost harmony to the outermost harmony",[27] thus expressing the characteristically Chinese "anthropocosmic"[28] vision (which also finds expression in its landscape paintings) of human, social, earthly, and cosmic harmony, the oneness of humanity and nature, and the union of the human and the heavenly.

## Attitude towards law and litigation

The Confucian attitude to law has been introduced above in connection with the Confucian-Legalist debate. In this regard, there is a much-quoted passage from the *Analects*:

> Guide them by edicts, keep them in line with punishments, and the common people will stay out of trouble but will have no sense of shame. Guide them by virtue, keep them in line with the rites, and they will, besides having a sense of shame, reform themselves.[29]

26. John C.H. Wu, "Chinese Legal and Political Philosophy" in Moore (N14) 213, 230–231.
27. *Ibid.*, 231.
28. Tu (N24) 145.
29. Confucius (N20) 11 (Book II, section 3).

While Confucian thinking was rich and deep on the question of moral obligations, there was no concept of "rights" (in the sense of a person's self-interests that are legitimate and deserving to be asserted as against others),[30] and litigation for the purpose of enforcing rights in the modern sense was clearly discouraged. Traditional Chinese culture held up as an ideal a society free of litigation and internal conflicts. In the *Analects*, we find a passage dealing directly with this issue:

> The Master said, "In hearing litigation, I am no different from any other man. But if you insist on a difference, it is, perhaps, that I try to get the parties not to resort to litigation in the first place."[31]

The concept and vision of harmony mentioned here provide at least a partial explanation for this antipathy to litigation. Some scholars have also suggested that the glorification of *wusong* (litigation-free) is also related to the Confucian "doctrine of the mean" (*zhongyong*) and the Confucian emphasis on drawing a distinction between "righteousness" (*yi*) and "profit" (*li*, which may also be translated as "gain" or "benefit" — this is a different Chinese character from that of "rites and norms of propriety").

According to *The Doctrine of the Mean* (*Zhongyong*), one of the four books comprising the core of the Confucian classics, "[b]eing without inclination to either side is called *zhong*; admitting of no change is called *yong*. ... The superior man embodies the course of the Mean; the mean man acts contrary to the course of the Mean".[32]

The person who insists on his "rights" to the full, refuses to compromise for the sake of social harmony and good relations, and takes his opponent to court would be perceived as going to extremes and departing from the moderation called for by the doctrine of the mean. Furthermore, insofar as "rights" in the modern sense constitute no more than a kind of self-interest on the part of the person asserting the right, rights-enforcement could be perceived as selfish, morally suspect, and, given the Confucian emphasis on moral self-cultivation and devotion to altruistic values, below the honour and dignity of a morally

---

30. See generally Albert H.Y. Chen, "The Rise of Rights: Some Comparative Civilizational Reflections" (1998) 25 *Journal of Chinese Philosophy* 5, especially at 6–8.
31. Confucius (N20) 115 (Book XII, section 13).
32. From James Legge's translation of the introduction and ch. 2 of *The Doctrine of the Mean, in The Four Books* (Hong Kong: International Publication Society, 1955). The Four Books are *The Analects, Mencius, The Great Learning (Daxue)*, and *The Doctrine of the Mean (Zhongyong)*.

upright person. For Confucius said: "The gentleman is versed in what is moral. The small man is versed in what is profitable."[33] When Mencius was asked by a king whom he was visiting, "You have come all this distance … You must surely have some way of profiting my state?" Mencius answered, "Your Majesty, what is the point of mentioning the word 'profit'? All that matters is that there should be benevolence and rightness."[34]

## The political order: fusion of politics, ethics, and education

The Confucian doctrine of government is characterised by the concepts of "the kingly way" (*wangdao*) (as opposed to "the hegemonic way" or *badao*; hence the celebrated phrase "inner sagehood and outer kingliness" or *neisheng waiwang*). The kingly way of rule is based on the king's virtues and moral education for the people, while the hegemonic way of rule is based on coercion and fear. The latter also involves "humane government" (*renzheng*), concern for the people's welfare or "people-as-the-basis" (*minben*), and rule by man, by virtue (*de*), by the *li*, and by inculcating in the people the virtues and the *li*. As one leading scholar puts it:

> The Chinese philosophy of political authority may be summed up in a few words. Political authority is a trust conferred by the Mandate of Heaven upon the government for the welfare of the people. The government is created for the people, not the people for the government. ... [T]he ruler is a steward of the common good, who must forget his own interests.[35]

The emperor, holding the Mandate of Heaven, was the Son of Heaven, and the ruler-subject relationship was conceived of as being duplicated from the father-child relationship. Thus, there is a saying, which may sound surprising to a Western audience, that the ruler should rule through filial piety.[36] However, this is not surprising if one understands that, as mentioned above, filial piety was considered a cardinal virtue and a foremost moral obligation of human beings. The ruler should practise the virtues himself and set a good example for his subjects to follow. He and his officials (sometimes called "father-

33. Confucius (N20) 33 (Book IV, section 16).

34. *Mencius*, translated by D.C. Lau (London: Penguin Books, 1970) 49 (Book I, pt. A, section 1).

35. Wu (N26) 214–215.

36. Yu, "Traditional Chinese Legal Culture" (N6). For the traditional Chinese concept of the State as an extended family and the family as a microcosm of the State, see Chen (N7) 79–82.

mother officials" or *fumuguan*) should teach their subjects the true principles of ethics (as embodied in the *li*) and care for them in the same manner as a father cares for his children. On their part, the subjects owed to the ruler the absolute moral (rather than political) obligation of loyalty (*zhong*), which ran parallel to their obligation of filial piety (*xiao*) towards their own parents. The theory was that if *xiao* reigned in all families, *zhong* would reign in society and the State, and social order and universal harmony would be achieved. Hence, Confucian thought fuses the realms of government, morality (based on familial ethics and the "five relationships"), and education. Traditional China knew no separation of secular-political power and spiritual-ethical power, or of State and Church.

## CHARACTERISTICS OF CONFUCIAN LEGAL CULTURE

Some of the salient features, particularly those which are noteworthy from the perspective of comparative legal traditions, of the Chinese legal tradition as shaped by Confucianism since the Han and reaching a definitive form during the Tang, may be summarised as follows.

### Sources of law

As indicated in the historical survey above, the major source of written law promulgated by the Chinese State was a comprehensive and systematic code prescribing criminal sanctions for unlawful acts, usually incorporating an official article-by-article commentary having the same force as the code — for example, the *Tanglü Shuyi* in the Tang dynasty, or the Code and Statutes of the Great Qing (*Daqing Lüli*) in the Qing dynasty. In some dynasties, comprehensive codes of administrative law also existed — for example, the "Six Books" of the Tang (*Liudian*), and the Administrative Code (*Huidian*) of the Qing and its Implementing Regulations (*Zeli*).[37]

However, a focus on the comprehensive and systematic codes would belie the actually complex and multifarious nature of the sources of law in traditional China. There were in fact a large number of legislative instruments bearing a wide variety of types of titles, all of which had the force of law in the sense

37. Chen (N7) 29.

that they were observed and enforced by the State machinery. They related to different areas of government activities, and were of different levels of generality.

Apart from legislation, two other major sources of law were case law and customary law. The role of case law, or records of previously decided cases which were consulted as precedents by decision-makers in subsequent cases, has been increasingly recognised by Chinese legal historians.[38] Customary law also existed at local and regional levels and among various trades, religious communities, and ethnic minorities, and, given the limited reach of State power in traditional China, played significant roles in regulating people's lives.[39]

## Legislative authority

Perhaps the most striking contrast between the histories of Chinese and Western civilisations is that in China, for most of the time since the Qin dynasty more than two millennia ago, political authority over a vast territory and a correspondingly huge population was unified and concentrated in an imperial bureaucracy — and politically significant counteracting forces such as a powerful church, an hereditary land-owning aristocracy with administrative and military capacity, or urban commercial capital with a significant degree of political autonomy were non-existent. Neither had China any experience of democracy or republicanism of the kind practised in ancient Greece and pre-imperial Rome.

The intense concentration of power in the hands of the emperor (even though in practice the exercise of power was usually delegated to bureaucratic officials recruited since the Tang largely on the basis of merit through civil service examinations) was evidenced in the legal system. The emperor *was* the legislative authority; there were no law-making institutions in the form of advisory councils or deliberative assemblies. The great dynastic codes were drafted by officials specially appointed by the emperor and then promulgated in the emperor's name. The emperor reserved the power to issue any decree on a specific matter or any regulation of general application which would override any provision in the code or any other law.[40] The emperor could also personally

38. See, for instance, Wu Shuchen (ed.), *Zhongguo chuantong falü wenhua* [*Traditional Chinese Legal Culture*] (Beijing: Peking University Press, 1994) chs. 5 and 7.

39. See generally Gao Qicai, *Zhongguo xiguanfa lun* [*Chinese Customary Law*] (Changsha: Hunan chubanshe, 1995); Liang Zhiping, *Qingdai xiguanfa: shehui yu guojia* [*Qing Customary Law: Society and State*] (Beijing: Zhongguo zhengfa daxue chubanshe, 1996).

40. Chen (N7) 94, 107–108.

intervene in any judicial proceeding and pronounce the verdict himself.[41] However, apart from the emperor, all other persons in the empire, including the highest officials, were subject to and bound by the law.

Scholars have pointed out that the theoretically absolute power of the emperor was in practice subject to constraints.[42] For example, he was bound to uphold the institutions established by the founder of the dynasty, and to observe immemorial constitutional customs and the commands left by his ancestors. He would be conditioned by Confucian teachings (teachers were specially appointed to educate young princes). He would also pay regard to how his actions would be assessed by future historians (the writing of history was a well-established State institution).[43] An institution of counsellors (*jianguan*) existed whose office expressly charged them with the solemn duty of scrutinising the emperor's conduct and advising him of his faults.[44] A similar institution, known as the censorate (*yushitai*) performed the supervisory function with respect to officials.[45]

## Attitude towards the law

As mentioned above in discussing the Tang Code as the perfection of the Confucianisation of Chinese law, the basic attitude towards the law (*fa*, or legal norms backed by coercive sanctions) was that it was only of secondary importance compared to ethical teachings, the cultivation of moral virtues, and the observance of the *li*, and had the status of a supplementary means to ensure social harmony. Rulers and officials had the moral obligation to educate their subjects regarding moral and social norms, and the law should only be invoked as a last resort, as a necessary evil, in cases where the *li* failed to work and violations of the social order — which were also conceived of as violations of the moral, natural, and cosmic order, which in the Chinese cultural vision constituted a single continuum — indeed occurred.

---

41. *Ibid.*, 68.

42. *Ibid.*, 24–27, 70–73; Wu (N14) 345; Qian Mu, *Zhongguo lishi jingshen* [*The Spirit of Chinese History*] (Taipei: Guomin chubanshe, 1954) ch. 2; Qian Mu, *Guoshi xinlun* [*New Essays on Chinese History*] (Taipei: Dongda tushu, 1989) chs. 4 and 5.

43. John Y. Kwei, "The Chinese Tradition and the Chinese Law", paper presented at a symposium on "Chinese and European Concepts of Law" organised in Hong Kong by the Chinese Law Programme, Chinese University of Hong Kong and the Goethe Institute, 20–25 March 1986, p. 4.

44. Chen (N7) 71–73.

45. Qian, *Guoshi xinlun* (N42) 88–92.

Regarding the authority and status of the law (*fa*) as norms for judicial decision-making, the traditional view was that three kinds of considerations were all relevant in deciding a case: *tianli* (heavenly reason or heavenly principles), *guofa* (the law of the State), and *renqing* (human feelings).[46] There is also a Chinese saying that "the law is no other than human feelings". Scholars have pointed out that in recorded judgments of cases decided since the Tang and Song dynasties, judges often mentioned all three types of considerations.[47] This suggests that traditional Chinese legal culture inclined against a strict and literal application of the letters of the written law, preferring instead a more flexible and liberal approach to achieve what is just and equitable in the particular circumstances of the case.

Although *tianli* (sometimes also referred to as *tiandao*, or the Way of Heaven) was, in theory, of the highest normative status, it is doubtful that it is the functional equivalent of natural law in Western tradition.[48] In the history of Western legal thought, there was a clear tension between the positive law made by a particular ruler and the natural law, which was conceived of as existing objectively in the moral order of the universe independently of man. Man should seek it by the use of reason, but grasping it would not be an easy task. In contrast, traditional Chinese thought, particularly Confucian thought, advanced the thesis that the sages of antiquity had *already* achieved union with *tianli* (heavenly reason) and given full expression to it by formulating the *li* which governed the "five relationships", prescribed what virtues were, and stipulated the true principles of ethics. In subsequent ages, the *fa* was also made in accordance with the *li* and with *tianli*. Hence, it has hardly been asserted that a law (*fa*) or a norm in the *li* should not be followed because it was contrary to heavenly reason. On the contrary, the concept of *tianli* was often used to confer legitimacy on the *fa*. When heinous crimes were committed, a more powerful way of condemning it than saying that it was a serious violation of the law (*fa*) would be to say that it was a severe injury or damage to *tianli*.

---

46. Chen (N7) 50; Fan Zhongxin, Zheng Ding, and Zhan Xuenong, *Qinglifa yu Zhongguoren* [*Feeling, Reason, Law, and the Chinese*] (Beijing: Zhongguo renmin daxue chubanshe, 1992), especially at 9–28.

47. Guo Jian, "Confucian ren and Chinese Legal Culture" in *Ruxue yu falü wenhua* (N6) 102, 107.

48. Yu Ronggen, "The Dao of Confucianism: A Legal Cultural Review" in *Ruxue yu falü wenhua* (N6) 57; Yu Ronggen, "Natural Law and Ethical Law: A Comparison of Chinese and Western Legal Culture" in Yang Haikun (ed.), *Jiaqi faxi jian de qiaoliang* [*Erecting a Bridge between Legal Families*] (Suzhou: Suzhou daxue chubanshe, 1995) 49.

## The under-development of civil law

One of the most remarkable differences between the Chinese and Western legal traditions is that whereas Rome's greatest legal achievement lay in the domain of civil law (e.g., the law of contract, property, family, inheritance, and the law of civil procedure), the development of China's civil law lagged far behind its criminal and administrative law.[49] It is true that some civil matters (e.g., family and inheritance) were already regulated by the *li*, and some were regulated indirectly in the legal codes by provisions regarding penal sanctions, but the fact remains that as far as formal compilation and the scholarly exposition of normative provisions are concerned (what are known as civil law relationships in the West) were neglected in traditional China. The lack of attention given to these matters is also reflected in the fact that while criminal cases were meticulously handled by magistrates and the legal system provided a careful and elaborate procedure for review, particularly in cases involving capital punishment by top-level central government departments, civil disputes were largely left to mediation by clan and village elders or local notables, and even if litigated, would only be dealt with at the local or regional level without the possibility of appeal to or review by the central national authorities.

The following points provide a tentative explanation of this phenomenon. First, Confucian ideology discouraged litigation and looked down on those seeking to advance their self-interests at the cost of disturbing social harmony. The strong duties-based ethics of Confucianism are inconsistent with civil law which is inherently rights-based. Second, the traditional Chinese State during most periods did not govern intensely or penetrate deeply into local society. It managed to govern through an extremely small number of bureaucratic officials relative to the enormous population. It simply could not afford to devote the financial and manpower resources to give minute attention to trying civil cases in accordance with precise legal norms.[50] Third, one reason why priority in the employment of such limited resources was given to criminal matters might be that criminal offences were considered violations of the public social order which threatened the State. Civil matters involving private property or monetary matters were of lesser concern to the State. Fourth, if the

---

49. Chen (N7) 51–57.

50. Huang Renyu, *Wanli shiwu nian* (Taipei: Shihuo chubanshe, 1985) 163–166. The English edition of this book is Ray Huang, *1587: A Year of No Significance* (New Haven: Yale University Press, 1981).

mercantile class were influential enough in China, they might have succeeded in pressing for better formal legal protection of commercial and proprietary interests. In fact, however, in the political system of traditional China, the State, in alliance with the small but powerful class of scholars-officials-gentry, usually pursued policies deliberately to restrain the power and growth of mercantile capital. In the Confucian value system, merchants had the lowest status among the four classes of scholars-officials, peasants, craftsmen, and merchants, and even merchants wanted their children to become scholars-officials. Mercantile interests never became sufficiently organised politically to lobby successfully for the protection of civil and commercial law.[51]

## Confucian influence on the law

There are many ways in which traditional Chinese law was shaped by Confucian ethics, so that it acquired certain unique characteristics from the point of view of comparative law. The following are examples which are often cited in modern literature on Chinese legal history.

The prime moral and political importance assigned by Confucianism to the family can be observed from the fact that among the "Ten Abominations" (*shi'e*)[52] — the most serious crimes to which no pardon could be applicable — four and part of the fifth were designed to protect familial relationships (the others to protect the ruling power of the State), and involved acts which, if committed against non-relatives, would not fall within the Ten Abominations. They included, for example (and this is by no means exhaustive): battery or murder of one's parent or grandparent (punishable by death); murder of certain relatives (punishable by death); being unfilial (which included scolding one's parent or grandparent) (punishable by death); making an accusation (of a crime other than the most serious ones such as treason) against one's parent or grandparent (even if the accusation is true, the accuser was liable to punishment by beatings, and if the accusation turned out to be false, capital

51. Chen (N7) 75. For the mercantile class in Chinese history, see John K. Fairbank, *The United States and China* (Cambridge, Mass: Harvard University Press, 4th edition, 1979) 46–52; Etienne Balazs, *Chinese Civilisation and Bureaucracy,* translated by H.M. Wright (New Haven: Yale University Press, 1964).

52. Chen (N7) 90–91.

punishment);[53] setting up of a separate household or division of property while the parents or grandparents were still alive or marrying during the mourning period for one's parent, grandparent, or husband (punishable by penal servitude in the Tang dynasty and by beatings in the Qing); failing to mourn the death of one's parent, grandparent, or husband in accordance with the *li* (punishable by penal servitude in the Tang and by beatings and penal servitude for a shorter period in the Qing); disobeying one's parent or grandparent or failing to maintain them financially (punishable by beatings if a party concerned brought a complaint); murder or battery of or making an accusation against certain types of relatives; and adultery committed with certain types of relatives.

The categorisation of relatives whom a person had, and the classification of the various degrees of closeness of kinship between a person and a relative, both of which were highly relevant factors in the application of the law, were defined by reference to five modes of mourning applicable to the death of different kinds of relatives.[54] Each mode of mourning was characterised by a particular kind of mourning garb to be worn, a specified period of mourning (amounting to several years in the case of close relatives) and a defined degree of severity of mourning (e.g., a person who, being bereft of a parent, married or begot a child during the mourning period violated the *li* and was punishable under the Tang Code — the idea being that the *li* relating to filial piety required a person under such circumstances to refrain from any activity of a pleasurable nature).[55] The system of mourning relationships was first established as a fundamental part of the *li* in the Western Zhou dynasty,[56] and was enshrined in the Tang Code one and a half millennia later and in the Qing Code two and a half millennia after the Zhou.

Foreign readers consulting the Qing Code will be surprised to discover that the opening page shows a diagram illustrating the five kinds of mourning garbs corresponding to the five modes of mourning and the relatives to which each

53. Confucius himself expressly approved the idea of a father and son concealing each other's crimes; see Wu (N26) 222–223 and Wu (N14) 347. A commentator has remarked that China is probably "the world's only country where the true reporting of a crime to the authorities could entail legal punishment for the reporter"; see Bodde and Morris (N9) 40.

54. Bodde and Morris (N9) 35–38.

55. Ma (N14) 462.

56. Lin Yongrong, *Zhongguo guyou falü yu xiyang xiandai falü zhi bijiao* [*A Comparative Study of Traditional Chinese Law and Modern Western Law*] (Taipei: Zhongyang wenwu gongyingshe, 1982) 87.

mode was applicable.[57] This was clearly designed to emphasise the categorisation of degrees of kinship as a fundamental part of the law (as it was of the *li*) and to facilitate understanding of the many provisions in the Code whose operation depended on drawing distinctions between different degrees of kinship.

Another use of the differentiation of degrees of kinship can be seen in the legal provisions providing for widely different degrees of severity of punishment for the same criminal act (e.g., assault and battery), depending on the kind of kinship relationship that existed between the offender and the victim. There were also highly asymmetrical penal provisions that applied differentially for the same kinship relationship but with the positions of the offender and victim reversed. Generally speaking, the provisions testified unequivocally to the superiority of the old over the young, and the male over the female.

Examples of this abound in the Qing Code.[58] Battery committed by a son against a parent was punishable by death, while battery committed by a parent against the son attracted no penalty at all. Battery committed by a wife against her husband was punishable by 100 blows with heavy bamboo, whereas battery committed by a husband against the wife was only punishable when the wife sustained a significant injury, and then only by 80 blows with heavy bamboo. Battery committed by a younger brother against an elder brother was punishable by 90 blows with heavy bamboo plus penal servitude for two and a half years, while battery committed by an elder brother against a younger brother attracted no penalty at all.[59]

The subordination of the wife to the husband, being one of the three bonds, was also reflected in family law. According to the doctrine of the "seven grounds for repudiating a wife" (*qichu*) which dated back to the *li* of the Zhou, a husband may divorce his wife if she failed to bear a son, was wanton, did not serve her parents-in-law, talked too much, stole, was jealous and envious, or had a malignant disease, though this right to divorce was subject to "three impediments to repudiation" — that the wife had carried on three years of mourning for the husband's parents, the husband was previously poor and they had now become rich, or the home from which she was married no longer existed. There was however no reciprocal right on the part of the wife to divorce the husband.[60]

57. *Ibid.*

58. See *The Great Qing Code*, translated by William C. Jones (Oxford: Clarendon Press, 1994).

59. Bodde and Morris (N9) 37–38.

60. Lin (N56) 98–99; *The Great Qing Code* (N58) 133–135.

Other institutions dating back to the *li* of the Zhou which were reflected in both the Tang and Qing Codes include the "eight groups qualified for special consideration" (*bayi*) and the "three groups qualified for special leniency" (*sanshe*). The former was first codified in law during the Wei dynasty (220–265 AD), and reflected the Confucian conception of a hierarchical social order. The concept of *bayi* conferred privileges on members of eight specified groups which they would enjoy when accused or convicted of crimes other than the Ten Abominations.[61] The privileged groups were relatives of the sovereign, old friends of the sovereign, persons of great virtue, persons of great ability, persons who had achieved great merit, high-ranking officials, persons who had served the government with exceptional zeal and diligence, and descendants of former imperial houses. The privileges extended also to the immediate family members of these groups.[62]

This does not however imply that officials were always treated more leniently in traditional Chinese law than other subjects. As officials were supposed to be ethical exemplars for the subjects, they were liable to heavier punishment than those prescribed for ordinary subjects in respect of some offences.[63] Moreover, there were many legal provisions specially applicable to officials which punished them severely for misbehaviour in the course of their work, such as corruption or dereliction of duty.[64]

*Sanshe* refers to the young (under 15 years old), the old (over 70), the sick, and the mentally handicapped.[65] Notably, women were eligible for more lenient modes of punishment as they were considered the weaker sex.[66] These can be thought of as manifestations of "Confucian humanitarianism".[67] Furthermore, exemptions from or reductions in punishment were usually granted to convicted persons to enable them to take care of aged or ailing

61. Lin (N56) 95; Wu (N14) 346, where he states: "Now, what were the privileges they were entitled to? For one thing, they could not be arrested or investigated before special permission was granted by the emperor. In some dynasties, they could not be fettered. In other words, they were not privileged to commit crimes, but only to have their cases reported to the emperor for his final decision, and be immune to certain procedures and methods of trial. Taken all in all, these privileges did not amount to much."

62. Bodde and Morris (N9) 34–35.

63. *Ibid.*, 35.

64. Chen (N7) 74–75.

65. Lin (N56) 97–98; Bodde and Morris (N9) 42.

66. Chen (N7) 75–76; Bodde and Morris (N9) 42.

67. Bodde and Morris (N9) 42.

parents if no other family member was available to perform the foremost filial duty in Confucian morality.[68]

Other features of the traditional Chinese legal system that are often cited to illustrate Confucian influence include admonitions frequently voiced by Confucian scholars in various dynasties regarding *minde shenxing*. These include that criminal law should be cautiously and, if possible, sparingly used as it was much more important to provide moral education for the people to inculcate in them the virtues and the *li*;[69] the frequent granting by emperors of general or special amnesties throughout the country (which were not however applicable to the Ten Abominations) as a demonstration of the Confucian ideal of benevolent rule;[70] the abolitions during the Han, Sui, and Tang dynasties of some cruel modes of punishment of the past, interpreted as being motivated by Confucian benevolence;[71] and the famous provision in the Tang Code and subsequent codes for clemency for those who turn themselves in and confess their crimes before they were discovered (this was supposed to reflect the Confucian emphasis on the inner moral life and the importance of repentance and rehabilitation).[72]

## Contemporary assessments of China's legal heritage

At the beginning of the twenty-first century, how should we assess the legal heritage of the long and rich Chinese tradition? In this regard, it is useful to start by examining the works on this subject that have been produced by scholars in mainland China since the 1980s, when the revival of interest in traditional Chinese legal culture began. It would appear from these works that there is a high degree of consensus on several main points.[73]

First, many writers point out that although the basic doctrines, modes of law-making, legal institutions, and procedures of traditional Chinese law have been discarded in the course of China's revolutionary transformations in the twentieth century, many of the traditional attitudes, perceptions, ideas, and values, and

68. Chen (N7) 85–87; Bodde and Morris (N9) 41.

69. Chen (N7) 61–63. See also Guo (N47); Yang Hegao, "Traditional Legal Culture and its Influence" in *Ruxue yu falü wenhua* (N6) 134; Liu Xin, "The Inheritance and Development of Traditional Chinese Legal Culture" in *Ruxue yu falü wenhua* (N6) 147.

70. Bodde and Morris (N9) 42; Guo (N47) 104.

71. Guo (N47) 103–104; Chen (N7) 105–106; Lin (N56) 101.

72. Bodde and Morris (N9) 42.

73. The following discussion is mainly based on the works cited in N6.

much of the traditional mentality, psychology, and behaviour relating to law still survive even today, and they constitute part of the "deep structure" of the consciousness, psychology, and character of the Chinese people. Some scholars express this point in the language of historical materialism, stating that unlike the West which underwent centuries of capitalist development after the decline of feudalism, China's present socialist society (albeit theoretically a more advanced social formation than capitalism) still exhibits features of the culture of "feudalism" (referring to China's economy, society, and polity from the time of the Warring States Period more than two millennia ago all the way to the Qing dynasty) which only ended relatively recently.

Second, several leading scholars suggest that the criterion used in evaluating China's legal heritage should be based on the contemporary needs of China's modernisation. These are interpreted to include the development of a socialist market economy, the construction of socialist democracy and legality, and the consolidation of China's "spiritual civilisation". Thus, those elements of traditional legal culture that are contrary to or constitute obstacles to these needs should be rejected and purged, while those elements that make a positive contribution to these contemporary objectives should be preserved and further developed.

Third, mainland Chinese scholars are almost unanimous in holding that Confucian legal culture is so tied to the traditional Chinese society that was based on an agricultural subsistence economy (or what many of them call the "natural economy" or *ziran jingji*, as opposed to the "commodity economy" or *shangpin jingji*, which is also known as the market economy), a clan and family-based social structure governed by familial ethics in the form of the three bonds, and an authoritarian and paternalistic imperial power which deliberately curtailed the development of commerce and the merchant class, that its basic structure and content are fundamentally unsuitable to the needs of China's modernising society.

Fourth, using the criterion above, the negative characteristics of traditional Chinese legal culture which scholars have identified include the suppression of the individual, individuality, and the individual's interests and freedom as a result of an over-emphasis on familial ethics, social morality, and the collective interest; the over-emphasis on obligations and the absence of a concept of rights; the Confucian consolidation of the hierarchical nature of the social order which discriminated against women and merchants; the authoritarian and paternalistic nature of political rule under which the people were "children-subjects" (*zimin*) rather than right-bearing citizens; the discouragement of civil litigation and the denigration of "profits" (*li*) as being opposite to "righteousness" (*yi*); and the "worship" of political power and the Rule of Man.

Fifth, some scholars have also associated many of the negative phenomena of contemporary Chinese society with traditional ideas and practices, sometimes strengthened by a symbiotic relationship with Marxism-Leninism, the communist party-state apparatus, and the socialist planned economy. They include, for example, the over-emphasis on obligations and absolute obedience and the relative neglect of rights and individuals' initiative, the top-down direction of the exercise of authority, the over-emphasis on the needs of order and stability, the instrumental view of law as only a means of dealing with social deviants, the overriding status of ideology and policy relative to the law, the power of senior officials to override the law, and the enjoyment of privileges by officials.

Sixth, most scholars also point out that it would be wrong to adhere to national cultural nihilism and reject the heritage of China's traditional legal culture as totally worthless and a complete failure. They write positively of traditional features such as the emphasis on moral education as the prime means of social control and the use of punishment only as a supplementary means, the humanitarian elements in the criminal law, the practice of mediation as a means of dispute settlement, the affirmation of the value of harmony (including harmony in society and harmony of humanity and nature), the use of a powerful ideology to hold the nation together, the existence of a central unifying political force over the whole of China for long historical periods, and the preaching of the virtues of internal moral self-cultivation and altruistic commitment to the nation.

In considering these views, it is noteworthy that contemporary writers in mainland China, in their reflections on and evaluation of China's legal heritage, are unanimous in affirming the Enlightenment values of liberty, equality, the rights of individuals and citizens, the Rule of Law, and the sovereignty of the people. Their strongest critique of traditional Chinese legal culture relates to its being part of a society with hierarchies and inequalities that subsumed the human individual in a familial, moral, social, and political order which knew nothing of the individual's rights or the concept of citizenship. However, it is possible that these scholars have not gone far enough in exposing the fact that in some ways more fundamental than those already identified, contemporary China has not yet grown out its past. For instance, the one-party rule by one single ideology, with no toleration of pluralism in political and social thought, is still a reproduction or duplicate of the China that for over two millennia upheld Confucianism as the orthodoxy in matters of thought, so that the free and vibrant intellectual climate of the "hundred schools of thought" in the Spring and Autumn Period and the Warring States Period never returned until the twentieth century, and then only briefly. Even today, the officials and cadres who control the fate of the most populous nation of the world are not subject to the kind of public accountability that is embodied in the political institutions of Western liberal democracies. The moralistic tone of the State-controlled media and educational system is reminiscent of the traditional style of Confucian moral instruction, even though the content of the messages is quite different from the content of Confucianism. China is still ruled by paternalistic rulers answerable primarily only to their own consciences (as the emperors were answerable only to heaven); thus, the transformation which many generations of modern Chinese intellectuals have hoped for of the people from children-subjects to citizens has yet to be seen.

## THE FUTURE

It is still possible to be optimistic about the future and believe that modern human rights, liberal democracy, constitutionalism, and the Rule of Law can and will be synthesised with the Chinese Confucian tradition in what Professor Tu Wei-ming calls the "third era of Confucianism".[74] The intellectual history of Confucianism demonstrates that it has been a dynamic and evolving tradition, and has the capacity to be open and receptive to new ideas and concepts introduced from the outside. What happened in the second great era of Confucianism — the period of the construction of Song and Ming *lixue* (which can be translated as the science of reason or of principles, sometimes also called neo-Confucianism) — provides a good example of this. In those times, the indigenous traditions of Confucianism and Daoism achieved a successful synthesis with Buddhism, originally a completely foreign system of thought and practices introduced from India, to produce neo-Confucianism.[75] Now that China has opened itself extensively to the West, the set of political and legal ideas born in the European Enlightenment as a new secular and universal

74. Tu (N5).
75. See generally W. Theodore de Bary, *East Asian Civilisations* (Cambridge, Mass: Harvard University Press, 1988), especially ch. 3; Herrlee G. Creel, *Chinese Thought from Confucius to Mao Tse-tung* (Chicago: University of Chicago Press, 1953), especially ch. 10.

religion will have the opportunity to make as many Chinese converts as Buddhism did one and a half millennia ago.

It is also heartening that the leading neo-Confucian philosophers of this century, while committed to the Confucian tradition as the best and most precious contribution of Chinese heritage to human civilisation, were also unanimous in holding that China's political future lies in institutionalising a liberal constitutional democracy.[76] They pointed out that there existed seeds for the development of democracy in the Confucian tradition, such as the principle of "the-people-as-the-basis" (*minben*), and the doctrine that all persons have the potential to develop and realise themselves fully as moral agents. Their vision is that political democracy will enable the moral life that Confucianism treasures and defends to be extended to the political arena and hence enrich it. Therefore, they believed that the introduction of democracy in China would be the next step in the self-perfection of the Confucian tradition, a momentous development which is however called for by the inner logic of growth of that tradition.

Some opponents of twentieth-century neo-Confucianism, who are more committed to the cause of liberalism than to Confucianism, have disputed the thesis that there are sufficient resources in the Confucian tradition to propel a development towards liberal democracy in China, and have drawn attention to the fact that in some ways Confucianism is more consistent with authoritarianism.[77] However, I think the debate is of academic rather than practical significance, as even these scholars agree that certain elements in the Confucian tradition are indeed compatible with liberal democracy. The main

---

76. The most representative and influential statement in this regard is "A Declaration to the World on Behalf of Chinese Culture" jointly issued by four leading Confucian thinkers, Mou Zongsan, Xu Fuguan, Zhang Junmai, and Tang Junyi, first published in Taiwan in the January 1958 issue of *Minzhu pinglun* and *Zaisheng*, and reprinted as an Appendix in Tang Junyi, *Shuo Zhonghua minzu zhi huaguo piaoling* [*On the Scattering and Withering of the Flowers and Fruits of the Chinese Nation*] (Taipei: Sanmin shuju, 1974), and in Zhang Junmai, *Zhongxiyin zheshe wenzhi* [*Essays on Chinese, Western, and Indian Philosophy*] (Taipei: Taiwan xuesheng shuju, 1981) vol. 2, 849. Other important works in this regard include Mou Zongsan, *Zhengdao yu zhidao* [*The Way of Politics and the Way of Administration*] (Taipei: Taiwan xuesheng shuju, revised edition, 1991); Xu Fuguan, *Rujia zhengzhi sixiang yu minzhu ziyou renquan* [*Confucian Political Thought and Democracy, Liberty, and Human Rights*] (Taipei: Taiwan xuesheng shuju, revised edition, 1988).

77. Lin Yusheng, "The Difficulties faced by the Neo-Confucian Theory on the Promotion of Democracy in China" in his book, *Zhengzhi zhixu yu duoyuan shehui* [*Political Order and Pluralistic Society*] (Taipei: Lianjing chuban, 1989) 337.

point of disagreement relates only to whether the importation of intellectual and philosophical resources from Western tradition is a necessary and indispensable condition for China's evolution towards liberal democracy. Both camps agree that liberal democracy is good and worth striving for. Further, the camp which is most committed to the cause of Confucianism and its revival is not at all in favour of "neo-authoritarianism" of the kind advocated by some mainland Chinese intellectuals.[78]

In the early 1990s, with the publication of a State Council White Paper on human rights in China,[79] the concept of human rights, which had been totally rejected since the 1950s as a bourgeois idea and irrelevant to socialist China, has been rehabilitated. Unlike some other Southeast Asian countries, no significant attempt has been made in the White Paper or in other official Chinese publications to water down human rights by reference to Asian or Confucian cultural values. Neither has any such attempt been made by scholars writing on the subject of human rights.[80] On the contrary, some actually put forward the thesis that modern human rights and the principle of toleration are compatible with, and converge with, the Confucian precepts of benevolence (*ren*) and tolerance (*shu*, alternatively translated as "altruism") as taught in the *Analects*, hence "the modern concept of human rights is not alien to Chinese soil".[81]

Writing about traditional culture, Professor Lao Siguang, a leading contemporary Hong Kong Chinese philosopher, draws a distinction between the open elements and the closed elements of culture.[82] While the closed elements are associated with particular historical, social, economic, and political circumstances, the open elements constitute, as it were, the spirit of

---

78. Qi (N4).
79. Information Office of the State Council, "Human Rights in China" Beijing Review, 4–10 November 1992, p. 8 (also available in a booklet form).
80. See generally Albert H.Y. Chen, "Developing Theories of Rights and Human Rights in China" in Raymond Wacks (ed.), *Hong Kong, China and 1997: Essays in Legal Theory* (Hong Kong: Hong Kong University Press, 1993) ch. 5.
81. Du Ganjian and Song Gang, "Relating Human Rights to Chinese Culture: The Four Paths of the Confucian Analects and the Four Principles of a New Theory of Benevolence" in Michael C. Davis (ed.), *Human Rights and Chinese Values* (Hong Kong: Oxford University Press, 1995) 35, 36.
82. Lao Siguang, *Zhongguo zhi luxiang* [*China's Way and Direction*] (Hong Kong: Shangzhi chubanshe, 1981) 56–61; Lao Siguang, *Zhongguo wenhua luxiang wenti de xin jiantao* [*A New Review of the Way and Direction of Chinese Culture*] (Taipei: Dongda tushu, 1993) 184–188.

a people, and is of more enduring significance. Applying this distinction, as economic and social changes sweep through China as a result of the current economic reforms, the social context for the closed elements of traditional legal culture will, in the course of time, be replaced by a context more favourable to elements more consistent with liberalism, democracy, human rights, and the Rule of Law. They will thus find their place in a rejuvenated Chinese culture, which can and will continue to be informed and inspired by the open elements of the Chinese tradition, such as Confucian benevolence, moral self-cultivation, and the quiet but unending spiritual quest for harmony of heaven, earth, and humanity.

## Acknowledgement

This chapter was first published as "Confucian Legal Culture and its Modern Fate" in Raymond Wacks (ed.), *The New Legal Order in Hong Kong* (1999), chapter 16, pp. 505–533. This edited version is reprinted with permission from the publisher, Hong Kong University Press.

# 7

# Three Political Confucianisms and Half a Century

## INTRODUCTION

Modern Chinese intellectual history has been dominated by rejection and criticism of much of Chinese traditional culture and thought in general and of Confucianism in particular.[1] "Down with the Confucian school" (*dadao kongjiadian*) was one of the slogans of the all-powerful May Fourth Movement in which Chinese intellectuals embraced Western science and democracy and saw China's Confucian heritage as an obstacle to its modernisation and its quest for power and wealth in competition with the nations of the world. Chinese communism, which was subsequently triumphant in giving rise to the People's Republic of China (PRC), was one of the products of the May Fourth tradition of radical anti-traditionalist thought. So was Chinese liberalism, although it failed to exert significant influence on Chinese politics and society in the mainland or on the island of Taiwan during the authoritarian era of one-party rule by the Nationalist Party.

In the early twenty-first century, the fates and prospects of both Confucianism and liberal democracy in China seem to be changing. There has been a revival of interest in classical learning (*guoxue*) and Confucianism. In Taiwan, the transition from authoritarianism to liberal democracy that was initiated by the Nationalist Party in the late 1980s has been successful, as evidenced by several democratic handovers of power from one political party to another. The case of Taiwan, as well as the progress made in the democratisation of Hong Kong (though much more limited than Taiwan) and the successful practice of liberal democracy in South Korea, raise the spectre of "Confucian democracy" — can a Chinese society with a Confucian heritage become a liberal democracy in which civil liberties and human rights flourish and top government leaders are elected by universal suffrage in free periodic elections in which multiple political parties can freely compete? Furthermore, if this is possible, is it desirable? This can and should be one of the central issues of contemporary Chinese political philosophy.

Jiang Qing, the protagonist in this chapter, opposes the introduction of Western-style liberal democracy in China (his book *Political Confucianism* is abbreviated hereinafter as "PC",[2] while his other book *Life Faith and the Kingly*

1. Yu-sheng Lin, *The Crisis of Chinese Consciousness: Radical Antitraditionalism in the May Fourth Era* (Madison: University of Wisconsin Press, 1979).
2. Qing Jiang, *Zhengzhi ruxue* [*Political Confucianism*] (Beijing: Sanlian shudian, 2003).

*Way of Politics* is abbreviated hereinafter as "LF"[3]). So does Kang Xiaoguang, another influential contemporary Chinese thinker who advocates Confucian benevolent governance (*renzheng*) instead of democracy (his book *Renzheng* is abbreviated hereinafter as "RZ").[4] On the other hand, the most well-known neo-Confucian philosophers of the twentieth century fully embrace liberal constitutional democracy in the form that has evolved in the West. In the *Manifesto to the World of Behalf of Chinese Culture* published in 1958,[5] they argued that not only are there seeds of democracy in the Confucian tradition, but "constitutional democracy is required by the internal development of the moral spirit in Chinese culture".[6] In his book *Between Scholarship and Politics* (abbreviated hereinafter as "XS"),[7] Xu Fuguan, who is considered one of these scholars, wrote: "I often say that whoever really understands and respects Chinese culture will believe that the efforts to build democratic politics today … are a development mandated by Chinese culture itself."

3. Qing Jiang, *Shengming xinyang yu wangdao zhengzhi: rujia wenhua de xiandai jiazhi* [*Life Faith and the Kingly Way of Politics: The Modern Value of Confucian Culture*] (Taipei: Yangzhengtang wenhua, 2004).

4. Xiaoguang Kang, *Renzheng: Zhongguo zhengzhi fazhan de disantiao daolu* [*Benevolent Rule: The Third Way for Chinese Political Development*] (Singapore: Bafang wenhua [Global Publishing], 2005).

5. The authors of the Manifesto were Tang Junyi, Mou Zongsan, Xu Fuguan, and Zhang Junmai (Carson Chang). The Manifesto was first published in 1958 in Hong Kong and Taipei in the magazines *Minzhu pinglun* [*Democratic Critique*] and *Zaisheng* [*National Renaissance*]. The full Chinese version has been re-published under the title "Zhongguo wenhua yu shijie" [Chinese Culture and the World] as an Appendix; see Junyi Tang, *Shuo Zhonghua minzu zhi huaguo piaoling* [*On the Withering Away of the Fruits of the Chinese Nation*] (Taipei: Sanmin shuju, 1974) 125–192. It has also been published in Junyi Tang, *Zhonghua renwen yu dangjin shijie* [*Chinese Humanities and the Contemporary World*] (Taipei: Xuesheng shuju, 1975); Junyi Tang, *Tang Junyi quanji* [*Complete Works of Tang Junyi*] (Taipei: Taiwan xuesheng shuju, 1991) vol. 4, pt. II; Junmai Zhang, *Zhong Xi Yin zhexue wenji* [*Essays on Chinese, Western and Indian Philosophy*] (Taipei: Xuesheng shuju, 1981). An abbreviated English version of the Manifesto has been published under the title "A Manifesto for a Re-appraisal of Sinology and Reconstruction of Chinese Culture" in Carson Chang, *The Development of Neo-Confucian Thought* (New York: Bookman, 1962) vol. 2. For an English summary of and commentary on the Manifesto, see Hao Chang, "New Confucianism and the Intellectual Crisis of Contemporary China" in F. Charlotte (ed.), *The Limits of Change* (Cambridge, Mass: Harvard University Press, 1976) ch. 11. For my earlier article on the Manifesto, see Albert H.Y. Chen, "Is Confucianism Compatible with Liberal Constitutional Democracy?" (2007) 34 *Journal of Chinese Philosophy* 195–216.

6. Tang, *Shuo Zhonghua minzu zhi huaguo piaoling* (N5) 166.

7. Fuguan Xu, *Xueshu yu zhengzhi zhi jian* [*Between Scholarship and Politics*] (Taipei: Xuesheng shuju, First published 1957, 1980) 126.

This chapter introduces the key elements of Jiang Qing's political thought. It then compares it with that of Kang Xiaoguang, whose thought demonstrates that Jiang is by no means a lone voice in contemporary Chinese political discussion. The discussion continues with the political thought of Xu Fuguan, probably the most insightful thinker on political philosophy among the neo-Confucian scholars of his generation.

## JIANG QING

One of the main themes of Jiang's PC is to highlight the inadequacies of twentieth-century neo-Confucianism in failing to provide a true Confucian political philosophy for China in the modern age. Jiang argues that such neo-Confucianism, which adheres to the tradition of the Song-Ming learning of the mind-heart and human nature, may be labelled "life Confucianism" (*shengming ruxue*) or "heart-nature Confucianism" (*xinxing ruxue*).[8] He identifies at least two other strands of Confucianism in the Chinese tradition, which he labels "political Confucianism" and "politicised Confucianism" respectively.[9] Political Confucianism is exemplified by the *Gongyang* learning on *Chunqiu* (the *Spring and Autumn Annals*) and much of Han Confucianism; it follows Xunzi in recognising the darker sides of human nature, emphasises the rites (*li*) more than benevolence (*ren*), and deals with the practical tasks of the reconstruction and maintenance of political and social institutions. It may also be called "institutional Confucianism".[10] Jiang is of the view that while political Confucianism as an official ideology did serve a legitimising function for the Imperial State, it also provided standards for the critical evaluation of the exercise of political power. On the other hand, politicised Confucianism, as exemplified by the Ancient Text Classics school (*guwen jingxue*) of the Han dynasty, which emphasised the sacred status and absolute authority of the emperor, was an ideology serving only the interest of the rulers. Jiang also points out that political Confucianism was actually a dominant strand in Confucianism for most of the time after the Han dynasty.

The strength of neo-Confucianism or what he calls life Confucianism lies in its theory of conscience and the heart-mind, the development of the human

8. PC, ch. 1.
9. PC, chs. 1 and 2.
10. PC, 32.

person and moral self-cultivation. Jiang points out that life Confucianism is grossly inadequate in failing to generate any specifically Confucian institutional proposal for the construction of the political and social order in modern China.[11] He also criticises the neo-Confucian scholars for their embrace of Western-style liberal constitutional democracy in an uncritical manner.[12] While the neo-Confucians suggest that the evolution of Confucian thinking in modern times logically and necessarily leads to democracy, Jiang argues that it is neither possible nor desirable that Confucian thinking should lead to Western-style democracy.[13] In particular, he criticises Mou Zongsan's famous theory that democracy may be achieved through the "self-negation of conscience".[14] Unlike Mou, Jiang does not consider democracy as it has evolved in the West to be universally valid for all humankind.[15] In his view, if China were to democratise in the same way as the West, it will lose its cultural identity and depart from the Confucian way.[16]

Although Jiang provides a critique of life Confucianism, his purpose is not to denigrate its importance, but only to point out that life Confucianism is not the whole of Confucianism, and that what he calls political or institutional Confucianism is equally important, particularly in this day and age. He believes that both strands of Confucianism have their rightful domains of existence and can nicely complement one another, and he argues this in both PC and LF.[17] For example, in LF, life Confucianism when practiced by political leaders will ensure that they will be persons of virtue, integrity, and moral character, and will be genuinely qualified for the task of governance.[18] Political Confucianism constructs institutions, structures, and norms that are conducive to the realisation of Confucian ideals and that ensure that such realisation is not solely dependent on the moral self-cultivation of individuals. In LF, Jiang also identifies a third positive strand of Confucianism — social Confucianism, which is preached and practiced in the community or what is

11. PC, ch. 1.

12. PC, 47.

13. PC, 91.

14. PC, 57–95. For this theory of Mou's, see Zongsan Mou, *Zhengdao yu zhidao* [*The Way of Politics and the Way of Administration*] (Taipei: Taiwan xuesheng shuju, revised edition, 1991) 55–62.

15. PC, 46–47, 91.

16. PC, 3.

17. PC, 5, 38, 117; LF, 406.

18. LF, 435.

today called civil society, as distinguished from the State or the government apparatus.[19] He theorises that the full revival of Confucianism in China would entail the simultaneous development of all three strands of Confucianism.

What, then, is the precise institutional proposals of political Confucianism for the purpose of political and social reconstruction in contemporary China? The answer was not clear from Jiang's PC but becomes much clearer in LF. The central premise of the book is that China should develop a political order that is simultaneously rooted in three sources of legitimacy: transcendent-sacred legitimacy, historical-cultural legitimacy, and democratic legitimacy, or legitimacy based on the will of the people. Jiang then puts forward a proposal for a tricameral Parliament,[20] consisting of the House of Confucians (*tongru yuan*) (providing transcendent-sacred legitimacy), the House of the Nation (*guoti yuan*) (providing historical-cultural legitimacy), and the House of the People (*shumin yuan*) (providing democratic legitimacy).[21] The proposal relating to the House of Confucians seems to be derived from the Chinese tradition of governance by Confucian scholars-officials and also partly inspired by Islamic theocratic institutions in contemporary Iran.[22] Indeed, the House of Nations seems to be inspired by the House of Lords as the Upper House of Parliament in English history,[23] and the House of the People is apparently derived from Parliamentary institutions elected by universal suffrage in the contemporary world.

Legitimacy is a modern Western concept and it is not clear why Jiang uses this concept as the basis of his political philosophy for the programmatic reconstruction of the political order for China's future. He stresses the importance of legitimacy for any political order, pointing out that no political order can rest entirely on physical coercion and every political order needs to win the voluntary acceptance and support of the people.[24] He believes that his theory of triple legitimacy is not his own invention but can be derived from

---

19. LF, 407.
20. LF, 313–315.
21. Other details of the proposed tricameral Parliament are provided in Daniel Bell, "Jiang Qing's *Political Confucianism*" in Ruiping Fan (ed.), *The Renaissance of Confucianism in Contemporary China* (New York: Springer, 2011). Note that Bell's translations of some of Jiang's terms are different from the translations here.
22. LF, 316.
23. LF, 316, 380.
24. LF, 326–327, 438.

Confucian classical texts.[25] A political order has transcendent-sacred legitimacy insofar as it is based on the Way of Heaven or expresses the will of Heaven. A political order has historical-cultural legitimacy insofar as it is rooted in the historical traditions of the people as evolved over time and is consistent with the culture and values of the people. A political order has democratic legitimacy insofar as it is consistent with the will of the people or public opinion. Jiang considers Western liberal democracy inadequate and inappropriate for China because it only has democratic legitimacy but lacks the two other kinds of legitimacy. Jiang claims that he is not against democracy, but believes that democratic legitimacy alone does not constitute a sufficient basis of legitimacy for the Chinese political order. He attempts to theorise on a political order that embraces and yet surpasses democracy.[26]

Jiang criticises liberal democracy as practiced in the West as a system in which people's material interests and lower-order desires prevail and transcendent moral principles are disregarded.[27] This is because liberal democracy has no built-in institutional safeguards to ensure that transcendent moral principles will not be violated and that the political order has transcendent-sacred legitimacy.[28] Regarding historical-cultural legitimacy, Jiang suggests that liberal democracy may have such legitimacy in the West because it is itself a product of the history of Western civilisation,[29] but it lacks historical-cultural legitimacy in China (even if it is imported or transplanted from the West).

It is apparent from Jiang's writings that all three sources of legitimacy can be understood in Confucian terms. A political order that is consistent with the Way of Heaven is a Confucian political order that practices rule by virtue (*dezhi*) and benevolent government (*renzheng*).[30] As far as China is concerned, a political order can have historical-cultural legitimacy only if it is Confucian, because (as interpreted by Jiang) Confucianism has been the dominant tradition in Chinese history and dominant force in Chinese culture.[31] A Confucian political order also has democratic legitimacy because

25. LF, 320–321, 350–352.

26. LF, 430.

27. LF, 295–296, 342.

28. LF, 299–300.

29. LF, 358–359.

30. LF, 333.

31. LF, 324, 443–445.

Confucianism requires the ruler to govern in the interests of the people and in accordance with the wishes of the people (thus Heaven's will is understood as the will of the people, as in the saying "Heaven sees as the people see, Heaven hears as the people hear").[32] In modern times, democratic legitimacy is associated with the election of the government by the people. Jiang recognises popular election as a vehicle of democratic legitimacy, and his tricameral Parliament includes one house that is popularly elected. It seems that Jiang considers both the Confucian *minben* (people-as-the-basis or government for the people or in the interests of the people) and *renzheng* tradition and the modern practice of electoral democracy or *minzhu* (people-as-the-master or government by the people) as instances of democratic legitimacy.[33]

In Jiang's thought, not only is Confucianism privileged as supplying all three sources of legitimacy, but Confucian scholars and personalities also have guaranteed roles in State institutions. For example, the House of Confucians consists of Confucian scholars nominated by the people as well as Confucian scholars who have graduated from a State-established Confucian college and are appointed by the State to the House. The President or Chairman of the House of the Nation is a descendant of Confucius himself. In a controversial article published on the Internet in 2006,[34] Jiang advocates that Confucianism should be recognised as the official religion (*rujiao*) and that the State should confer privileges on a Confucian Association formed in civil society. Jiang expressly points out that this proposal has its parallels in some Western countries that have established official churches, such as the Anglican Church in Britain.[35] He points out that his proposal does not mean that the Confucian Association should be controlled by the State, for in the Chinese tradition, there exists a distinction between the tradition of the Way (*daotong*) (as developed by true Confucian thinkers) and the tradition of politics (*zhengtong*) (as developed by the State).[36] He also clarifies that the proposed State endorsement of and support for the Confucian religion does not mean the suppression of freedom of religious beliefs and freedom of thought, and he specifies that different

32. Oft-quoted passage from "Taoshi" in *Shangshu*.

33. LF, 441–443.

34. Qing Jiang, "Guanyu chongjian Zhongguo rujiao de gouxiang" [Thoughts on the Re-establishment of the Chinese Confucian Religion], available at: www.cccrx.com/2006-1/2006115174902.asp, last accessed 25 February 2020.

35. *Ibid.*

36. LF, 428–429.

religions and thoughts should be allowed to exist freely in civil society.[37] However, he also suggests that if the majority of the Chinese people were to become Christians, China's national and cultural identity would perish.[38]

In his later writings,[39] Jiang puts forward concrete proposals and strategies for the revival of Confucianism and the reconstruction of China's political order. One set of strategies relates to the State, and the other relates to civil society. At the level of the State, Jiang proposes that Confucianism should be affirmed in the Constitution as the State ideology (in effect replacing Marxism-Leninism and the thoughts of Mao Zedong and Deng Xiaoping, which are affirmed in the existing Constitution of the PRC); officials should have received education in classical Confucian texts and passed examinations based on them (a modern keju, or examination, system resurrected from the traditional Chinese system for the recruitment of officials). In the domain of civil society, Jiang proposes the establishment of a Chinese Confucian Association (*Zhongguo rujia xuehui*) which should be given privileged status in the religious life of the nation (e.g., the Association will design and prescribe the rites for official ceremonies), and the revival of social Confucianism (Confucianism as practiced in people's daily life), including the promotion of the study of Confucian texts among children and students.

It is apparent by now that Jiang is in effect proposing the substitution of Confucianism for Communism as the ruling ideology of the Chinese State. He also considers that the existing political system in China is grossly deficient in legitimacy,[40] particularly since the adherence to Marxism is now no more than lip service, unlike the case in the first few decades of the PRC. In fact, if one applies Jiang's theory of triple legitimacy to the existing Chinese State, its legitimacy deficit is clear and obvious. This probably explains why some of Jiang's writings have apparently experienced difficulties in getting published in mainland China. His book LF was published in Taiwan but not in mainland China. Some of the articles in this book can however be found on the Internet.[41]

37. Ruiping Fan (ed.), *Rujia shehui yu daotong fuxing: yu Jiang Qing duihua* [*Confucian Society and the Revival of the Tradition of the Dao: Dialogues with Jiang Qing*] (Shanghai: East China Normal University Press, 2008) 37.

38. Jiang (N34).

39. *Ibid*.

40. LF, 294.

41. See, for example, the collection of Jiang's articles at www.cccrx.com/ind5.asp, last accessed 25 February 2020.

Although Jiang is critical of Western liberal democracy and criticises neo-Confucian political philosophy for its wholesale Westernisation, he is not against the borrowing of elements of the Western democratic tradition. Like many neo-Confucian philosophers, he recognises that a primary weakness in the Chinese political tradition is that it has not developed adequate objective institutional or procedural safeguards to prevent the abuse of political power and to ensure the fulfilment of the requirements of triple legitimacy when rulers fail to practice rule by virtue, rule by the *li* and benevolent governance.[42] He praises the Western institutional innovation of securing peaceful transfer of power by periodic elections as a great contribution to the civilisation of humankind.[43] He also affirms that there is much which China can learn from Western political practices such as the separation of powers, judicial independence, parliamentary government, and constitutionalism.[44] However, he stresses that any borrowing from Western political institutions can be based purely on pragmatic considerations, and there is no need to engage in the philosophical project (which he thinks the neo-Confucians engaged in but failed) of trying to integrate or synthesise Western political theories of liberal democracy with Confucian political philosophy.[45]

It is clear that Jiang rejects some of the main tenets of liberalism and democracy that are taken for granted by most contemporary Western thinkers. For example, his proposal that the State should adopt Confucianism as its official ideology is the exact opposite of the liberal principle of the neutrality of the State, although this is by no means original in the Chinese context since both the contemporary Chinese State and the traditional Chinese State have embraced their own official ideologies — Marxism and Confucianism, respectively. As Joseph Chan points out in his comments on Jiang's political thought,[46] drawing on Rawls's theory in this regard, adopting a "comprehensive doctrine" like Confucianism as the basis of political rule would mean disrespecting Chinese citizens who subscribe to other religious, philosophical, and political beliefs. Jiang's outlook seems to be out of place in a modern

42. LF, 334–335, 374–375.
43. LF, 426–427, 429.
44. LF, 378–380.
45. Qing Jiang, "Chaoyue xifang minzhu, huigui rujia benyuan" [Transcending Western Democracy, Returning to Confucian Roots] (1996) 17 *Zhongguo shehui kexue jikan* [*Chinese Social Sciences Quarterly*] (Hong Kong) 123.
46. Fan (N37) 37–38.

pluralistic and open society in which people with radically different values and lifestyles seek to live together in social cooperation. Whereas Max Weber's thesis that the disenchantment of the world seems to be increasingly applicable to China even though it originally described the conditions of Western modernity, Jiang expressly seeks the re-enchantment of the world through political reconstruction.[47] However, even those who share Jiang's despair about the secularisation and materialism of modern life and believe in the validity of transcendent-sacred principles will doubt whether Jiang is justified in assuming that as far as the Chinese people are concerned, Confucianism has an exclusive claim to the representation or interpretation of the transcendent and sacred.

Regarding democracy, Jiang expressly rejects the principle, taken for granted since the Age of Enlightenment in the West, that all persons are equal and are the sovereign in the State.[48] Jiang points out that according to Confucianism, although all persons equally have the potential to grow as human beings and to become sages, in practice people are different in terms of experience, learning, wisdom and virtues.[49] Only the learned and virtuous are qualified to exercise political power; thus, it is not true that all people in the State are equally qualified to participate in the running of the State. He therefore rejects the principle of equal rights of political participation on the part of all citizens of the State.[50] He refers to the Confucian distinction between "the superior (or noble or cultivated) persons" (*junzi*) and "ordinary (or mean) people" (*xiaoren*), who are different in terms of learning, cultivation, and intellectual and moral calibre. Democratic politics based entirely on "one person, one vote" is, according to Jiang, the politics of *xiaoren*.[51] It will only seek the satisfaction of the lower-level desires of ordinary people and ignore the claims of the transcendent and the scared, and of history and culture. Thus, Jiang openly advocates rule by the virtuous (*xianren zhengzhi*) or rule by scholars (*shiren zhengzhi*) rather than rule by all the people, denies that rulers and the people (the ruled) should be considered equal, and defends paternalism to be practiced by rulers with regard to the people.[52]

47. *Ibid.*, 60.

48. *Ibid.*, 5.

49. LF, 384.

50. Fan (N37) 6.

51. *Ibid.*, 9, 10, 27.

52. *Ibid.*, 16, 61.

## KANG XIAOGUANG

We now turn to Kang Xiaoguang, another leading advocate of the application of Confucianism in China's political reconstruction. Although he does not himself use the term "political Confucianism", a term coined by Jiang Qing as discussed above, his theory can be regarded as another version of political Confucianism.

Kang notes that many intellectuals in contemporary China consider liberal democracy a panacea to China's ills.[53] He disagrees,[54] arguing that the introduction of Western-style democracy in China would not be able to solve the major problems that it currently faces, such as corruption, poverty, economic problems, and social injustice.[55] Such problems can only be gradually overcome as China achieves further successes in economic development.[56] Kang is of the view that democratisation will not only fail to solve China's current problems but may give rise to new problems, such as political instability and risks of secession arising from ethnic conflicts (as the cases of the former Soviet Union and Yugoslavia demonstrate).[57]

Like Jiang, Kang believes that the current Chinese State suffers from a severe legitimacy deficit.[58] He, again like Jiang, advocates the substitution of Confucianism — particularly Confucian benevolent government (*renzheng*) — for Marxism as the fundamental belief system of the Chinese State. This probably explains why his book RZ was not published in mainland China but was instead published in Singapore.

Given the legitimacy crisis faced by the Chinese regime, Kang suggests that there are basically two options for China to choose from in mapping its future: either "re-Westernisation" (as the embrace of Marxism was also Westernisation) (i.e., wholesale Westernisation) or re-Sinicisation.[59] Jiang theorises that if the first option is chosen and Western culture triumphs in China, then China will become a Western-style liberal democracy. On the other hand, if Confucian culture revives, then *renzheng* will be practiced as the

53. RZ, xlvii.
54. RZ, viii, xviii–xix.
55. RZ, xix–xx.
56. RZ, xxi.
57. RZ, xx, xxiii–xxiv.
58. RZ, xv, 119–122.
59. RZ, xlv.

Chinese system of government. Kang himself advocates re-Sinicisation, which includes restoring Confucianism and Confucian *renzheng* as the foundation of the Chinese State. Only such a return to China's tradition and indigenous culture can supply the legitimacy that the existing Chinese State desperately needs. Kang does not object to learning and borrowing from the West, but insists (like Jiang) that this should be done on the basis of the principle of "Chinese learning as the body, Western learning for use" (*zhongxue weiti, xixue weiyong*).[60]

Kang argues that the Confucian doctrine of *renzheng* is less concerned with how political power originates (e.g., whether the government is elected by the people) than with how it is exercised.[61] *Renzheng* is practiced where such power is held as a trust for the people and is exercised for the benefit of the people. Like Jiang, Kang characterises the essence of the Confucian tradition of government as government by the community of Confucian scholars.[62] He proposes that the Chinese Communist Party (CCP)-run government be replaced by a new community of Confucians which may be produced by a metamorphosis of the CCP.[63] In Kang's view, paternalistic rule by such a group of political elites is justified, with the State educating the people in the virtues (instead of maintaining neutrality as advocated by liberalism) and encouraging their pursuit of the good life and of moral and spiritual excellence.[64]

Like Jiang, Kang proposes a two-fold strategy for the realisation of what he calls the "Confucianisation" (or re-Confucianisation) of Chinese politics and society. The first strategy relates to the State, and the second to civil society.[65] Regarding the State, Kang advocates the "Confucianisation" of the CCP, the substitution of "the Way of Confucius and Mencius" (*Kongmeng zhidao*) for Marxism-Leninism as the official ideology, the inclusion (or re-inclusion) of the Confucian classics (*sishe wujing*) in the syllabus of the civil service examination, and the re-establishment of the link between the Confucian tradition of scholarship (*xuetong*) and the tradition of politics (*zhengtong*).[66] Moving from the domain of politics and government to that of society itself,

60. RZ, xlv.
61. RZ, 124.
62. RZ, xxx.
63. RZ, xlviii.
64. RZ, 128–130.
65. RZ, xlvii.
66. RZ, xxxii.

Kang proposes that Confucianism should be included in the school curriculum and that Confucianism as a religion (*rujiao*) should be recognised as the official religion (*guojiao*) of China.[67] Kang holds that freedom of religion should be allowed, while at the same time certain privileges should be accorded to the Confucian religion.[68] These proposals are very much in line with those of Jiang Qing's as discussed above.

As mentioned above, Jiang recognises peaceful political transition in accordance with electoral arrangements to be a great achievement of Western civilisation. Interestingly, Kang argues that a transfer of power by competitive elections is not essential in the Confucian political order he advocates for China's future; instead, he recommends a modern equivalent to the traditional practice of *chanrang* (handover of power to those who merit it).[69] Kang actually suggests that this has already been practiced within the CCP in recent decades, with Deng Xiaoping handing over power to Jiang Zemin, and Jiang Zemin handing over power to Hu Jintao.[70]

Like Jiang Qing and the neo-Confucians, Kang acknowledges that in traditional China, safeguards against the abuse of political power were inadequate.[71] However, he believes that Western liberal-democratic institutions are not essential and that other safeguards can be devised for the political order of China's future. More specifically, he advocates a political, social, and economic system with the following features: market economy, welfare state, "administrative absorption of politics" (with the elites in society being co-opted into the government consultative system), corporatism (what Kang calls *shetuan zhuyi*) or freedom of association (with main social groups such as workers and entrepreneurs being organised into trade unions and associations representing their respective interests and the State coordinating with them), and freedom of the media (so that the press and other media can freely report matters of government errors and mismanagement and public opinion will be mobilised to supervise government performance and subject it to critical scrutiny).[72]

---

67. RZ, xlviii.
68. RZ, xlix.
69. RZ, xxxiii, 132–134.
70. RZ, xxxiii, 135.
71. RZ, xlii.
72. RZ, xxxv–xli.

It may be noted that although Kang rejects liberal democracy as the model for China's political reform, the implementation of some of his concrete proposals, including those relating to freedom of the media and freedom of association, would entail significant liberalisation of the existing Chinese political order. Like Jiang, Kang also draws on Confucianism in opposing the liberal-democratic premise of the political equality of all. Kang points out that although Confucianism affirms the equality principle in the sense that all persons have the possibility of becoming sages, it also recognises that in reality there are people with virtues and people without virtues, and only the virtuous are qualified to rule.[73] The tasks of government are a heavy responsibility placed on the intellectual and moral elite, who are subject to particularly onerous moral requirements, and the people are under a duty to accept their teachings.[74] Like Jiang, Kang believes that the will of Heaven is higher than the will of the people, and the Way of Heaven is more fully understood by the community of Confucian scholars than by ordinary people.[75] Kang also suggests that in recognising the inequality of persons, Confucianism is more "honest" than liberal-democratic theory, which propagates the myth of the equality of all and the sovereignty of the people.[76]

## XU FUGUAN

Xu Fuguan (1904–1982) lived more than half a century before Jiang and Kang, in the era of Republican China, Nationalist Party rule, the Sino-Japanese War, and the struggle between the Chinese Nationalist Party and the CCP. Unlike Jiang and Kang, he did not start his career as a scholar. He served in the army of the Nationalist regime and rose to senior ranks.[77] After the communist takeover, he lived his life in Taiwan and Hong Kong. He devoted himself to teaching and scholarship, writing many articles and books on contemporary

73. RZ, xxxi.

74. RZ, 127.

75. RZ, xxxi.

76. RZ, 127.

77. For biographical information about Xu, see Honghe Liu, *Confucianism in the Eyes of a Confucian Liberal: Hsu Fu-kuan's Critical Examination of the Confucian Political Tradition* (New York: Peter Lang, 2001) ch. 1.

political issues as well as Chinese history and philosophy. Together with several famous neo-Confucian scholars (Tang Junyi, Mou Zongsan, and Carson Chang), he co-authored the *Manifesto to the World on Behalf of Chinese Culture* ("the Manifesto") published in 1958,[78] which contains, among other things, the definite statement of twentieth century neo-Confucian political philosophy.

The thesis of the Manifesto as far as China's political development is concerned is that not only are there seeds of democracy within the Chinese tradition, particularly the Confucian tradition ("Proposition 1"), but the establishment of a liberal constitutional democracy in China is the internal requirement or necessity of the development of the Chinese cultural tradition itself ("Proposition 2"). According to Proposition 1, Confucianism is compatible with liberal constitutional democracy. According to Proposition 2, the development of democracy in China will (to quote from a passage in the Manifesto in both English[79] and the original Chinese[80]) "enable her national character to reach higher planes of perfection and her spiritual life to achieve a more comprehensive development" than ever before. It seems therefore that Proposition 2 is a stronger claim than Proposition 1.

Regarding Proposition 1, the authors of the Manifesto adduce as evidence both ideas and practices in the Chinese tradition which are considered to be consistent with the spirit of democracy.[81] The relevant *ideas* include, for example, rule by virtue (*weizheng yide*), and the ancient ideas that the will of Heaven is reflected in the people's will, that the ruler should heed the people's views, that political power should be exercised so as to realise the people's wishes, that all under Heaven belongs to the public (*tianxia weigong*) and does not belong to one person, and that everyone has the moral potential to become a sage, thus implying human equality. Very ancient ideas such as transfer of power to the meritorious (*chanyang*) (by Yao and Shun) and rebellion against tyranny are also referred to. The relevant *practices* include, for example, ministers' remonstrance with the ruler, impartial chronicles by court historiographers, institutions such as the prime minister and the censorate, and the recommendation and examination system for bureaucratic recruitment.

78. See references in N5.

79. Carson Chang (N5) 469.

80. Tang, *Shuo Zhonghua minzu zhi huaguo piaoling* (N5) 158.

81. *Ibid.*, 162–165.

The arguments for Proposition 2 are rather complicated in structure and dispersed in different passages in sections 8 and 9 of the Manifesto. The arguments may be reconstructed as follows:

(1) China's traditional political system was plagued by problems, resulting in dynastic cycles with alternating periods of order and chaos. "In order to break through this situation the only way is to establish a democratic government."[82]

(2) Some of the seeds for democracy in the Chinese tradition mentioned above "serve to offset the monarch's power and to bridge the gap between the central government and the populace, although their effectiveness depended ultimately solely on the personal integrity of the monarch, since there was no fundamental law or constitution to check him. It is therefore clear that the limitations on the powers of the ruler must be transferred from the ministers to the people outside the governmental structure if they are to be effectual. Towards democracy, therefore, is the natural direction of development for Chinese political history."[83] In this context, the Manifesto expressly advocates constitutionalism and peaceful transfer of political power as between political parties.[84]

(3) The ancient ideas of *chanyang* and rebellion against tyranny and that all under Heaven does not belong to one person imply that political power should be transferable. However, "the deficiency of Confucian thought in the past is that it did not understand that the legal system could be used to effect the transfer of the ruler's power so as to realise the wishes of the people".[85]

(4) The monarchical system is inconsistent with the idea of human equality mentioned above, because it denies that the people may have equal status as the ruler both politically and morally. In a democracy such equality can be secured.

82. Carson Chang (N5) 471; Tang, *Shuo Zhonghua minzu zhi huaguo piaoling* (N5) 162.

83. Carson Chang (N5) 472–473; Tang, *Shuo Zhonghua minzu zhi huaguo piaoling* (N5) 163–164.

84. Tang, *Shuo Zhonghua minzu zhi huaguo piaoling* (N5) 164.

85. *Ibid*.

(5) In the last paragraph of the section of the Manifesto on the question of democracy, the authors refer to "a more profound reason why the establishment of a democratic government is necessary for the development of China's culture and history".[86] They point out that even if the monarch practises the ideal of rule by virtue, the people in this case are no more than "passive recipients of virtuous rule, and their status as full moral agents (subjects, actors or *zhuti*) has not yet been secured".[87] Thus only the monarch is a full moral agent. Interestingly, it is further argued that in this case, the monarch can hardly be said to be truly virtuous and to be an authentic moral agent unless he is willing and ready to make his own position as ruler open and accessible to all and affirm the equal political rights of all. It concludes:

> The capacity for self-determination by the moral agent requires the possibility of his/her political participation. Here we see a fundamental contradiction between the moral spirit in Chinese culture and the monarchical system. The contradiction can only be resolved by a constitutional democracy that affirms that all are equal political agents (*zhuti*). Thus constitutional democracy is required by the internal development of the moral spirit in Chinese culture.[88]

In line with the Confucian faith of the authors, the Manifesto grants the moral consciousness a superior position and assumes that the subject (*zhuti*) in traditional Chinese culture is primarily a moral subject (agent). It is believed that it is the inner requirement of the development of Chinese culture in this modern age for this moral subject to become a political subject and a cognitive subject as well, so that China can embrace democracy and science. For this purpose, one of the authors of the Manifesto, Mou Zongsan, developed the theory of the "self-negation" (*kanxian*) of conscience (*liangzhi*), which holds that in order to develop (*kaichu*) democracy and science in the Chinese cultural tradition, the conscience needs to undergo temporarily a process of self-negation.[89] Traces of this idea can be found in the Manifesto itself, when it suggests that the moral subject should temporarily forget itself in order to

86. Chang (N5) 472; Tang, *Shuo Zhonghua minzu zhi huaguo piaoling* (N5) 165.
87. Tang, *Shuo Zhonghua minzu zhi huaguo piaoling* (N5) 165.
88. *Ibid*., 166.
89. See Mou (N14).

become a purely cognitive subject.[90] As mentioned above, Mou's self-negation theory subsequently became one of Jiang Qing's targets of criticism.

We now turn to Xu Fuguan's political thought,[91] which is closely linked to his study of Chinese political and intellectual history and of the classical texts of pre-Qin Confucian thought. One of the central notions he developed is the contradiction of "double subjectivity" (*shuangchong zhutixing*) in Chinese history.[92] By this he means that while true Confucian thinking stresses that the people should be the subjects (*zhuti*) or primary actors in the political order, in practice the monarch or emperor was the subject or primary actor in the political order. In his view, Confucianism requires the rulers to put aside their self-interests and to serve only the interests of the people. However, in the actual course of Chinese history, such Confucian ideal was seldom realised,[93] and Confucianism did not develop sufficient institutional safeguards to restrain the exercise of absolutist imperial power. It was only able to alleviate to some extent the oppressive use of political power.[94] Xu stresses that in the course of Chinese history, some Confucian scholars and intellectuals did practice true Confucianism and spoke up against the abuses of political power; their history has been written in blood and tears.[95]

Xu distinguishes between true or original Confucian thought which developed before the Qin unification and its subsequent distortion to serve the interests and needs of imperial rule during and after the Han dynasty.[96] For example, he believes that the theory of the Three Bonds (*sangang*) departs from the true spirit of classical Confucianism which emphasises the reciprocal obligations in and mutuality of the relationship between monarch and minister, father and son, and husband and wife. The ethics of the Three Bonds leads to the subordination of the minister, son, and wife to the absolute authority of the other (superior) party in the relationship and their absolute loyalty and

---

90. Tang, *Shuo Zhonghua minzu zhi huaguo piaoling* (N5) 160–161.

91. See generally Xu (N7); Fuguan Xu, *Rujia zhengzhi sixiang yu minzhu ziyou renquan* [*Confucian Political Thought and Democracy, Liberty and Human Rights*] (Taipei: Taiwan xuesheng shuju, 1988). For secondary sources, see Bin Xiao, *Chuantong zhongguo yu ziyou linian: Xu Fuguan sixiang yanjiu* [*Traditional China and the Concept of Liberty: A Study of Xu Fuguan's Thought*] (Guangzhou: Guangdong People's Press, 1999); Liu (N77).

92. XS, 104.

93. XS, 385.

94. XS, 54, 395.

95. XS, 386.

96. See generally Liu (N77).

obedience to that party, which is discussed in his Xu's book *Confucian Political Thought and Democracy, Liberty and Human Rights* (abbreviated hereinafter as "RJ").[97] Xu is also critical towards the traditional civil service examination, arguing that it was largely an instrument used by the regime to tame and control the intellectuals of traditional China.[98]

On the basis of his study of classical Confucian texts, Xu points out that Confucianism understands the system of political rule or government as being established by Heaven for the benefit of the people. "Heaven sees as the people see, Heaven hears as the people hear."[99] Rulers need to win the voluntary support of the people, and political rule should be based on morally exemplary conduct and virtues rather than coercion. Rulers should practice benevolent governance (*renzheng*), rule by virtue (*dezhi*), and rule in accordance with the rites (*lizhi*). In particular, rulers should govern in accordance with the interests and the wishes of the people themselves and should not impose their own political blueprint on the people.[100] This is Xu's interpretation of the concept of "doing nothing" (*wuwei*) as a political virtue.[101] He interprets the Confucian precept on the pursuit of righteousness rather than profit (*yili zhibian*) as requiring rulers to pursue the people's interests (righteousness) rather than the rulers' own interests (profit).[102]

One of Xu's most important and original interpretations of Confucianism lies in his distinction between the Confucian notions of self-cultivation (*xiuji*) and ruling the people (*zhiren*).[103] He stresses that the standards to be adopted in these two domains are different and should not be confused with one another. In practicing self-cultivation, practitioners of Confucianism should impose the highest ethical standards on themselves and practice utmost self-discipline. However, this does not mean that rulers, political leaders, or officials should impose such standards on the people. This would be oppressive, as encapsulated in the Chinese term *yili sharen* (killing people with ethics).[104] According to Xu, Confucianism applies a different set of standards in the domain of political

97. Xu (N91) 77, 137.

98. XS, 193.

99. XS, 51; See also Kang (N4).

100. XS, 389; RJ, 126, 213.

101. XS, 105, 111–112; RJ, 210.

102. RJ, 136.

103. RJ, 203–220.

104. RJ, 205; XS, 112.

rule. In political rule, feeding the people (*yangmin*) takes priority over teaching the people (*jiaomin*); the natural life (*ziran shengming*, or physical life) of the people is the uppermost consideration.[105] Furthermore, even when it comes to "teaching the people" (*jiaomin*, or education and cultivation of the people), what should be taught is no more than the basic principles of Confucian ethics, such as filial piety, benevolence, righteousness, and fulfilling one's duties to others in the context of ethical human relationships.[106] Thus, in Xu's view, Confucianism by no means justifies the kind of ideological indoctrination practiced in modern totalitarian governments.

One of Xu's main theses about Confucianism and democracy is that the Confucian theory of the goodness of human nature (*xingshan lun*) provides the moral foundation for democracy.[107] In his view, this positive and optimistic view of human nature affirms human dignity and leads to respect for and trust and faith in the people (or *min* in Chinese).[108] He argues that democracy is based on such respect for and trust and faith in the people. Xu also argues that the opposite view of human nature — that human nature is basically evil (*xing'e lun*) — would lead to the opposite of democracy: if people are evil and not to be trusted, then authoritarian rule would be justified to keep them from evil.[109] Xu's view in this regard may be contrasted with that of Chang Hao, who argues that Western liberalism is closely associated with the distrust of human beings (particularly rulers) that originates in the Christian notion of original sin.[110]

Xu fully embraces Western liberal democracy and believes that it is universally applicable; he expressly points out that there is no specifically Chinese style of democracy.[111] He suggests that if Confucius and Mencius were alive today, they would also be in favour of democracy.[112] Xu's writings also affirm a basic proposition in the 1958 Manifesto discussed above: the democratisation of China is not only consistent with its Confucian cultural

105. RJ, 18, 197–198, 203.

106. RJ, 199.

107. RJ, 99; For a critical discussion, see Xiao (N91) 225–232.

108. RJ, 152.

109. RJ, 110, 153.

110. Hao Zhang (Hao Chang), *You'an yishi yu minzhu chuantong* [*Darkness of Human Nature and the Democratic Tradition*] (Taipei: Lianjing Press, 1989).

111. XS, 42.

112. RJ, 191.

heritage but would be the natural development of the Confucian tradition and enable Confucian ideals to be better realised than before.[113] In particular, the historical tragedy of the contradiction of "double subjectivity" as mentioned above can be overcome.[114]

Although Xu was a firm believer in and was fully committed to Confucianism, he recognises that there were deficiencies and weaknesses in the Confucianism tradition. For example, he points out that the Confucian concept of the "five cardinal relationships" (ruler and minister, father and son, husband and wife, elder and younger brothers, friend and friend) does not sufficiently address the relationship between the government and the people.[115] He suggests that traditional Confucianism looks at politics mainly from the standpoint of the ruling elite rather than from the standpoint of the people.[116] He also noticed that in emphasising duties and obligations, Confucianism and traditional Chinese culture do not facilitate the development of the individual subject's self-consciousness and assertion of his subjectivity, legitimate interests, and rights.[117] Thus, he suggests that a modernised Confucian philosophy should not only preach the achievement of moral excellence by human beings but that it should also preach liberty, equality, and human rights.[118] At the same time, he believes that Confucian ideas of conscience and moral self-restraint in recognition of the interests of others can enable Western liberal democracy — which originated in the struggle for individuals' rights — to find a firmer moral foundation.[119] Thus, Confucianism can not only give rise to democracy in China but can also provide deeper roots for democracy in the West.

## CONCLUSION

Xu wrote at a time when communism was at its heights in mainland China and authoritarian rule was practiced by the Nationalist Party (Kuomintang or

113. XS, 59–60.

114. XS, 126.

115. XS, 390.

116. XS, 54–55; RJ, 72.

117. XS, 57–58.

118. RJ, 190.

119. XS, 53–54.

KMT) in Taiwan. He was critical towards both communist totalitarianism and the KMT's authoritarianism, and advocated Western-style liberal democracy for China's future. However, unlike many Chinese liberals in modern times who were critical of traditional Chinese political culture and Confucianism, Xu believed in the reconciliation and synthesis of Confucianism and Chinese culture, on the one hand, and liberal democracy, on the other. Xu and the other neo-Confucian thinkers who co-authored the 1958 Manifesto were of the view that democratisation in China does not mean wholesale Westernisation or the abandonment of China's cultural tradition. On the contrary, China's democratisation should be, as Xu pointed out, the quest and dream of all those who understand and love the Chinese cultural tradition and Confucianism and who are committed to defending and promoting them.[120]

Jiang and Kang wrote at a time when communism as a secular religion was on the wane in China, and indeed all over the world, and when China was experiencing an upsurge of nationalism and a renaissance of traditional Chinese culture and thought. Both of them question the legitimacy of the existing regime in China, which still proclaims communism as its official ideology. They also propose the adoption or re-adoption of Confucianism (as a substitute for communism) as the guiding philosophy for the Chinese people. This contrasts with Xu's endorsement of a liberal-democratic constitutional framework in which no preference will be accorded to any ideology or political, philosophical, or religious beliefs, and different political parties and programs can freely compete for people's votes in an electoral system.

Although Jiang and Kang do not support the liberal neutrality of the State, neither of them rejects extensive borrowing from Western political and social institutions. For example, Jiang is in favour of a parliamentary system in which one of the houses is popularly elected in periodic elections with multi-party competition. Kang proposes the freedom of media, freedom of association, and corporatism. Both support the market economy with welfare provisions, and a vibrant civil society in which different beliefs and opinions can freely co-exist, although they would also like Confucianism to be recognised by the State as the official religion and to be accorded a privileged status.

The differences between Jiang and Kang, on the one hand, and Xu, on the other, boil down to the following issues. First, should Confucianism be privileged as an ideology, religion, philosophy, or belief system endorsed

120. XS, 126; RJ, 72, 191.

by the State? Second, should there be equality of political rights among all Chinese citizens in the sense that the highest political institutions should be elected by universal and equal suffrage on the basis of free and fair elections? The first question concerns the extent to which the Chinese State should be a liberal entity. The second question concerns the extent to which it should be a democratic entity.

On the first question, Jiang's argument is apparently that Confucianism should be privileged because it expresses the transcendent-sacred reality and has also been the dominant force in Chinese history and culture. However, this may be questioned as to why Confucianism should monopolise spiritual truth and why other religions, philosophies, or belief systems that are subscribed to by some members of Chinese society should be discriminated against. As mentioned above, this would constitute disrespect to them and to their human dignity and freedom of belief. Regarding the second question, it may be argued that even if Confucianism was the dominant force in Chinese history and culture in the past, this is not a sufficient reason why it ought to be the dominant force in China's future. Whether it would be so should not be decided by the State but should be decided by the people in their daily life as Chinese society changes and evolves.

On the question of democracy, Jiang, Kang, and Xu all draw on Confucianism in defending their positions. Jiang and Kang argue that according to Confucianism, although everyone has the moral potential to become a sage, in practice some have achieved higher levels of learning, cultivation, and virtues than others. Thus, there is a Confucian distinction between "superior people" (*junzi*) and "ordinary people" (or mean people, or *xiaoren*). The Confucian thesis is that positions of power and responsibility should only be open to the virtuous. Therefore, they agree that it is not right that everyone, irrespective of their moral and intellectual qualities, should have completely equal rights to political participation, and it would not be wrong to accord privileges to "superior" people.

In contrast, Xu draws on the Confucian thesis that human nature is good rather than evil to argue that democracy (in terms of equal rights to political participation) has a Confucian foundation. He argues that because human nature is good, people have human dignity, they should be respected, and they can be trusted to make judgments and decisions for themselves. Insofar as democracy is a system that trusts the people and entrusts political power to them, it is consistent with this Confucian insight into human nature. Xu also points out that Confucianism requires holders of political power to exercise it in accordance with the interests and wishes of the people, and not to abuse it so as to promote the rulers' self-interest. This is also the principle and objective of democracy. Xu also makes an extremely important point about the distinction between self-cultivation (*xiuji*) and ruling the people (*zhiren*): Confucianism does urge practitioners of Confucianism and the ruling elite to engage in self-cultivation and to become *junzi*, but the distinction between *junzi* and *xiaoren* is only for the purpose of self-cultivation and not to be extended to politics and used to take away or diminish the political rights of ordinary people. Indeed, if ordinary people are to be regarded as *xiaoren* and not to be trusted, this would contradict the Confucian proposition that rulers should rule in accordance with the wishes of the people and win their hearts' support.

Ultimately, Xu's interpretation of Confucianism, which renders it consistent with and supportive of democracy, is more convincing than that of Jiang and Kang. It is true that, as stressed by Jiang and Kang, Confucianism has insisted that positions of political power and responsibility should be held by the learned, cultivated, and virtuous. However, it does not follow that these people (or those who claim that they are such people) should become a self-perpetuating ruling elite who rule without any need to be held accountable to ordinary people. If Xu is right, then ordinary people can be trusted to recognise who are learned, cultivated, and virtuous enough to deserve to be elected by them to positions of power and responsibility. This means that there is actually no inherent conflict between the Confucian thesis that positions of political power should be held by the learned, cultivated, and virtuous, and the democratic thesis (which, according to Xu's interpretation of Confucianism, is also a Confucian thesis) that ordinary people can be trusted to make judgments and decisions about who deserve to hold positions of political power. In a society with a Confucian culture, the people will recognise and elect into positions of power persons with the moral integrity and strength of character that Confucianism affirms and preaches. On the other hand, if a society does not have a Confucian culture, it would be impossible and un-Confucian for a self-proclaimed and self-appointed Confucian elite to impose their rule and their values on the people. This would not be Confucianism; it would be totalitarianism, known not to traditional China but well-known to modern China.

Taken together, the political Confucianism of Xu Fuguan and of the 1958 Manifesto is more persuasive than that of Jiang Qing or Kang Xiaoguang, as argued above. Though developed more than half a century ago, it still speaks to us today and resonates in our hearts. The mere substitution of Confucianism for communism as the ruling ideology of a non-liberal-democratic government is, as the Chinese saying goes, "changing the soup but not changing the medicine" (*huantang bu huanyao*). Instead, believers of Confucianism should push for more freedom of expression, freedom of association, and freedom of religion, so that Confucianism — together with other religions or faiths — can flourish in civil society. Furthermore, when Confucian culture revives and China democratises, the people of China will then be able to elect leaders with the moral integrity and strength of character that develops from Confucian self-cultivation, who will put the Confucian principles of benevolent governance and rule by virtue into practice.

## Acknowledgement

This chapter was first published as "Three Political Confucianisms and Half a Century" in Ruiping Fan (ed.), *The Renaissance of Confucianism in Contemporary China* (2011), chapter 13, pp. 205–223. This edited version is reprinted with permission from the publisher, Springer.

# 8

# Chinese Cultural Tradition and Modern Human Rights

## INTRODUCTION

In formulating the title of this chapter, I deliberately include the words "tradition" and "modern", because I would like to contrast tradition with modernity. If the title were "Chinese culture and Western human rights", then the theme would have been very different. The contrast would then between "Chinese" and "Western".

The twentieth century Chinese philosopher Fung Yulan wrote about the discourse and thinking which employed the distinction about "Chinese" and "Western", as well as the distinction between "ancient" and "modern". He points out that the correct description of the task or challenge for China in the twentieth century is not "Westernisation" but "modernisation". He writes:

> Some people say that Western culture is a motor car culture. … But motor cars did not exist in the West originally, [and only came into existence at a certain point in history.] Having motor cars and not having motor cars is a distinction between the ancient and the modern, and not a distinction between China and the West.[1]

I think the reference to "motor cars" in this passage can be perfectly substituted with "human rights". That is why I use the phrase "modern human rights". The concept and discourse of human rights is a unique phenomenon of modernity. It is true that it first appeared in the sphere of Western civilisation in the seventeenth and eighteenth centuries, but at the time, it represented an intellectual breakthrough and a political revolution. Something new was created that never existed before in the history of the West in the civilisations of ancient Greece, ancient Rome, or the Middle Ages. The concept and discourse of human rights was a new invention in modern times, just as the steam engine was a new invention in modern times. As the contemporary Argentinean thinker C.S. Nino points out: "There can be no doubt that human rights are one of the greatest inventions of our civilisation."[2]

Sceptics may say that human rights are simply beautiful slogans and that the reality of gross violations of human rights in modern history and in the

1. Chen Lai (陳來) (ed.), 《馮友蘭語萃》 [*Quotations from Feng Youlan*] (Beijing: Huaxia Press, 1993) 105.
2. C.S. Nino, *Eticay Derechos Humanos* (Buenos Aires: Paidos Studio, 1984) 13, quoted in Norberto Bobbio, *The Age of Rights*, translated by Allan Cameron (Cambridge: Polity Press, 1996) 64.

contemporary world demonstrates the futility of discussions about human rights. They also doubt the possibility of moral progress in humankind, as distinguished from progress in the spheres of science, technology, and material life. I do not share this view.

## THE CASE FOR MORAL PROGRESS

First, I think the fact that good ideas are often disregarded or not practised does not mean that the ideas themselves are worthless, or that the distinction between good ideas and bad ideas is irrelevant. The doctrine of human rights is an idea, so is Nazism, Fascism, the kind of Maoism that led to the Cultural Revolution in China, and the kind of Christianity that formed the background to the Inquisitions in medieval Europe. These are different ideas, and they led to different practical consequences in history. History is a tale of suffering, cruelty, oppression, and war, and some ideas do lead to the increase of human suffering, while others lead to the alleviation of human suffering.

Second, I think it can be demonstrated that the modern doctrine of human rights is a good idea and that the development of this doctrine is a sign of moral progress on the part of humankind. The possibility of humanity's moral growth in the course of history was first raised by Kant in his 1784 essay on the "idea for a universal history with a cosmopolitan purpose".[3] Following up on Kant's speculations, the contemporary Italian political thinker Norberto Bobbio writes:

> My theory, which is inspired by this extraordinary passage of Kant's, is that from the point of view of the philosophy of history, the current increasingly widespread and intense debate on human rights can be interpreted as a "prophetic sign" of humanity's moral progress, given that is it so widespread as to involve all the peoples of the world and so intense as to be on the agenda of the most authoritative international judicial bodies.[4]

Reflecting on the moral resources developed by modern civilisation, particularly the concept and discourse of human rights, the contemporary

---

3. Immanuel Kant, *Political Writings* (Cambridge: Cambridge University Press, 2nd edition, 1991) 41–53.

4. Bobbio (N2) 35.

Canadian philosopher Charles Taylor writes that the "imperative of benevolence" associated with the modern human rights consciousness

> carries with it the sense that this age has brought about something unprecedented in history, precisely in its recognition of this imperative. We feel that our civilisation has made a qualitative leap, and all previous ages seem to us somewhat shocking, even barbarous, in their apparently unruffled acceptance of inflicted or easily avoidable suffering and death, even of cruelty, torture, to the point of revelling in their display. ... [H]igher standards in the relevant regards [have been] built into the moral culture of our civilisation.[5]

Thus, human rights were not part of pre-modern Western civilisation; human rights are a modern invention; the rise and globalisation of human rights thinking may be interpreted as a sign of humanity's moral progress; and a quantum leap in the moral consciousness of humankind has indeed occurred. This summary of points can be correlated to the development of modern human rights thinking and discourse in Chinese cultural tradition.

Chinese people are proud of the manifold achievements of Chinese civilisation, which has enjoyed more than 3,000 years of cultural continuity. History produces tradition, and tradition shapes people's thinking and behaviour. The rationality, morality, values, and aspirations of human beings are embedded in the particular cultural tradition in which they find themselves. There are probably no absolute or objective standards with regard to rational thinking and moral judgment that are completely independent of tradition. There exists no "view from nowhere", no tradition-free ground, from which we can think and reason in a humanly meaningful way. This is the insight contributed by contemporary philosophers like MacIntyre[6] and Gadamer.[7] If this is right, then what are modern human rights? How can they be evaluated from the point of view of the Chinese cultural tradition?

In principle, there is no formal or structural difference between these questions and the same questions viewed from the perspective of pre-

---

5. Charles Taylor, *Sources of the Self: The Making of the Modern Identity* (Cambridge, Mass.: Harvard University Press, 1989) 396–397.
6. Alasdair C. MacIntyre, *Whose Justice? Which Rationality?* (Notre Dame, Indiana: University of Notre Dame Press, 1988).
7. Hans-Georg Gadamer, *Truth and Method*, translated by J. Weinsheimer and D.G. Marshall (London: Continuum, 2nd revised edition, 2000).

modern Western tradition.[8] Briefly, we can say that there were elements in the pre-modern Western tradition which were consistent with and probably contributed to the rise of modern human rights. These include, for example, the Christian conception of the equal worth and dignity of each human individual, the classical conception of natural law as based on a universal human nature and universal reason, the idea of legal rights implicit in Roman jurisprudence, and medieval political institutions providing for democracy and representation of interests.

At the same time, there were elements in the pre-modern Western tradition that were inconsistent with modern human rights, which is precisely why modern human rights are a new invention. Examples of such elements include religious intolerance and persecution of heretics, cruel and inhuman punishment, slavery, serfdom, aristocratic privileges and thus denial of equality under the law, arbitrary exercise of absolutist powers by rulers, and the idea of the king's divine right to rule.

However, when modern human rights have come into existence, people in the Western tradition can evaluate them positively and affirm them as indicators of progress, using pre-existing standards such as the principle of universal Christian love and that of the equal dignity and worth of all human beings. So we see how a tradition can evolve and even transform itself, but still rely on moral and spiritual resources within the tradition and achieving a reconfiguration of the elements, often mutually contradictory, that originally existed within the tradition.

In the Chinese tradition, as in the case of the West, there are elements that have affinities with, or can contribute to, the modern conception of human rights, as well as elements that contradict that conception. The former elements include the Confucian principle of benevolence as the basic norm governing relations between human beings, the ethics of benevolent rule on the part of the ruler who must cultivate their virtues and serve as a moral exemplar for their subjects, the recognition of the importance of consultation by the ruler and the need to follow the wishes of the people and winning their hearts instead of just their outward submission, the affirmation of the moral autonomy and perfectibility of each human being, the idea of the equality of all human beings in terms of the capacity for moral cultivation and growth,

8. Since this is not the topic of this chapter, I will deal with it very briefly, simply to illustrate the form which a possible answer can take.

the humanistic conception of the human being as the noblest creature in the natural and cosmic order, and the recognition of the existence of transcendent principles of Heaven (*tianli*) which govern the universe and which constitute the source of the principles of justice and ethics.

Elements in Chinese tradition that ran against the modern notion of human rights include despotic power in the hands of the emperor as the Son of Heaven, paternalistic thinking on the part of the scholar-official ruling class and hence denial of political participation from below, social relationships that are hierarchical and involving respective positions of absolute authority and subordination, the emphasis on social harmony and the subsuming of the individual within the family both of which operate to deny the individual's assertion of their rights and the individual's individuality, cruel and inhuman methods of punishment, and harsh punishment regarding potentially seditious publication, etc.

As in the case of Western tradition, the adoption of modern human rights by the Chinese tradition can be assessed as a morally positive development even by using certain traditional standards and concepts, such as the Confucian principles of benevolence and righteousness and the Confucian belief in each human being's rational propensity, moral autonomy, and spiritual capacity for growth and perfection. Indeed, certain more recently developed human rights can be regarded as particularly compatible with traditional Chinese values. This includes, for instance, the right to education, since Confucianism lays particular emphasis on education for the purpose of bringing out the good potential inherent in each human being, and to the recognition of the rights of various disadvantaged groups (e.g., women, children, the aged, the disabled), since the Confucian principle of benevolence draws special attention to the needs of the less fortunate members of society. Furthermore, as the contemporary philosopher Richard Rorty argues,[9] the actualisation of respect for modern human rights depends on the development of the human sentiment of sympathy for those who do not belong to one's own ethnic, cultural, or social community, and this view converges with the Confucian perspective that the principle of benevolence is to be realised by first cultivating oneself morally and caring for those with whom one has a social relationship (such as

9. Richard Rorty, "Human Rights, Rationality, and Sentimentality" in Stephen Shute and Susan Hurley (eds.), *On Human Rights: The Oxford Amnesty Lectures 1993* (New York: BasicBooks, 1993) 111–134.

family member or friend), and then extending one's sentiment of sympathy to those situated further and further away from one's immediate social circles and finally to all humankind.

Since the extensive contacts between China and the West began in the nineteenth century, many Western political and legal doctrines, including the idea of human rights, have gained a firm ground in the Chinese intellectual scene and in the Chinese consciousness. In the first half of this century, the discourse of human rights has been well received by many Chinese thinkers and often used among political activists, particularly those who criticised reigning governments for their human rights violations. The Chinese Communists themselves employed this tactic and used the human rights language in condemning the Kuomintang (KMT) and in winning public support. Sadly, soon after the Communist Revolution succeeded in 1949, human rights discourse disappeared from the mainland, and for nearly four decades the topic of human rights was a "forbidden zone" for Chinese scholars. This was mainly because human rights were regarded as bourgeois political and ideological devices, and were therefore alien to and inconsistent with the socialist project. It was only in 1991 that there occurred a turnabout in the Chinese Government's official position, and it declared its endorsement of the doctrine of human rights in its White Paper on the subject.[10] Since then, many scholarly writings on human rights have emerged in mainland China, and a survey of these writings suggests that most scholars enthusiastically embrace the concept of human rights. In recent decades, the Chinese Government has been a more active participant in international activities and dialogue on human rights matters. This culminated in China's signature of the International Covenant on Economic, Social and Cultural Rights (ICESCR) in 1997 and the International Covenant on Civil and Political Rights (ICCPR) in 1998 (the former covenant was ratified by China in 2001, but the latter has not been ratified). China has also been a party to a number of other international conventions relating to more specific areas of human rights.

A development which occurred almost simultaneously with China's entry into the international dialogue on human rights is the debate about human rights and Asian values. The central issue here is whether there can be a universal doctrine of human rights equally applicable to peoples of all nations

10. Information Office of the State Council of the PRC, *White Paper on Human Rights in China* (1991).

and cultures, and the extent to which culture can make or justify a difference in the application of human rights thinking, discourse, and standards to different countries. For example, are there particular elements in human rights thinking and discourse in the West that are culturally specific to the West and less applicable to a cultural tradition like China?

Such a question raises the fundamental issue of what is the Chinese cultural tradition. Who is to interpret what this tradition is? Is the government the legitimate spokesman for this tradition? Professor Michael Freeman has argued that it is the people who live in the culture or tradition, rather than their government, who are in the best position to speak on the content of their culture or tradition.[11] There is also significant value in the works of scholars who are learned in the history, philosophy, and culture of the tradition concerned. This is emulated in the views of Mou Zhongsan, probably the greatest Confucian philosopher of this century, who devoted his whole life to reconstructing the Chinese philosophical tradition.

Mou was certainly not a liberal in the Western sense, and he was also a strong critic of Marxism. He was totally committed to Confucianism and believed that Confucianism is at the core of the Chinese cultural, intellectual, and philosophical tradition. He placed his hope for China's future on a renaissance of the Confucian tradition. What is remarkable about Mou in the context of human rights discourse is that despite his great Confucian learning and deep commitment to Confucian philosophy, he also advocated for the adoption of Western notions of democracy, human rights and freedoms, constitutionalism, and the Rule of Law. His view is that such developments would not only be compatible with the Chinese cultural tradition, but would enable it to fulfil itself better than before. In other words, the establishment of constitutional democracy and institutional guarantees for human rights are in fact required by Confucian values themselves and will facilitate their better realisation. Drawing on the ancient phrase describing the best life as "inner sagehood and outward kingliness", Mou described China's challenge and the challenge for contemporary Confucians as "the opening up of a new

11. Michael Freeman, "On Culture, Values and Human Rights", paper presented at an international workshop on "Human Rights and Asian Values", Nordic Institute of Asian Studies and the University of Copenhagen, Copenhagen, 15–16 May 1997.

mode of outward kingliness", which he identified as the way of democracy and human rights.[12]

Like a number of twentieth century Confucian thinkers, Mou believed that the seeds for democracy and human rights lie within the Chinese cultural tradition itself. He developed his own philosophical vocabulary to discuss this aspect of the Chinese cultural tradition and the mechanics of its modernisation. In his theory, the Chinese cultural tradition, particularly Confucianism, was already generated and developed to the full rationality or reason in its "intensional" meaning (i.e., the content and application of the spirit of democracy and respect for human rights). What it lacked was rationality in its "extensional" meaning (i.e., the form and institutional structures of democracy and respect for human rights). Confucian ethics and doctrines about human nature, human relationships, and, in particular, the moral obligations of rulers, exemplify the intensional aspect of rationality. However, it is in the West that the extensional aspect of rationality first matured, and this aspect comprises elements such as democracy, human rights, constitutionalism, popular sovereignty, parliamentary institutions, and the Rule of Law. Yet Mou pointed out that this development in the West is not culturally specific to the West, but has universal significance and general applicability for all rational human beings, people, and cultures.

## CONCLUSION

As pointed out by Zhai Zhicheng — another contemporary Confucian philosopher[13] — the cultural sphere of a tradition includes ethics, the arts, politics, and science. In modern times, China has fallen behind the West in the domains of politics and science, but the realm of ethics and the arts are where the strengths of the great Chinese cultural tradition lie. Thus, Chinese people should re-discover these strengths in their own tradition and restore their confidence in the achievements of this tradition, while at the same time learning from the political and scientific achievements of modern Western civilisation.

---

12. See generally Mou Zongsan, 《政道與治道》 [*The Way of Politics and the Way of Administration*] (Taipei: Taiwan xuesheng shuju, revised edition, 1991).

13. Zhai Zhicheng (翟志成), 《當代新儒學史論》 [*On the History of Contemporary Neo-Confucianism*] (Taipei: Yunchen wenhua chuban, 1993) 395–409.

In doing so, it would be possible to rehabilitate the virtues and insights of Confucianism and other precious elements in the rich and great Chinese cultural tradition which modern Chinese deserve to feel proud of, and simultaneously work for the further democratisation and better protection of human rights in twenty-first-century China. This is the way forward for China. This is the lesson finally learnt from the immense sufferings which the Chinese people have endured in the throes of modernisation in the last two centuries.

## Acknowledgement

This chapter was first published as "Chinese Cultural Tradition and Modern Human Rights" (2000) 1:5 *Perspectives* (e-journal), translated to German and published in "Menschenrechte Made in China" in *KulturAustausch* (Ausgabe II, 2006), pp. 51–53.

# 9

# Legal Thought and Development in the People's Republic of China

## INTRODUCTION

China and Vietnam share much in common. In terms of the history of civilisation, China, together with Korea and Vietnam, and also to some extent Japan, may be regarded as belonging to an East Asian Confucian cultural sphere. There is also a striking similarity between the history of communism in China and Vietnam in the modern era. In the choice of their model of development after the success of their indigenous communist revolutions, both countries were under the heavy influence of the Soviet Union (or USSR), although Maoist China consciously chose to depart from the Soviet path after the 1950s. Again, in recent decades, both countries have embarked upon the road of economic reform towards privatisation, marketisation, and opening to the global economy, and have thereby achieved spectacular economic growth. In China, this journey began with the famous Third Plenum of the Eleventh Central Committee of the Chinese Communist Party (CCP) in December 1978, which adopted the new policy of *gaige kaifang* (reform and opening). In Vietnam, a journey in the same direction was marked by the new policy of *doi moi* (renovation) inaugurated by the Sixth National Congress of the Vietnamese Communist Party in December 1986.[1]

The CCP and Chinese Government have given China's new policy of development the label of "socialism with Chinese characteristics".[2] However, "capitalism with Chinese characteristics" — the title of a book on China's economic reform[3] — is probably a more realistic description. Similarly, there has emerged a new capitalism with Vietnamese characteristics. Both the Chinese and Vietnamese economies are now characterised by the simultaneous existence of State-owned enterprises and private firms financed by both domestic and foreign capital. The main "socialist" feature of the two nations is the monopoly of political power by the respective Communist Party which has been in firm control of all organs of the State apparatus and

1. Peerenboom points out that "Vietnam has closely followed the economic, legal, and political reforms in China, and modeled its foreign investment regime on China's". See Randall Peerenboom, *China Modernizes: Threat to the West or Model for the Rest?* (Oxford: Oxford University Press, 2007) 9.
2. See the Constitution of the Chinese Communist Party, in *Zhongguo gongchandang zhangcheng* [*Constitution of the Chinese Communist Party*] (Beijing: Renmin Press, 2007).
3. Yasheng Huang, *Capitalism with Chinese Characteristics: Entrepreneurship and the State* (Cambridge: Cambridge University Press, 2008).

important social organisations, and which has consistently tried its best to avoid any political liberalisation that might lead to the introduction of Western-style multi-party democracy. Despite such rejection of fundamental political change, both China and Vietnam have embarked on various legal reforms.

China has experienced a chequered legal history, which is itself part of the chequered history of Chinese law in the modern era. Modern Chinese law has been marked by radical discontinuities with the past.[4] The Chinese dynastic empires used to have elaborate legal codes and highly developed bureaucracies for administration,[5] but as imperial rule came to an end with the 1911 Revolution, Chinese law entered an era of doubt (about its own past), uncertainty, and attempted Westernisation, modernisation, and reconstruction, first by drawing inspiration from Continental Europe and Japan in the Republican era,[6] and then from the Soviet Union in the early years of the People's Republic of China (PRC).[7] A fairly sophisticated set of codes (of civil, criminal, and procedural laws) modelled on Continental European law was enacted by the Nationalist Party regime of the Republic of China (ROC) in the late 1920s and early 1930s.[8] These codes, subject to various amendments, are still in force in Taiwan today.[9] However, when the PRC was established in 1949, the Chinese Communists decided to completely abolish the laws and legal system of the Nationalist regime. After a brief attempt in the mid-1950s to establish a new socialist legal system modelled on that practiced by the Soviet Union, China saw two decades of deteriorating standards of legality ending

4. See generally Jianfu Chen, "The Transformation of Chinese Law — From Formal to Substantial" (2007) 37 *Hong Kong Law Journal* 689.
5. See generally Derk Bodde and Clarence Morris, *Law in Imperial China* (Cambridge, Mass: Harvard University Press, 1967); *The Tang Code*, translated by Wallace Johnson (Princeton, NJ: Princeton University Press, 1979); *The Great Qing Code*, translated by William C. Jones (Oxford: Clarendon Press, 1994).
6. See generally Herbert H.P. Ma, "General Features of the Law and Legal System of the Republic of China" in Herbert H.P. Ma (ed.), *Trade and Investment in Taiwan: The Legal and Economic Environment in the Republic of China* (Taipei: Institute of American Culture, Academia Sinica, 2nd edition, 1985) ch. 1.
7. See generally Albert H.Y. Chen, "Socialist Law, Civil Law, Common Law, and the Classification of Contemporary Chinese Law", Chapter 10 of this volume.
8. Ma (N6); Albert H.Y. Chen, *An Introduction to the Chinese Legal System* (Hong Kong: LexisNexis, 5th edition, 2019) ch. 3.
9. Ma (N6); Tay-sheng Wang, "Taiwan" in Poh-ling Tan (ed.), *Asian Legal Systems* (Sydney: Butterworths, 1997) ch. 4.

in total lawlessness (which was actually praised as something good) in the Cultural Revolution era of 1966–1976.[10]

In 1978, the Dengist era of "reform and opening" began. The last 30 years have seen not only rapid economic development in China, but also significant efforts in the reconstruction and development of its legal system.[11] These efforts were guided by and reflected a new and continuously deepening understanding of the value of law and legal institutions and of the Rule of Law[12] on the part of the scholarly and governing elites of China which has also spread among the populace, civil society, and the mass media. It is the purpose of this chapter to examine the history of legal thought in the PRC, and to review how such thought has produced "an event of epic historic proportions"[13] — a phrase used by Professor William Alford of Harvard Law School to describe China's "post-Cultural Revolution project of legal development".[14]

## LEGAL HISTORY AND THOUGHT

### 1949–1956

Before the CCP took over the government and established the PRC in 1949, it had already been in existence for nearly three decades and had experience of governance of parts of China.[15] Thus, although the PRC disinherited the legal system of the former Nationalist regime and all its laws, the PRC's legal thought and practice was not built up from scratch after 1949, but was a continuation and development of the communist tradition. The influence of the Soviet Union was also considerable in the 1950s, when the PRC viewed it as a model of both economic and legal development. A Soviet-style political

---

10. See Chen (N8) ch. 3.
11. See generally Randall Peerenboom, *China's Long March Toward Rule of Law* (Cambridge: Cambridge University Press, 2002).
12. See generally Albert H.Y. Chen, "Toward a Legal Enlightenment: Discussions in Contemporary China on the Rule of Law" (1999) 17 *UCLA Pacific Basin Law Journal* 125.
13. William P. Alford, "A Second Great Wall? China's Post-Cultural Revolution Project of Legal Construction" (1999) 11:2 *Cultural Dynamics* 193–213, at 193.
14. *Ibid.*, 193.
15. See, for example, W.E. Butler (ed.), *The Legal System of the Chinese Soviet Republic 1931–1934* (Dobbs Ferry, New York: Transnational Publishers, 1983); Zhang Xipo (ed.), *Geming genjudi fazhishi* [*Legal History of the Revolutionary Bases*] (Kaifeng: Henan University Press, 1999).

and legal system were introduced into China by the 1954 Constitution, the first Constitution of the PRC. For example, the Chinese system of people's congresses and procuratorates had their Soviet counterparts.[16] In the 1950s, work on the drafting of codes of civil law and criminal law and procedure began. A system of lawyers started to develop.[17] In 1956, the Eighth National Congress of the CCP affirmed both economic modernisation and the development of the legal system as important objectives to be pursued by the nation. Chinese Communist thought at this time recognised that the construction of a legal system was necessary both for economic development and the protection of the people's "democratic rights".[18] Dong Biwu, a leading jurist and CCP leader, advocated that State organs should act in accordance with the law, and CCP members should take the lead in complying with the law. "Legal educational propaganda" for the purpose of popularising legal norms among the people was also promoted. Chinese legal thought in this period is epitomised by the phrase "the concept of the legal system of people's democracy" (*renmin minzhu fazhi guan*).[19]

## 1957–1976

The political and legal history of the PRC took an abrupt turn in 1957 with the Anti-Rightist Movement of that year. In this political movement, many jurists and others working in the legal field were purged. Those who had advocated the Rule of Law and the improvement of standards of legality during the Hundred Flowers Campaign (in which freedom of speech was encouraged by Mao) that immediately preceded the Anti-Rightist Movement were accused of "using the law to resist the Party".[20] Principles such as the equality of all before the law, judicial independence, and the right of the accused in criminal proceedings to be defended by lawyers were all criticised as reactionary bourgeois ideas

16. See Chen (N7).
17. See generally Wu Jianfan, "Building New China's Legal System" (1983) 22 *Columbia Journal of Transnational Law* 1.
18. See Chen Jingliang (ed.), *Dangdai Zhongguo falü sixiangshi* [*The History of Contemporary Chinese Legal Thought*] (Kaifeng: Henan University Press, 1999) 21–25; Cheng Liaoyuan, *Cong fazhi dao fazhi* [*From Legal System to Rule of Law*] (Beijing: Law Press, 1999) 5–7.
19. Chen (N18) 21.
20. See Wu (N17); Chen (N18) 25–26, 157–166; Cheng (N18) 7–10. See also Guo Daohui, Li Buyun, and Hao Tiechuan (eds.), *Zhongguo dangdai faxue zhengming shilu* [*Jurisprudential Debates in Contemporary China*] (Changsha: Hunan Renmin Press, 1998).

that should be rejected. Mao Zedong even said that "what is needed is the Rule of Man, not the Rule of Law".[21] After 1957, legislative activities and legal scholarship both declined. The situation became even worse when Mao launched the Cultural Revolution in 1966.[22] Mao openly advocated the idea that revolutionary violence and the dictatorship of the proletariat need not be subject to legal restraint.[23] Lawlessness was considered good in the Cultural Revolution era — an era of legal nihilism and massive killings and beatings of persons and massive violations of all kinds of human rights.[24]

## 1977–1981

The most important turning point in the history of the PRC came in 1976 with the death of Mao Zedong and the downfall of the "Gang of Four" (Jiang Qing, Mao's wife, and three other ultra-leftist leaders at that time). Under the transition leadership of Hua Guofeng, Mao's successor, a new Constitution was promulgated in early 1978, which replaced the ultra-leftist Constitution of 1975. In late 1978, Deng Xiaoping rose to power as China's paramount leader, and his policies were adopted by the CCP at the now legendary Third Plenum of the Eleventh Central Committee of the CCP. The cornerstone of Deng's policies was "reform and opening" to the outside world (also known as "reform and open door", or *gaige kaifang*) for the purpose of promoting economic development, and the abandonment of the Maoist pursuit of class struggle as a means for building a communist society. Dengist thought and policies also included an important legal component, which was to strive to develop "socialist democracy" (*shehui zhuyi minzhu*) and "socialist legality", or a "socialist legal system" (*shehui zhuyi fazhi*). In this regard, Deng made a famous speech in December 1978,[25] the main content of which was incorporated into the communiqué of the Third Plenum:

> In order to safeguard people's democracy, it is imperative to strengthen the socialist legal system so that democracy is systematized and written into law in such a way as to ensure the stability, continuity, and full authority of this democratic system and

21. Cheng (N18) 9.
22. See Chen (N18) 26, 175–203; Cheng (N18) 10–11.
23. Cheng (N18) 9–11.
24. See Wu (N17).
25. For the relevant section (on issues of law and democracy) in the Chinese text of the speech, see *Deng Xiaoping wenxuan* [*Selected Works of Deng Xiaoping*] (Beijing: Renmin Press, 1994) vol. 2, 146–147.

> these laws; there must be laws for people to follow, these laws must be observed, their enforcement must be strict, and law breakers must be dealt with.[26]

The Third Plenum of December 1978 inaugurated an era of economic, political, and legal reforms in China. There was a renaissance of legal thought in the years immediately following 1978. Many scholars of law who had been purged twenty years ago in the Anti-Rightist Movement or ten years ago in the Cultural Revolution were now rehabilitated and allowed to teach and research again in the newly re-opened law schools and institutions of legal research. Many law-related subjects which had been "forbidden zones" in academic writing, teaching, and discussion since the late 1950s could now be freely discussed and debated. For example, one of the more lively debates in the late 1970s and early 1980s among legal intellectuals in China concerned the "Rule of Man" and the "Rule of Law". Three schools of thought emerged. One advocated the Rule of Law, another the synthesis of the Rule of Law and the Rule of Man, and the third school advocated socialist legality and abandoning the terms "Rule of Law" and "Rule of Man" altogether.[27] Other subjects of revitalised scholarly discussion included the principle of equality of all before the law, the extent to which the law reflects class interests and class struggles or the common interest of all in society, and the "heritability" in the socialist State of the capitalist law and legal institutions of the pre-revolutionary era.[28]

## 1982–1991

The enactment in 1982 of a new Constitution, the Fourth Constitution of the PRC (which, subject to five sets of amendments introduced in 1988, 1993, 1999, 2004, and 2018 respectively, is still in force today) further promoted legality in China and reflected the legal thinking of the post-Mao ruling elite. The 1982 Constitution moved the topic of citizens' rights from chapter 3 (in which citizens' rights were provided for in all three previous

26. My translation from the Chinese in *Shiyijie sanzhong quanhui yilai zhongyao wenxian xuandu* [*Selected Documents of the Period Since the Third Plenum of the Eleventh Central Committee*] (Beijing: Renmin Press, 1987) vol. 1, 11.

27. See *Fazhi yu renzhi wenti taolunji* [*Collected Essays on the Rule of Law and the Rule of Man*] (Beijing: Qunzhong Press, 1980); Cheng (N18) ch. 2.

28. See Chen (N18) 230–234, 240–242; Liu Xuebin, Li Yongjun, and Wei Fei, "Gaige kaifang sanshi nian de Zhongguo falixue: 1978–2008" [Chinese Legal Theory in the Three Decades of Reform and Opening: 1978–2008] (2008) 5 *Fazhi yu shehui fazhan* [*Legal System and Social Development*] 3–36, especially 4, 8–9.

constitutions) to chapter 2, intending to give this topic more prominence. The principles of the equality of all citizens before the law and the independent exercise of judicial power, both of which had existed in the 1954 Constitution but disappeared from the 1975 and 1978 Constitutions, were restored in the 1982 Constitution.[29] The principle of legality was enshrined in article 5, which provides, *inter alia*, that "the state upholds the unity and dignity of the socialist legal system"; "all state organs, the armed forces, all political parties and public organizations and all enterprises and institutions must abide by the Constitution and the law"; and "no organization or individual is privileged to be beyond the Constitution or the law". The principle that the CCP should operate within the framework of the Constitution and the law was also affirmed in the new 1982 constitution of the CCP itself. The official line was that the CCP leads the people in making the law, and also leads the people in complying with and enforcing the law. The law is made by people under the leadership of the Party; through the law-making processes in the National People's Congress (NPC) and its Standing Committee (NPCSC), party policies are elevated into legal provisions. It is thus explained that there is no conflict between the principle of Party leadership and the supremacy of the law. This view of the relationship between the Party and the law has been consistently advocated by the Chinese leadership since the early 1980s and is still the official line today.[30]

After the enactment of the 1982 Constitution, the next milestone in the development of Chinese legal and political thought was the Thirteenth National Congress of the CCP in 1987, when Zhao Ziyang was General Secretary of the Party. At this party congress,[31] the theory of the "preliminary stage of socialism" was developed. It was said that China was still at such a stage where socialist ideals could not yet be fully realised and adaptations

29. See arts. 33 and 126 of the 1982 Constitution, and arts. 78 and 85 of the 1954 Constitution. For the texts of the pre-1982 Constitutions, see Chen Hefu (ed.), *Zhongguo xianfa leibian* [*Collection of Chinese Constitutions*] (Beijing: Chinese Academy of Social Sciences Press, 1980).

30. See Albert H.Y. Chen, "The Developing Legal System in China" (1983) 13 *Hong Kong Law Journal* 291–315, at 309–313; Chen (N18) 26–27, 34–36; Chinese Government, *White Paper on China's Efforts and Achievements in Promoting the Rule of Law* (2008), available at: www.china.org.cn/government/news/2008-02/28/content_11025486.htm, last accessed 4 May 2009.

31. See Zhao Ziyang, *Yanzhe you Zhongguo tese de shehui zhuyi daolu qianjin: zai Zhongguo gongchandang di shisanci quanguo daibiao dahui shang de baogao* [*Marching on the Path of Socialism with Chinese Characteristics: Report at the 13th National Congress of the Chinese Communist Party*] (Hong Kong: Sanlian shudian, 1987); Zhao Ziyang, *The 13th Party Congress and China's Reforms* (Beijing: Beijing Review, 1987).

of orthodox Marxist doctrines to China's circumstances were called for. For example, instead of practicing a strictly planned economy, China should introduce elements of the socialist "commodity economy" (*shangpin jingji*). In this context, the role of law and the legal system was emphasised. The Party Congress adopted Deng's idea of "working on (economic) construction with one hand and working on the legal system with the other hand" (*yishou zhua jianshe, yishou zhua fazhi*),[32] and called for the development of a system of economic laws (*jingji fagui tixi*). According to Deng's idea of "one center and two basic points",[33] the one central task of the CCP was economic construction for China, and in order to achieve this it was necessary to insist on two basic points: the "Four Cardinal Principles" (in practice the most important of which is the leadership of the CCP),[34] and "reform and opening".

After the Thirteenth Party Congress and before the Tiananmen tragedy of 1989, legal scholarship that had started to revive since the late 1970s reached a climax in its development. The vitality of scholarly discussion on law-related issues was exemplified by the great debate initiated in 1988 on whether the concept of rights should be recognised as the most fundamental category in legal thought, and whether law and the legal system should be understood as rights-oriented, duties-oriented, or consisting of a combination of rights and duties that are equally basic to legal thought.[35] At the same time, the constitutional amendment of 1988 liberalised the concept of State ownership of land by allowing "land use rights" to be granted by the State to private developers and to be traded in the market.[36]

The suppression of the "counter-revolutionary rebellion" of June 1989 was followed by a revival of leftist ideology, and liberal legal thought became suspect for being inclined towards "bourgeois liberalisation", the critique of which had previously brought about the downfall of the liberal-minded

32. *Deng Xiaoping wenxuan* (N25) vol. 3, 154; Zhao (N31) 42.

33. Zhao (N31) 11–12.

34. The other three principles are insisting on the socialist road, on the people's democratic dictatorship, and on Marxism-Leninism and Mao Zedong thought. The "four principles" are mentioned in both the Constitution of the PRC and the Constitution of the CCP.

35. See Liu (N28) 10–11; Albert H.Y. Chen, "Developing Theories of Rights and Human Rights in China" in Raymond Wacks (ed.), *Hong Kong, China and 1997: Essays in Legal Theory* (Hong Kong: Hong Kong University Press, 1993) ch. 5.

36. For the Chinese text of the 1982 Constitution and its subsequent amendments, see *Zhonghua renmin gongheguo xianfa* [*Constitution of the People's Republic of China*] (Beijing: Law Press, 2004).

Party General Secretary Hu Yaobang in 1986. This leftist trend proved to be temporary, however. In 1991, the first White Paper was published by the Information Office of the State Council, which was followed by many more White Papers in subsequent years. The first White Paper was on the subject of human rights.[37] Hitherto, the concept of human rights had long been rejected by the Chinese Government and most Chinese scholars as a bourgeois idea and slogan that was not relevant to socialist China. However, the 1991 White Paper performed an about-turn by rehabilitating the concept and discourse of human rights, and alleging that for the Chinese people, as for the other peoples of the world, human rights represent noble ideals the gradual realisation of which are worth struggling for. It is believed that the embrace of the language of human rights in the White Paper was largely a strategic move to defend China against international criticisms of China's human rights record in the light of the events of 1989. Be that as it may, in retrospect this new official recognition of the legitimacy of human rights discourse proved to be an important positive step in the development of legal thought in China,[38] which ultimately culminated in the 2004 constitutional amendment discussed below.

## 1992–1995

The Tiananmen tragedy of 1989 was soon followed by other events that shook the world, leading quickly to the dramatic collapse of communism in Eastern Europe and then in the Soviet Union, which met the fate of disintegration. It looked for a while in the 1990s that the CCP was to call a halt to the "reform and opening" policy in order to protect itself from the worldwide trend of communism's decline and to ensure its self-survival. Deng Xiaoping, still paramount leader of China although Jiang Zemin had succeeded Zhao Ziyang as Party General Secretary, made the bold move in 1992 to maintain the communist regime in China not by halting or reversing the "reform and opening" policy but by intensifying and deepening economic reform. In a number of speeches made during his now legendary "Tour to Southern China" in 1992,[39] Deng declared that the market economy was not the monopoly of

37. Information Office of the State Council, *White Paper on Human Rights in China*, available at: www.china.org.cn/e-white/7/index.htm, last accessed 4 May 2009.

38. See Chen (N35); Albert H.Y. Chen, "Human Rights in China: A Brief Historical Review" in Raymond Wacks (ed.), *Human Rights in Hong Kong* (Hong Kong: Oxford University Press, 1992) ch. 5.

39. See Jin Chunming, *Zhonghua renmin gongheguo jianshi (1949–2004)* [*A Brief History of the People's Republic of China (1949–2004)*] (Beijing: Zhonggong dangshi Press, 2007) ch. 35.

capitalism, and that socialism did not necessarily mean a planned economy, but it was possible and legitimate (particularly in the preliminary stage of socialism) for China to operate a socialist market economy. This concept of the socialist market economy, now hailed as a key ingredient of the Dengist theory of socialism with Chinese characteristics, was officially adopted by the CCP at its Fourteenth National Congress in 1992, and was then enshrined in China's Constitution by the constitutional amendment of 1993.

The official designation of the development of a socialist market economy as the target of Chinese economic reform paved the way for yet another wave of legal discourse among Chinese scholars and intellectuals. The most commonly discussed subject at this time was the thesis that the socialist market economy is an "economy based on a legal system" (*fazhi jingji*) or an "economy based on the Rule of Law"[40] (also *fazhi jingji* in pinyin Romanisation, but *fazhi* here stands for "Rule of Law" rather than "legal system"). It was also argued that to facilitate the operation of such a market economy, private law — which had hitherto been relatively neglected in China — was important and should be actively developed.[41]

The importance of law for the socialist market economy was also emphasised in official Party documents. The report of the Fourteenth Party Congress in 1992 called for the strengthening of legislative work, particularly in the making of laws related to economic matters. The Third Plenum of the Fourteenth Central Committee of the CCP, which took place in 1993, emphasised that in the socialist market economy, there would be greater reliance than before on legal means for the purpose of economic regulation, and thus the speeding up of legislative work on economic matters was called for. It also stipulated the goal of the completion of the work of the "preliminary formation" (*chubu jianli*) of a legal system suitable for a socialist market economy by the end of the century.[42]

40. Cheng (N18) ch. 4.

41. See Albert H.Y. Chen, "The Developing Theory of Law and Market Economy in Contemporary China" in Wang Guiguo and Wei Zhenying (eds.), *Legal Developments in China: Market Economy and Law* (Hong Kong: Sweet & Maxwell, 1996) 3–20, at 11–12.

42. See Zhou Yezhong and Yi Shiguo, "Zhongguo tese shehuizhuyi falü tixi de fazhan yu huigu: Gaige kaifang sanshi nian Zhongguo lifa jianshi" [Development and Review of the Chinese Socialist Legislative System: Three Decades of Reform and Opening] (2008) 4 *Faxue luntan* [*Legal Forum*] 13–20; Cheng (N18) 131.

## 1996–2002

1996 marks yet another stage of development of official thinking about law in China, which stimulated another wave of scholarly discourse on law. In February 1996, PRC President and CCP General Secretary Jiang Zemin delivered a widely publicised address on the importance of "ruling the country according to law" (*yifa zhiguo*).[43] He pointed out that "ruling the country according to law" is an important mark of social progress and of the degree to which a society can be considered civilised, and is a necessary requirement of the construction of a modern socialist state. In March 1996, the NPC adopted its "Ninth Five-Year Plan and Outline of Objectives for Long-term Developments towards 2010". The document included among the objectives to be pursued by the nation "ruling the country according to law and constructing a socialist state based on a legal system" (*shehui zhuyi fazhi guojia*, where *fazhi* stands for "legal system"). In April 1996, the Institute of Law of the Chinese Academy of Social Sciences organised a conference on "ruling the country according to law and constructing a socialist Rule of Law state (Rechtsstaat)" (*shehui zhuyi fazhi guojia*, where *fazhi* stands for "Rule of Law").[44] This was the beginning of several years of lively scholarly discussion of the meaning and significance of the Rule of Law for China's development.[45] Unlike the situation in the late 1970s and early 1980s, when proponents of the Rule of Law and of the Rule of Man debated with one another, now in the late 1990s scholarly opinion unanimously supported the Rule of Law.

Chinese scholars succeeded in persuading the authorities that the "socialist Rule of Law state" should be preferred as a concept, term, and slogan to the "socialist state based on a legal system".[46] This was highly significant because whereas the latter term connotes the use of law as an instrument of rule by the State, the former term may be taken to imply that the State itself is subject to and governed by law, which stands above the State. The report adopted at the Fifteenth Party Congress in 1997 officially embraced the policy of

43. For the Chinese text of the speech, see Liu Hainian (ed.), *Yifazhiguo jianshe shehuizhuyi fazhi guojia* [*Ruling the Country According to Law, Building a Socialist Rule of Law State*] (Beijing: Chinese Legal System Press, 1996) 1–5.

44. The papers presented at the conference have been published in Liu (N43).

45. See generally Chen (N12).

46. See Li Buyun, "Yifa zhiguo lishi jincheng de huigu yu zhanwang" [The Historical Process of Ruling the Country According to Law: Retrospect and Prospects] (2008) 4 *Faxue luntan* [*Legal Forum*] 5–12; Chen (N18) 307–311; Cheng (N18) ch. 7.

"ruling the country according to law and constructing a socialist Rule of Law state (Rechtsstaat)". This principle was then written into the PRC Constitution itself by the constitutional amendment of 1999. Chinese scholars have pointed out that the adoption of this principle means nothing less than a fundamental and institutional change in China's mode of governance that will promote long-term order and stability in China.[47] The Fifteenth Party Congress also set the year 2010 as the target date for the basic completion of the construction of a socialist legal system with Chinese characteristics.

The late 1990s and the early years of the twenty-first century were a time of flourishing legal thought in China, not only on the Rule of Law but on related topics such as human rights, judicial reform, and judicial enforcement of the Constitution (or "judicialisation (*sifa hua*) of the Constitution", a topic of debate generated by the famous interpretation issued by the Supreme People's Court in the *Qi Yuling* case in August 2001).[48] The PRC's signature of the International Covenant on Economic, Social, and Cultural Rights (ICESCR) in 1997 (which has been ratified) and of the International Covenant on Civil and Political Rights (ICCPR) in 1998 (which has not yet been ratified up to this date), as well as the PRC's accession to the World Trade Organization (WTO) in 2001, further stimulated scholarship on how China's legal and judicial systems and laws should be reformed so as to converge with international standards in the domains of human rights, commerce, trade, investment, and intellectual property.

In 2002, the Sixteenth Party Congress of the CCP was held. The report for the Congress[49] introduced the concept of "political civilisation" (*zhengzhi wenming*), and suggested that democracy, the Rule of Law, and human rights are all ingredients of "political civilisation".[50] The strengthening of socialist legal construction was again called for, and the target re-affirmed the formation of a socialist legal system with Chinese characteristics by 2010. Regarding the CCP's ideology, the Sixteenth Congress introduced Jiang Zemin's "important

47. Chen (N18) 39–40.

48. See Kui Shen, "Is It the Beginning of the Era of the Rule of the Constitution? Reinterpreting China's 'First Constitutional Case'" (2003) 12 *Pacific Rim Law and Policy Journal* 199. However, the Supreme People's Court judicial interpretation in the *Qi Yuling* case was repealed by the court in December 2008. See the forum ("Bitan") on this topic in (2009) 3 *Faxue* [*Legal Science Monthly*] 3–35.

49. The Chinese texts of the reports and documents at various National Congresses of the CCP, are available at: http://cpc.people.com.cn/GB/64162, last accessed 4 May 2009.

50. See Li (N46) 7.

thought of 'the three represents'"[51] into the CCP Constitution as a supplement to Marxism-Leninism, Mao Zedong thought, and Deng Xiaoping theory.

## 2003–2008

The last period in PRC legal history to be identified in this chapter was inaugurated by the Sun Zhigang incident[52] in 2003 and the constitutional amendment of 2004. Whereas the *Qi Yuling* case mentioned above highlighted the extent to which the Constitution may be directly relied on by the courts in deciding a case, the Sun Zhigang incident prompted a wave of discussion among scholars and in civil society on the related and equally crucial issue of constitutional review — how to determine the constitutionality of existing laws and regulations and to enable unconstitutional legal rules (for example, rules that violate constitutionally guaranteed rights) to be struck down. Sun was a young university graduate from Wuhan who was arrested and detained by the police in Guangzhou simply because he was not able to produce proper identification documents. He was subsequently beaten to death while in detention. The detention was pursuant to the Measures on the Custody and Repatriation of Vagrants and Beggars in Cities enacted by the State Council in 1982. There was a public outcry and scholars called for the NPCSC to follow the procedures provided for in the Law on Legislation enacted in 2000 to review the constitutionality of the Measures. In the end, the NPCSC did not formally exercise its power of review, but the State Council took the initiative in repealing the Measures. Despite this act, scholarly discussion has continued since then on how China should move forward in developing an effective system of constitutional review and on the concept of constitutionalism (*xianzheng*), which has not yet received official recognition in the Constitution or by the Party. In civil society, the term "defence of rights" (*weiquan*) became increasingly used, particularly in the context of

51. The "three represents" are that the CCP signifies (a) the requirement for the development of progressive forces of productivity in China, (b) the direction of movement of progressive culture in China, and (c) the fundamental interest of the great majority of the Chinese people.

52. For a comment in Chinese, see Chen Hongyi (Albert H.Y. Chen), "2004 nian de xiuxian yu Zhongguo xianzheng de qianjing" [The 2004 Constitutional Amendment and the Prospects for Chinese Constitutionalism] (2005) 88 *Ershiyi shiji* [*Twenty-First Century*] 67–77, at 72–74.

lawyers who resort to the Chinese legal and judicial systems to fight for the rights and interests of the underprivileged and persecuted.[53]

In 2004, the 1982 Constitution was amended for a fourth time. From a legal point of view, the most significant amendments are the express mention of human rights in the amended version of the Constitution, and the enhanced protection of private property rights. The question of the legal protection of private property rights came to the fore in the debate initiated in 2005 by Peking University law professor Gong Xiantian on the draft Law of Property (LP) (*wuquan fa*). Gong alleged that the draft law was unconstitutional and violated the socialist principles enshrined in the Constitution.[54] Despite the opposition and criticisms from Gong and other leftist elements in China, the LP was ultimately passed by the NPC in 2007.

An updated version of the ideology of the CCP was stated in Hu Jintao's report to the Seventeenth Party Congress in 2007. Whereas Deng's ideological contribution had previously received codification as Deng's theory of socialism with Chinese characteristics and Jiang's as the "theory of the three represents",[55] the elements of the "scientific concept of development", "harmonious society", and "people as the basis" now mark the Hu Jintao era. Before and after the Party Congress, there was a new wave of discourse among scholars of law on how law can contribute to the construction of a harmonious society and to China's development in accordance with the "scientific concept of development" and governance with the "people as the basis".[56]

Regarding law and legal development, the Seventeenth Party Congress[57] decided to "insist on the basic strategy of ruling the country according to law and establish a socialist rule of law".[58] It pointed out that "ruling the country

53. See, for example, Hualing Fu and Richard Cullen, "*Weiquan* (Rights Protection) Lawyering in an Authoritarian State: Building a Culture of Public-interest Lawyering" (2008) 59 *China Journal* 111–127.

54. See Liu Yiqing and Zhang Qinde (eds.), *Gong Xiantian xuanfeng shilu* [*Records of the Gong Xiantian Storm*] (Beijing: Zhongguo caizheng jingji Press, 2007).

55. See the meaning of this in N51.

56. See Zhang Wenxian, "Fazhi xuanyuan, faxue wenxian: shiqi da baogao de faxue jiedu" [A Declaration on the Rule of Law, a Jurisprudential Document: A Legal Reading of the Report to the 17th Congress] (2007) 6 *Fazhi yu shehui fazhan* [*Legal System and Social Development*] 3–6; Liu (N28) 17.

57. The documents are available at the website cited in N49.

58. For the concept of the socialist Rule of Law (*shehuizhuyi fazhi linian*), see articles by Zhang Wenxian and others in (2006) 5 *Faxuejia* [*The Jurist*] 6–39.

according to law is the basic requirement of socialist democratic politics". It reiterated the importance of the "path of political development of socialism with Chinese characteristics" and the "organic unity of the leadership of the Party, the people being the masters of the nation, and ruling the country in accordance with law". The Party itself should "exercise its power of governance scientifically, democratically, and in accordance with law".

## MAJOR LEGAL DEVELOPMENTS

To briefly explain China's legal developments over the last three decades, this section outlines the legislative developments in several basic areas of the law and then turns to institutional developments in the administrative system, judicial system, legal profession, and legal education.

It was pointed out in the report of the NPCSC in March 2008[59] that by this time, "a socialist legal system (*shehuizhuyi falütixi*) with Chinese characteristics consisting of three levels of legal norms and seven departments or areas of law has basically been formed". The three levels are (a) the laws made by the NPC and the NPCSC, (b) approximately 600 administrative regulations made by the State Council, and (c) more than 7,000 local regulations made by the provincial people's congresses and their standing committees and other legal norms at the same level. The seven areas of law are classified as (1) constitutional law, (2) civil and commercial law, (3) administrative law, (4) economic law, (5) social law, (6) criminal law, and (7) law on litigation and non-contentious procedures.

Criminal law and the law of criminal procedure constitute parts of the core of any modern legal system as they concern the liberty of a subject — or the freedom of the body of the person. The Criminal Code and the Code of Criminal Procedure were among the first seven laws enacted by the NPC in the post-Mao era (the other laws enacted in the same year of 1979 were on the courts, the procuratorates, the structure of the local people's congresses and local governments, the elections of the NPC and local people's congresses, and Sino-foreign joint ventures). The two codes were actually the first of their

59. See "Quanguo renmin daibiao dahui changwu weiyuanhui gongzuo baogao" [Report of the NPCSC] in *Zhonghua renmin gongheguo quanguo renmin daibiao dahui changwu weiyuanhui gongbao* [*Gazette of the Standing Committee of the National People's Congress of the PRC*], No. 3, pp. 335–369 (2008).

kind in the history of the PRC. The codes were based on drafts produced in the 1950s and early 1960s when the Soviet influence on Chinese legislative drafting was strong.[60] They were rather crude and rudimentary, and were extensively amended and improved in 1996 and 1997. The 1996 revision of the Law of Criminal Procedure[61] improved, to some extent, the protection of the rights of the accused and introduced a form of presumption of innocence (but not the right to silence or the exclusion of unlawfully obtained evidence). It also abolished the much criticised procedure of "detention for examination" (*shourong shencha*), but did not reform the notorious procedure of "re-education through labour" (*laodong jiaoyang*) under which persons may be detained for one to three years without any criminal trial.[62] The 1997 revision of the Criminal Law[63] introduced the principle, long accepted since the beginnings of modern legal history in the West, of *nulla poena sine lege* (no crime or punishment in the absence of an express legal provision on it), substituted the concept (generally used in other countries) of "offences against national security" for that of "counter-revolutionary offences", and generally adapted the criminal code to the changing social and economic circumstances. The crime rate in China rose dramatically in the era of reform and opening. To cope with waves of crime, severe punishment (including the extensive use of the death penalty) and "strike hard" campaigns against crimes during which criminals were promptly and severely dealt with were used. Three major "strike hard" campaigns were conducted in 1983–1987, 1996–1997, and 2001–2003.[64] In 2007, the Supreme People's Court introduced stricter measures of review for death sentences imposed by lower courts to control the excessive use of capital punishment.[65]

60. See Chen (N7).

61. See Lawyers Committee for Human Rights, *Opening to Reform? An Analysis of China's Revised Criminal Procedure Law* (New York: Lawyers Committee for Human Rights, 1996).

62. "Re-education through labour" was subsequently abolished in December 2013; see Chen (N8) 257–258, 341.

63. See Lawyers Committee for Human Rights, *Wrongs and Rights: A Human Rights Analysis of China's Revised Criminal Law* (New York: Lawyers Committee for Human Rights, 1996).

64. See Bin Liang, *The Changing Chinese Legal System, 1978–Present* (New York: Routledge, 2008) ch. 4.

65. See the Supreme People's Court's work report to the National People's Congress in March 2008, in *Zhonghua renmin gongheguo quanguo renmin daibiao dahui changwu weiyuanhui gongbao* [Gazette of the Standing Committee of the National People's Congress of the PRC], No. 3, pp. 370–383 (2008).

Civil, commercial, and economic law are the domains of the law that have been most intimately connected with the far-reaching economic reforms in China in the last three decades. In the 1980s, the milestone for the development of Chinese civil law was the enactment of the General Principles of Civil Law (GPCL) in 1986. As in the case of the Codes of Criminal Law and Criminal Procedure, the GPCL was also shaped by the socialist legal tradition. The sources of reference for the drafting of the GPCL included the relevant laws of the USSR, Czechoslovakia, East Germany, and Hungary.[66] The GPCL also reflected the indigenous concerns of Chinese economic reform. For example, it recognised as a "property right related to property ownership" the "*chengbao* operational rights" over collectively owned land that had emerged as a result of the rural reform of introducing the *chengbao* or contract responsibility system for peasant households. Another "right related to property ownership" that was recognised by the GPCL was the "operational right" of State enterprises with regard to property that the State has given to them for the purpose of operational management.

The 1980s were a time when the foundation for contemporary Chinese civil law was laid. Apart from the GPCL, other major enactments in this area include the Marriage Law 1980, the Law of Economic Contracts 1981, the Trademark Law 1982, the Patent Law 1984, the Succession Law 1985, the Law of Foreign-related Economic Contracts 1985, the Land Management Law 1986, the Law of Technology Contracts 1987, and the Copyright Law 1990.

Since the early 1990s, Chinese civil, commercial, and economic law progressed even more rapidly, prompted by the decision to move towards a socialist market economy in 1992 and to introduce relevant economic legislation, the decision to implement socialist Rule of Law in 1997, and the PRC's accession to the WTO in 2001. Sources of reference for legislative drafting in this era were broadened to include the continental European legal tradition (including the laws that are in force in Taiwan), the Anglo-American common law tradition, and international law. The conceptual divisions between civil, commercial, and economic law have become clearer.[67] Civil law is primarily concerned with the personal and property relationships between civil subjects of equal status. Commercial law builds upon the principles of civil law

66. See generally Albert H.Y. Chen, "The Developing Chinese Law and the Civil Law Tradition" in M. Brosseau, S. Pepper, and S.K. Tsang (eds.), *China Review 1996* (Hong Kong: Chinese University Press, 1996) 29–59.

67. Chen (N8) 288–290.

and specialises in dealing with the relationships between business entities of equal legal status. Economic law regulates the economic relationships generated by government actions in the coordination and regulation of economic activities and the government's intervention in the market economy, and includes laws to control unfair trade practices and to promote competition.

Major enactments in civil law since the 1990s include the Guarantee Law (GL) 1995 (which is significant in providing for property interests that can serve as security for loans),[68] the Law of Contract 1999 (highly significant in that it unifies the rules of contract law applicable to contracts involving only domestic business entities and contracts involving business entities with foreign sources of capital, thus replacing the three separate contract laws mentioned above), the Law of Trust 2001, the Law of Rural Land Contracts (LRLC) 2002 (significant in codifying the legal norms and property rights generated by the rural land reform), and, most significantly, the LP 2007 (which formulates a set of property rights, particularly those relating to land, and gives private property rights a legal status equal to that of State property, thus affirming the value and importance of private property rights). In late 2002, a draft Civil Code — usually considered the most important and comprehensive code in a legal system belonging to the Continental European tradition — was tabled before the NPCSC, but further work on it was subsequently postponed for more than a decade.[69]

In the domain of commercial law, a milestone was set by the enactment of the Company Law in 1993.[70] Its innovation lies in its equal application to enterprises irrespective of the source of their capital (domestic or foreign). This was a departure from the previous approach in business regulation, and was said to facilitate fair competition in the market on the basis of legal equality. The law was also partly aimed at fostering the reform of State-owned enterprises in China, and was thus hailed as an important step in the development of a "modern system of enterprise" in China.

Other major enactments in the field of commercial law include the Maritime Law 1992, Law of Negotiable Instruments 1995, Insurance Law 1995, Law on Commercial Banks 1995, Law of Partnership Enterprises 1997, Law of Individuals' Solely-owned Enterprises 1999, Securities Law 1998, and

68. See Chen (N66).

69. In December 2019, the draft Civil Code was approved by the NPCSC, and the draft was passed into law by the NPC in May 2020.

70. See Chen (N66).

the Enterprise Bankruptcy Law 2006. Regarding economic law, notable enactments include the Consumer Protection Law 1993, Law Against Improper Competition 1993, Product Quality Law 1993, Law on Advertisements 1994, Law on the Management of Urban Real Estate 1994, Law on Foreign Trade 1994, Pricing Law 1997, and the Anti-Monopoly Law 2007.

The last area of law to be surveyed here is administrative law. In this area, the most important milestone was the enactment in 1989 of the Law of Administrative Litigation, which, for the first time in the legal history of the PRC, enabled citizens to take the government to court and courts to strike down government actions.[71] This was followed in the 1990s by the enactment of the Law of State Compensation 1994 (enabling citizens to obtain compensation for violations of their rights by administrative organs and their officials),[72] the Law of Administrative Punishment 1996 (which is highly significant in introducing some principles of administrative procedure, including the right to a fair hearing), the Law of Administrative Supervision 1997, and the Law of Administrative Review 1999.

In the early years of the twenty-first century, administrative law and the related area of public law continued to grow, with the making of several major laws by the NPCSC, including the Law on Legislation 2000 (which delineates the spheres of legislation by the NPC and NPCSC, administrative regulations by the State Council, and local regulations by local authorities),[73] the Law of Administrative Licensing 2003, the Law on Civil Servants 2005, the Law on Security Administrative Punishment 2005, and the Law on Supervision 2006 (which codifies the supervisory powers of the people's congresses). Also significant are the ground-breaking Regulations on Openness of Government Information (*zhengfu xinxi gongkai tiaoli*) introduced by the State Council in 2007. However, a comprehensive Law of Administrative Procedure (of the kind that exists in Taiwan, Korea, and Japan) has not yet been enacted though this has been recognised as an eventual objective.

The development of administrative law has been accompanied by the government's effort to shift from the previous practice of government by policy

71. See Pitman B. Potter, "The Administrative Litigation Law of the PRC: Judicial Review and Bureaucratic Reform" in Pitman B. Potter (ed.), *Domestic Law Reforms in Post-Mao China* (Armonk: M.E. Sharpe, 1994) 270.

72. See Chen (N66).

73. See Li Yahong, "The Law-making Law: A Solution to the Problems in the Chinese Legislative System?" (2000) 30 *Hong Kong Law Journal* 120.

documents and of decision-making not being subject to any procedural norms that protect an affected persons' rights to what has been termed "administration in accordance with law" (*yifa xingzheng*), which requires legal norms to be enacted to serve as the basis of administrative actions as well as compliance with legal norms in the administrative process, including procedural norms. For example, following the constitutional amendment in March 1999 on "ruling the State in accordance with law" and "building a socialist Rechtsstaat", the State Council later in the same year promulgated a Decision on the Comprehensive Promotion of Administration in Accordance with Law. This Decision was followed by the very detailed and elaborate Implementation Outline for the Comprehensive Promotion of Administration in Accordance with Law promulgated by the State Council in 2004.[74] The Outline sets a 10-year timetable for achieving the target of a government based on the Rule of Law (*fazhi zhengfu*), implicitly recognising that the present system is still far away from this target.[75]

We now turn from the administrative to the judicial system. From an institutional point of view, much progress has been made in the development of the Chinese judiciary in the last three decades. Over the years there has been a steady and significant rise in the number of judges, in their average levels of education and professional training, and in the number of cases tried by the courts.[76] In 1978–2008, the caseload of the Chinese courts increased 20-fold.[77] Increasing numbers of citizens have become aware of the legal system and have resorted to the courts for the purpose of dispute settlement.[78] However, as in many developing countries, there are serious concerns regarding the professional quality and judicial ethics of the Chinese judiciary, corruption,

74. For the Chinese text, see www.gov.cn/zfjs/2005-08/12/content_22212.htm, last accessed 28 January 2009.

75. See generally Luo Haocai and Song Gongde, "Linking the Rule-of-Law Government" in Luo Haocai (ed.), *Xingzhengfa luncong* [*Essays on Administrative Law*] (Beijing: Law Press, 2006) vol. 9, 441–459.

76. For relevant figures and statistics, see Liang (N64); Zhu Jingwen (ed.), *Zhongguo falü fazhan baogao* [*Chinese Legal Development Report*] (Beijing: Chinese Renmin University Press, 2007).

77. See the Work Report of the Supreme People's Court to the National People's Congress in March 2009, available at: www.npc.gov.cn/npc/xinwen/syxw/2009-03/17/content_1493653.htm, last accessed 12 May 2009.

78. Pierre Landry, "The Institutional Diffusion of Courts in China: Evidence from Survey Data" in Tom Ginsburg and Tamir Moustafa (eds.), *Rule By Law: The Politics of Courts in Authoritarian Regimes* (Cambridge: Cambridge University Press, 2008) ch. 8. See also the special issue on "Markets, Courts and Leninism in China" (2009) 9:1 *China Review* 1–163.

susceptibility to political interference (which in the case of China may sometimes be legitimised by the supreme principle of the leadership of the Party in all spheres of State activities, including the judicial function), and problems in the enforcement of court judgments.[79] Apparently genuine efforts have been made to address and to alleviate these problems. For example, the Law on Judges 1995 represented a major step towards the institutionalisation and professionalisation of the Chinese judiciary. The year 2001 saw the introduction of the Basic Norms of Professional Ethics of Judges of the PRC. Earlier, in October 1999, the Supreme People's Court published a Five-year Outline Plan for the Reform of the People's Courts, which sets out 39 tasks relating to judicial reform.[80] The Second Five-year Reform Outline Plan for 2004–2008 was announced in October 2005.[81] This plan was divided into eight sections containing a total of 50 tasks to be pursued. The Third Five-year Reform Outline Plan for 2009–2013 was issued in March 2009, setting out 30 tasks.[82]

Like the judicial system, the legal profession is also a pillar of any modern legal system. China has made strenuous efforts to build up its legal profession in the last three decades.[83] The first law on lawyers in the PRC — the Provisional Regulations on the Work of Lawyers — was enacted by the NPCSC in as early as 1980. Since then the size, nature, and mode of operation of lawyers have changed beyond recognition. Economic reform and economic development have created tremendous opportunities for China's legal profession; the number of full-time practicing lawyers in China multiplied 10-fold, from 10,000 in 1984 to 100,000 in 2004.[84] By the end of 2006, the total number of practicing lawyers reached 130,000, working

79. See generally Hualing Fu, "Putting China's Judiciary into Perspective: Is It Independent, Competent, and Fair?" in Erik G. Jensen and Thomas C. Heller (eds.), *Beyond Common Knowledge: Empirical Approaches to the Rule of Law* (Stanford: Stanford University Press, 2003) ch. 6.

80. See Chen (N8) 164.

81. The Chinese text is available at: www.dffy.com/faguixiazai/xf/200512/20051214221735.htm, last accessed 27 February 2009.

82. *Renmin fayuan disange wunian gaige gangyao* (2009–2013), available at: www.chinacourt.org/public/detail.php?id=350101, last accessed 4 May 2009.

83. See generally William P. Alford, "Of Lawyers Lost and Found: Searching for Legal Professionalism in the People's Republic of China" in William P. Alford (ed.), *Raising the Bar: The Emerging Legal Profession in East Asia* (Cambridge, Mass: Harvard University Press, 2008) ch. 7.

84. Zhu (N76) 340.

in 13,000 law firms all over the country.[85] A milestone in the development of China's legal profession was the enactment of the Law on Lawyers in 1996, which substituted "practitioners who have obtained lawyers' practicing certificates in accordance with the law and provide legal services to society" for the concept of "State legal workers" in the old Provisional Regulations on the Work of Lawyers as the official understanding of what lawyers are. Although most lawyers are in private practice today and not employed by the State and lawyers' associations have been formed with some self-regulatory powers, Chinese lawyers are still much more closely regulated and supervised by the government and the Party (through the Ministry of Justice and the organs of judicial administration under the Ministry) and enjoy less autonomy than in many other countries. The latest revision of the Law on Lawyers in 2007 has not changed this position. Regarding the professional qualification of lawyers, a major development was the introduction in 2002 of the unified national judicial examination for all intending lawyers, judges, and procurators, which replaced the national professional qualifying examination introduced in 1986.[86]

Important developments have also taken place with regard to legal aid[87] and legal education. The developing legal aid system was only formalised in 2003, with the enactment of the Legal Aid Regulations by the State Council.[88] The amount of funding for legal aid increased from 78 million RMB in 2002 to 152 million in 2003 and then to 217 million in 2004.[89] Legal education has been a spectacular area of growth within the system of higher education in China. Starting with a handful of law schools three decades ago, the total number of law schools in China has now exceeded 600, with an undergraduate law student population of 300,000.[90]

Apart from promoting legal education for university students, the Chinese Government has, since 1985, consistently set "legal educational propaganda" — the popularisation of legal knowledge among officials, cadres,

85. *White Paper* (N30) ch. 6.

86. See Chen (N8) 204–205.

87. See, for example, Benjamin L. Liebman, "Legal Aid and Public Interest Law in China" (1999) 34:2 *Texas International Law Journal* 211; Benjamin L. Liebman, "Lawyers, Legal Aid, and Legitimacy in China" in Alford (N83) ch. 8.

88. See Chen (N8) 217–220.

89. Zhu (N76) 408.

90. *White Paper* (N30) ch. 7.

and the populace — as one of its high-priority tasks.[91] Since 1985, several five-year programs for popularising legal knowledge have been launched in accordance with decisions of the NPCSC. An example is the NPCSC's Decision in 2006 on the Strengthening of Legal Educational Propaganda. Since 4 December 2001 — the anniversary of the enactment of the 1982 Constitution — has been celebrated every year as the "national legal propaganda day". Many newspapers specialising in legal news have been published, and law-related programs developed by State television and radio stations. It has been pointed out that as of 2008, more than 300 television stations at provincial and municipal levels broadcasted law-related programs. The Internet has also been used as a vehicle for legal educational propaganda. Legal knowledge has been incorporated into secondary and primary school curricula. Lectures and seminars on legal knowledge have been organised for top leaders of the Party, members of the NPCSC, as well as for officials and cadres at various levels. Slogans such as "ruling the province in accordance with law" or "ruling the city in accordance with law" have also been introduced to promote the Rule of Law at local levels.

## THE MODERNISATION PARADIGM

China is the most populous nation on earth, with a proud history of a glorious civilisation since ancient times; it has, however, trodden a tortuous path while grappling with the challenges of modernity. The Chinese legal system today only has three decades of continuous and uninterrupted development behind it. How do we make sense of it? Is it a child still learning to walk? How much has it grown up? The following two quotations capture the ethos of these questions:

> The accomplishments of the legal reform to date are impressive given the need to overcome the burden of Chinese tradition, thirty years of Maoism, and the hostility of the institutional environment in which reform must take place. Law has gained more importance than it has ever possessed in Chinese history.[92]

> China's legal construction is still facing some problems: The development of democracy and the rule of law still falls short of the needs of economic and social

91. *Ibid.*

92. Stanley B. Lubman, *Bird in a Cage: Legal Reform in China After Mao* (Stanford: Stanford University Press, 1999) 2.

> development; the legal framework shows certain characteristics of the current stage and calls for further improvement; in some regions and departments, laws are not observed or strictly enforced, violators are not brought to justice; local protectionism, departmental protectionism, and difficulties in law enforcement occur from time to time; some government functionaries take bribes and bend the law, abuse their power when executing the law, abuse their authority to override the law, and substitute their words for the law, thus bringing damage to the socialist rule of law; and the task still remains onerous to strengthen education in the rule of law, and enhance the awareness of law and the concept of the rule of law among the public.[93]

These two quotations, one from an American scholar of Chinese law and the other from the Chinese Government's latest White Paper on the Rule of Law, actually express the commonly held views that (a) the PRC has indeed made great progress in the development of its legal system, which has risen quickly and sharply from the "low baseline" from which it started at the end of the Cultural Revolution era; and (b) the existing Chinese legal system still suffers from many problems, defects, and imperfections, and a long way still lies ahead in overcoming various obstacles and developing a more satisfactory Rule of Law in China.

These views seem to presuppose what may be called a "modernisation" paradigm for thinking about legal development. Such a paradigm would affirm some standards or criteria for evaluating legal development. Without such standards, it would not be possible to say that China has made progress in terms of the building of its legal system in the last three decades. Also, without such standards, it would not be possible to measure or identify where China's existing legal system still falls short of what should be the case, and thus to conclude that there is still much room for improvement and much to be done.

Such standards may be considered elements of a "modernisation" paradigm of law because they are standards applicable to what we would call a "modern legal system", but were not generally followed by legal systems of many civilisations in the pre-modern world. Insofar as modernity began in the West, the modern legal system was initially a product of Western civilisation, and the modernisation of legal systems in the non-Western world has been largely a process of their Westernisation. Thus the "modernisation" paradigm of law not only affirms principles of legality or the Rule of Law that as a matter of world history first

93. *White Paper* (N30) concluding section.

emerged in the West, but also implies that as non-Western legal systems transform and re-make themselves in the image of the modern Western legal system, they will be modernised and adapted to the conditions of modernity.[94]

It may be argued that the kind of legal modernisation presupposed by such a paradigm is part and parcel of globalisation, and that once China has chosen to open itself to and integrate itself into the global economy of transnational capital and to become a member of the WTO, there is no alternative other than to develop a legal system that that provides a hospitable environment for business. In this sense, the logic of economic globalisation may to a significant extent dictate the direction and content of legal reform.[95] One is reminded here of Weber's thesis on rational law and the rise of capitalism,[96] as well as Marx's idea that law is part of the superstructure of a society, the base of which is constituted by economic and property arrangements and class structures which the law would simply seek to serve.[97] However, China's "opening" to the world has opened it not only to global economic forces but also to external cultural, social, and even political influences. As a major player in the United Nations and the international community, China has now signed large numbers of treaties, undertaken many international obligations (including obligations in the domain of human rights), and participated actively in global discussions and dialogues on various matters (including human rights).[98] China has also opened itself to

---

94. See generally Clarke's discussion of what he calls the "Ideal Western Legal Order" model in contemporary Chinese law; Donald C. Clarke, "Puzzling Observations in Chinese Law: When Is a Riddle Just a Mistake?" in C. Stephen Hsu (ed.), *Understanding China's Legal System: Essays in Honor of Jerome A. Cohen* (New York: New York University Press, 2003) ch. 3.

95. See generally David M. Trubek and Alvaro Santos (eds.), *The New Law and Economic Development: A Critical Appraisal* (Cambridge: Cambridge University Press, 2006). According to the Washington Consensus, Western-style Rule of Law is one of the prerequisites for economic development; for a critical discussion of this, see Peerenboom (N1) ch. 1.

96. See David M. Trubek, "Max Weber on Law and the Rise of Capitalism" (1972) 3 *Wisconsin Law Review* 720; Donald C. Clarke, "Economic Development and the Rights Hypothesis: The China Problem" (2003) 51 *American Journal of Comparative Law* 89.

97. See generally Hugh Collins, *Marxism and Law* (Oxford: Clarendon Press, 1982).

98. For recent statements by the Chinese Government on human rights, see China's national report submitted to the UN's Human Rights Council for the Universal Periodic Review, February 2009, available at: http://lib.ohchr.org/HRBodies/UPR/Documents/Session4/CN/A_HRC_WG6_4_CHN_1_E.pdf, last accessed 12 May 2009; State Council Information Office, *National Human Rights Action Plan of China (2009–2010)*, available at: www.gov.cn/test/2009-04/14/content_1284725.htm (Chinese version), http://english.gov.cn/official/2009-04/13/content_1284128.htm (English version), last accessed 12 May 2009.

international agencies and foreign governments that seek to provide assistance to China in improving or strengthening its law drafting, legal system, judiciary, legal aid, human rights, and so on. Thus, globalising forces act not only on China's commercial and economic laws, but on all fronts of its developing legal system.[99]

However, insofar as the "modernisation" paradigm of law and legal development appears to be Western-centric, it is susceptible to being resisted by those in the non-Western world who wish to defend their own culture, to develop laws and legal institutions that are home-grown and responsive to indigenous circumstances instead of transplanting Western laws and legal institutions, or to resist Western hegemony. In the case of contemporary China, such resistance has been exemplified by the late Deng Zhenglai's critique of what he also terms the "modernisation paradigm" in the debate initiated by him in 2005 on "Whither Goes Chinese Jurisprudence".[100] Deng, a leading social and legal theorist, chastised his colleagues engaged in legal scholarship in the last two decades for uncritically adopting the Western vision of law and legal development as the ideal model for China's legal development.[101] Similar sentiments may also be seen in the writings of Zhu Suli, an influential legal thinker and former Dean of the Law School at Peking University. One of his most famous works is titled *The Rule of Law and Its Indigenous Resources*,[102] which challenges the unquestioning importation of Western legal concepts and norms into China.

Deng's and Zhu's views, however, do not represent all those who are committed to the Chinese tradition and are concerned about China's destiny in the modern world. For example, the leading neo-Confucian philosophers of the mid-twentieth century advocated unequivocally that China should embrace Western-style constitutionalism and democracy, and argued that such a movement would not be inconsistent with the Confucian humanistic tradition and that it would actually enable the Chinese cultural tradition to fulfil itself better and to reach a higher plane of development.[103] Mou Zongsan,

99. See generally Pitman B. Potter, *The Chinese Legal System: Globalization and Local Legal Culture* (London: RoutledgeCurzon, 2001); Chen (N4) 708–713.

100. See Deng Zhenglai, *Zhongguo faxue xiang hechuqu* [*Whither Goes Chinese Jurisprudence*] (Beijing: Shangwu yinshuguan, 2006).

101. See Deng Zhenglai, *Shui zhi quanqiuhua? He zhong fazhexue?* [*Whose Globalisation? What Kind of Legal Theory?*] (Beijing: Shangwu yinshuguan, 2009).

102. Su Li, *Fazhi ji qi bentu ziyuan* [*The Rule of Law and Its Indigenous Resources*] (Beijing: China University of Political Science and Law Press, 1996). See also Chapter 12 of this volume.

103. See Albert H.Y. Chen, "Is Confucianism Compatible with Liberal Constitutional Democracy?" (2007) 34:2 *Journal of Chinese Philosophy* 195–216.

probably the most sophisticated philosopher among them, wrote that although the Rule of Law, constitutionalism, human rights, and democracy "originated in the West, once they have appeared they are no longer localized; so long as they are the truth, then they are universal; so long as they are universal, every nation and people should recognize and accept them".[104] Thus, the crux of the matter is whether values like the Rule of Law are universal to humankind, or whether they are culturally specific to Western civilisation.

It is significant that the official and mainstream scholarly discourse of law in China in the last three decades has not resisted Western notions of the Rule of Law on cultural grounds. Baptised in the Marxist tradition, most Chinese scholars of law adopt a critical perspective towards the law, legal and political institutions, and legal culture of "feudal" China (referring to the long pre-modern era of imperial rule), and accept that modern ideas of the Rule of Law that emerged in the era of the "bourgeois revolutions" represented forces of historical progress.[105] The official and scholarly reservation regarding total conversion to Western notions of law and legality stems rather from fidelity to socialism.

What is currently advocated in China is not the Rechtsstaat, but the socialist Rechtsstaat, not Rule of Law, but socialist Rule of Law.[106] Thus, embracing the Rule of Law does not mean giving up or diminishing the leadership of the CCP. On the contrary, the Chinese authorities' "conversion" to legality may be interpreted as an attempt to use the legitimacy of law to bolster the legitimacy of the CCP at a time when the ideological attraction of communism has all but disappeared.[107] Further, although notions of checks on and supervision of the exercise of power have been incorporated into official discourse in contemporary China,[108] issues like "separation of powers" and "multi-party

---

104. Mou Zongsan, *Zhengdao yu zhidao* [*The Way of Politics and the Way of Governance*] (Taipei: Taiwan xuesheng shuju, revised edition, 1991) preface to the new edition, 21.

105. See generally Chapter 6 of this volume.

106. See forum on this topic cited in N58; the Supreme People's Court's Third Five-year Reform Outline Plan for 2009–2013 (N82). For a controversial speech on "The Difference Between Socialist Rule of Law and Capitalist Rule of Law" by Zhu Suli, Dean of the Law School at Peking University, see www.chinaelections.org/newsinfo.asp?newsid=130716, last accessed 12 May 2009.

107. See generally Bin Liang, *The Changing Chinese Legal System, 1978–Present: Centralization of Power and Rationalization of the Legal System* (London: Routledge, 2008).

108. See, for example, the Supreme People's Court's Third Five-year Reform Outline Plan for 2009–2013 (N82); the National People's Congress Standing Committee's Report to the National People's Congress in March 2009, available at: www.npc.gov.cn/npc/xinwen/syxw/2009-03/16/content_1493462.htm, last accessed 4 May 2009.

elections" are still within the "forbidden zone" of discourse. Thus, in the report of the NPCSC presented to the annual session of the NPC in March 2009, Wu Bangguo, Chairman of the NPCSC, emphatically declared that China "would definitely not adopt a Western-style political system, and would definitely not practice multi-party politics, 'separation of three powers' or bicameralism".[109]

The Chinese legal system today may be characterised as (1) a "modernising" or "developing" legal system, (2) a "socialist" legal system, and (3) a "Chinese" legal system that exhibits characteristics of Chinese culture. It is a modernising or developing legal system in the sense that it has not yet reached a mature state of development as measured by modern standards of legality or the Rule of Law as understood both inside China (among top Chinese officials and scholars) and internationally (among foreign observers of China's legal development). It is a socialist legal system, both because this is how the Chinese Government and scholars describe it, and because from a comparative perspective, it is the legal system of a communist one-party state rather than one of a Western-style liberal democracy. It is also a legal system that is still very much "Chinese", in the sense that it bears characteristics that are explicable in terms of traditional Chinese culture.

Three examples may be given to illustrate the thesis that the Chinese legal system is still in the process of development or modernisation and is not yet sufficiently developed even by the standards proclaimed by its government. First, the system of legal norms is still incomplete, and in some areas the NPC or its NPCSC has not yet enacted relevant laws (even though there may exist lower-level norms such as regulations enacted by the State Council). The areas of freedom of publication and freedom of association — very important civil liberties recognised in the Constitution itself — furnish such examples.[110] Second, despite the enactment of the Law on Legislation 2000 which in theory delineates the scope of power of various authorities in the making of legal norms and provides for the possibility of review of inconsistent norms, in

---

109. National People's Congress Standing Committee's Report, *ibid*. This position has been reiterated in the Xi Jinping era.

110. Regarding the freedom of association, the main piece of administrative regulations was the Regulations on the Management and Registration of Social Organizations (1998), but no relevant laws have been enacted by the NPC or NPCSC. Regarding freedom of speech and publication, one of the demands put forward by the signatories of the famous "Charter '08" (*lingba xianzhang*) was the enactment of a Press Law and a Publications Law. For the Chinese text of the Charter, see *Kaifang zazhi* [*Open Magazine*], Hong Kong, January 2009, 8–10.

practice there is not yet in operation any effective system by which the legality or constitutionality of legal norms or rules may be challenged and reviewed.[111] Third, despite the significant growth in the number of legal personnel, such as judges, procurators, and lawyers, and the steady improvement in their average educational and professional qualifications, legal talent is very unevenly distributed across the country and concentrated in large cities and economically prosperous parts of the nation. In the rural areas and poor areas of the country, the legal infrastructure is much less developed than in large cities and rich areas of the country.[112]

Regarding the "socialist" nature of the legal system, this is evident from the tension between the supremacy of the law (which is a core element of the Rule of Law) and the supremacy of the CCP in the Chinese legal system. The principle of the leadership of the Party is not only proclaimed in all important official discourse relating to law, but is also institutionalised in the authority of Party committees and Party secretaries at different levels of the State hierarchy and in non-governmental but State-sponsored institutions.[113] Even the NPC — the "supreme organ of State power" under the Constitution — and local people's congresses are subject to the leadership of the Party,[114] which in practice means, *inter alia*, that the Party can decide from time to time how much freedom of debate will be allowed in the congresses and how vigorously they will be allowed to exercise their supervisory powers over State organs. The courts and the judiciary are also expressly subject to CCP leadership and are called upon to realise the requirements of the "three supremes" — the supremacy of the Party's cause, the supremacy of the interests of the people, and the supremacy of the Constitution and the law.[115]

The CCP jealousy guards its monopoly of power and is careful not to allow any other State organs to acquire too much power. For example, the courts have not been given complete freedom to deal with socially controversial or

111. See Chen (N8) 132–138.

112. See generally Zhu (N76).

113. See Chen (N8) 96–111.

114. See, for example, the NPCSC's Report to the NPC in March 2009 (N108).

115. See, for example, the Supreme People's Court's Third Five-year Reform Outline Plan for 2009–2013 (N82).

politically sensitive cases that citizens would like to litigate.[116] The Party does not want to encourage litigants to use the judicial system to fight for their rights in such cases. It should also be noted that there is no law regulating the power or operation of the Party, and unlike acts of administrative organs which can be challenged under the Law of Administrative Litigation, acts of Party organs and officials as well as the rules or policies made by them are not justiciable before the courts. The highest priority accorded to the maintenance of Party monopoly of power at all costs necessarily leads to excessive restrictions on civil liberties and human rights. As Susan Shirk points out:

> China's leaders face a troubling paradox. The more developed and prosperous the country becomes, the more insecure and threatened they feel. The PRC today is a brittle, authoritarian regime that fears its own citizens ... Chinese leaders are haunted by the fear that their days in power are numbered.[117]

Finally, vestiges of traditional Chinese culture still shape the life of law and society in China today. For example, the official emphasis on mediation of civil disputes, both before disputes get into court and after litigation has commenced when mediation will still be conducted by the court, is partly explicable in terms of the long Chinese tradition of mediation, the Confucian preference for mediation and harmony, and the Confucian aversion to confrontation and litigation.[118] Furthermore, the contrast between the rule of *guanxi* and the Rule of Law has often been drawn in the discussion of law in China.[119] Traditional Chinese culture privileges *guanxi* or personal and social relationships or connections and de-emphasises law. *Guanxi* may be used to find solutions to problems that might otherwise be dealt with by impersonal law and law-related processes, or even to by-pass or violate the requirements of the law.

---

116. See generally Randall Peerenboom, "More Law, Less Courts: Legalized Governance, Judicialization, and Dejudicialization in China" in Tom Ginsburg and Albert H.Y. Chen (eds.), *Administrative Law and Governance in Asia: Comparative Perspectives* (London: Routledge, 2009) ch. 9, 175–201.

117. Susan L. Shirk, *China: Fragile Superpower* (Oxford: Oxford University Press, 2007) 5, 7.

118. See generally Albert H.Y. Chen, "Mediation, Litigation, and Justice: Confucian Reflections in a Modern Liberal Society" in Daniel A. Bell and Hahm Chaibong (eds.), *Confucianism for the Modern World* (Cambridge: Cambridge University Press, 2003) ch. 11, 257–287.

119. See generally Albert H.Y. Chen, "Rational Law, Economic Development and the Case of China" (1999) 8 *Social and Legal Studies* 97–120; Michael Trebilcock and Jing Leng, "The Role of Formal Contract Law and Enforcement in Economic Development" (2006) 92 *Virginia Law Review* 1517.

The prevalence of *guanxi* in Chinese society is well known and is sometimes regarded as an obstacle to the Rule of Law. Finally, the legalist tradition in China of Rule *by* Law, of law being used by power-holders as an instrument of power while the power-holders themselves stand above the law, still survives to a considerable extent today.[120]

## CONCLUSION

In the first 30 years of the history of the PRC, law in China was interesting from the perspective of comparative law precisely because it was so different from law in other countries of the world. Such "deviance" or "abnormality" was indeed fascinating for overseas scholars and observers, but the people of China paid an extremely heavy price for it. The Cultural Revolution era was without doubt one of the darkest episodes in Chinese history and in the history of civilisation. The suffering and tragedy of lawlessness testifies to the value of law and legality.

In 1979, the following passage appeared in an article published in the official *Beijing Review* magazine:

> History always leaves behind something instructive. We have paid dearly, but we have learnt important lessons which we did not understand before. … There must be a legal system and its genuine enforcement. These are convictions gained at the cost of our people's blood and lives.[121]

The decision taken by the CCP in the late 1970s to re-build a legal system from scratch may be interpreted partly as a response to the lessons of the Maoist era, and partly as a move to provide the legal basis for economic development and foreign investment in the new era of reform and opening. As demonstrated above, since 1978 there has been a steady and consistent trend of increasing emphasis on legality and the Rule of Law, and of expansion and improvement of laws and legal institutions in the PRC. Whereas the first 30 years of legal history in China was a case of "deviance" or "abnormality" relative to other countries in the world, the developments in the next 30 years have brought into existence a legal system that looks more and more similar to the legal systems

120. See generally Chen Hongyi (Albert H.Y. Chen), "Modern Reflections on the Ancient Legalist Tradition" in Chen Hongyi, *Falixue de shijie* [*The World of Jurisprudence*] (Beijing: Zhongguo zhengfa daxue chubanshe, 2003) 151–177 (in Chinese).

121. "Prospect and Retrospect: China's Socialist Legal System" (1979) 22:2 *Beijing Review* 25, at 27.

of other countries. Ironically, this seems to suggest that Chinese law is now less interesting from the perspective of comparative law.

There is, however, another way to look at this movement of Chinese law and the Chinese legal system towards "normality" and towards "convergence" with worldwide trends and practices relating to law and legality. This is to understand the deep significance for China and for the world of China's "conversion" to the universalist ideals of human rights and the Rule of Law. The 1991 White Paper on "Human Rights in China"[122] begins:

> It has been a long-cherished ideal of mankind to enjoy human rights in the full sense of the term. Since this great term — human rights — was coined centuries ago, people of all nations have achieved great results in their unremitting struggle for human rights. ... [N]umerous people with lofty ideals are still working determinedly for this cause.

The 2008 White Paper on the Rule of Law[123] begins:

> The rule of law signifies that a political civilization has developed to a certain historic stage. As the crystallization of human wisdom, it is desired and pursued by people of all countries.
>
> The Chinese people have made protracted and unremitting struggles for democracy, freedom, equality, and the building of a country under the rule of law. They know well the significance and value of the rule of law, and thus cherish the fruits they have achieved in building China into a country under the rule of law.

These statements reflect the genuine desire of the Chinese leadership to promote the Rule of Law and some degree of human rights in China and to participate in international and global discourse on the Rule of Law and human rights as a responsible and respectable member of the international community. At the same time, the same leadership is also committed to retaining the CCP's monopoly of political power in China. Taken together, there is still much room for growth and improvement in Chinese law and legal institutions in the foreseeable future as the Chinese legal system is still in the process of modernisation. Further progress will undoubtedly be made in this regard as China moves further towards what Professor Peerenboom calls the

122. Information Office of the State Council (N37).

123. *White Paper* (N30).

"thin version" of the Rule of Law.[124] As Professor Lubman states in his book on legal reform in post-Mao China, *Bird in a Cage*,[125] the future of the "cage" and where the bird will fly remain to be seen.

## Acknowledgement

This chapter was first published as "Legal Thought and Legal Development in the People's Republic of China, 1949–2008" in John Gillespie and Albert H.Y. Chen (eds.), *Legal Reforms in China and Vietnam: A Comparison of Asian Communist Regimes* (2010), chapter 3, pp. 51–77. This edited version is reprinted with permission from the publisher, Routledge.

124. Peerenboom (N11) 2–6.
125. Lubman (N92).

# 10

# Socialist Law, Civil Law, Common Law, and the Classification of Contemporary Chinese Law

# INTRODUCTION

The question of how the diverse legal systems of the countries of the world can be classified into families or types of legal systems stands at the core of comparative law scholarship. As pointed out in a leading text in this field: "In a sense, classification is the ultimate purpose of any kind of comparative scholarship: comparison implies a statement about the relationship between peculiar objects of study, their resemblances and their differences".[1]

Before the fall of communism in the former Soviet Union (or USSR) and Eastern Europe, the dominant paradigm in comparative law scholarship in the West classified the world's legal systems into the Civil Law Family, the Common Law Family, the Socialist Law Family, and other residual categories (such as traditional, religious, or some *sui generis* forms of legal systems).[2] A number of leading comparativists located the legal system of the People's Republic of China (PRC) among the residual categories rather than the Socialist Law Family, despite the Chinese Communists' professed commitment to Marxism-Leninism.[3] This view was grounded on the sharply divergent paths that the Soviet Union and the PRC took in the late 1950s, when China began to discard the Soviet concept of "socialist legality".[4] Some scholars also questioned the validity of the orthodox distinction between the Civil Law Family and the Socialist Law Family.[5] It was argued that given the Civil Law roots of the socialist legal systems in the Soviet Union and other Eastern European countries, and "the continuing relevance in socialist law of civil law rules, methods, institutions, and procedures",[6] socialist legal systems should not be placed outside the Civil Law Family.

---

1. R.B. Schlesinger, H. Baade, M. Damaska, and P. Herzog, *Comparative Law* (Mineola, N.Y.: Foundation Press, 5th edition, 1988) 68.
2. See, for example, René David and J.E.C. Brierley, *Major Legal Systems in the World Today* (London: Stevens and Sons, 3rd edition, 1985); K. Zweigert and H. Kötz, *An Introduction to Comparative Law*, translated by Tony Weir (Oxford: Clarendon Press, 2nd revised edition 1992).
3. This approach was adopted in both of the works cited in N1.
4. For Soviet legal history and modern Chinese legal history, see respectively Harold J. Berman, *Justice in the U.S.S.R.* (Cambridge, Mass.: Harvard University Press, revised edition, 1963); Albert H.Y. Chen, *An Introduction to the Chinese Legal System* (Hong Kong: LexisNexis, 5th edition, 2019) ch. 3.
5. See, for example, John Quigley, "Socialist Law and the Civil Law Tradition" (1989) 37 *American Journal of Comparative Law* 781.
6. *Ibid.*, 808.

Since the age of colonisation and imperialism that began 500 years ago, Western Europeans have introduced their legal ideas and institutions to all corners of the earth. There is hardly any country in the world today that has not incorporated elements of Western law to some extent in their own legal systems. Both Civil Law and Common Law were products of Western civilisation, but they have been transplanted to many non-Western jurisdictions. For example, if one looks at East and Southeast Asia today, Japan, South Korea, and Taiwan have legal systems that, at least in terms of formal legal rules and institutions, closely resemble the Civil Law system, whereas Hong Kong (as a Special Administrative Region of China), Malaysia, and Singapore are widely regarded as fully Common Law jurisdictions.

In the case of China, the legal tradition that had thrived for more than two millennia was largely abandoned in its desperate attempts at modernisation in the course of the twentieth century. From the point of view of legal concepts and doctrines, the legal system developed by the Nanjing Nationalist Government of the Republic of China (ROC) in the late 1920s and early 1930s was one among the Civil Law family of legal systems.[7] After the Chinese Communists established the PRC in 1949, the Soviet Union was the main source of external influence in Chinese legal system building, until the late 1950s when the socialist legality model was repudiated. This model was only rehabilitated after the end of the Cultural Revolution era in 1977.[8]

Some of the first laws enacted by the PRC since 1978 were still closely modelled on the corresponding laws in the Soviet Union. Examples were the Criminal Code and the Code of Criminal Procedure (both promulgated in 1979).[9] In the 1980s and 1990s, the policy of economic reform and opening to the outside world brought about fundamental changes in Chinese society. At the same time, much progress was made in legal system building. In the legal field, there was much interaction and scholarly and professional exchange between China and the Western world, including countries belonging to both the Civil Law and Common Law families of legal systems.

To what extent can the Soviet heritage still be identified in the contemporary Chinese legal system? To what extent has this system incorporated elements

---

7. See, for example, William S.H. Hung, *Outlines of Modern Chinese Law* (Arlington, Va.: University Publications of America, 1976; Shanghai: Kelly and Walsh, reprint of original, 1934).
8. See generally Albert H.Y. Chen, "The Developing Legal System in China" (1983) 13 *Hong Kong Law Journal* 291.
9. See the discussion below on the Soviet heritage of contemporary Chinese law.

of the Civil Law family and the Common Law family? To what extent is the distinction between Civil Law and Common Law still significant, given the globalisation of the law in fields as varied as trade, investment, and finance, on the one hand, and human rights and constitutionalism, on the other? Finally, to what extent is the Chinese legal system still constrained by indigenous tradition and circumstances so that external influences, whether Socialist, Civil Law, or Common Law, are only of limited significance? It is the purpose of this chapter to tackle these fundamental questions.

## THE SOVIET HERITAGE

Unlike Eastern European countries which decided after their communist revolutions to retain most of their original laws,[10] all the pre-existing laws of the Nationalist (Kuomintang or KMT) regime were abolished when the PRC was established. Preceding the 20-year period of the abandonment of socialist legality from 1957 to 1976, there was a brief "Golden Age" of legal system construction in the middle of the 1950s.[11] This was a time when China was attempting to learn from and to borrow the ideology, institutions, and practices of the Soviet Union in many domains of political, economic, and social life. The Soviet model was also followed in law-related matters. Soviet legal scholars were invited to teach in Chinese law schools, and Soviet legal literature was translated into Chinese for use as teaching materials in legal education. In law drafting, Soviet legislative texts were also heavily relied on as reference materials.

A comparison of the text of the first Constitution of the PRC enacted in 1954 with the USSR Constitution of 1936 would reveal a remarkable degree of similarity in terms of both structural arrangement and substantive content. The 1954 Constitution was passed at the First Plenary Session of the National

10. As pointed out by Quigley (N5).

11. The term "Golden Age" was used to describe Chinese legal developments in the mid-1950s in Jerome A Cohen, *The Criminal Process in the People's Republic of China 1949–1963* (Cambridge, Mass.: Harvard University Press, 1968) 11. However, it was only a Golden Age in a relative sense when compared to the situations in China in the early 1950s and the late 1950s (and all the way until 1977). It was not a real Golden Age in terms of there being highly satisfactory progress in the construction of a legal system.

People's Congress (NPC), during which Liu Shaoqi, then President of the PRC, said to the Congress:

> When the Constitution Drafting Committee worked on the draft, it used as reference materials the earlier and later constitutions of the Soviet Union and the constitutions of other people's democracies. Obviously, the experience of the advanced socialist countries headed by the Soviet Union has been of great assistance to us. Our draft constitution combines Chinese experience and international experience. Our draft constitution is not only the product of the people's revolutionary movement in our nation, but is also a product of the international socialist movement.[12]

The same session of the NPC also enacted five basic "organic laws" relating to the structural organisation of the State: the Organic Laws of the NPC, the State Council, the People's Courts, the People's Procuratorates, and the Organic Law of Local People's Congresses and Local People's Councils. Soviet influence was significant in shaping the content of these laws. The contemporary significance of such Soviet influence lies in the fact that there is a high degree of continuity and similarity between the 1954 Constitution and the current 1982 Constitution (which differs substantially from the 1975 Constitution that reflected Maoist and Cultural Revolution ideology, and is also closer to the 1954 Constitution than to the 1978 Constitution in affirming the concept of socialist legality), and between the organic laws mentioned above and the current organic laws on the NPC (1982), State Council (1982), People's Courts (1979), People's Procuratorates (1979), and Local People's Congresses and Local People's Governments (1979).

The Soviet influence on the making of these basic Chinese laws accounts for the fact that even today, the constitutional organisation of the PRC replicates to a significant extent that of the former USSR. Soviet constitutional doctrine rejected the "bourgeois concept" of separation of powers, and concentrated (at least in theory) all power in the Supreme Soviet, which appointed the Council of Ministers and leading members of the Supreme Court and the Procurary, and to which these executive, judicial, and procuratorial organs were all accountable. Similarly, the Chinese Constitution establishes the NPC as the

---

12. My own translation from Chen Hefu (ed.), *Zhongguo xianfa leibian* [*Collection of Chinese Constitutions*] (Beijing: Zhongguo shehui keshe chubanshe, 1980) 248.

"supreme organ of State power",[13] and confers constitutional status not only on the State Council and the Supreme People's Court but also on the Supreme People's Procuratorate,[14] all appointed by and responsible to the Congress.[15]

In a sense, and particularly in its initial stage, the post-Mao drive in rehabilitating socialist legality and reconstructing a legal system in China can be seen as a continuation of the project of legal modernisation (on the basis of the Soviet model) that started in the 1950s but was largely abandoned after the Anti-Rightist Movement of 1957 and completely repudiated in the Cultural Revolution era (1966–1976). It was as if after having gone astray for twenty years, China decided in the late 1970s to return to the trajectory of legal development that had started in the 1950s. This interpretation can be supported by examining two basic codes of law enacted in 1979, the Criminal Code and the Code of Criminal Procedure.

The origins of these codes were explained by Peng Zhen, Chairman of the Legislative Affairs Commission of the NPC Standing Committee (NPCSC), when he presented the bills to the NPC.[16] He pointed out that more than thirty drafts of a criminal code had been produced before the Cultural Revolution, and the bill for the Criminal Code now presented was based on the 33rd draft. The bill for the Code of Criminal Procedure was also a revision based on various drafts produced before the Cultural Revolution. The extent of Soviet influence on the drafting of these laws can easily be inferred from this historical background. Harold Berman, a leading authority on Soviet law, pointed out

13. Art. 57 of the 1982 Constitution of the PRC.

14. See arts. 3, 85, 124, 127, 130, and 132 of the 1982 Constitution. The 5th Amendment of the 1982 Constitution enacted in 2018 establishes the National Supervisory Commission (NSC) and local supervisory commissions under it. See arts. 123–127 of the Constitution as amended in 2018. (By virtue of the 2018 Amendment, arts. 123–138 of the 1982 Constitution have been re-numbered arts. 128–143. In this chapter, references to articles of the Constitution are references to the articles as numbered in the 1982 Constitution.) The NSC has the same constitutional status as the Supreme People's Court and the Supreme People's Procuratorate, and is also appointed by and responsible to the NPC.

15. For the principle of responsibility to the Congress, see arts. 3, 128, and 133 of the 1982 Constitution. For the appointment of members of the court and the procuratorate, see art. 35 of the Organic Law of the People's Courts (1986); art. 21 of the Organic Law of the People's Procuratorates (1986). The President of the Supreme People's Court and the Procurator-General of the Supreme People's Procuratorate are elected by the NPC, while other members of the court and the procuratorate are appointed by the NPCSC.

16. *Main Documents of the 2nd Session of the 5th National People's Congress of the PRC* (Beijing: Foreign Languages Press, 1979) 190–220.

that it is clear from a textual analysis of the respective Chinese and Soviet codes on criminal law and criminal procedure that the Chinese draftsmen had the corresponding Soviet codes in front of them when they drafted their own codes: even the chapter headings and the order of arrangement of articles in the codes were similar, although the Chinese codes were shorter and simpler.[17]

Soviet influence on Chinese law can be traced not only in legislative texts and legal concepts but also in institutions, procedures, and practices. A prominent example is that of the institution of the procuracy or procuratorate. The constitutional status and functions of the contemporary Chinese procuratorate can only be fully understood in the light of its Soviet origin, as it has no direct counterpart in Common Law or Civil Law systems.[18] The procuratorates are mentioned in the Chinese Constitution as a branch of the State, in the same way as the courts and the people's governments are mentioned as branches of the State, and all three types of organs (procuratorial, judicial, and executive) are similarly derived from and subordinated to the people's congress system.[19] The procuratorates are constitutionally defined as the legal supervisory organs of the State.[20] They not only conduct public prosecutions but exercise supervision over the work of the public security organs (police) and the organs responsible for labour reform and imprisonment (prisons, etc.), and can protest (appeal) against a court decision by way of cassation or by way of adjudicatory supervision in both criminal and civil proceedings (even where the government is not a party). They may also (instead of leaving it to the police) initiate direct investigation into certain categories of offences committed by government officials.[21]

These were also functions of the Soviet procuracy, a key institution in the Soviet legal system and almost a fourth branch of the State.[22] The Russian procuracy was first established in early eighteenth century by Tsar Peter

17. Chen (N8) 297.

18. For the Soviet Procuracy, see W.E. Butler, *Soviet Law* (London: Butterworths, 2nd edition, 1988) ch. 7.

19. Art. 3 of the 1982 Constitution.

20. Art. 129 of the 1982 Constitution.

21. See generally the Organic Law of the People's Procuratorates, the Code of Criminal Procedure, the Code of Civil Procedure, and the Law on Prisons.

22. See Butler (N18) 107–116; M.A. Glendon, M.W. Gordon, and C. Osakwe, *Comparative Legal Traditions* (St. Paul, Minn.: West Publishing Co., 1982) 322–324.

the Great. It was to be "an eye of the Tsar"[23] for the purpose of supervising conformity to the law. Although the procuracy was abolished in 1917 immediately following the revolution, it was re-established in the 1920s, and its powers and functions were expressly recognised in the 1936 Constitution of the USSR. It was often regarded as the most prestigious component of the Soviet legal profession. Its powers were even more extensive than its Chinese counterpart, in that it could protest governmental acts, whether normative (legislative) or non-normative (in relation to a specific case only), as being contrary to law.

Other examples abound of Chinese adoption of Soviet legal thinking and practice. The extensive power of the Supreme People's Court (sometimes acting jointly with the Supreme People's Procuratorate) to issue "judicial interpretations" of the law can be traced to the practice of Supreme Courts in the USSR issuing similar "guiding explanations". In both the Chinese and Soviet systems, the interpretations or guidelines may be issued without reference to the context of any specific case that has actually arisen, and some of these interpretations are in fact in the form of comprehensive and systematically laid out rules for the purpose of supplementing and elaborating on legislative texts.[24]

In relation to appeals against decisions at first instance in criminal and civil cases, both the Chinese and Soviet systems draw a distinction between judgments that have not yet become legally effective and those that have already become so.[25] Judgments do not become legally effective until the time limit for lodging a cassational appeal or cassational protest has expired, or the right of cassational appeal or protest has been exhausted. The accused (in a criminal case) or either party (in a civil case) may appeal against a judgment that has not become legally effective, and the procuracy may protest such a judgment (in both criminal and civil cases). After a judgment has become legally effective (whether or not there has already been a cassational appeal or protest), the procurary still has the right to protest the judgment "by way of

23. Butler (N18) 107.

24. For the Soviet practice in this regard, see Butler (N18) 104–106; Quigley (N5) 792. For the Chinese practice, see Chen (N4) 141–152; Liu Nanping, *Judicia l Interpretation in China* (Hong Kong: Sweet & Maxwell Asia, 1997).

25. For the Chinese system, see the Code of Criminal Procedure and the Code of Civil Procedure. For the Soviet system. See also Butler (N18) ch. 19; Harold J. Berman, *Soviet Criminal Law and Procedure* (Cambridge, Mass.: Harvard University Press, 2nd edition, 1972).

adjudicatory supervision". Courts can also review such judgments on their own initiative, and parties may petition the court or the procurary to request such review or protest. This peculiar system is shared by China and the Soviet Union.

Other significant features of Chinese law which have counterparts in Soviet law include the following:

(1) the distinction between detention and arrest:[26] under certain conditions the police may detain suspects for a limited period, but confinement for a longer period is only lawful if it takes the form of an arrest approved by the procuratorate or the court;

(2) the concept of dereliction of duty crimes in criminal law[27] (by officials, resulting in serious loss of public property and serious damage to the interests of the State and the people) which corresponds to that of "official crimes" in Soviet law;

(3) the existence of the "administrative" measure of "re-education through labour", which could result in a person being deprived of their liberty (on the ground, for example, that the person persistently refuses to work and disrupts production) and sent to re-education through labour for one to three years by the judicial administrative organs under the Ministry of Justice without going through any court procedure.[28] The Soviet counterpart was the "anti-parasite legislation" under which persons could be sent for re-settlement for two to five years (on the ground that they have avoided socially useful work and committed anti-social acts which enabled them to lead a parasitic way of life);[29]

(4) the existence of the "administrative penalty" of detention by the police for up to 15 days for minor violations of the law under the Security Administration Punishment Regulations, which corresponds to a similar sanction of administrative confinement of 15 days (but by order of a court) in the Soviet Union;[30]

26. See the PRC Code of Criminal Procedure; Butler (N18); Berman (N25).
27. See pt. II, ch. 9 of the Criminal Code (originally pt. II, ch. 8 before its amendment in 1997).
28. "Re-education through labour" was subsequently abolished in December 2013; see Chen (N4) 257–258, 341.
29. Butler (N18) 315; Berman (N25) 8.
30. Berman (N25) 10.

(5) all land and natural resources are the subject of socialist public ownership, which takes the form of either State ownership (meaning ownership by the whole people) (which is applicable to land in the urban areas) or collective ownership by labouring masses (applicable to land in rural areas).[31] The doctrine of socialist ownership was first developed in the Soviet Union, where it included both State ownership and ownership by cooperatives and mass organisations;[32]

(6) before the marketisation of the Chinese economy, the concept in Chinese criminal law of crimes against the socialist economic order (e.g., speculation for profit)[33] had its counterpart in the concept of "economic crimes" in Soviet criminal law,[34] and the law of economic contracts in both countries was designed to ensure the fulfilment of State economic plans by State enterprises. Also, in both countries, economic law (as distinguished from civil law) was conceived as the area of the law that regulated the "vertical" relationships between different organs and units situated in a hierarchical administrative order designed to implement State economic plans.[35] These features are now losing their relevance as economic reforms proceed in both countries.

## THE CIVIL LAW TRADITION

When China started to re-build its legal system in the late 1970s on the basis of work done in the 1950s, one possible scenario was that it would develop a legal system closely modelled on that of the Soviet Union, where socialist legality was in a much more advanced state of development relative to that of China. However, it soon became apparent that the economic reforms introduced in China were faster and much more liberal than those in the Soviet Union, in terms of the development of a non-State sector in the economy, the shift

31. Arts. 9 and 10 of the PRC Constitution.
32. Zweigert and Kötz (N2) 303; Butler (N18) 180–181.
33. See pt. II, ch. 3 of the 1979 Criminal Code, titled "Crimes Against the Socialist Economic Order". The 1997 amendment changed the title of this chapter to "Crimes Against the Socialist Market Economic Order", and substantially altered the content of the chapter.
34. Berman (N25) 171–175.
35. See Chen (N4) 287–289.

from a planned economy to one increasingly regulated by market forces, and the rapid expansion of foreign investment in and trade with China. In these circumstances, Soviet legal models would not be adequate for China's bold experiment in "socialism with Chinese characteristics". At the same time, the broader and deeper contact between China and the Western world enabled China to learn actively from the West — a situation that was impossible and unimaginable in the 1950s. Hence, the external influences on Chinese legal development were much richer and more diverse.

This provides the context for our investigation of the extent of Civil Law influences on contemporary Chinese legal development. Indeed, given the Civil Law roots of the socialist legal systems in the former Soviet Union and Eastern European countries, and in the light of those scholarly opinions that deny that the degree of socialist legal innovation was such as to justify the creation a new family of legal systems in the classification scheme,[36] it is not easy to separate the socialist Soviet and the Civil Law elements in the Chinese legal system. One example is the right of the victim in a criminal case to bring a supplementary civil suit for damages at the same time as the criminal prosecution by the State against the suspected offender, so that the criminal charge and the civil claim can be tried at the same time.[37] This procedure is both a feature of Soviet litigation procedure and of Civil Law jurisdictions such as France, Italy, and Germany. The inquisitorial nature of litigation procedure in China and the Soviet Union can also be traced back to the same Civil Law origin. A further example is supplied by China's General Principles of Civil Law (GPCL). It has been pointed out that the sources of reference in drafting the GPCL were the civil codes of the Soviet Union, East Germany, Hungary, and Czechoslovakia.[38] However, the structures of and concepts employed by these codes are themselves clearly products of the Civil Law tradition.

Civil codes in the Civil Law tradition usually deal with basic concepts such as civil law, the "civil juristic act" (*Geschäftshandlung* in German, a concept that has no parallel in Common Law), and limitation periods, as well as the core areas of the civil law — the law of obligations (including both the law of contract and the law of tort in Common Law), the law of things (also called the law of real rights or rights in *rem*), the law of persons (including

36. See, for example, Quigley (N5).

37. Art. 77 of the PRC Code of Criminal Procedure (1996 version).

38. As pointed out in Qian Mingxing, *Wuquanfa yuanli* [*Principles of the Law of Rights over Things*] (Beijing: Beijing daxue chubanshe, 1994) 58.

family law), and the law of inheritance. This framework has been inherited by some Eastern European communist countries (e.g., East Germany, Poland, Romania), which retained their original civil codes after their communist revolutions.[39] Although the Soviet Union repudiated its pre-revolutionary laws, the Civil Code enacted by the Russian Federation in 1922 was modelled on the civil codes of Germany and Switzerland as well as the draft imperial Russian code.[40] It included a General Part dealing with the subjects of rights, legal transactions, and limitation periods, and Special Parts on the law of things, the law of obligations, and the law of inheritance, respectively.

The GPCL enacted in China in 1986 was not a full civil code (which has yet to be enacted, although drafts of a comprehensive civil code were produced in the mid-1950s, the early 1960s, and the early 1980s),[41] but was designed to provide a basic framework and a set of general principles to facilitate the operation of a number of laws in the area of civil law that had already been enacted (such as the Marriage Law, the Succession Law, and various laws on contracts and intellectual property). The GPCL, like civil codes in other socialist countries, has adopted the structure and concepts of the Civil Law tradition.[42] This may be seen from its general principles (on the subjects of civil law, the civil juristic act, limitation period, etc.), its treatment of the law of obligations, and, to a limited extent, its treatment of ownership and other property rights. However, the GPCL conceded to socialist ideology by omitting any express mention of the fundamental Civil Law concept of "rights over things". This reflected the political situation in the mid-1980s. In the 1990s, "rights over things" have been openly recognised and affirmed in Chinese textbooks on civil law and in articles in leading law journals, and a law on "rights over things" has been in the process of being drafted.

When we turn to Chinese legislative developments in the 1990s, we can find further evidence of transplanted elements of the Civil Law tradition that went beyond the Civil Law elements in Soviet law.[43] The laws providing such evidence include enactments in the area of civil and commercial law and

39. As pointed out in Quigley (N5) 801.

40. See Butler (N18) 176.

41. Chen (N4) 290.

42. See the collection of articles in the special issue on "The Emerging Framework of Chinese Civil Law" (1989) 52:2/3 *Law and Contemporary Problems*.

43. See generally Albert H.Y. Chen, "The Developing Chinese Law and the Civil Law Tradition" in M. Brosseau, S. Pepper, and S.K. Tsang (eds.), *China Review 1996* (Hong Kong: Chinese University Press, 1996) 29.

enactments in the area of administrative law. The first law that deserves to be examined in this regard is the Guarantee Law (GL; alternatively translated as the Law on Security for Credit) enacted in 1995. The enactment of this important law in the area of civil law can be regarded as an intermediate step between the introduction of rudimentary principles on ownership and property rights in the GPCL and the eventual enactment of a comprehensive law on "rights over things" (*wuquan*) either on its own or as part of a civil code.

The GL provides for five legal devices that can serve as security for credit: guarantee, mortgage (*diya*), pledge (*zhiya*), lien, and deposit. The Civil Law background of this law is most obvious in the nature of the distinction drawn by the law between mortgage and pledge, and its sub-dividing pledge into pledge of movables (*dongchan zhiya*) and pledge of rights (*quanli zhiya*).[44] In Common Law jurisdictions, the concept of pledge (involving delivery of the pledged property to the pledgee) applies only to movable property. Rights (e.g., shares in a company) may be assigned by way of security for credit, but this is regarded as a mortgage rather than a pledge. However, the division of pledges (*Pfand* in the German language) into pledge of movables and pledge of rights can be found in the German Civil Code, as well as the Civil Code that is currently in force in Taiwan today (originally made by the Nanjing Nationalist Government of the ROC in 1929–1931 and modelled on the German and Swiss Civil Codes). Furthermore, the provision in the GL that in effect imposes an obligation on the mortgagor to maintain the economic value of the mortgaged property and not to cause its depreciation,[45] and another provision that any new building erected on the mortgaged property after the creation of the mortgage will not form part of the mortgaged property,[46] both have almost identical counterparts in the Civil Code of Taiwan.[47] The similarity is all the more striking as the laws are both written in the Chinese language.

The second law to be considered is the Company Law enacted in China at the end of 1993. The law provides for two types of companies, the limited liability company (*youxian zeren gongsi*) and company limited by shares (*gufen youxian gongsi*). Members of both kinds of companies are called shareholders (*gudong*), but the concept of shares (*gufen*) is only applicable to the company limited by shares (the interest of shareholders in the limited

44. See chs. 3 and 4 of the GL.

45. Art. 51.

46. Art. 55.

47. Arts. 871, 872, and 877.

liability company is called "capital contribution", *orchuzi* or *chuzi'e*, instead). This contrasts with the case of companies in English law, under which both private companies and public companies are companies limited by shares. However, the limited liability company in Chinese law has a direct counterpart in the limited company (*youxian gongsi*) in Taiwan, the *Gesellschaft mit beschränkter Haftung* (GmbH) in Germany, the *société à responsabilité limitée* (SARL) in France, and the *yugen-gaisha* in Japan. As for the Chinese company limited by shares, its counterparts in Taiwan, Germany, France, and Japan are the company limited by shares (*gufen youxian gongsi*), the *Aktiengesellschaft*, *société anonyme*, and *kabushiki-gaisha*, respectively. There are also technical terms in the German and French languages corresponding to the concepts of capital contribution and shares in the context of the two types of Chinese companies. Hence, the Chinese Company Law falls clearly within the Civil Law rather than the Common Law tradition, at least in terms of the basic conceptual framework it employs.[48]

Another area of Chinese law that has made considerable progress, beginning from the enactment of the Law of Administrative Litigation in 1989, is administrative law. The structure, sub-divisions, and basic concepts in Chinese administrative law are largely alien to the Common Law tradition, and can only be understood from the perspective of the Civil Law tradition. For example, administrative liability (resulting from a breach of administrative law) stands together with civil liability and criminal liability as the three principal forms of legal liability in China.[49] Key concepts in Chinese administrative law, such as administrative act, administrative penalty (alternatively translated as administrative punishment), administrative enforcement, administrative procedure and State compensation, are also borrowed from the Civil Law tradition. For example, administrative liability flows from a contravention of traffic regulations (part of administrative law), and the administrative penalty of revocation of the driving licence may be imposed by the relevant administrative authority. The Law of Administrative Punishment defines the

48. For a more detailed analysis and references to sources on the systems in Taiwan, Japan, Germany, and France, see Chen (N43) 37–41.

49. See, for example, State Law and Administrative Law Unit of the Legislative Affairs Commission of the NPC Standing Committee (ed.), *Zhonghua renmin gongheguo Xingzheng chufa fa shiyi* [*Commentary on the Law of Administrative Punishment of the People's Republic of China*] (Beijing: Falü chubanshe, 1996) 1; Chen Yanqing and Zhang Shicheng, "The Significance and Basic Principles of the Administrative Punishment Law" (1996) 2 *Zhongguo faxue* [*Chinese Legal Science*] 40, at 41.

right to be heard on the part of the licensee in such a situation,[50] and the Law of State Compensation provides compensation for any unlawful exercise of the power to revoke licences.

The Law of State Compensation enacted in 1994 is an important law that demonstrates the Civil Law orientation of the developing Chinese legal system. Even before the enactment of this law, compensation could already be claimed in respect of unlawful administrative action under the GPCL[51] and the Law of Administrative Litigation.[52] The State Compensation Law elaborates and extends further the right to State compensation.

The concept of State compensation does not exist in Common Law jurisdictions. The traditional Common Law approach upheld a doctrine of the State's immunity: the sovereign could do no wrong, and officials could only be sued in respect of their personal liability for unlawful acts committed in the execution of their duties that resulted in harm or loss to persons affected. This position was only abandoned in Britain and the United States with the enactment of the Crown Proceedings Act 1947 and the Federal Tort Claims Act 1946, respectively. The contemporary Common Law position is therefore that the State is vicariously liable to affected persons for tortious acts committed by its employees in the execution of their duties (such as unlawful acts of its officials).

In Germany, the liability of the State for loss caused by officials' breach of duty was affirmed as early as 1910 when a State compensation law was enacted. The German State compensation system has been widely admired and adopted as a model in Japan, Korea, and Taiwan (Taiwan enacted a State Compensation Law in 1981). In France, the Law of State Compensation was developed by its Conseil d'État through case law and is highly sophisticated.[53]

The Chinese State Compensation Law of 1994 extends the citizen's right to compensation to situations other than administrative acts, such as assault, battery, and torture. It also goes beyond the existing law in extending the cause of action to cover acts done by judges and procurators in the course of their work. Two principal types of compensation are provided for — administrative compensation and criminal procedure compensation.[54]

---

50. See the Law of Administrative Punishment enacted in 1996; Chen (N4) 311–313.

51. Art. 121.

52. Ch. 9 of the Law of Administrative Litigation (1989).

53. For further information on the comparative materials, see Chen (N43) 47–50.

54. See chs. 2 and 3 respectively of the State Compensation Law (1994).

Administrative compensation is available in respect of violations of the rights of the body of the person or property rights by administrative organs or their personnel in the course of the exercise of their powers and duties. Examples are unlawful detention, battery, or other acts of violence, and unlawful administrative penalties (administrative penalties include fines, confiscation of property, and revocation of licences).

Criminal procedure compensation is available in respect of violations of rights by officials in the course of criminal investigation, procuratorial work, adjudication, and management of prisons. Examples include wrongful detention and arrest, wrongful conviction, torture, wrongful fines, or freezing of property.

Given the Civil Law orientation of Chinese legal reforms introduced in the late Qing dynasty and the Republican period before the Communist revolution, the decline of the socialist family of legal systems formerly led by the Soviet Union, and the existence of a Civil Law system operated fully in the Chinese language in Taiwan (which therefore facilitates learning and borrowing by mainland China), it may be expected that the Civil Law tradition will be the dominant influence in the development of Chinese law in the foreseeable future. The following passage, written by two leading mainland Chinese jurists in 1993, is instructive:

> As two stages in the history of the development of Chinese law, the law of the Guomindang [Kuomintang] period and the present law of the PRC have a necessary historical and cultural connection. This is an objective manifestation of the national character and continuity of Chinese legal development in the contemporary age. It is true that for long periods after 1949, particularly in the 1960s, Chinese legislative work and the legal system could not undergo normal development. But since the 1980s, the legislative work and legal system of contemporary China have been able to develop rapidly and to perfect themselves step by step, even though there have existed many deficiencies in this process. It may now be predicted that the rapid progress of the Chinese legal system in future is an irreversible trend of history. And in this process, the characteristics of the Civil Law tradition will continue to stamp themselves upon the Chinese legal system.[55]

55. My own translation from Jiang Ping and Mi Jian, "The Civil Law Tradition and Contemporary Chinese Law (part II)" (1993) 3 *Zhengfa luntan* [*Tribune of Political Science and Law*] 1, at 7. The article has been reprinted in (1993) 11 *Faxue* [*Science of Law*] 82.

## COMMON LAW INFLUENCE

The predominance of Soviet and Civil Law influences on modern Chinese law has eclipsed that of Common Law, and this is easily explicable with reference to the twentieth-century history of Chinese legal and political development. However, this does not mean that the Common Law tradition will not exert any force in shaping the future of Chinese law. Indeed, the American version of the Common Law tradition has even become a leader in Western law and in the international arena of legal ideas.[56] Increasing numbers of Chinese law students and professors are receiving training in the United States, and the global influence of American law firms and their legal culture is also increasing. Since July 1997, the PRC has one Special Administrative Region (SAR) in which the Common Law is fully in force — that of Hong Kong (HKSAR). Therefore, the potential for Common Law influence on future Chinese legal development cannot be under-estimated in the domains of legal theory, legal culture, legal scholarship, and legal institutions as well as in substantive and procedural law.

A clear sign of Common Law influence may be seen in the move to reduce the inquisitorial elements and increase the adversarial elements in both criminal and civil procedure in the Chinese courts. In the domain of litigation procedure, the inquisitorial system has been a hallmark of the Civil Law tradition, and the adversarial system that of the Common Law tradition.

The inquisitorial system was developed by the Canon Law in medieval Europe. According to this approach, the main objective of the judicial process is to find out the truth about the facts of the case, and to reach a just decision by applying the law to the facts. The court has the duty and power to actively investigate the case and is not limited to the evidence adduced by the parties to the litigation. The inquisitorial system in Continental Europe is often characterised by a pre-trial stage (not open to the public) of full investigation into the case by an examining judge (e.g., the *judge d'instruction* in France), who interrogates the accused (in a criminal case) or the parties (in a civil case) and other persons, and also collects evidence from other sources. The dossier of the case compiled in the course of the investigation has enormous weight in the subsequent trial. During the trial, the court plays an active role in questioning parties and witnesses, and the scope for examination and cross-

56. Ugo Mattei, "Why the Wind Changed: Intellectual Leadership in Western Law" (1994) 42 *American Journal of Comparative Law* 195.

examination by the parties and their lawyers is limited. The court's inquiry is not restricted to the evidence adduced and the legal issues raised by the parties.

The adversarial system, also known as the accusatory system, originated from ancient Greek and Roman republican times, and was further developed in England as the home of the Common Law tradition. It conceives of the litigation process as a contest between the parties (whether prosecutor and accused or plaintiff and defendant), who themselves or through their lawyers provide to the court the evidence that supports their case and define the legal issues to be argued before the court. The court's function is no more than that of an umpire for the purpose of deciding which side wins and which side loses in the case. The court does not have the power to initiate the judicial process, nor does it collect evidence not supplied by the parties. During the trial, the judge maintains a low profile while the questioning and cross-examination of witnesses are conducted by the parties or their lawyers. Unlike the inquisitorial system in which non-public pre-trial investigation and written documentation play a dominant role, the Common Law judicial process emphasises public trial, oral presentation of evidence, and oral arguments in court.

Inquisitorial procedure was largely adopted by the Soviet legal system and is thus another element of affinity between the Civil Law tradition and socialist law. In China, the inquisitorial orientation of the judicial process was even more pronounced, because in addition to the Soviet heritage, both traditional legal culture and indigenous circumstances in the early history of the Chinese Communists also favoured the inquisitorial style. The traditional magistrate was at once inquisitor, prosecutor, and judge. The "mass line" has been part of Chinese Communist ideology, and its application to judicial practice meant that judges should work closely with the people, actively investigate cases (by, for example, going out of the courtroom to various places to collect evidence and interview people, or even conducting investigation on their own initiative before any suit is filed by private litigants) and see to it that justice is done.[57]

However, in recent years, there has been a move in China towards reducing the investigative role of the courts, requiring the parties (including the prosecution in a criminal case) to assume the greater share of the burden of proof, and allowing the parties to take a more active part in trial proceedings. Both scholars and officials have called for a shift from the inquisitorial system

57. Chen (N4) 263.

to the adversarial system, or at least one that incorporates more adversarial elements in the judicial process. The original system was criticised for resulting in the case being pre-judged before the actual trial, for failing to enable the litigants themselves to perform their proper roles and responsibilities, and for overburdening the court.[58]

The reform of the inquisitorial system was evidenced in the amendment to the Code of Criminal Procedure in 1996. The amended code changed the nature of the pre-trial review of cases by the court (for the purpose of determining whether the case should go to trial) from a review of the substance of the case to a review of whether the relevant formal criteria have been satisfied.[59] The amendment also shifted the primary role in questioning the accused and witnesses and in producing physical evidence from the court to the parties and their lawyers.[60]

Reform of civil procedure has also proceeded in the same direction. At an important national conference on the reform of the mode of adjudication in 1996,[61] the Vice-President of the Supreme People's Court called for a reduction of the courts' pre-trial activities in the interrogation of relevant persons, investigation, collection of evidence, and mediation. He pointed out that the Code of Civil Procedure provides that the parties have the burden of adducing evidence to prove their case,[62] although courts also have the power to investigate and collect evidence,[63] and the current situation was that parties did not do enough in providing evidence, so that judges had to do the parties' job in collecting evidence.

---

58. See, for example, Wang Liming and Yao Hui, "A Study of the Reform of the Institutional Structure of the People's Courts and the Mode of Trial" (1998) 2 *Zhongguo faxue* [*Chinese Legal Science*] 3 (pt. I) (in Chinese); (1998) 3 *Zhongguo faxue* 23 (pt. II).

59. Art. 150 of the Code. See Chen Weidong and Liu Lifa, "The Change in Judges' Judicial Investigative Power in China's Criminal Procedure" (1998) 2 *Faxue pinglun* [*Law Review*] 51 (in Chinese).

60. Art. 157 of the Code.

61. Zhu Mingshan, "Seriously Studying and Implementing the Revised Law of Criminal Procedure, Comprehensively Reforming and Improving the Mode of Adjudication" (1996) 4 *Zhongguo renmin gongheguo Zuigao renmin fayuan gongbao* [*Gazette of the Supreme People's Court of the PRC*] 121 (in Chinese). The speech dealt with the reform of the mode of adjudication in both criminal and civil cases.

62. Art. 64 of the Code.

63. Arts. 64 and 116.

## THE GLOBAL AND THE LOCAL

It may be argued that this mode of categorising the external influences that have contributed to shaping contemporary Chinese law (namely as Soviet Law, Civil Law, or Common Law) is already out-of-date, in view of the collapse of Soviet communism, the movement towards European integration, the globalisation of market capitalism, and the rapid development of international human rights law and discourse. The socialist family of legal systems hardly exists any more, while there are signs of convergence between Civil Law and Common Law.[64] From this perspective, the external forces acting upon Chinese legal development are global in nature, and the future of Chinese law becomes a function of the interplay between global forces and local contexts.

China's participation in the international trading system and its active absorption of foreign investment have inevitably generated pressure for Chinese law and legal institutions to develop in such a way as to meet foreign and international expectations, and, where relevant, to incorporate norms of international law as set out in treaties or other sources, in areas such as investment protection, intellectual property, arbitration, laws on contractual and property rights, corporate securities, banking and finance, bills of exchange, insurance, admiralty, civil aviation, etc. As China builds up its market economy, it faces problems common to the industrial nations of the West and develops similar legal solutions in areas such as environmental protection law, labour law, social security law, consumer protection law, unfair trade practices law, etc. Chinese developments in the last few decades in many areas of the law may therefore be interpreted as a sign of the globalisation of modern legal doctrines and institutions that were born in the West but have universal applications to all humankind.

The globalising force of legal values and institutions that have universal relevance is not only applicable to the laws relating to commerce, finance, and investment but has extended to the domain of human rights. The extension of legal safeguards for the rights of the accused in criminal proceedings and the expansion of judicial scrutiny of governmental actions are both worldwide trends in contemporary legal development, and some major legislative steps in China suggest that China is moving with the tide. For example, the 1996

64. See generally Jonathan E. Levitsky, "The Europeanization of the British Legal Style" (1994) 42 *American Journal of Comparative Law* 347; Pierre Legrand, "European Legal Systems are not Converging" (1996) 45 *American Journal of Comparative Law* 52.

Law on Administrative Punishment rationalises the system for administering administrative penalties and clearly delineates the scope of power of different levels of State organs in enacting rules on administrative penalties.[65] The Law also states clearly for the first time in the PRC's history that administrative penalties imposed without legal authority or in breach of legal procedures are invalid[66] and affirms the principles of justice and openness in the imposition of administrative penalties.[67] Legal rules authorising administrative penalties must be published in order to be effective.[68] Persons on whom administrative penalties are to be imposed have the right to be informed of the charge against them and the right to be heard by an impartial authority.[69]

In 1996, China also extensively revised the Code of Criminal Procedure.[70] A form of the presumption of innocence was introduced (by the provisions that no person should be considered guilty until and unless convicted by a court, and that where there is insufficient evidence of guilt, the accused should be acquitted by the court).[71] The moment at which lawyers may participate in the criminal process was moved from (at least) seven days before the formal trial to the time when a coercive measure (e.g., detention or arrest) is used against the suspect or immediately after the first interrogation of the suspect by the authorities.[72] The notorious procedure of "shelter and investigation"[73] (or detention for a considerable period by the police for examination) has been abolished.[74] In line with international trends, particularly in Civil Law countries, the status of the victim of crime in relevant criminal proceedings has been enhanced by expanding the right of private prosecution.[75] Further, providing that the

65. See generally Chen (N4) 310–313.

66. Art. 3.

67. Art. 4.

68. Art. 4.

69. Arts. 6, 31, 32, and 42.

70. See generally Chen (N4) 244–255; H.L. Fu, "Criminal Defence in China: The Possible Impact of the 1996 Criminal Procedural Law Reform" (1998) 153 *China Quarterly* 31.

71. Arts. 12 and 162 of the Code.

72. Art. 96.

73. See Albert H.Y. Chen, *An Introduction to the Legal System of the People's Republic of China* (Hong Kong: Butterworths Asia, 1998) 164–166.

74. Huang Taiyun, "Major Reforms of the System of Criminal Procedure" (1996) 2 *Zhongguo faxue* [*Chinese Legal Science*] 29, at 32–33.

75. Arts. 88, 145, and 170 of the Code of Criminal Procedure (1996 version).

victim (even in a public prosecution) is party to the case,[76] they can appoint a lawyer to represent them in the proceedings[77] as well as petition to procuratorate to request it to protest (by way of appeal) a relevant court decision.[78]

The extensive amendment introduced in 1997 to the Criminal Code is also in some respects a sign of progress.[79] For the first time in Chinese criminal law, the Code states the three basic principles of criminal law — *nulla poena sine lege* (there is no crime or punishment in the absence of an express legal provision on it, which principle is expressly affirmed in many criminal codes in Civil Law countries),[80] the equality of all persons before the applicable law,[81] and the appropriate correspondence (which can also be translated as "proportionality") between the punishment of an offender, on the one hand, and the crime committed by and the criminal responsibility borne by the offender, on the other hand.[82] Another important feature of the amendment is the substitution of the concept of "crimes endangering State security"[83] for the original concept of "counter-revolutionary crimes", which was abandoned because being a "counter-revolutionary" is a political rather than a legal concept, and the definition of counter-revolutionary crimes emphasised the counter-revolutionary objective in the mind of the offender rather than their actual behaviour.[84]

Can it therefore be said that the forces of legal globalisation are now helping to modernise and civilise China's legal system, which has lagged behind the rising standards of legality, rationality, and humanism that have been achieved in the West since the advent of modernity? Although there are valid points to this perspective, the theory must not be pushed too far. Post-modern thinking has warned us against the naivety, over-optimism, pride, and prejudice in the meta-narratives of modernity and Enlightenment, and the totalising discourse of reason, progress, and the necessary and inevitable trend

76. Art. 82.

77. Art. 40.

78. Art. 182.

79. See generally Chen (N4) 280–287.

80. Art. 3 of the Criminal Code (1997 version).

81. Art. 4.

82. Art. 5.

83. Pt. II, ch. 1 of the Criminal Code (1997 version).

84. Chen Xingliang, *Xingfa shuyi* [*A Commentary on the Criminal Code*] (Beijing: Zhongguo renmin gong'an daxue chubanshe, 1997) 49–50.

of history. Indeed, there has been a revealing debate[85] among Chinese legal scholars in recent decades about the extent to which post-modern philosophy is relevant to contemporary China, given that China has not yet achieved the goals of legal modernisation in the sense of constructing a "logically formal and rational" legal system in the Weberian sense (consisting of a comprehensive set of rationally constructed and general legal rules which are impartially and effectively applied to concrete situations by an independent judiciary in a predictable manner). While many Chinese scholars believe in and advocate the universality of the doctrine of the Rule of Law and are very enthusiastic about transplanting Western legal ideals to China, there are others who stress the need for any form of the Rule of Law to be indigenised, localised, and contextualised, and who even question the desirability of the uncritical endorsement of Western notions of formal legality.[86]

The view that the benefits of modern legality are universal (that the Rule of Law is, in the words of E.P. Thompson, an "unqualified human good"[87]) and the view that there is no context-free and perfectly transplantable form of legality should not however be considered contradictory and mutually exclusive. Indeed, each of the two perspectives provides a useful framework for the purpose of studying, evaluating, and mapping out the future of the contemporary Chinese legal system. Thus, based on the premise that modern legality is good and China is still far from having achieved it, we can point to various existing defects and deficiencies in the Chinese legal system and call for its improvement. For example, there is still too wide a gap between the law in the books and the law in action; many judges and lawyers are inadequate in legal competence or professional ethics; the court system is plagued by local protectionism and corruption;[88] higher courts sometimes give instructions to lower courts on how to decide particular cases; there is not yet any effective system to resolve conflicts between different legal norms at different levels of the hierarchy of the legal order; the operation of the legal system is still not

85. See, for example, Ji Weidong, "Towards 21st Century Law and Society" (1996) 3 *Zhongguo shehui kexue* [*Social Sciences in China*] 104 (in Chinese); Zhu Suli, "Postmodern Thought and the Jurisprudence and Legal System of China" (1997) 3 *Faxue* [*Jurisprudence*] 11 (in Chinese).

86. See, for instance, Su Li, *Fazhi ji qi bentu ziyuan* [*The Rule of Law and its Indigenous Resources*] (Beijing: Zhongguo zhengfa daxue chubanshe, 1996).

87. E.P. Thompson, *Whigs and Hunters: The Origin of the Black Act* (Harmondsworth: Penguin Books, 1977) 266.

88. Jerome A. Cohen, "Reforming China's Civil Procedure: Judging the Courts" (1997) 45 *American Journal of Comparative Law* 793.

completely autonomous vis-à-vis the Chinese Communist Party (CCP); full reasons for the decision are not yet given in court judgments; the death penalty is still too widely used; and judicial safeguards are not fully adequate against the unlawful deprivation of the liberty of the person.

On the other hand, the perspective that there is no universal form of modern legality enables us to identify, appreciate, and explain the special characteristics of Chinese legal culture, as well as elements of legal experimentation and innovation that have been developed to meet the unique problems of the transition from a socialist planned economy to a socialist market economy. For example, the prevalence in contemporary China of mediation as an alternative means of dispute settlement is indeed an important feature from the point of view of comparative law. The much criticised practice of adjudicative committees (consisting of the most senior judges of the court) in courts (instead of the collegiate bench that hears the case) deciding on difficult or important cases needs to be understood as a largely necessary adaptation of the judicial system to the poor quality of many judges in various localities.[89] The legal form of township and village enterprises[90] is an innovation that evolved from the "third realm" of Chinese society[91] (a realm that stands between the public realm or State sector, on the one hand, and civil society or private sector, on the other hand). The concept of land use rights (with regard to land subject to socialist public ownership) which in fact comes close to private property rights is an interesting legal experiment and an ingenious solution to problems that are unique to China's circumstances.[92]

## CONCLUSION

Like all countries in the non-Western world, modern China has incorporated into itself many elements of the Western legal tradition. The influence of the Soviet Union was significant in the early legal history of the PRC, and traces of this can still be easily identified today. The socialist legal system that was developed in the Soviet Union was itself largely shaped by the Civil Law

89. Chen (N4) 169–172.

90. See the Law of Township and Town Enterprises (1996).

91. Philip C.C. Huang, "'Public Sphere'/'Civil Society' in China? The Third Realm between State and Society" (1993) 19:2 *Modern China* 216.

92. See the Land Management Law (first enacted in 1986).

tradition, and we have seen in this chapter that the Civil Law tradition, which had already been received by China before the Communist Revolution, is now re-emerging as an important force in legislative developments in contemporary China. At the same time, elements of the Common Law tradition are also finding their way into the Chinese legal system, particularly in the area of the law of procedure. Indeed, there now exists a fully Common Law jurisdiction within the PRC — the HKSAR.

Both Civil Law and Common Law are no more than branches of the same Western legal tradition.[93] In this age of globalisation and the increasing dominance of Western legal values and institutions on a global scale, the distinction between Civil Law and Common Law is becoming less significant. At the centre of this is the contest between the global and the local. Are China and other developing countries going to converge towards the same global legal modernity, or will there be different local legal modernities? This will be a question for the future.

Professor Ugo Mattei, a leading scholar of comparative law, has proposed[94] to replace the orthodox classification of the world's families of legal systems (Civil Law, Common Law, Socialist Law, and residual categories) with a new taxonomy based on three "patterns of law" — the rule of professional law, the rule of political law, and the rule of traditional law. All three patterns of law may exist to some extent in the legal system of a particular country, and each legal system is a "plurality of patterns of law" and a "layered complexity",[95] whereby different patterns of law may be dominant at different layers of the system. In different legal systems, the three competing patterns of law may co-exist in different ratios. A legal system may be classified according to the pattern of law that enjoys "hegemony"[96] within the system.

In Mattei's theory, each social structure is also a legal structure, and a pattern of law is no more than a pattern of social control. Law, politics, and philosophical or religious tradition represent three sources of norms for the purpose of social organisation and social interaction. They correspond respectively to the rule of professional law, the rule of political law, and the rule

93. Harold J. Berman, *Law and Revolution: The Foundation of the Western Legal Tradition* (Cambridge, Mass.: Harvard University Press, 1983).

94. Ugo Mattei, "Three Patterns of Law: Taxonomy and Change in the World's Legal Systems" (1997) 45 *American Journal of Comparative Law* 5.

95. *Ibid.*, 13, 17.

96. *Ibid.*, 15.

of traditional law. The rule of professional law is exemplified by modern Western legal systems which are secularised and autonomous from politics. The rule of political law is found in many countries in Latin America, Africa, and Eastern Europe, and is characterised by the weakness of law and courts before political power. In the rule of traditional law, formal law is subordinate to informal and non-professional institutions, lawyers have a limited role to play, and the dominant social values are harmony, duties, and hierarchy. Mattei places East and Southeast Asia (including both China and Japan), India, and countries that practise Islamic law under the category of the rule of traditional law.[97]

Although one may disagree with Mattei's classification of contemporary China as under the rule of traditional law, his classification scheme does draw attention to the importance of investigating the role of law in society, different conceptions of, attitudes towards, and unspoken assumptions about the law in different cultures and societies, and the social, economic, and political context in which the formal law operates in different parts of the world. The recognition of layers and plurality within each legal system is particularly insightful. Once we are able to understand legal systems as "layered complexities" with "plural legal formants",[98] we can realise the inadequacy, for instance, of using the orthodox classification scheme and simply identifying China's legal system as a member of either the Civil Law or Socialist family of legal systems.

Mattei also criticises the orthodox classification scheme for being too Euro-American-centric, for placing the Western legal tradition in a "privileged position", and for marginalising "radically different cultures" such as China and Japan.[99] His substitute scheme would overcome this limitation if and only if one adopts a position of total neutrality in terms of value judgment as between the rule of professional law, the rule of political law, and the rule of traditional law. However, the problem is that Mattei identifies the rule of professional law with the Western legal tradition, with judicial decision-making according to law, the protection of the rights of the individual, and the subordination of political power to law. Are these not the universal goods claimed for the modern Rule of Law? Are these not the ideals postulated by the contemporary international and cross-cultural discourse of human rights? Are these not also the aspirations

97. *Ibid*. He also points out (at 40) that while both China and Japan fall within the rule of traditional law, China tends towards the rule of political law, whereas Japan tends towards the rule of professional law.

98. *Ibid*., 20.

99. *Ibid*., 8, 11, 19.

expressed in the writings of contemporary Chinese jurists? If so, then perhaps one cannot be value-neutral with regard to the three patterns of law identified by Mattei's theory. Some vision of evolution or progress of the legal civilisation of humankind will be needed. The challenge, then, for the builders of China's legal system is to articulate such a vision, and to work towards its realisation, without losing sight of the reality of context and the contingency of history.

## Acknowledgement

This chapter was first published as "Socialist Law, Civil Law, Common Law, and the Classification of Contemporary Chinese Law" in J.M. Otto, M.V. Polak, J. Chen, and Y. Li (eds.), *Law-Making in the People's Republic of China* (2000) chapter 4, pp. 55–74. This edited version is reprinted with permission from the publisher, Kluwer.

# 11

# The Law of Property and the Evolving System of Property Rights in China

## INTRODUCTION

The enactment of the Law of Property (LP) (*wuquan fa*, alternatively translated as Property Law) in March 2007 in China — after a long process stretching over 14 years[1] during which some of the most heated debates[2] in contemporary Chinese legislative history took place — has been hailed as a milestone in the development of contemporary Chinese law and as one of the most important core components of the evolving civil law in the People's Republic of China (PRC). This chapter attempts to understand some of the key concepts and provisions in the LP in the context of the evolving Chinese law relating to property rights, the changing economic system as China moves from a socialist planned economy to a socialist market economy or "socialism with Chinese characteristics", and from the perspective of comparative law. This chapter also seeks to answer the following two questions:

(1) To what extent is the LP a product of borrowing from or transplant of foreign legal ideas versus a reflection of indigenous circumstances and needs in China?

(2) To what extent has China moved away from the orthodox socialist system of public ownership of the means of production towards a regime of private property rights?

It should be noted at the outset that the property rights which this chapter focuses on are those covered by the LP or the Chinese term *wuquan* (which may be literally translated as "rights relating to *wu*" or "rights over *wu*"). *Wu* can be literally translated as "things". In the LP, *wu* includes movable property and immovable property.[3] Both species of property are tangible property. *Wuquan* is thus property (*caichan*) in a narrow sense, as distinguished from property (also *caichan* in Chinese) in a broad sense, which includes "invisible" forms of

---

1. For the history of the legislative process, see Zhihui Liu (ed.), *Wuquan fa lifa guannian yu yinan zhidu pingzhu* [*The Law of Property: A Commentary on the Legislative Concepts and Problems in the System*] (Beijing: Jiangsu Renmin Press, 2007) 15–28.
2. A famous debate was initiated in 2005 by Peking University law professor Xiantian Gong, who criticised the draft LP as an unconstitutional departure from the socialist principles enshrined in the Constitution of the PRC. See, for example, Yiqing Liu and Qinde Zhang (eds.), *Gong Xiantian xuanfeng shilu* [*Records of the Going Xiantian Storm*] (Beijing: Zhongguo caizheng jingji, 2007).
3. Art. 2 of the LP. It is also provided that rights may also be the object of *wuquan* where the law so provides.

property such as rights under shares in companies and negotiable instruments, intellectual property rights, or what are known as "choses in action" in English Common Law.[4] Indeed, from the perspective of continental European law, rights under a contract or under the law of tort (the law of contract and the law of tort both being components of the law of obligations in the civil law tradition) also fall within the concept of property in the broad sense.[5]

## THE HISTORICAL TRAJECTORY

The history of the PRC is commonly perceived as consisting of two periods: the first 30 years of Maoist rule, and the subsequent decades of "reform and opening" (*gaige kaifang*) inaugurated by Deng Xiaoping's rise to power and the Third Plenum of the Eleventh Central Committee of the Chinese Communist Party (CCP) in December 1978. As far as legal history is concerned, the existing legal system and laws of the PRC are largely a product of the era of "reform and opening",[6] although the basic institutions (such as the system of people's congresses and the legislative, administrative, judicial, and procuratorial institutions) were established in the 1950s during which China briefly followed the mode of socialist legality as practised in the Soviet Union (or USSR).

In the era of "reform and opening", the fundamental legal source of the regime of property and property rights in the PRC lies in the Constitution of the PRC enacted in 1982. This is the fourth Constitution in the history of the PRC (the former ones were enacted in 1954, 1975, and 1978), and was amended in 1988, 1993, 1999, 2004, and 2018.[7]

4. See generally E.L.G. Tyler and N.E. Palmer, *Crossley Vaines' Personal Property* (London: Butterworths, 1973) 11–14.
5. In the civil law tradition, the law of "things" (*res*) in the broad sense included the law of "things" in the narrow sense (i.e., tangible assets such as land and goods), the law of "obligations" (including the functional equivalents of the law of contract and the law of tort in the common law tradition), and the law of inheritance. See generally B. Nicholas, *An Introduction to Roman Law* (Oxford: Clarendon Press, 1962); Albert H.Y. Chen, "The Developing Chinese Law and the Civil Law Tradition" in M. Brosseau, S. Pepper, and S.K. Tsang (eds.), *China Review 1996* (Hong Kong: Chinese University Press, 1996) ch. 2, 29–59.
6. See generally Albert H.Y. Chen, "Legal Thought and Legal Development in the People's Republic of China 1949–2008" in J. Gillespie and Albert H.Y. Chen (eds.), *Legal Reforms in China and Vietnam: A Comparison of Asian Communist Regimes* (London: Routledge, 2010) ch. 3, 51–77.
7. See generally Albert H.Y. Chen, *An Introduction to the Chinese Legal System* (Hong Kong: LexisNexis, 5th edition, 2019) chs. 4 and 11.

The 1982 Constitution provides for the "socialist public ownership of the means of production" which takes two forms — ownership by the whole people (also known as State ownership[8]) and collective ownership by the labouring masses (*laodong qunzhong* or working people, alternatively translated as "ownership by collectives of labouring masses").[9] It provides that all land in the cities is owned by the State.[10] This provision actually had the effect of nationalising, without compensation, privately owned urban land on which privately owned residential buildings stood at the time of enactment,[11] while land in the rural and suburban areas is collectively owned (*jiti suoyou*).[12] The Constitution specifies: "The State may, in the public interest, requisition land for its use in accordance with law. No organization or individual may appropriate, buy, sell or lease land or otherwise engage in the transfer of land by unlawful means."[13] It goes on to say that "[s]ocialist public property is sacred and inviolable"[14] and that "[t]he State protects the right of citizens to own lawfully earned income, savings, houses and other lawful property. The State protects according to law the right of citizens to inherit private property".[15]

The first major development relating to property law after the making of the 1982 Constitution was the enactment of the General Principles of Civil Law (GPCL) in 1986. The GPCL was largely modelled on the corresponding legislation in the USSR and Eastern European communist countries, such as the Soviet Union's Basic Principles of Civil Legislation (BPCL).[16] The GPCL was designed to provide some general principles of the civil law and some rudimentary rules governing particular areas of the civil law pending the enactment of a full civil code in the continental European tradition. Chapter 5

8. See arts. 7, 9, and 10.
9. Art. 6.
10. Art. 10(1).
11. See P.A. Randolph and Jianbo Lou, *Chinese Real Estate Law* (The Hague: Kluwer, 2000) 9–11; T.A. Lo, "Debate Surrounding the New Property Law in China" (2008) 4 *Cambridge Student Law Review* 182, 187–188.
12. Art. 10(2). This rule is subject to the exception that some such land is State-owned as provided by law.
13. Art. 10(3) and (4). The prohibition on "lease" was deleted by the 1988 constitutional amendment.
14. Art. 12.
15. Art. 13.
16. Chen (N5) 30; Xianzhong Sun, *Zhongguo wuquan fa zonglun* [General Principles of Chinese Property Law] (Beijing: Law Press, 2nd edition, 2009) 190–191; E.L. Johnson, *An Introduction to the Soviet Legal System* (London: Methuen, 1969) 106.

of the GPCL is titled "Rights in Civil Law" (*minshi quanli*), and it consists of four sections: property ownership and property rights related to ownership; rights over obligations (*zhaiquan*) (such as rights under a contract); intellectual property; and rights of the person (*renshen quan*). In the first of the four sections, there are express provisions on ownership by the State, by collectives of labouring masses and by individual citizens.[17] The property rights related to ownership provided for in this section include operational rights under *chengbao* contracts (*chengbao jingying quan*) related to farmland, forests, grassland, waste land, etc.; State-owned enterprises' operational rights (*jingying quan*) with regard to property which the State has granted to them for the purpose of operational management; and rights arising from "neighbourhood relationships" (*xianglin guanxi*) between occupiers of neighbouring land.

The *chengbao* or "contract responsibility" system that has given rise to the *chengbao* contracts mentioned above was a major measure of economic reform in China's rural areas that began in the early 1980s.[18] Under this system, the relevant authority in the rural areas enters into contracts with peasant households pursuant to which the households enjoy the right to possess, control, use, and derive economic benefits from (collectively owned) land covered by the contract subject to payment of consideration. For example, the *chengbao* contractor may decide what to grow on the land, sell his produce directly in the market, and receive the income. The system may be understood as a partial privatisation of agricultural production which had been collectivised since the mid-1950s, and contributed significantly to China's rapid economic growth since the 1980s. The *chengbao* system in agriculture, though an important element of China's economic reform involving re-allocation of property rights, was largely defined by CCP and government policy documents rather than by formal law, at least until the enactment of the Law of Rural Land Contracts (LRLC) in 2002, discussed further below.

In section 2 of chapter 5, the GPCL provides for two forms of property-related security for credit — mortgage (*diya*) of property and lien (*liuzhi*).[19] The context in which these provisions appear is that of security for payment of debt,

17. Arts. 73–75 of the GPCL. Art. 77 provides for the property of "social organizations" (including "religious organizations").

18. See, for example, Chen (N7) 297–298.

19. Art. 89(2) and (4). The term mortgage (*diya*) in the GPCL covers both mortgage (in English law) and pledge, and no distinction has been drawn between these two security devices in the GPCL. See Chen (N5) 35.

and the section they appear in is that on "rights over obligations" rather than "property rights". The concept of *wuquan* is absent from the GPCL.

In 1986, the Land Administration Law (LAL) (alternatively translated as the Land Management Law) was also enacted. The LAL sets out the rules of ownership of both urban and rural land (under State ownership and collective ownership, respectively), as well as the procedural and substantive rules governing the use of land for various purposes. *Chengbao* contracting of land by collectives or individuals for agriculture, forestry, animal husbandry, and fishery is authorised by the LAL.[20] The LAL also provides for requisitioning of land — particularly agricultural land under collective ownership — by the State for purposes of construction and development, and the compensation therefor.

The next major development in Chinese property law came in 1988. In April 1988, the National People's Congress (NPC) adopted the first set of amendments to the 1982 Constitution. One amendment recognises the importance and legitimacy of "the private sector of the economy" as a "supplement to the socialist public economy". The other amendment provides that "the right to the use of land may be transferred according to law".[21] The latter amendment is the constitutional foundation for the emergence of a new regime of private property rights in urban land that will be elaborated below.

Following this constitutional amendment, the LAL was amended in December 1988. According to the amendment, the right to use (*shiyong quan*) State-owned or collectively owned land may be transferred (*zhuanrang*) in accordance with the law.[22] It also specified the establishment of a system for the use of State-owned land by payment of consideration (*youchang shiyong*).[23]

The legal regime for the acquisition of the right to use State-owned land by real estate developers was established by the State Council when it enacted the Provisional Regulations on the Grant (*churang*) and Transfer (*zhuanrang*) of the Right to Use State-owned Land in Cities and Towns (PRCT) in 1990. The PRCT provides for various aspects of the operation of the system, including the duration and conditions of grant, modes of grant (agreement, tender, and auction), assignment (transfer), leasing and mortgage of land use rights, and requisition by the State. The system of land use rights resembles and

20. Art. 12.

21. At the same time, the prohibition on lease of land in art. 10 of the Constitution was deleted by this constitutional amendment.

22. See art. 2 of the LAL, as amended in 1988.

23. *Ibid*.

was probably influenced in its conception by colonial Hong Kong's system of property rights, in which almost all land was owned by the Crown (i.e., the Hong Kong Government), and it granted (sold) Crown leases of long duration to developers.[24] It should also be noted that the PRCT distinguishes between granting (*churang*) land use rights which is subject to payment of consideration, and the allotment (*huabo*) of land use rights which does not require payment of consideration.[25] Although some of the provisions in the PRCT overlap with and may be considered superseded by later laws, some provisions are still relevant and applicable today. For example, the maximum terms of the grant for various purposes are still governed by the PRCT:[26] 70 years for residential land; 50 years for industrial land; 50 years for land for educational, technological, cultural, public health, and sporting purposes; 40 years for land for commercial, tourism, and entertainment purposes; and 50 years for combined or other purposes.

In 1993, the 1982 Constitution was amended for a second time. The most significant amendment was that the PRC would now practise a "socialist market economy" instead of practising a "planned economy on the basis of socialist public ownership" as previously provided in the Constitution.[27] The family household *chengbao* contract responsibility system, which had already been practised in the 1980s, was also given constitutional recognition in this amendment.[28]

In 1994, the Law on the Administration of Urban Real Estate (LAURE) was enacted. The LAURE further elaborates the legal regime for granting land use rights in urban areas to developers and the sale of units in buildings erected on such land to ultimate users, as well as raising these stipulations to the level of law[29] (from the level of administrative regulations). It also provides for property transactions regarding apartments in buildings and houses, including

---

24. See, for example, Albert H.Y. Chen, "The Basic Law and the Protection of Property Rights" (1993) 23 *Hong Kong Law Journal* 31, 40–41.
25. Land use rights obtained by such allotment may not be assigned, leased, or mortgaged; see art. 44 of the PRCT (which is subject to the exception in art. 45). The circumstances in which allotment of land use rights is permissible are now set out in the Law on the Administration of Urban Real Estate (art. 23) and the LAL (art. 54, as amended in 1998).
26. Art. 12.
27. See the amendment to art. 15 of the Constitution.
28. See the amendment to art. 8 of the Constitution.
29. Laws are enacted by the NPC or the NPC Standing Committee (NPCSC), while administrative regulations are enacted by the State Council. See arts. 58 and 89 of the Constitution.

assignment (*zhuanrang*), sale of uncompleted flats, mortgage and leasing, and for property agents and registration of title.

The Guarantee Law (GL) (*danbao fa*) was enacted in 1995. The GL sets out the rules governing the creation, effect, operation, and enforcement of five legal devices that can serve as security for credit: guarantee (*baozheng*); mortgage (*diya*); pledge (*zhiya*); lien (*liuzhi*) and deposit (*dingjin*). Although the concept of *wu* or *wuchan* is not used in the GL, the mortgage, pledge, and lien provided for in it may be used as security over movable and immovable property. Furthermore, whereas the concept of mortgage (*diya*) as used in the GPCL does not distinguish between mortgage and pledge, these two security devices are now separately provided for in the GL. The pledge is further divided into pledge of movables (*dongchan zhiya*) and pledge of rights (*quanli zhiya*).

In 1998, the LAL was amended extensively for better regulation of rural land use. New chapters on the protection of arable land and on arrangements for supervision and inspection were added. Some provisions in the amendment also relate to the *chengbao* system, and the term of a *chengbao* contract is specified as 30 years.[30] Further, provisions were added to ensure that adjustments to *chengbao* arrangements and the grant of *chengbao* contracts to persons outside the village were subject to the approval of a two-thirds majority in a villagers' meeting.[31] The amendment also improves the compensation arrangements for the requisition of peasants' land for purposes of development.[32]

In 1999, a third amendment to the Constitution was introduced. The following aspects of the amendment are noteworthy for this discussion. First, the original provision that "the basis of the socialist economic system of the PRC is socialist public ownership of the means of production" was amended by adding that China is in "the preliminary stage of socialism" and its economic system shall be one in which "public ownership is the main body and the economic activities of multiple forms of ownership shall develop

30. Art. 14 of the amended law. In 1993, when many *chengbao* contracts were due to expire, the CCP decide that they should all be renewed for 30 years; see the speech of Suinian Liu introducing the bill for the LRLC to the NPCSC on 26 June 2001, reprinted in Chaoying Wang (ed.), *Zhonghua renmin gongheguo nongcun tudi chengbao fa shiyong wenda* [*Practical Questions and Answers on the PRC Law of Rural Land Contracts*] (Beijing: Zhongguo fazhi, 2002) 204.

31. Arts. 14 and 15 of the new law.

32. Arts. 46–49 of the amended law. Dissatisfaction with the compensation arrangements has been a primary source of conflict and popular unrest in China's rural areas as land was taken away from peasants for purposes of development.

together".[33] Second, it is provided that the individual and private sectors of the economy (*geti jingji* and *siying jingji*) constitute important components of the socialist market economy.[34] Third, the provision on the *chengbao* system in the rural areas is further refined.[35]

Codification of the legal rules governing the *chengbao* system came in 2002 with the enactment of the LRLC. The declared objective of the LRLC is to ensure that peasants under the *chengbao* system can enjoy secure and long-term rights to the use of *chengbao* land.[36] The terms of the *chengbao* contracts in different contexts are provided for: 30 years for farmland; 30 to 50 years for grassland; 30 to 70 years for forest land.[37] Different types of *chengbao* arrangements are also provided for, including family *chengbao* (under which every peasant household in a village has a right to be granted a *chengbao* contract)[38] and *chengbao* of wasteland by means of tender, auction, or open discussion (*gongkai xieshang*).[39] The LRLC provides in detail for the rights of the *chengbao* contracting party and for the extent to which rights under a *chengbao* contract may be sub-contracted, leased, exchanged, assigned, used as capital contribution to a business, mortgaged, or inherited. These provisions suggest that the rights under a *chengbao* contract are in the nature of *wuquan* or property right,[40] but the term *wuquan* does not appear in the LRLC itself.

The fourth amendment to the 1982 Constitution was introduced in 2004. This amendment contains provisions that are directly relevant to the recognition and protection of private property rights. The most important amendment for this purpose is article 13, the original text of which has been quoted above. The article is now replaced by the following provision:

> The lawful private property (*siyou caichan*) of citizens shall be inviolable. The State shall protect in accordance with law citizens' private property rights (*siyou caichanquan*) and inheritance rights. The State may, as necessitated by public

33. See amended art. 6 of the Constitution.
34. See amended art. 11 of the Constitution.
35. See amended art. 8 of the Constitution.
36. Art. 1.
37. Art. 20.
38. Arts. 5–6 and ch. 2 of the law.
39. Ch. 3 of the law.
40. See also Suinian Liu's speech (N30) 206–207. According to Liu, the intention of the LRLC was to protect family *chengbao* as *wuquan*, while other forms of *chengbao* would only enjoy protection as *zhaiquan* (i.e., as a contractual rather than property right).

> interest, expropriate (*zhengshou*) or requisition (*zhengyong*) citizens' private property and pay compensation therefor.

Another provision introduced by the constitutional amendment requires the payment of compensation for expropriation or requisition of land by the State in the public interest (in circumstances not limited to those in which private property is affected).[41]

Following this constitutional amendment in 2004, the LAL was slightly amended in the same year to bring it in line with the language of the constitutional amendment. The existing version of the LAL provided for requisition (*zhengyong*) of land by the State. The constitutional amendment introduces the distinction between requisition (*zhengyong*) (where the State assumes control of the property without however transferring ownership of the property to itself) and expropriation (*zhengshou*) (where ownership of the property concerned is transferred to the State).[42] The term *zhengyong* as used originally in the LAL covered both situations, and thus the LAL was now amended to refer to and include both requisition and expropriation.

The above legislative and constitutional developments thus paved the way for the enactment of the LP in 2007. Indeed, prior to 2007, no code of property law existed governing movable and immovable property (or *wu* as now defined in the LP) in a comprehensive and systematic manner. Unfortunately, the relevant law has developed in a piecemeal fashion, and the relationship between different these pieces is not easy to understand. In the course of China's economic reform, new practices were often introduced by policy documents and administrative directives before relevant laws and regulations were enacted. For example, in the case of the *chengbao* contracting system for rural land, the practices evolved in the 1980s, the system only received constitutional recognition in 1993, and the precise rights of the *chengbao* contracting party were not specified in law until the enactment of the LRLC in 2002. In the case of the urban land reform involving grants of State-owned land to developers, the system gradually evolved since the constitutional amendment of 1988, and has been regulated by the LAL, PRCT, and LAURE. It is noteworthy that the PRCT — a set of provisional regulations enacted by the State Council in 1990 — is still in force despite the enactment of the LAURE

41. See the amendment to art. 10(3) of the Constitution.

42. See Dingjian Cai, *Xianfa jingjie* [*A Commentary on the Constitution*] (Beijing: Law Press, 2nd edition, 2006) 197.

and LAL, and has not been updated or made no longer "provisional". Similarly, the GPCL has not been updated, even though the GL has superseded the provisions in the GPCL on mortgage and lien, and even though the land use rights in State-owned land granted to developers should certainly fall within the concept of "property rights related to property ownership" in the GPCL.

Although the relevant law is by no means well-organised or clear, the trend since the 1980s of giving increasing scope to private (as distinguished from State-controlled) economic activities on land and to the private sector of the economy is obvious based on these legislative and constitutional developments. There has also been an increasing degree of reliance on the Constitution and the law for the purpose of legitimising, specifying, and clarifying the private property rights that have been allowed to emerge in the course of economic reform.

## THE TRANSLPANTED AND THE INDIGENOUS

The LP consists of 247 articles divided into 19 chapters (and two supplementary provisions) organised into five parts. The five parts are titled "General Principles", "Ownership" (*suoyou quan*), "Rights of Use and Enjoyment over Things" (*yongyi wuquan*), "Security Rights over Things" (*danbao wuquan*), and "Possession". In designing the basic conceptual framework of the LP, Chinese lawmakers borrowed much from continental Europe, particularly the German legal tradition, while the provisions on socialist ownership can be traced back to the legal tradition of the former USSR. On the other hand, the substantive content of the LP caters for the indigenous circumstances of China, and there are important innovations in the LP for this purpose.

The concepts of *wuquan* and *wuquan fa* can be traced directly to the German Civil Code (*Bürgerliches Gesetzbuch*, or BGB) enacted in 1896 rather than the Roman civil law tradition generally. Although both the BGB and the French Civil Code enacted in 1804 were shaped by this civil law tradition which distinguished between actions *in rem* (concerning *jura in re* or real rights) and actions *in personam* and had developed the concept of *jura in re aliena* (rights of a limited nature over property owned by another, or rights *in rem* other than ownership),[43] the French Civil Code does not contain any textual equivalent of *wuquan fa*. The French Civil Code consists of three books, titled "Of Persons", "Of Property (*biens*) and the Different Modifications

43. See Nicholas (N5) 140–141.

of Property (*propriété*)", and "Of the Different Modes of Acquiring Property (propriété)", respectively.[44] Property (*propriété*) (alternatively translated as "ownership") is defined in Book II of the Code as "the right of enjoying and disposing of things in the most absolute manner, provided they are not used in a way prohibited by the laws or statutes".[45] Property (*biens*) is divided into movable and immovable property.[46] Apart from ownership, Book II of the Code also provides for usufruct (*usufruit*),[47] right of common (*usage*), right of habitation, and servitudes. Pledge and mortgage of property are provided for in Book III of the Code (on the modes of acquisition of property), which also contains the law of contract. All these species of property rights are embraced by the concept of *droits réels* (real rights or rights *in rem*, as distinguished from *droits de créance*, or rights of credit, such as rights under a contract)[48] developed by French jurists, although this term does not appear in the French Civil Code itself.

The BGB, hailed as the most "scientific" legal code of its kind[49] at the time of its enactment almost one century after the French Civil Code, is divided into five books, titled "The General Part", "The Law of Obligations" (*Recht der Schuldverhältnisse*), "The Law of Things" (i.e., "The Law of Property"; *Sachenrecht*), "Family Law", and "The Law of Succession", respectively.[50] For this discussion, Book III (*Sachenrecht*) of the BGB deserves closer examination.

*Sachenrecht* means the law relating to *Sachen*, which means corporeal things including movable things (*bewegliche Sachen*) and immovable things (*unbewegliche Sache*), such as land (*Grundstücke*).[51] Book III of the BGB starts with the topic of possession, then stipulates general principles relating to rights over land. It then provides for ownership (*Eigentum*) and

---

44. See *The Code Napoleon* (London: C. Hunter, 1824) in HeinOnline.
45. Art. 544.
46. Art. 516.
47. Art. 578: "Usufruct is the right of enjoying things of which the property is in another, in the same manner as the proprietor himself, but on condition of preserving them substantially." The concept of usufruct can be traced back to ancient Roman law; see Nicholas (N5) 144–148.
48. See generally C. Dadomo and S. Farran, *French Substantive Law* (London: Sweet & Maxwell, 1997) 11–15, 62–69.
49. E.J. Cohn, *Manual of German Law* (London: British Institute of International and Comparative Law, 2nd revised edition, 1968) vol. 1, 57.
50. See generally *The German Civil Code*, translated by Simon L. Goren (Littleton, Colo.: F.B. Rothman, revised edition, 1994).
51. N. Foster, *German Law and Legal System* (London: Blackstone Press, 1993) 238.

other kinds of property rights such as hereditary building rights (*Erbbaurecht*), servitudes (*Dienstbarkeit*), usufruct (*Niessbrauch*), mortgage (*Hypothek*), land charge (*Grundschuld*), annuity charge (*Rentenschuld*), right of pledge on movable things (*Pfandrecht an beweglichen Sachen*), and right of pledge on rights (*Pfandrecht an Rechten*), etc. In German jurisprudence, ownership and the various forms of property rights over things owned by another person (*beschränkte dingliche Rechte*) are collectively known as *dingliche Recht* (real rights). These may be further divided into rights of use and enjoyment (*Nutzungsrechte*) and disposal or security rights (*Verwertungsrechte* or *Sicherungsrechte*).[52]

Thus, a comparison of the text and jurisprudence of the *Sachenrecht* and the Chinese *wuquan fa* would suggest that each of the following pairs of German and Chinese legal terms has the same meaning: *Sachen* (*wu*); *Sachenrecht* (*wuquan or wuquanfa*); *dingliche Recht* (*wuquan*); *Eigentum* (*suoyou quan*); *Nutzungsrechte* (*yongyi wuquan*); and *Sicherungsrechte* (*danbao wuquan*). Article 2 of the LP, which consists of three provisions and reads as follows, can therefore be easily understood in the light of German jurisprudence:

> This Law governs the civil relationships arising from the assignment of rights over, and the use of, things (*wu*).
>
> The things mentioned in this Law include immovable and movable property. Where the law provides for rights as objects of rights over things (*wuquan*), such law shall be applied.
>
> The *wuquan* mentioned in this Law means the right of the right-holder to control directly specific things to the exclusion of others, and includes ownership (*suoyou quan*), rights of use and enjoyment over things (*yongyi wuquan*) and security rights over things (*danbao wuquan*).

It should be pointed out, however, that although the term and concept of *wuquan* only appeared for the first time in PRC legislation when the LP was enacted, this was by no means the first time Chinese lawmakers borrowed from the German concepts of *Sachen* and *Sachenrecht*. In fact, the draft civil code produced in 1911 just before the fall of the Qing dynasty (when Chinese lawmakers borrowed actively from the contemporary Japanese and continental

52. *Ibid.*, 239, 251.

European law in their attempt to modernise the Chinese legal system) already included *wuquan* as one of its five books, which were on general principles, rights over obligations (*zhaiquan*), rights over things (*wuquan*), family law, and law of succession, respectively.[53] It is no coincidence that the BGB and the Japanese Civil Code (1896)[54] consist also of five books on exactly the same subjects as the draft civil code of China.[55] The same structure of books and their topics appeared in the Civil Code of the Republic of China (ROC) enacted in 1929–1930 by the Nanking Government of the Chinese Nationalist Party (Kuomintang or KMT). This is the civil code which, subject to various amendments, is still in force in Taiwan today.

Book III of the ROC Civil Code as originally enacted in 1929 consists of 210 articles divided into ten chapters:[56] (1) general principles; (2) ownership (*suoyou quan*); (3) superficies (*dishang quan*);[57] (4) emphyteusis (*yongdian quan*); (5) easements (*diyi quan*, alternatively translated as "servitudes"); (6) mortgage (*diya quan*);[58] (7) pledge (*zhiquan*), including pledge of movable property (*dongchan zhiquan*) and pledge of rights (*quanli zhiquan*); (8) *dianquan*;[59] (9) lien; and (10) possession. Although the terms *yongyi wuquan* and *danbao wuquan* do not appear in the text of the Civil Code itself, they are used by jurists in Taiwan to explain and categorise the various species of *wuquan* in

53. For the history of the drafting of civil codes in twentieth-century China, see, for example, Sun (N16) 188–190; Jianyuan Cui, Weixing Shen, Hongliang Wang, and Xiao Cheng, *Wuquan fa* [*Property Law*] (Beijing: Tsinghua University Press, 2008) 10; Honglie Yang, *Zhongguo falü fazhan shi* [*History of the Development of Chinese Law*] (Shanghai: Shanghai Shudian, originally published in 1930, reprinted in 1990).

54. See H. Oda, *Japanese Law* (London: Butterworths, 1992) 133.

55. While the five books of the draft civil code of the late Qing dynasty followed the same order as the BGB, in the Japanese Civil Code, the order of the second and third books was reversed: book II is on the law of things, and book III is on the law of obligations.

56. For the Chinese text of this part of the Civil Code, see *Zuixin liufa quanshu* [*The New Book of Six Codes*] (Taipei: Dazhongguo Tushu Gongsi, 1989) 94–101.

57. This is the right to use another's land for the purpose of owning buildings or other works, trees, or bamboo on the land, as provided in art. 832.

58. This is the perpetual right to cultivate or raise livestock on another's land subject to payment of rent, as provided in art. 842.

59. This is the right to possess, use, and derive benefits from another's immovable property on payment of consideration, as provided in art. 911. (Art. 912 provides that the duration of the *dianquan* shall not exceed 30 years, while art. 913 touches upon the issue of redemption.) This is a form of security for credit in the Chinese tradition.

Book III of the Code: superfices, *yongdian quan*, and easements are all *yongyi wuquan*, while mortgage, pledge, *dianquan*, and lien are all *danbao wuquan*.[60]

If the concepts of *wuquan*, *yongyi wuquan*, and *danbao wuquan* have all been part of Chinese jurisprudence since the enactment of the ROC Civil Code in 1929–1930, why did they disappear completely from Chinese law in mainland China and were only resurrected by the enactment of the LP in 2007? The answer lies in the communist revolution, the abolition at the time of the establishment of the PRC of all laws enacted by the KMT Government, and the transplant to China of the Soviet Union's Marxist system of property law.[61] Indeed, the provisions on ownership in the LP today are only fully explicable in the light of Soviet property law.

Jurists in the former Soviet Union adopted the Marxist view that law is an instrument of the ruling class. In a capitalist society, property law is thus an instrument of the bourgeoisie to maintain their class domination by legal provisions on the private ownership of the means of production. Private property was therefore a principal target of Marxist criticism of the injustice and oppression of a capitalist society. If the communist revolution means anything, it must mean the abolition of the private ownership of the means of production and its substitution by a system of socialist public ownership. Soviet lawmakers and jurists thus embarked upon the task of translating the concept of socialist public ownership into legal provisions and institutions.[62]

The basic sources of Soviet property law included the Constitution, the BPCL enacted in 1961 (which as mentioned above influenced the making of the GPCL in the PRC), and the civil codes of the union republics of the USSR such as the Civil Code of the Russian Socialist Federal Soviet Republic (RSFSR). In the USSR Constitution of 1936 (the principal model which the PRC drew upon in drafting its first Constitution of 1954), two forms of "socialist ownership" were provided for: State ownership (the wealth of the whole people) and cooperative-collective farm ownership (ownership by

60. Meiling Chen, Taizhen Li, and Lianshun Chen, *Minfa rumen* [*Introduction to Civil Law*] (Taipei: Yuedan, 1994) 393.

61. Sun (N16) 190–191. For the Soviet influence on PRC law, see generally Albert H.Y. Chen, "Socialist Law, Civil Law, Common Law, and the Classification of Contemporary Chinese Law" in J.M. Otto, M.V. Polak, J. Chen, and Y. Li (eds.), *Law-Making in the People's Republic of China* (The Hague: Kluwer Law International, 2000) ch. 4, 55–74.

62. See generally O.S. Ioffe, *Soviet Civil Law* (Dordrecht: Martinus Nijhoff, 1988) 91–111.

individual collective farms and ownership by cooperative associations).[63] Land, natural resources, factories, enterprises, etc. were under State ownership.[64] Citizens had the "right of personal ownership" (*lichnaya sobstvennost*, as distinguished from *chastnaya sobstvennost*, or private ownership)[65] of "their income and savings from work, dwelling house, ... articles of domestic and everyday use" and the "right to inherit the personal property of citizens".[66] In the BPCL, a third form of socialist ownership was provided for — ownership by public bodies or social organisations such as trade unions.[67]

Notably, under Soviet law a collective farm was recognised as a "separate juridical entity with the rights of a legal person"[68] and could therefore own property.[69] This contrasts with the Chinese system of collective ownership by the labouring masses, where the "collective" that owns property was never clearly defined in law until the LP.[70] Three other features of Soviet law are also relevant for the purpose of comparative study of PRC law. First, there is the concept of the "right of operative management" on the part of State enterprises in respect of property or assets allocated to them by the State.[71] This concept also appears in the GPCL. Second, houses or buildings may be privately owned, though not the land on which they stand.[72] This is also the case in the PRC.[73] Third, ownership was the only core concept recognised in Soviet property law, which contained no concepts of *Sachenrecht*, *beschränkte dingliche Rechte*, or *Nutzungsrechte*. Following the Soviet approach, PRC law also did not recognise these concepts until the enactment of the LP. Ownership was defined in the Civil Code of the RSFSR as follows: "The owner has the

---

63. Art. 5.
64. Art. 6.
65. Johnson (N16) 108.
66. Art. 10 of the Constitution.
67. Johnson (N16) 106; Ioffe (N62) 96.
68. Johnson (N16) 107.
69. Ioffe (N62) 105–106.
70. See the section of this chapter on collective ownership.
71. Johnson (N16) 107; Ioffe (N62) 93–95, 98–99.
72. Johnson (N16) 110.
73. See generally K. Wilhelm, "Rethinking Property Rights in Urban China" (2004) 9 *UCLA Journal of International Law and Foreign Affairs* 227.

right to possess, use, and dispose of property within the limits established by law."[74] A similar provision can be found in the GPCL.[75]

In the course of the drafting of the LP, there was some debate regarding whether the LP should codify the threefold classification of property (i.e., State ownership, collective ownership, and ownership by individual citizens) or whether an alternative approach closer to that adopted by other civil law jurisdictions should be adopted.[76] One view was that the threefold classification was applicable only to systems of ownership (*suoyou zhi*) and need not be provided for in the LP, which should make provisions for ownership of property rather than systems of ownership which concern the "economic base" of society (according to Marxist theory) and which belong to the province of constitutional law rather than civil law.[77] A related view was that as the GPCL had already provided that the subjects of civil law are natural persons and legal persons, the subjects of ownership that the LP should recognise are the State, natural persons, and legal persons.[78] Another view was that the LP should follow the approach in the BGB and the ROC Civil Code of having separate sets of provisions for ownership of movable property and immovable property (land).[79]

Despite these views, the LP eventually adopted the conservative or orthodox approach of reiterating the threefold classification of State ownership, collective ownership, and ownership by individuals. However, the provisions of the LP on ownership do go beyond the existing law in (1) defining the nature and mode of operation of collective ownership;[80] (2) substituting the term "ownership by private persons" (*siren suoyouquan*, alternatively translated as "private ownership") for "ownership by individual citizens";[81] (3) declaring

---

74. Art. 92. See Ioffe (N62) 92.

75. Art. 71.

76. See, for instance, Baoyu Liu, *Wuquan tixi lun* [*The System of Property Rights*] (Beijing: Renmin Fayuan Press, 2004) 120–125, 136–145.

77. Sun (N16) 26, 122–127.

78. *Ibid.*, 123; Liu (N76) 138.

79. This approach was adopted in the draft LP prepared by Professor Huixing Liang of the Chinese Academy of Social Sciences; see Huixing Liang, *Zhongguo wuquanfa cao'an jianyi gao* [*A Proposed Draft Bill for the Chinese Law of Property*] (Beijing: Shehui Kexue Wenxian Press, 2000), especially 212–213.

80. Arts. 58–63 of the LP.

81. Arts. 64–66 of the LP. Ownership by "citizens" rather than "private persons" was the concept employed by the 1982 Constitution and the GPCL.

equal protection for the *wuquan* of the State, collectives, private persons, and other right-holders[82] (hailed as a major breakthrough in Chinese legal and political thinking and a victory of the reformers over the conservatives who had criticised the draft LP as unconstitutional and a departure from socialism);[83] and (4) introducing the concept of ownership by owners of apartments in condominium buildings (*jianzhuwu qufen suoyouquan*).[84] Furthermore, although there is no express provision in the LP on ownership by legal persons, there are provisions in the LP on the property rights of enterprise legal persons (*qiye faren*),[85] other legal persons,[86] and social organisations (*shehui tuanti*).[87]

We now turn from ownership (*suoyouquan*) to *yongyi wuquan* (rights of use and enjoyment over things) and *danbao wuquan* (security rights over things). During the drafting process of the LP, some PRC scholars suggested that the LP use the same terms for various species of *yongyi wuquan* and *danbao wuquan* that are used in the ROC Civil Code, including *dishang quan* (superficies) and *yongdian quan*, which they considered to be sufficiently similar to the land use rights granted to developers and the rights under the *chengbao* contract, respectively.[88] In the end, the LP adopted neither of the terms. The *yongyi wuquan* (defined to mean the right to possess, use, and derive benefits from immovable or movable property owned by another)[89] provided for in the LP include (1) the *chengbao* operational right in land (CORL),[90] (2) the right to use construction land (RUCL),[91] (3) the right

---

82. Art. 4 of the LP.

83. See, for example, Lo (N11) 192–194; Mo Zhang, "From Public to Private: The Newly Enacted Chinese Property Law and the Protection of Property Rights in China" (2008) 5 *Berkeley Business Law Journal* 317, 343–345; Cui et al. (N53) 123; Sun (N16) 138.

84. Ch. 6 (arts. 70–83) of the LP.

85. Art. 68(1) of the LP. On the question of ownership by legal persons, see, for example, Tian Yin, *Wuquanfa lilun pingxi yu sikao* [*The Theory of Property Law: Analysis and Reflections*] (Beijing: Zhongguo renmin daxue, 2nd edition, 2008) 95–110.

86. Art. 68(2).

87. Art. 69.

88. See Liu (N1) 117–124; Liu (N76) 120–125, 176–182.

89. Art. 117 of the LP.

90. Ch. 11 of the LP.

91. Ch. 12 of the LP.

to use land for house sites (RUHS),[92] and (4) easements (*diyiquan*).[93] The *danbao wuquan* provided for in the LP are (1) mortgage,[94] (2) pledge (including pledge of movable property and pledge of rights — following the dual mode of pledge in the BGB),[95] and (3) lien.[96] Following the two parts of the LP on *yongyi wuquan* (Part III) and *danbao wuquan* (Part IV), respectively, there is a final part (Part V) of the LP on the subject of "possession" — which is also the subject of a separate chapter in both the BGB and the ROC Civil Code.

The provisions regulating the types and content of *yongyi wuquan* in the LP can be considered the most original features of Chinese property law that distinguish it from its counterparts in other jurisdictions. In non-communist civil law jurisdictions where private ownership of property is the dominant form of ownership, property ownership rather than *yongyi wuquan* (*Nutzungsrechte*) is the central concept in the LP as well as the most important concept in property practice. The peculiarity of "socialism with Chinese characteristics" or the "socialist market economy" in China is such that ownership in land cannot be privately held and cannot enter the market, but *yongyi wuquan* can, hence the crucial importance of the conceptual category of *yongyi wuquan* within the Chinese system of property law.

Actually, the four species of *yongyi wuquan* provided for in the LP are not entirely new and existed in PRC law and practice well before the enactment of the LP.[97] The most significant advance made by the LP in this regard is the recognition of the *chengbao* operational right in rural land as a *yongyi wuquan*. Before the enactment of the LP, the exact legal nature or status of the rights

---

92. Ch. 13 of the LP.

93. Ch. 14 of the LP. These are the main types, but not the only types, of *yongyi wuquan* provided for in the LP. See arts. 122–123 of the LP; Liming Wang, *Wuquanfa lun* [*The Law of Property*] (Beijing: Zhongguo zhengfa daxue, 2nd revised edition, 2008) 216, 306; Ping Jiang (ed.), *Wuquanfa jiaocheng* [*Textbook on the Law of Property*] (Beijing: Zhongguo zhengfa daxue, 2007) 176; Cui et al. (N53) 178–180.

94. Ch. 16 of the LP.

95. Ch. 17 of the LP.

96. Ch. 18 of the LP.

97. Regarding easement (*diyiquan*), this did not exist in Chinese law before the enactment of the LP, but the GPCL provided for a related concept of "neighbourhood relations" (*xianglin guanxi*). See art. 83 of the GPCL; Liming Wang, *Wuquanfa lun* [*The Law of Property*] (Beijing: Zhongguo zhengfa daxue, revised edition, 2003) ch. 17.

under the *chengbao* contract was not entirely clear.[98] While many scholars believed that they were in the nature of *wuquan* (property right), some pointed out that insofar as they were derived from contract and the law (at least before the enactment of the LRLC in 2002) did not regulate the content of the contract, they properly belonged to the realm of rights in contract (*zhaiquan*) rather than property rights.[99] In the absence of legislation clearly spelling out the nature of *chengbao* rights, the courts had for a long time treated them as contractual rights rather than property rights.[100] The recognition of *chengbao* rights as a species of *wuquan* has ultimately strengthened the degree of protection afforded to the holder of the rights.[101] For example, the mechanisms and remedies for the enforcement of all *wuquan* specified in chapter 3 (on "the protection of *wuquan*") of the LP are now available to the *chengbao* rights holder, and the rights can be enforced against third parties.

In terms of rules of substantive law, the provisions on *danbao wuquan* in the LP introduced more changes to the existing law than those on *yongyi wuquan*. Although the law on security for credit was previously contained in the GL (*danbao fa*) enacted in 1995, the provisions on *danbao wuquan* in the LP considerably changed the existing law and have largely superseded the GL (although the GL has not been formally repealed). The LP expands the scope of property that may be used as security as credit. For example, one provision stipulates that a mortgage may be created in respect of "all other property which is not prohibited from being mortgaged by law or administrative regulations", in addition to certain specified categories of property.[102] Moreover, a mortgage in the nature of the floating charge in common law is also made possible by the LP,[103] and the scope of rights that may be the subject matter of a pledge of rights is expanded to include "accounts receivables".[104]

Taken together, while the basic conceptual framework and textual structure of the LP borrowed significantly from the continental European, particularly the German, legal traditions, it has also retained certain ideas regarding

98. See, for example, Huixing Liang and Huabin Chen, *Wuquanfa* [*Law of Property*] (Beijing: Law Press, 3rd edition, 2005) 9.

99. See Wang (N97) 454–455; Jiang (N93) 200–201.

100. *Ibid*.

101. Wang (N93) 225.

102. Art. 180.

103. Art. 181.

104. Art. 223(6).

socialist ownership which China imported from the Soviet Union after the communist revolution. However, although conceptual categories such as *yongyi wuquan* and *danbao wuquan* have German origins and formed part of the "old" jurisprudence of republican China (that had developed before the establishment of the PRC), the precise content of the *yongyi wuquan* and *danbao wuquan* provided for in the LP is largely a response to indigenous circumstances and needs. It also testifies to the unique combination of socialist and private property rights that is a product of the era of "reform and opening" in China that began 30 years ago.

## A MOVE TOWARDS PRIVATE PROPERTY RIGHTS?

There is a significant body of literature, by lawyers, economists, philosophers, and other scholars in the humanities and social sciences, on theories of property rights[105] and the relationship between the delineation, protection, and enforcement of property rights and economic development.[106] It is however beyond the scope of this chapter to investigate property law and economic development in contemporary China. The much more modest objective here is to examine to what extent the less conventional property rights (less conventional in the sense that there are hardly any counterparts in other jurisdictions) provided for in the LP can be considered private property rights or contain elements of private property rights. The species of rights to be explored here include (1) RUCL, (2) RUHS, (3) CORL, and (4) collective ownership.

First, the criteria for determining what are private property rights need to be set. According to Harold Demsetz, property should be understood as a bundle of rights, including rights of control, income, and transfer.[107] Similarly, Lawrence C. Becker points out that "to have a property right in a thing is to have a bundle of rights that defines a form of ownership". In his view, the concept of "full ownership" comprises 13 elements: the right to possess; the

105. For a review of some of these theories, see, for example, Chen (N24) 31–39.

106. See, for instance, D.C. North, *Structure and Change in Economic History* (New York: Norton, 1981); Y. Barzel, *A Theory of the State: Economic Rights, Legal Rights, and the Scope of the State* (New York: Cambridge University Press, 2002); Albert H.Y. Chen, "Rational Law, Economic Development and the Case of China" (1999) 8 *Social and Legal Studies* 97.

107. H. Demsetz, "Toward a Theory of Property Rights" in E.G. Furubotn and S. Pejovich (eds.), *The Economics of Property Rights* (Cambridge: Ballinger, 1975) ch. 3.

right to use; the right to manage (i.e., to decide how and by whom a thing shall be used); the right to the income; the right to consume or destroy; the right to modify; the right to alienate; the right to transmit (i.e., devise or bequeath); the right to security (immunity from expropriation); the absence of term (time limit); the prohibition of harmful use; liability to execution; and residuary rules. According to Becker, any of the first eight rights, when supplemented by some version of the right to security, can be considered legal ownership.[108]

Becker's detailed analysis of various elements of ownership is useful, but Steven Cheung has provided a simpler formulation:

> Any productive resource is a *private* property if, within well-defined limits, its owners has:
>
> (a) the right to exclude others so that he alone may decide on its use;
>
> (b) the right to extract exclusive income from its use; and
>
> (c) the right to transfer or sell the property or resource to anyone as he sees fit.
>
> ... An economic system based on private property rights implies that each individual is necessarily an owner of property (of his own labour, if nothing else), and that he is free to contract with others for its use.[109]

## The Right to Use Construction Land

The RUCL is defined by the LP as the right to possess, use, and derive benefits from State-owned land, including the right to use the land for the construction of buildings, structures, and ancillary facilities.[110] Two species of this right may be distinguished:[111] RUCL obtained by *churang* (granted by the government, usually on the basis of tender or auction, upon payment of a premium, or *churang jin*, by the grantee),[112] and RUCL obtained by *huabo* (allotted

108. L.C. Becker, *Property Rights: Philosophical Foundations* (London: Routledge & Kegan Paul, 1977); L.C. Becker, "The Moral Basis of Property Rights" in J.R. Pennock and J.W. Chapman (eds.), *Property: Nomos XXII* (New York: New York University Press, 1980) 187.
109. Steven N.S. Cheung, *Will China Go "Capitalist"?* (London: Institute of Economic Affairs, 2nd edition, 1986) 33 (emphasis in original).
110. Art. 135 of the LP.
111. Art. 136 of the LP.
112. Arts. 138 and 141 of the LP.

by the government for use by government organs or the military, or for urban infrastructural development, etc.,[113] where no premium payment is required).[114] In both cases, the types of permitted land use are specified.[115] The term of the RUCL obtained by grant varies from 40 years to 70 years depending on the type of land use,[116] while the RUCL obtained by allotment is for an indefinite duration.[117] An important legal rule introduced by the LP is that the RUCL in residential land shall be "automatically renewed" upon expiry of the term of grant.[118] However, the LP has not made such a guarantee for non-residential land.[119]

The LP provides that subject to any contrary provision in other laws, the holder of the RUCL has the right to assign (*zhuanrang*), exchange (*huhuan*), use as capital contribution (*chuzi*), give as a gift or mortgage the RUCL.[120] It should also be noted that lease and inheritance are not mentioned in this provision. The PRCT provides, *inter alia*, for leasing of land use rights together with the buildings or structures on the land,[121] while the LAURE also provides for leasing of housing (*fangwu*).[122] The RUCL may also be the subject matter of inheritance.[123]

The LP provides that where RUCL is assigned, exchanged, or made a capital contribution or a gift, the buildings, structures, or ancillary facilities shall be disposed of together with the RUCL.[124] Conversely, where the

113. See art. 54 of the LAL and art. 23 of the LAURE.

114. Jiang (N93) 197; Cui et al. (N53) 212.

115. Art. 140 of the LP.

116. Art. 12 of the PRCT; Jiang (N93) 198; Cui et al. (N53) 222.

117. Jiang (N93) 198; Cui et al. (N53) 213.

118. Art. 149(1) of the LP. "Automatic renewal" means that there is no need for the holder of the RUCL to apply for renewal. However, the LP has made no provision for the terms and conditions of renewal, including the question of whether it requires a premium, and, if so, how much premium is payable for renewal. It seems that the legislative intention was to leave these matters for future determination. See Songyou Wang (ed.), *Zhonghua renmin gongheguo wuquanfa tiaowen lijie yu shiyong* [*The PRC Law of Property: Interpretations and Applications*] (Beijing: Renmin Fayuan Press, 2007) 446–450.

119. See art. 149(2). See, however, art. 21 of the LAURE (regarding applications for renewal).

120. Art. 143 of the LP.

121. Arts. 28–31 of the PRCT.

122. Arts. 52–55 of the LAURE. On the contract of lease, see ch. 13 of the PRC *Law of Contract*.

123. Wang (N93) 244.

124. Art. 146 of the LP.

buildings, structures or ancillary facilities are disposed of, the RUCL of the underlying land shall be disposed of together with them.[125]

The right to assign, mortgage, or otherwise dispose of RUCL obtained by allotment is subject to more restrictions than RUCL obtained by grant. In the latter case, the LAURE provides that the grantee may not assign the real estate (*fangdichan*) until 25 percent of the total amount of the required investment has been provided (in the case of housing development) or the conditions for forming industrial or other construction land have been fulfilled.[126] For RUCL obtained by allotment, the allottee may not assign the real estate until government approval has been obtained. Furthermore, while no premium is required for an RUCL obtained by allotment, as mentioned earlier, a premium is required if the RUCL is transfered.[127]

Like other property rights provided for in the LP, RUCL and the buildings thereon are subject to possible expropriation or requisition by the State with payment of compensation.[128] In addition, failure to develop the land in accordance with the conditions in the grant may result in the resumption of the land by the State without compensation.[129]

In light of the above, it appears that the RUCL obtained by grant (as distinguished from allotment) is a private property right close to the right of ownership, subject to the term (limited duration) of the grant. Indeed, the RUCL is very similar to the property right acquired by purchasers of government land in Hong Kong who are lessees of the government (or the Crown in colonial Hong Kong) for the term of the lease. When a real estate developer is granted RUCL, constructs buildings on the land, and sells the apartments in them to end users, the end users also obtain a property right akin to ownership — including the ownership of the apartment of the building and a share of the RUCL in the land on which the building stands. In this regard, the system for the development and use of urban land in socialist China is very similar to that in capitalist Hong Kong.

---

125. Art. 147 of the LP.

126. Art. 38 of the LAURE. For sale of uncompleted flats, see art. 44.

127. Art. 39 of the LAURE.

128. Arts. 42, 44, and 121 of the LP; art. 19 of the LAURE (on resumption in the public interest before expiry of term). The compensation is generally considered inadequate. The practice of *chaiqian* (demolition and relocation) is such that the protection of urban property rights is weak in China. See, for instance, Wilhelm (N73).

129. Art. 25 of the LAURE; art. 37 of the LAL.

## The Right to Use Land for House Sites

The LP provides for RUHS in four articles. RUHS is defined as the right to possess and use collectively owned land, including the right to use the land for the construction of a residence and ancillary facilities.[130] As in the case of buildings on urban land, the residence may be privately owned.[131] Apart from recognising RUHS as a *yongyi wuquan*, the LP does not change but preserves the existing law on house sites on rural land. The LP provides that the LAL and other relevant provisions made by the State shall govern the acquisition, exercise, and transfer of RUHS. It also expressly provides that RUHS (and other rights of use over collectively owned land) may not be mortgaged save where authorised by law[132] (and the existing law does not authorise such mortgage).

Before its amendment in 1998, the LAL provided that when rural residents constructed their residence, they should use existing house sites (*zhai jidi*) or vacant land within the village with the approval of the township government.[133] Agricultural land may also be used for this purpose subject to consideration of the application by the township government and approval by the county government.[134] It was also provided that "if one sells or leases his residence and applies again for a house site, such applications shall not be approved".[135]

The LAL as amended in 1998 largely preserves the existing rules, but requires all applications for house sites on the part of rural residents to be considered by the township (or town) government and approved by the county government.[136] It also introduces the limitation that each household of villagers is entitled to only one house site.[137] The rule prohibiting fresh applications after the sale or leasing of a residence is preserved.[138]

The RUHS is in the nature of a social benefit made available to rural residents largely for their own use rather than for transfer. Only members of

---

130. Art. 152 of the LP. In practice the use of the land is not limited to residential use; small-scale family business operations have not been prohibited; Jiang (N93) 206; Cui et al. (N53) 233.

131. Cui et al. (N53) 231.

132. Art. 184(2).

133. Art. 38(1).

134. Art. 38(1).

135. Art. 38(3).

136. Art. 62(3).

137. Art. 62(1).

138. Art. 62(4).

a village are entitled to apply for RUHS,[139] and applicants are households rather than individuals.[140] No payment of consideration is needed.[141] Further, the RUHS is not subject to any time limit,[142] survives the death of individual members of the household,[143] and may be inherited by family members.[144] Regarding the extent to which the RUHS and the residence built on the land may be leased or sold, the law is not completely clear. The rule mentioned above prohibiting fresh applications after the sale or leasing of a residence seems to presuppose that such sale or leasing may occur.[145] However, a State Council notice in 1999 provides that peasants' residences may not be sold to urban residents, and urban residents should not be given approval to build residences on peasants' collectively owned land.[146] A State Council decision in 2004 prohibits urban residents from purchasing house sites in villages.[147]

There was much debate during the drafting process of the LP regarding whether free transfer of RUHS should be permitted.[148] In the end, it was decided to leave the question open in the LP.[149] Some localities have however started to experiment with the practice of permitting transfer of land use rights in collectively owned land for construction purpose.[150] There are different scholarly interpretations of the existing law on whether residences built on

139. Jiang (N93) 206, 208; Cui et al. (N53) 177, 232; Wang (N93) 275.

140. Wang (N93) 275; Cui et al. (N53) 177.

141. Jiang (N93) 207; Cui et al. (N53) 232.

142. Jiang (N93) 207; Cui et al. (N53) 178, 232.

143. Jiang (N93) 207.

144. Cui et al. (N53) 232.

145. Liu (N1) 96.

146. Wang (N93) 282.

147. Cui et al. (N53) 235. In practice, it is common for urban residents to purchase houses in rural areas. The doubtful legality of such practice is referred to by the term *xiao chanquan fang* ("house with mini-property right"). See, for example, Ping Jiang, "Wuquanfa de maodun yu chongtu" [The Law of Property: Contradictions and Conflicts] (2008) 10 *Hongfan pinglun* [*Journal of Legal and Economic Studies*] 1; Sun (N16) 139–140.

148. Wang (N93) 282.

149. Art. 153 of the LP simply provides that the acquisition, exercise, and transfer of RUHS shall be subject to relevant laws (such as the LAL) and provisions. It has been pointed that that this leaves open the possibility of future liberalisation regarding the transfer or sale of RUHS. See, for instance, Wang (N93) 282.

150. Wang (N93) 282.

house sites by holders of RUHS may be assigned (sold), leased (to fellow villagers or to outsiders), or even mortgaged.[151]

From the perspective of economic efficiency, RUHS should be made freely transferable. There is a demand on the part of some urban residents to live in rural areas either after retirement or for other reasons. Holders of RUHS may want to migrate away from the village or to raise money for their own purposes. However, there is fear on the part of the government that a free market in RUHS may result in many peasants losing their residence and rich people or corporations buying large amounts of RUHS.

In light of the above, RUHL may be understood as a private property right of a limited nature, the main limit being on the transfer or other similar dispositions of the right. In other respects it bears resemblance to RUCL, particularly RUCL as applied to owners of residential accommodation in the urban areas.

## The *Chengbao* Operational Right in Land

As mentioned above, CORL dates back to the rural economic reform of the 1980s and was systematically codified in the LRLC. The chapter on CORL in the LP begins by reproducing the provisions in the Constitution that rural collective economic organisations should practise a two-level operational system based on family *chengbao* operation and the combination of centralised and decentralised operations.[152] It goes on to provide that the system of *chengbao* operation of land is applicable to farmland, forest land, grassland, and other agricultural land collectively owned by peasants or owned by the State but collectively used by peasants.[153] CORL is defined as the right to possess, use, and derive benefits from the land that is subject to *chengbao* operation, including the right to engage in various agricultural activities.[154] The periods of *chengbao* operation are specified in the LP, and vary from 30 years to 70 years depending on whether the land is farmland, grassland, or forest land.[155] The LP provides that on the expiry of the relevant period, the *chengbao*

151. See Wang (N93) 276–277, 282; Jiang (N93) 207–208; Cui et al. (N53) 235–236; Liu (N1) 95. Regarding mortgage, art. 184 of the LP expressly prohibits the mortgage of land for house sites unless otherwise provided for by law.

152. Art. 124(1) of the LP; art. 8(1) of the Constitution.

153. Art. 124 of the LP.

154. Art. 125.

155. Art. 126(1). Previously this was provided for in art. 20 of the LRLC.

may be continued in accordance with relevant provisions made by the State.[156] The grantor of the *chengbao* land cannot adjust the land during the *chengbao* period[157] and cannot resume the land save where the law otherwise provides.[158] Compensation is payable for expropriation of *chengbao* land.[159]

*Chengbao* operation of rural land may be classified into two types — family *chengbao* and *chengbao* of wasteland (*huangdi*, commonly referred to as *sihuang* or four types of wasteland).[160] All members of a village are entitled to be granted family *chengbao* contracts,[161] and the relevant authority is under a legal obligation to grant *chengbao* contracts to members of the village.[162] *Chengbao* rights are allocated to peasant households (*nonghu*)[163] in accordance with the numbers of persons and manpower of peasant households.[164] On the other hand, *chengbao* contracts in respect of wasteland are awarded on the basis of tenders, auctions, or open negotiations (*gongkai xieshang*)[165] and upon payment of a premium (*chengbaofei*).[166] "Outsiders" (persons who are not members of the village) may bid for such contracts, although members of the village are given some priority in the award of such contracts.[167] Contracts to outsiders are also subject to the consent of a two-thirds majority at a villagers' meeting and the approval of the township or town government.[168] The *chengbao* periods are usually longer in the case of wasteland *chengbao*.[169] However, the abovementioned provision on the continuation of the *chengbao*

156. Art. 126(2). This provision provides an important assurance regarding the long-term nature or indefinite duration of the *chengbao* arrangement. Thus, CORL may in practice be the functional equivalent of a property right without a time limit (*wuqi wuquan*); Cui et al. (N53) 195.
157. Art. 130.
158. Art. 131.
159. Art. 132.
160. Art. 3 of the LRLC.
161. Art. 5 of the LRLC; see also the speech of Liu (N30) 206.
162. Jiang (N93) 203; Cui et al. (N53) 198.
163. Art. 15 of the LRLC.
164. Cui et al. (N53) 195.
165. Art. 44 of the LRLC.
166. Art. 45 of the LRLC.
167. Art. 47.
168. Art. 48.
169. Originally some contracts for wasteland *chengbao* were for periods as long as 100 years. After 1996, the State Council's policy was that the maximum period for wasteland *chengbao* was 50 years. See Cui et al. (N53) 195.

arrangement after the expiry of the *chengbao* period is apparently not applicable to wasteland.[170] In family *chengbao*, the land may be resumed by the grantor before the expiry of the *chengbao* contract if the whole family of the *chengbao* operator has migrated to a city and has become a non-agricultural household (*fei nongye hukou*).[171]

The right to transfer or otherwise engage in dealings in the CORL is also more extensive in the case of wasteland *chengbao* than family *chengbao*. The LP provides that wasteland *chengbao* operators who are awarded their contracts on the basis of tender, auction, or open negotiation may assign, use as capital contribution, mortgage, or otherwise transfer their CORL in accordance with the LRLC and other relevant laws and provisions.[172] In family *chengbao*, the LP provides that the *chengbao* operator may sub-contract (*zhuanbao*), exchange, or assign their CORL in accordance with the LRLC.[173] The LRLC permits assignment of CORL under limited circumstances: the consent of the grantor (the village authority) must be obtained; the assignor must have a stable non-agricultural occupation or stable source of income; and the assignee must be a peasant household engaged in agricultural production.[174] In the case of sub-contracting, leasing (note that leasing is not mentioned in the LP but is mentioned in the LRLC), and exchange, no consent by the grantor is required, but the matter should be reported to the grantor for the record.[175] However, mortgage of CORL is not permitted by law.[176]

Family *chengbao* and wasteland *chengbao* also differ with regard to inheritance. In the former, as the grant of the *chengbao* contract is made

170. This means that it is not mandatory for the grantor to renew the *chengbao* contract when it expires; Cui et al. (N53) 208; Jiang (N93) 205.

171. Art. 26(3).

172. Art. 133.

173. Art. 128. It should also be noted that art. 184(2) of the LP provides that the right to use farmland and other collectively owned land may not be mortgaged unless there is a contrary provision in other laws.

174. Arts. 37 and 41 of the LRLC. Members of the same village enjoy priority in obtaining the assignment, according to art. 33(5).

175. Art. 37 of the LRLC. Again, members of the same village enjoy priority in becoming parties to these transactions, according to art. 33(5).

176. Art. 184 of the LP; Wang (N93) 236, 239–240. Unlike the case of wasteland *chengbao*, the law does not permit CORL to be used as capital contribution. However, localities such as Chongqing have experimented with permitting peasants to use their CORL as capital contribution to a business; see Sun (N16) 137.

to the peasant household, the death of an individual member of the household will not affect the continuation of the COLR.[177] If all members of the household die, the COLR is extinguished and the land should be returned to the grantor.[178] A special provision is made in the LRLC regarding *chengbao* of forest land (where the *chengbao* period may be as long as 70 years): on the death of the *chengbao* operator, their successor under the law of inheritance (irrespective of whether the successor is a member of the household or the village) may continue the *chengbao* arrangement for the remainder of the original *chengbao* period.[179] In the case of wasteland *chengbao* on the basis of tender, auction, or open negotiation, upon the death of the *chengbao* operator, the successor may also continue the *chengbao* arrangement for the remainder of the original term.[180]

As in the case of house sites in rural areas, the question of whether to allow free transfer of CORL was much debated in the course of the drafting of the LP.[181] Relaxation of the existing restrictions on transfer would improve economic efficiency: peasants who want to migrate to cities may sell their CORL, and persons or companies which have skills, expertise, and capital can acquire large amounts of CORL and introduce large-scale agricultural operations.[182] However, there were reservations about the emergence of large numbers of people from the rural areas (originally peasants) being left without any means of livelihood and the possible depletion of agricultural land. For a long time, the CORL has performed a "social security" function for peasants in China's rural areas.[183] With the development of the socialist market economy, economic and social inequality in China has risen sharply. There was concern that marketisation of rural land would lead to still greater inequality in China.

177. Wang (N30) 78–79. The benefits due to the deceased under the *chengbao* arrangement may be inherited by their successors; art. 31(1) of the LRLC.

178. Wang (N30) 78. Thus, successors under the law of inheritance who are not members of the original household living in the same village are not entitled to continue the original *chengbao* contract.

179. Art. 31 of the LRLC; Wang (N30) 79.

180. Art. 50 of the LRLC.

181. See, for example, Jiang (N147) 3; Sun (N16) 137.

182. Wang (N93) 236.

183. *Ibid.*, 239.

Thus, in the end, the LP did not directly address the issue of such marketisation but left it open (for resolution by future legislative change).[184]

Similar to the RUHS, the CORL (in the case of family *chengbao*) is a private property right which is fairly extensive in terms of the right to use and derive benefits, and in terms of the long duration which in view of the provision on continuation is almost indefinite. The main limitation on this right concerns transfer and mortgage. In the case of wasteland *chengbao*, the CORL is a more extensive property right because of the existence of the right of transfer and mortgage, although the right (as in the case of RUCL obtained by grant) is not one of indefinite duration.

## Collective ownership

As mentioned, collective ownership by the labouring masses is one of the two modes of socialist public ownership in the PRC. Unlike State ownership, the rights of which are ultimately exercised by the State Council and persons or bodies authorised by it, the subject of collective ownership has never been clarified in PRC law.[185] As mentioned above, in the Soviet Union, there were also two forms of socialist ownership — State ownership and cooperative-collective ownership. However, the collective farms were subjects of separate juridical entities and legal persons.[186] In the PRC, however, there is no corresponding concept of collective farms. The question therefore arises of what is meant by saying that a particular piece of land (in rural areas, as urban land is State-owned) is under collective ownership.[187]

Historically, collective ownership was intended to be something other than private ownership or ownership by private individuals. As far as rural land is concerned, the origins of collective ownership can be traced back to the 1950s. The communist revolution was accompanied by a massive redistribution of

---

184. See generally Wang's speech to the NPC on 8 March 2007 on the bill for the LP in *Zhonghua renmin gongheguo quanguo renmin daibiao dahui changwu weiyuanhui gongbao* [*Gazette of the Standing Committee of the National People's Congress of the PRC*], No. 3, pp. 309–314 (2007).

185. Sun (N16) 130–131.

186. Johnson (N16) 107.

187. Notably, collective ownership of enterprises (as in the case of township and village enterprises), though equally important, is outside the scope of this chapter; see, for example, Wang (N93) 150–151; J.C. Oi and A.G. Walder (eds.), *Property Rights and Economic Reform in China* (Stanford: Stanford University Press, 1999).

land, and land owned by rich landowners was confiscated. Under the Land Reform Law of 1950, peasants were allocated land which they could own privately.[188] In subsequent years, however, there was a movement towards the socialisation or collectivisation of all means of production. By 1957, private ownership of rural land had been largely abolished, with peasants being required to transfer their land to peasants' cooperatives.[189] Thus, the system of collective ownership of rural land was established. The system was further expanded by the Regulations on Rural People's Communes in 1962, which introduced the principle of "three-level ownership with the production team as the basis".[190] The three levels were the people's communes, the production brigades (*shengchan dadui*, at a level below the communes), and the production teams (*shengchan dui*, at a level below the brigades).[191] After the end of the Cultural Revolution era, the people's communes were abolished, and a new system of rural governance and rural economic organisation was introduced. In this new system, the structural equivalents (in terms of the hierarchy of rural organs) of the people's communes, production brigades, and production teams are the townships (*xiang*), the villages (or "administrative villages"), and the villagers' groups (*cunmin xiaozu*, or "natural villages"). Notably, one "administrative village", or village for administrative purposes, may comprise more than one natural village or villagers' group).[192] These three divisions are administered by the township governments,[193] the villagers' committees,[194] and the heads of villagers' groups (*xiaozuzhang*), respectively.[195]

188. Wang (N97) 292; Yifan Yang and Hanfeng Chen (eds.), *Zhong huaren mingongheguo fazhishi* [*Legal History of the People's Republic of China*] (Harbin: Heilongjiang Renmin Press, 1997) 221–224.

189. Wang (N97) 293; Cui et al. (N53) 11, 109; Xianzhong Sun, *Lun wuquan fa* [*The Law of Property*] (Beijing: Law Press, 2008) 363.

190. Wang (N97) 293.

191. Peter Ho, "Who Owns China's Land? Policies, Property Rights and Deliberate Institutional Ambiguity" (2001) 166 *China Quarterly* 394, 404–405.

192. Cui et al. (N53) 109; Wag (N97) 293; Ho (N191) 405–406.

193. See the Organic Law of Local People's Congresses and Local People's Governments.

194. See the Organic Law of Villagers' Committees.

195. See art. 10 of the Organic Law of Villagers' Committees. According to figures in the early 1990s, there were 55,800 governments of townships and towns in the rural areas, 743,300 villagers' committees, and 5 million villagers' groups; see Wang (N97) 294.

At the time of the enactment of the LP, the existing law recognised three modes of collective ownership of rural land,[196] which correspond to these three levels of rural organisation. According to the GPCL, collectively owned land is collectively owned by the peasants of the village and should be managed by the agricultural production cooperative of the village or the villagers' committee, except where the land is already owned by the collective economic organisation of the township or town.[197] Thus, the GPCL recognised two modes of collective ownership of rural land — at the village level and the township level. A third mode was provided for in the LAL, which added the rule that where rural land is already collectively owned by peasants of two or more rural collective economic organisations within a village, it had to be managed by the respective collective economic organisations or villagers' groups.[198] In practice, collective ownership at the township level is rare, and the dominant forms of collective ownership are collective ownership by the village[199] and by the villagers' group.[200]

The law regulates the extent to which those in charge of collectively owned land may deal with or dispose of such land, although it has been pointed out that such restrictive rules are often disregarded in practice.[201] For example, agricultural land may not be used for construction without government approval.[202] Even where rural land has been designated as land for construction purpose, the use by rural collective economic organisations of such land for establishing business enterprises is subject to government approval.[203] The law also provides that the right to use collectively owned land may not be transferred or leased for non-agricultural construction.[204] Generally speaking, those in charge of collectively owned land may not sell it for development purposes. In fact, the land (i.e., the right to use land) may only be sold for

196. Wang (N97) 290.
197. Art. 74 of the GPCL.
198. Art. 10 of the LAL.
199. Cui et al. (N53) 109.
200. Wang (N97) 295.
201. *Ibid.*, 294, 296.
202. Art. 44 of the LAL.
203. Art. 60 of the LAL.
204. Art. 63 of the LAL.

development purposes after it has been expropriated (requisitioned) by the State and converted into State-owned land.[205]

Before the enactment of the LP, there existed two sets of problems, one theoretical and one practical, related to collective ownership in rural land. These problems have been addressed in the LP to some extent. The first problem was that the nature of collective ownership had not been clarified by law. According to one leading scholar, there existed at least four schools of thought regarding its nature.[206] The second set of problems flowed from the fact that, in practice, those in charge of collectively owned land[207] often abused their powers and engaged in illegal dealings in the land to the detriment of fellow members of the village or the collective that in theory owned the land, who may not have the standing to take the matter to court.[208]

The LP now clearly defines the nature of collective ownership and provides more specifically for the rights of the members of the collective body that owns rural land. It states that the immovable and movable property that is collectively owned by peasants is "collectively owned by *the members of* the relevant collective".[209] This provision is significant in that it makes it clear that the property does not merely belong to the collective as an abstract entity, but that individuals as members of the collective may enjoy property rights of some kind with regard to the collectively owned property.[210] Although the LP does not define the meaning of the "collective", it recognises that, as provided by the existing law, the collective may be the township, the village, or the villagers' group by providing that the relevant township collective economic organisation, villagers' committee, or villagers' group may exercise ownership on behalf of

205. Wang (N97) 296; Wang (N93) 145; Cui et al. (N53) 109. The expropriation of peasants' collectively owned land has been a major source of social unrest in contemporary China. See, for instance, E. Pils, "Land Disputes, Rights Assertion, and Social Unrest in China: A Case from Sichuan" (2005–2006) 19 *Columbia Journal of Asian Law* 235. It may be noted that in recent years, some provinces and localities (e.g., Guangdong) have experimented with the practice of allowing collectively owned land (i.e., the right to use it) to be directly sold in the market; see Wang (N93) 282; Jiang (N147) 5–6.

206. Wang (N97) 283–288.

207. In practice, those in charge of townships, villages, or villagers' groups which hold collectively owned land have the power to engage in dealings in the land; Liu (N1) 123–124.

208. Wang (N97) 291; Sun (N189) 120.

209. Art. 59 of the LP (emphasis added). See the discussion in Wang (N93) 146–147.

210. For further analysis, see Cui Jianyuan, *Wuquanfa* [*Law of Property*] (Beijing: Zhongguo renmin daxue, 2009) 185–188.

the collective.[211] The LP seeks to protect the rights of members of the collective by providing that certain matters (e.g., *chengbao* plans, the use and distribution of land compensation, etc.) must be decided by members of the collective in accordance with legally prescribed procedures,[212] and that where the collective economic organisation, villagers' committee, or other responsible persons have made a decision infringing upon the lawful rights and interests of members of the collective, aggrieved members may apply to court for the decision to be quashed.[213] The LP also requires information related to the state of the collectively owned property to be made available to members of the collective.[214]

In practice, apart from the rights of participation in decision-making and of taking court actions that are expressly provided for in the LP, members of the collective also enjoy the right to share in the income or benefits derived from the use (e.g., leasing[215] or *chengbao* operation[216]) of the collectively owned land managed by relevant authorities.[217] This right may be the subject of inheritance, but may not be transferred to others.[218]

Taken together, collective ownership of rural land in China is a complex phenomenon that is only partially provided for in law, and much depends on practices that are continuously evolving. It can be argued that although collective ownership is, in theory, a form of socialist public ownership, there are elements of private property in it insofar as members of the collective as private individuals may enjoy certain private rights (including income) and assert certain private claims as to the use of the collectively owned property. Indeed, it has been suggested by a leading Chinese scholar that collective ownership may be conceived of as a special form of common ownership;[219] whereas under the ordinary form of common ownership, the owner may exercise the right of

211. Art. 60 of the LP. See the discussion in Wang (N93) 147–148; Cui et al. (N53) 113.

212. Art. 59 of the LP. See also arts. 5 and 19 of the Organic Law of Villagers' Committees; Wang (N93) 148–149.

213. Art. 63 of the LP. See also Wang (N93) 149–150.

214. Art. 62 of the LP. See also art. 22 of the Organic Law of Villagers' Committees; Cui et al. (N53) 114.

215. Wang (N97) 296.

216. Members may share in the income derived from the *chengbao* operation of wasteland managed by the collective. See Jiang (N93) 204; art. 46 of the LRLC.

217. Jiang (N93) 291–292; Cui et al. (N53) 112.

218. Wang (N97) 292.

219. *Ibid.*, 288. However, in the 2008 edition of his book, Wang no longer suggests that collective ownership may be understood as a special form of common ownership; see Wang (N93) 147.

severance over the commonly owned property, exercise certain rights directly over the commonly owned property, or join together with the other co-owners to dispose of the property. This is not so under collective ownership.[220]

## CONCLUSION

Economic reform in China during the past three decades of "reform and opening" has been accompanied by significant legal developments related to property rights, which culminated in the enactment of the LP in 2007. However, the LP has not revolutionised the existing law. The LP's main significance and contribution lies in providing a conceptual framework for the purpose of organising, consolidating, and systematising the existing law relating to property rights for movable and immovable property. This conceptual framework has largely been borrowed from the continental European, particularly the German, legal tradition. The concepts of *wu*, *wuquanfa*, *suoyou quan*, *yongyi wuquan*, and *danbao wuquan* all have their counterparts in German jurisprudence.

These concepts, though largely new (except *suoyou quan*) to the text of PRC legislation, already existed in the twentieth-century Chinese legal tradition that preceded the establishment of the PRC. The LP suggests that this tradition, embodied in the Civil Code of the ROC that is still in force in Taiwan today, is being resurrected in the PRC. From this perspective, there is not only a trend of convergence in the domain of property law between contemporary Chinese law and continental European law, but also one of convergence between the laws on both sides of the Taiwan Straits.

However, the similarities in basic concepts and textual structure belie some big differences between PRC property law and that in Taiwan or Europe, and in the many unique features of the LP that respond to the indigenous circumstances of the PRC. For example, the LP still maintains the system of socialist public ownership that was transplanted from the Soviet Union after the Chinese communist revolution. What is most interesting is that the LP has grafted onto it a regime of *yongyi wuquan* that is uniquely Chinese in content. Such combination of socialist ownership with *yongyi wuquan* represents at once a synthesis of Soviet and German legal ideas, and a synthesis of socialist property and private property.

220. Wang (N97) 288; Cui et al. (N53) 112.

The three main types of *yongyi wuquan* (including their sub-species) provided for in the LP are to varying degrees private property rights. Furthermore, collective ownership in respect of rural land also contains elements of private property. The species of *yongyi wuquan* that come closest to private property rights are the RUCL obtained by grant and the CORL of wasteland obtained by auction, tender, etc. The RUHS and the CORL (in the case of family *chengbao*) also exhibit important elements of private property rights, and their limitations as property rights relate mainly to restrictions on sale (transfer) and mortgage.

In his seminal paper asking "Will China Go Capitalist?" published in 1982,[221] Professor Steven Cheung argues that China will "go capitalist", and that capitalism depends on an effective regime of private property rights. To a large extent, Cheung's forecast has proved to be accurate. Various species of private property rights (including but not limited to those covered in this chapter) have indeed emerged in China and have probably contributed significantly to the spectacular economic growth observed in China over the last three decades. However, in terms of the clarity of legal delineation of private property rights and the security of such rights, there is still much to be desired. There is also room for the further privatisation and commodification of property rights in rural land. Whether that will happen eventually will be a crucial policy choice for the Chinese Government and the CCP. However, whatever choice they make, it will be reflected and embodied in new legislative action, which, like the enactment of the LP, may become the subject of intense debate. Thus, the story of Chinese law will continue to unfold, together with the story of China's quest for modernisation and for the building of a "wealthy, powerful, democratic and civilized" nation.[222]

## Acknowledgement

This chapter was first published as "The Law of Property and the Evolving System of Property Rights in China" in Guanghua Yu (ed.), *The Development of the Chinese Legal System: Change and Challenges* (2011), chapter 4, pp. 81–112. This edited version is reprinted with permission from the publisher, Routledge.

---

221. Cheung (N109).

222. Quoted from the preamble to the PRC Constitution.

# 12

# Socio-legal Thought and Legal Modernisation in Contemporary China: A Case Study of the Jurisprudence of Zhu Suli

## INTRODUCTION

Rapid, large-scale, and far-reaching economic and social changes have occurred in China since the Chinese Communist Party (CCP) decided in 1978 that China should embark upon the path of "reform and opening to the outside world". These changes include, among others, the transition from the socialist planned economy to a market economy, the gradual emergence of civil society, the reconstruction of the legal system (which had been totally devastated in the Cultural Revolution era of 1966–1976), and the establishment of a socialist Rechtsstaat. These developments have provided a fertile soil for socio-legal thought in contemporary China.

Legal sociology was an under-developed field of study in China before the 1980s. From the 1980s up to the present, much progress has been made in the development of Chinese legal sociology. Western works on legal sociology have been translated into Chinese and introduced to the Chinese academic world.[1] Books and articles on both the theoretical and empirical dimensions of legal sociology have been published.[2] There are vibrant debates on key issues relevant to the future development of Chinese law. Examples of these issues include (1) the pathway of legal modernisation in China,[3] (2) the relationship between traditional Chinese legal culture

1. For example, Lawrence M. Friedman, *The Legal System: A Social Science Perspective* (New York: Russell Sage Foundation, 1975) was translated in Li Qiongying and Li Xin, *Falu zhidu: cong shehui kexue jiaodu guancha* (Beijing: Zhongguo zhengfa daxue chubanshe, 1994); Donald J. Black, *The Behavior of Law* (New York: Academic Press, 1976) was translated in Tang Yue and Su Li, *Falu de yunzuo xingwei* (Beijing: Zhongguo zhengfa daxue chubanshe, 1994); Philippe Nonet and Philip Selznick, *Law and Society in Transition: Toward Responsive Law* (New York: Harper and Row, 1978) was translated in Zhang Zhiming, *Zhuanbian zhong de falu yu shehui: maixiang huiying xing fa* (Beijing: Zhongguo zhengfa daxue chubanshe, 1994); Roberto M. Unger, *Law in Modern Society* (New York: The Free Press, 1976) was translated in Wu Yuzhang and Zhou Hanhua, *Xianda shehui zhong de falu* (Beijing: Zhongguo zhengfa daxue chubanshe, 1994). These works form part of a series of translated works under the general editorship of Ji Weidong.
2. See, for example, Zhao Zhenjiang (ed.), *Falu shehui xue* [*Legal Sociology*] (Beijing: Beijing daxue chubanshe, 1998); Li Dun (ed.), *Falu shehui xue* [*Legal Sociology*] (Beijing: Zhongguo zhengfa daxue chubanshe, 1999); Zhu Jingwen, *Bijiao fa shehui xue de kuangjia he fangfa* [*The Framework and Methodology of Comparative Sociology of Law*] (Beijing: Zhongguo renmin daxue chubanshe, 2001).
3. See, for example, Gong Pixiang, *Fazhi xiandaihua de lilun luoji* [*The Theoretical Logic of Legal Modernisation*] (Beijing: Zhongguo zhengfa daxue chubanshe, 1999).

and the quest for legal modernisation,[4] (3) faith in law,[5] (4) civil society and legal development,[6] (5) judicial reform,[7] and (6) the contextual approach to legal research.[8]

This chapter, however, does not attempt to survey the whole field of socio-legal thought in contemporary China. Instead, it provides a case study of the socio-legal thought of one scholar — Zhu Suli, law professor at Peking University. Professor Zhu Suli (hereafter called "Zhu") is one of the best-known legal theorists in China and probably the most original and controversial among them. It is hoped that by studying his work, which as of 2002 consisted of over 60 articles (most of which have been collected and re-printed in four books[9]), one can get a glimpse of the exciting "legal revolution" that is taking place in China today and the interesting theoretical issues raised by it. This chapter consists of some biographical information on Zhu and introduces his general orientation to jurisprudence. It also discusses his thoughts on law and China's modernisation and outlines his work on the relationship between formal law and informal law as well as his work on the judicial system in China. This assessment highlights a distinct paradox: Zhu as a committed member of the CCP[10] and an adherent to historical materialism, on the one hand, and as a believer in the market and Hayek's "spontaneous order", in

4. See, for example, Zhang Jinfan, *Zhongguo falu de chuantong yu jindai zhuanxing* [*The Tradition and Modern Transformation of Chinese Law*] (Beijing: Law Press, 1997).

5. See, for example, Xie Hui, *Falu xinyang de linian yu jichu* [*The Concept and Foundation of Faith in Law*] (Beijing: Law Press, 1997).

6. See, for example, Ma Changshan, *Guojia, shimin shehui yu fazhi* [*The State, Civil Society and the Rule of Law*] (Beijing: Shangwu yinshuguan, 2001).

7. See, for example, Zuo Weimin and Zhou Changjun, *Bianqian yu gaige: fayuan zhidu xiandai hua yanjiu* [*Change and Reform: A Study of the Modernisation of the Judicial System*] (Beijing: Law Press, 2000).

8. See, for example, Su Li, "Contextualism: An Approach to and Methodology of Research on Legal Systems" (2000) 1 *Zhongwai faxue* [*Peking University Law Journal*] 40 (in Chinese).

9. Su Li, *Fazhi ji qi bentu ziyuan* [*The Rule of Law and its Indigenous Resources*] (Beijing: Zhongguo zhengfa daxue chubanshe, 1996); Su Li, *Yuedu zhixu* [*The Order of Reading*] (Jinan: Shandong jiaoyu chubanshe, 1999); Su Li, *Zhidu shi ruhe xingcheng de* [*How Institutions are Formed*] (Guangzhou: Zhongshan daxue chubanshe, 1999); Su Li, *Songfa xiaxiang: Zhongguo jiceng sifa zhidu yanjiu* [*Bringing the Law to the Villages: A Study of the Basic-level Judicial System in China*] (Beijing: Zhongguo zhengfa daxue chubanshe, 2000).

10. As revealed by himself in *Yuedu zhixu* (N9) 3.

Foucault's understanding of power and knowledge, and in Posner's pragmatic and economic approach to jurisprudence, on the other hand.[11]

## ZHU'S GENERAL ORIENTATION TO JURISPRUDENCE

Zhu was born in Hefei of Anhui in eastern China in 1955. He grew up in the eras of the Anti-Rightist Campaign (1957), the Great Leap Forward and the People's Communes Movement (in the late 1950s), and the Great Proletarian Cultural Revolution (now officially periodised as 1966–1976). Before he gained entrance as an undergraduate to the Department of Law at Peking University in 1978, he had been in the army and had worked in a factory. He graduated from Peking University in 1982. In 1984, he began his postgraduate legal study at Peking University. In 1985, he won a scholarship which enabled him to study in the United States, where he subsequently obtained degrees in commercial law and tax law (LLM), the American legal system (MA), and interdisciplinary legal study (PhD). In September 1992, he returned from the United States and began his academic career in the School of Law at Peking University. In 2001, he was appointed Dean of the School (a position which he held until 2010).

Zhu's approach to jurisprudence is unconventional by contemporary Chinese standards. How he positions himself on the contemporary Chinese jurisprudential scene can best be seen from his categorisation of the types of legal scholarship in contemporary China. He distinguishes between three types of Chinese legal scholarship that emerged after the rehabilitation of the legal system and of law as an academic discipline in 1978.[12] The first is what he calls "political-legal discourse", which was the first type of legal scholarship that arose after 1978. Examples of this kind of scholarship are discussions of the nature of law, the legal system, the Rule of Law, and legal transplant. While he recognises that this kind of legal scholarship played a positive role in asserting the autonomy of law as a discipline, he seems to suggest that it is of limited intellectual value, and he predicts that it will decline in the course of social development. The second type of legal scholarship is a technical and specialised professional discourse based on the analysis and interpretation of legal concepts and rules. Zhu recognises that there is a strong demand for this kind of scholarship on the

11. Zhu has single-handedly translated most of Posner's books into Chinese.

12. Su Li, "Maybe This is Happening: An Overview of the Development of Contemporary Chinese Jurisprudence" (2001) 3 *Bijiao fa yanjiu* [*Studies in Comparative Law*] 1 (in Chinese).

part of the legal and judicial professions (or what he in his economistic language calls "consumers in the market for such products of legal researchers"). The third kind of legal scholarship explores the social life, reality, and history that lies behind the law and employs the concepts and methodology of the social sciences. Zhu believes that the kind of work he is doing is of this kind.

In another essay, Zhu labels his methodology of legal scholarship as a "contextual" approach.[13] Scholars who adopts this approach attempt to understand a particular legal institution or rule in its historical and social context. His working assumption is that if the legal institution or rule has had a stable existence in the society concerned for a long time, then it must have been performing some useful functions in responding to some real needs of people or providing effective solutions to some real problems in society. In this sense, it should be considered legitimate and reasonable: scholars should try to understand it in its social context instead of simply evaluating and condemning it on the basis of certain moral values that are regarded as absolute and eternal.

Zhu demonstrates how his contextual approach works by applying it to analyse what he believes to be the basic legal features of the traditional Chinese family, including marriage at an early age, arranged marriage, prohibition of marriage between persons with the same surname, and the rules governing divorce. He attempts to explain them in terms of the prevailing social and material conditions of life in traditional China. For example, since life expectancy was low (he referred to studies which estimated the average age of death at 35 years old), early marriage was necessary to ensure reproduction. Early marriage in turn necessitated arranged marriage. The prohibition on marriage between persons with the same surname was designed to avoid birth defects.

Zhu distinguishes between this contextual approach and two other approaches he has identified. One is an approach emphasising values, while the other is an approach emphasising culture. The "values approach" would, for example, condemn the institution of the traditional Chinese family as patriarchal and oppressive; the "culture approach" would understand it as uniquely expressive of Chinese culture. Zhu criticises the former for simplistically dismissing history as a mistake, and the latter for ignoring the material and social conditions in which people actually lived. Both approaches, as he sees them, have limited explanatory power.

13. Su Li (N8).

Zhu is however at pains to point out that the contextual approach does not mean the rejection of legal reform, but it does mean that more attention should be paid to the social transformations underlying legal change. He comments that "slavery as an institution collapsed not because people came to understand what is justice and human rights, but because of [the change in] the efficiency of slavery".[14] Changes in the social, technological, economic, environmental, and other material conditions of life may mean that some of the existing legal institutions and rules (which are based on past social and material conditions) are no longer appropriate. New legal institutions and rules may therefore be necessary, and the ultimate test for their legitimacy should be based on a cost-benefit analysis.

However, it should be stressed that Zhu does not believe that it lies within the responsibility or capacity of legal scholars or jurists to construct new legal institutions and rules for society. In the preface to one of his books, Zhu writes:

> I have always doubted whether jurists have the capacity to undertake the task of the construction of the Rule of Law. I still insist on my view that the Rule of Law is a nation's enterprise, and the task for jurists is largely no more than the legitimation and understanding of this enterprise. Therefore, it is not superfluous but constantly necessary for jurists, on the basis of social praxis — particularly social change in China, to reflect on the characteristics of jurisprudence, on the formation of modern Chinese jurisprudence and on legal scholarship and its methodology.[15]

What, then, is jurisprudence as Zhu sees it? His view of jurisprudence is based on his view of knowledge and of law. Knowledge, to him, is always local rather than abstract and universal in nature. It is directed towards problem-solving in concrete and specific situations. Similarly, law is a problem-solving enterprise directed towards social problems and social needs. As Zhu doubts the existence of knowledge as universal truth, he also rejects the proposition that the concept and practice of the Rule of Law as it exists in the Western world today has universal validity or ought to be taken as the norm by the Chinese people. As Zhu said to an interviewer:

> There is no absolute knowledge, and the same applies to jurisprudence. Law is for solving practical problems. As different societies have different practical

---

14. *Ibid.*, 52.

15. Su Li, *Zhidu shi ruhe xingcheng de* (N9) 1–2. This is my own translation from the Chinese. Other quotations in this chapter from Professor Zhu's works are similarly my own translations.

> problems, so they need different knowledge. If we assume that all societies develop in the same way according to some principles of evolution, then all legal systems in the same stage of development are the same, and the relevant legal knowledge is the same. But this is impossible. Individuals and peoples form different traditions in their own society. So much of the existing knowledge, including foreigners' knowledge or knowledge of people in the past, may not be applicable to China today. ... What we need to solve is China's problems. So you must study in detail China's problems, and in researching these problems you will obtain a unique knowledge.[16]

Thus, Zhu is against three kinds of discourse in mainstream Chinese jurisprudence. One advocates "ruling the country according to law" and engages in philosophical and theoretical expositions of the Rule of Law on the basis of Western Enlightenment and liberal thinking. Zhu calls upon his colleagues to turn their attention away from "words and concepts" to real "problems and things"[17] instead. A second kind of discourse promotes the use of law as a means for social change and presupposes that jurists can play an important role in this regard. Here Zhu cautions that the law is not so powerful, and whether the law is effective depends on the choice of the people. He states: "In this regard, the law, like language in society, is a public instrument. It is not the creation of one or a few geniuses, but is shaped collectively by and manifested in the actions of the people."[18] He stresses that "the people will make their own choices; ... they themselves know what they need",[19] and it is not for jurists to impose a legal system on the people. Zhu also rejects a third kind of discourse which urges the Chinese law and the Chinese legal system to "connect to the international railroad" (i.e., converge with the international norms). He points out that the real questions are why and what should China learn from the West, and he qualifies his position by saying that he is not against "referring to and borrowing from" (*jiejian*) the Western experience:

> In introducing Western scholarship, we should not regard it as Truth or as a remedy for the backwardness of traditional Chinese law or legal thought. ... When I look back on the social development in China in the last ten or twenty years, I often feel strongly that the power of theory is not as big as what we imagine it to

16. Su Li, *Yuedu zhixu* (N9) 278.
17. Su Li (N8) 51.
18. Su Li, *Zhidu shi ruhe xingcheng de* (N9) 158.
19. Su Li, *Yuedu zhixu* (N9) 281.

> be when we inflate our self-image. The development of civil rights in Chinese society is largely a result of social and economic development rather than of the influence of theory or so-called enlightenment.[20]

## CHINA'S LEGAL MODERNISATION

The mainstream paradigm of contemporary Chinese jurisprudential thinking is that of legal modernisation. The premise is that China is not only economically backwards (relative to the West) but also legally backwards, and it therefore needs to "catch up" in terms of both economic development (primarily by the "reform and open-door policy", or *gaige kaifang*, and establishing a socialist market economy) and the construction of the Rule of Law. The latter is to be achieved largely by legal reform and legal transplant — transplanting to China from the West advanced legal ideas, institutions, and practices, particularly those that are conducive to the development of a market economy. Zhu, however, dissents from this mainstream paradigm of legal modernisation. He is probably the leading critic of the concept of "legal reform" (*bianfa*, which also be translated as "institutional reform" or "using the law to promote social change"), of the thesis that "the market economy is a legal-system-based or Rule-of-Law-based economy", and of the idea of legal transplant. He advocates the contrary view that China's "indigenous resources" (*bentu ziyuan*) can supply the foundation for the development of the Rule of Law in China. In order to understand this thesis, we need first to consider Zhu's conception of the Rule of Law and of the nature of the social change that characterises modernity.

Zhu's understanding of the Rule of Law draws on the thought of Fuller, Hayek, and Weber. Zhu agrees with Fuller[21] that the Rule of Law is the enterprise of subjecting human conduct to the governance of rules,[22] thus providing order and predictability in social life and human interactions. He defines the Rule of Law as "the rule of rules" (or "governance by rules").[23] However, the rules in this regard are not limited to rules enacted by the State,

20. *Ibid.*, 64.
21. See generally Lon L. Fuller, *The Morality of Law* (London: Yale University Press, revised edition, 1969).
22. Su Li, *Zhidu shi ruhe xingcheng de* (N9) 242; Su Li, *Yuedu zhixu* (N9) 148; Su Li, "Dispute Resolution and Governance by Rules in Rural Basic-level Courts" (1999) 2:1 *Beida falu pinglun* [*Peking University Law Review*] 80 (in Chinese).
23. Su Li, *Yuedu zhixu* (N9) 148.

or legislation. They also include, more importantly, the rules and norms that emerge in social life and the expectations and predictability generated by them.[24] These rules and norms are unwritten and customary in nature (but Zhu does not use the term "customary law" to refer to them) and are based on long-standing practices, habits, and mores. They supply the basis for a "spontaneous order" (as conceived by Hayek) of social interaction and cooperation. Insofar as this order has stability over time and predictability in its operation, it is an order under the Rule of Law.

Zhu adopts Hayek's distinction between "law" and "legislation".[25] State-enacted legal rules can be of two kinds. One kind of State-enacted rules merely codify the rules that emerge spontaneously in social life.[26] The other kind of rules (legislation) are consciously created or "rationally designed" by the State for the purpose of social engineering. Like Hayek, Zhu is sceptical about such legislation. He emphasises the limits of human reason or rationality in managing social change. He points out that the social order and its institutions, including its legal institutions and law, is the result of human actions (the sum total of the actions of countless people all rationally pursuing their own interests subject to the constraints arising from social institutions and rules) but not of human design.[27]

On the basis of his understanding, Zhu argues that the Rule of Law is not a unique product of modernity and that many traditional societies can also be said to be under the Rule of Law. Referring to Weber's classification of the types of authority and of legitimacy — that based on tradition, that based on charisma, and that based on formal and rational law — Zhu suggests that both traditional authority and legal authority can be regarded as based on the Rule of Law, whereas charismatic authority corresponds to the Rule of Man.[28] He points out that although the Rule of Law and the Rule of Man represent different modes of governance, they both aim to promote the people's well-being in terms of social stability and economic prosperity. Both respond to

---

24. Su Li, *Fazhi ji qi bentu ziyuan* (N9) 8.
25. Su Li, "Modernization and the Rule of Law in Twentieth-century China" (1998) 1 *Faxue yanjiu* [*CASS Journal of Law*] 3, at 7 (in Chinese). The English translation of a condensed version of this article is Suli Zhu, "Paradoxes of Legal Development in 20th Century China from the Perspective of Modernisation" (1998) 28 *Hong Kong Law Journal* 429.
26. Su Li, *Yuedu zhixu* (N9) 161.
27. *Ibid.*, 11; Su Li, *Fazhi ji qi bentu ziyuan* (N9) 20.
28. Su Li, *Zhidu shi ruhe xingcheng de* (N9) 234.

the needs of a particular society at a particular point in time. Zhu does not agree with the mainstream view in contemporary Chinese jurisprudence of simply dismissing the Rule of Man as inferior to the Rule of Law. The Rule of Man has also existed in some societies for significant periods, and it is reasonable within relevant social contexts (for example, he points out that under conditions of rapid social change, the Rule of Man might be the most appropriate mode of governance).[29] As far as China is concerned, Zhu is of the view that the Rule of Law and Rule of Man both existed in some periods of Chinese history, although in imperial China, whether the Rule of Law or the Rule of Man was adopted ultimately depended on the ruler's will.

Zhu's views on Rule of Law and Rule of Man are also related to his view of the social change that ushered in modernity.[30] Here he seems to employ Tönnies' paradigm of the transformation of a *Gemeinschaft* into a *Gesellschaft*,[31] and he also relies heavily on the Chinese sociologist Fei Xiaotong's works on rural China.[32] Traditional or pre-modern society is small in size (such as a village in rural China) in which people are well-known to each other, and interactions and transactions among the same group of people are frequent and form a continuous course of dealings. This contrasts with modern urban industrial-commercial society, which consists of strangers and involves many transactions that are one-off. In traditional society, people can engage in social cooperation on the basis of unwritten rules and customary practices (which provide predictability and stability and thus supply the basis of the Rule of Law), while in modern society, strangers will find it necessary to develop a modern form of the Rule of Law predicated on universalistic rules uniformly enforced within a large space by a centralised and bureaucratic State. Moreover, as the modern State is much more powerful and intrusive than the traditional State (which as in the case of imperial China did not really penetrate into local rural society), the modern Rule of Law attempts to control

29. *Ibid.*, 229–230, 237–238.

30. Su Li, *Yuedu zhixu* (N9) 151–166.

31. See Ferdinand Tönnies, *Gemeinschaft und Gesellschaft* [*Community and Society*] (New York: Harper & Row, 1963).

32. See, for example, Fei Hsiao-tung, *Xiangtu Zhongguo* [*From the Soil: The Foundations of Chinese Society*] (Shanghai: Shanghai renmin chubanshe, 2007), the first edition of which was translated into English by Gary G. Hamilton and Zheng Wang (Berkeley: University of California Press, 1992).

the exercise of State power by providing rules that are applicable to State institutions and officials. Zhu writes:

> I believe that the emergence and development of modern Rule of Law and its substitution for the "Rule of Man" in traditional society or its order is not the unfolding of a true moral philosophy or the realization of the moral ideal or rationality of humanity as described by traditional political and legal philosophers. It is instead an integral component of the social-structural transformation brought about by modernization as a historical movement that shaped the whole world in the last three or four centuries. It is true that modern Rule of Law is a requirement of modern society. But the meaning of this proposition is perhaps not as customarily understood or expressed by many people, who hold that modern Rule of Law is mainly used by the moderns to solve the problems of traditional rural society and the problems of so-called authoritarianism or the unlimited exercise of power: this would be a unidirectional evolutionary view of law. On the contrary, the problem confronted is and merely is the guarantee and maintenance of the social order brought about by the modernity that has made possible the modern Rule of Law.[33]

Turning to China's efforts in the twentieth century to "catch up" with the West by embarking upon legal reforms and attempting to develop a Western-style Rule of Law, Zhu argues that the rapid social and legal changes in China actually militated against the development of the Rule of Law. He points out that the Rule of Law, by its very nature, is a conservative force. It confers stability and predictability on social relationships; it tends towards the preservation of the status quo. However, China's quest for modernisation means that rapid and large-scale social and economic transformations have to be initiated by the State, using the law (State-centred law or legislation) as one of its principal means for achieving this objective — hence the frequent reference to *bianfa* (which, as pointed out above, can be translated alternatively as "legal reform", "institutional reform", or "using the law to promote social change"). In China, the law is also used to construct the modern nation-state itself.[34] This results in a situation in which the traditional order has broken down but no new legal order has been effectively put in its place.[35]

33. Su Li, *Yuedu zhixu* (N9) 166–167.

34. Su Li (N25) 3–4.

35. *Ibid.*, 8.

Zhu does not believe that the Rule of Law in China can be realised by the State's legislative efforts. Insofar as the Rule of Law is a rule-based social order in which rules are actually relied on by people for predictability and stability, it will largely depend on the people's customs, practices, and morals.[36] This is highlighted in Zhu's statement that "[w]ithout a spontaneous order endogenous to social life, without the support of compatible informal institutions, the State's formal institutions will lack a strong foundation" and that "it will be difficult to develop a reasonable and legitimate order that wins general and long-term acceptance".[37] Zhu cautions against superstition about the omnipotence of State power and of legislation, or the slogan that "the market economy is a legal-system-based (or Rule-of-Law-based) economy", for much legislation may be ineffective in practice. He points out that the problem in the Chinese legal system is that the law enforcement organs and judicial organs complain that the legislators are out of touch with reality, while at the same time legislators complain that legal scholars are out of touch with reality.[38] He also warns that if the law loses touch with the life of ordinary people, it may become no more than an instrument for the legal elite to promote their own interests.[39]

What, then, is to be done to promote the Rule of Law in China? Here Zhu warns against the uncritical "transplant" of Western legal norms and institutions to China by means of legislation and advocates the utilisation of "indigenous resources". Indigenous resources refer not to Confucian or other classical texts but to the "living law" among the people today — their customs, practices, and the informal institutions that have developed spontaneously in social life.[40] Zhu refers to the post-1978 developments of the household contract responsibility system of farming and of village and township enterprises as examples of how practices originating among the people themselves (rather than being initiated by the State) can play a creative role in forming and shaping new institutions.[41] Zhu calls upon scholars to pay more attention to the existing and developing practices and norms in Chinese society and that they "should not

36. *Ibid.*, 6.

37. *Ibid.*, 7.

38. *Ibid.*, 10.

39. *Ibid.*, 11.

40. See generally Su Li, *Fazhi ji qi bentu ziyuan* (N9) 13–14; Su Li, *Yuedu zhixu* (N9) 30.

41. Su Li, *Fazhi ji qi bentu ziyuan* (N9) 16.

simplistically, on the basis of Western scholars' formulations and criteria of the Rule of Law, deny that the customs and conventions that regulate social life in Chinese society are law".[42]

Zhu also stresses that the development of the Rule of Law in China is necessarily a gradual and time-consuming process:

> The formation and recognition of any institution, rule, custom and convention in social life takes time. ... Time is important in the formation of human concepts and modes of behaviour, and in the establishment of a social institution and its legitimacy. Time transcends the capacity of any individual or group of individuals; it is the work of "God". ... Time marks the accumulation of resources, the inheritance or transformation of tradition, and the establishment of legitimacy.[43]

However, Zhu is optimistic about the long-term prospects for a modern-style Rule of Law in China. This is because in his assessment, after all the turmoil and trials of the twentieth century, China has largely completed its task of social transformation.[44] The basis of China's economy has been transformed from agriculture to industry and commerce, and a modern nation-state has been constructed. The social structure and culture have also been transformed. Zhu believes that "the great transformations in Chinese society in the twentieth century have laid a firm foundation for the ultimate establishment of modern Rule of Law in Chinese society".[45] He thinks that the social conditions for developing the Rule of Law in China are more favourable now than in any other time in modern Chinese history. "In this sense, we are blessed."[46]

## FORMAL AND INFORMAL LAW

Zhu recognises that as a result of urbanisation and the marketisation of the economy, China is becoming a society of strangers, or a *Gesellschaft*, and that the modern Rule of Law is indeed appropriate for such a society. Even so, he is concerned about the negative consequences of the imposition of Western legal

---

42. *Ibid.*, 21.
43. *Ibid.*, 21–22.
44. Su Li, *Yuedu zhixu* (N9) 33; Su Li (N25) 13.
45. Su Li (N25) 14.
46. Su Li, *Yuedu zhixu* (N9) 33.

norms on rural China where the *Gemeinschaft* still prevails. The traditional rural community and the urbanised community may have different legal needs:

> We should not simplistically and easily sacrifice the order presently needed by Chinese rural society on the pretext of modernization. How to coordinate between the different needs in terms of law and the Rule of Law of the modernized cities on the one hand and the traditional rural communities on the other hand is a question which ought to be taken seriously by Chinese jurists and legislators. This is not only a technical issue but also a moral issue.[47]

In a series of articles on the legal situation in rural China, Zhu argues against the view that Western notions of legal rights and legal relationships embodied in contemporary Chinese legislation are universal and objective. He suggests that they may not be appropriate for rural China, and may also conflict with its informal law and culture. He also points out that in such situations, it may be reasonable for people to behave in such a way as to avoid the operation of imported legal norms. The first article[48] in the series reflects on the issues raised by two movies, *Qiuju Goes to Court* and *The Defendant Shangangye*. Both movies depict the contemporary operation of the law in a small village community.

Qiuju was the wife of a man who was kicked in the lower part of his body by the village head. Qiuju went to various authorities and various levels of the court system trying to obtain a *shuofa* (which may be translated as "words of justice"). She probably only wanted some form of official criticism or apology acknowledging that a wrong had been done to her husband, but in the end, the village head was arrested and punished by administrative detention. This was an outcome which Qiuju did not expect and could not understand, particularly as the village head was otherwise a conscientious official who saved Qiuju's life on a separate occasion.

In the second movie, Shangangye is a Party secretary in a village. He is of good character and well respected by the people. A young village woman seriously maltreated her mother-in-law and continued the maltreatment despite warnings. Shangangye had the woman arrested and paraded her in the village — a severe mode of punishment under local custom that is not authorised by State law. As a result, the woman committed suicide. Shangangye

47. Su Li (N25) 13.

48. Su Li, *Fazhi ji qi bentu ziyuan* (N9) 23–37.

was arrested by the police for false imprisonment and violation of the citizen's right to freedom of the person.

Zhu disagrees with one common interpretation of the two movies, which is that they demonstrate that China is moving towards the Rule of Law. Instead he suggests that the two stories illustrate the tragic result of the conflict between the Westernised legal norms and institutions of the State and the local customs, expectations, and "local knowledge"[49] in rural China. The local customs and legal culture are simply disregarded by the imported law, which operates in such a way as to destroy the existing community bonds and relationships of solidarity in the local community. The imported system and the legal instruments under its disposal are not able to satisfy the needs and aspirations of the local people, and yet it refuses to give recognition to or be tolerant of the customary norms in which such needs and aspirations are expressed. Zhu states: "From Qiuju's perplexity, we can say that the operational logic of the formal law in contemporary China is in some ways divorced from the social reality."[50]

Since the imported law may not operate in a practical manner in the circumstances of rural China, it may be reasonable for people to devise ways of avoiding the operation of the imported law. In another article,[51] Zhu describes the following case as an example of the "avoidance" of the law and hence of "legal pluralism". M was in love with W, who was from another village. When they were having a date, M wanted to have sexual intercourse with W, and when W refused, M raped her. W subsequently told her parents about this, and they reported the matter to the police. Before the police took action against M, M's parents visited W's home, and W's parents agreed to enter into a settlement with M's parents: M would marry W; M's family would pay 5,000 yuan to W's family; and W's family would withdraw the case against M. Although neither M nor W had reached the minimum age for marriage, they were able with a friend's help to obtain a marriage certificate. However, this private settlement to avoid the law was discovered by the government, and the marriage was declared null and void. M was then prosecuted for and convicted of rape.

Zhu disagrees with the mainstream view on this case, which is that it shows that people are ignorant about the law and there should be more legal education for members of the public. Instead, Zhu argues that this

49. Su Li, *Fazhi ji qi bentu ziyuan* (N9) 27. "Local knowledge" is a concept developed by the anthropologist Clifford Geertz and is the title of one of his books.

50. Su Li, *Fazhi ji qi bentu ziyuan* (N9) 28.

51. *Ibid.*, 41–58.

is a case in which the parties concerned were aware of what the law was, and yet deliberately and rationally chose to by-pass it, the formal operation of which would make all the parties concerned worse off than under the private settlement. The law was effective in the sense that it constituted the background and provided the starting point for the parties' negotiation and bargaining. The parties rationally pursued their interests within the constraints of the formal and informal law, and the arrangement ultimately entered into by the parties was, in Zhu's view, reasonable in the circumstances: in the small rural community in which the parties lived, it was in their interest to compromise and cooperate; the local culture is such that it is difficult for a rape victim to get married; the two families were friends and wanted to maintain their social relationship; and W's family needed the money.

Zhu thus suggests that two kinds of law are in fact in existence in rural China: State law and *minjian fa* (which may be translated as "popular law" or "people's law"), the latter being constituted by the people's customs, traditional practices, behaviour, and culture. This is a kind of legal pluralism, albeit not the same as the legal pluralism of colonial law and indigenous law for which the term was originally coined. Zhu suggests that the popular law may be understood as a kind of resistance to the State legal system that is modelled on Western law. He writes:

> Some people simplistically regard legal modernization as a change in legislation and the legal system; they assume that once these are changed, the old law will disappear. Some people in their criticism of traditional Chinese culture consciously or unconsciously adopt an attitude of legal nihilism towards Chinese legal culture. They adopt the model and standards of the State law of modern Western states and deny that there was law in traditional China. On this basis, they think that a modern legal system can be constructed in China simply by strengthening legislation, strictly enforcing the enacted law and educating the public about such law. Thus they fail to see the power of the norms that in fact operate within Chinese society, and the difficult and long-term nature of building a modern unified legal system on the basis of such norms.[52]

In the sequel[53] to the article mentioned above, Zhu goes one step further to argue that people's avoidance of the law may in fact be a source of institutional

52. *Ibid.*, 54–55.

53. *Ibid.*, 59–73. The English translation of this article is Su Li, "More on Avoidance of the Law" (winter 1998) *Social Sciences in China* 145.

innovation of positive significance. He points out that in the course of the economic reform in China in the last two decades, many new practices emerged that were originally a form of avoidance of the existing law or policy, but they subsequently became acceptable and were institutionalised by formal legal rules. It would therefore be healthy and useful to have a system in which there is communication, compromise, and cooperation as between State law and popular law. The latter ought not be regarded as backward or something to be abolished.[54] On the contrary, jurists should try to engage from a hermeneutic perspective in empathetic understanding of popular law and contribute to the breaking down of the barrier between State law and popular law. He points to the development of a mixed system of law. One possible version of this system would assume that the State law normally prevails but provide room for private settlement or avoidance on the basis of popular law. Another possible version would give priority to popular law, restricting the role of State law to domains where State intervention is essential.[55]

In another article[56] Zhu discusses a case in rural China for the purpose of demonstrating how popular custom is, in practice, given recognition by Chinese courts even where it is not entirely consistent with State law. In this case, T committed adultery with M's wife W. M made threats to T and his family. T initiated legal proceedings against M, and M counter-claimed against T. The court detained T (partly to protect him against M), and finally a settlement was arrived at by court mediation. The settlement provided that T would pay compensation to M, and M would stop his threats against T. They would both contribute to pay the court fees for the case. Zhu points out that under State law, adultery is neither a crime nor a tort, thus M has no legal right to compensation from T and there is no legal basis for T's detention. Zhu, however, suggests that although the settlement is technically contrary to State law, it is reasonable and based on the recognition of an unwritten customary norm accepted by all parties concerned that adultery constitutes an injury to the husband. The judge applied this norm, not because he identified with it in the cultural or moral sense, but because of pragmatic considerations — disregard of this norm would lead to public anger in the local community in which the court was situated.

---

54. Su Li, *Fazhi ji qi bentu ziyuan* (N9) 65.

55. *Ibid*., 62–63.

56. Su Li, "Custom in Contemporary Chinese Law" (2000) 3 *Zhongguo shehui kexue* [*Chinese Social Science*] 124 (in Chinese).

## THE JUDICIAL SYSTEM

One of Zhu's most ambitious works is his book *Bringing the Law to the Villages*,[57] which is a masterpiece synthesising empirical socio-legal research with theoretical analysis. The focus of the book is the operation of the "basic-level" (*jiceng*) courts in China's rural areas, and the empirical research takes the form of interviews with judges of basic-level courts in Hubei province and fieldwork in Shanxi province. In the introduction to the book,[58] Zhu identifies four reasons why the basic-level courts in China, rather than courts at higher levels of the judicial hierarchy, deserve to be studied as a matter of priority. First, "China's problems are still mainly those of its rural areas. Most of China's population still live in the rural areas, and one of the most important tasks in the modernisation of Chinese society is the modernization of rural society." Second, modern law is mainly directed towards the urban and commercial society consisting of "strangers" to one another; there is a gap in legal research regarding the needs of people in the rural areas. Third, in terms of the numbers of judges and cases dealt with, the basic-level courts constitute the largest component of the Chinese judicial system. Finally, it is in the basic-level courts that the relationship between law and social reality is most vividly demonstrated and the most challenging issues are raised regarding the development of the Rule of Law in China.

Also in the introduction to the book, Zhu reiterates his approach to and methodology of socio-legal scholarship. He points out that he adopts the framework of historical materialism and rejects historical idealism or the premise that legal development is largely a product of the intellect, of concepts or moral ideas. He also acknowledges his debt to modern sociology, the thoughts of Foucault and Bourdieu, the new institutional economics, and the study of law and economics. Regarding methodology, he states:

> I have borrowed from the analytical perspectives of empiricism, functionalism and pragmatism (there is a degree of consistency among these three schools of thought). I emphasize that practice is the sole criterion for testing a theory, emphasize the practical functions of institutions and laws, and reject the a

57. Su Li, *Songfa xiaxiang* (N9).

58. The introductory essay for the book has also been published separately; see Su Li, "Weishenmo yanjiu Zhongguo jiceng sifa zhidu?" [Why Do I Study the Basic-level Judicial System in China?] (2000) 3 *Fashang yanjiu* [*Studies in Law and Commerce*] 82.

priori nature of metaphysics. I emphasize consequences that are observable and functions that are comparable, and reject empty talk or games of words such as conceptual analysis.[59]

In a chapter[60] in the first of the four substantive parts of the book, Zhu tackles the common criticism that the existence of adjudication committees in the Chinese courts is one of their gravest structural defects and obstacles to judicial independence. As all students of the Chinese judicial system would know, such committees have a legal basis in the Organic Law of the People's Courts.[61] Consisting mainly of the president, vice-presidents, and divisional heads of the court, the adjudication committee rather than the collegial bench that has actually heard the case has the power to decide on difficult, important, or sensitive cases. On the basis of his empirical study of the operation of adjudication committees in basic-level courts, Zhu comes up with the controversial thesis that their continued existence in the basic-level courts is justified.

Zhu cautions against the call for "convergence with international standards" and the elevation of judicial reform to an ideology. The fact that the adjudication committee as an institution does not exist in other jurisdictions does not necessarily imply that China must abolish it in its current drive for judicial reform. Zhu points out that insofar as an institution has enjoyed a relatively stable existence for a relatively long time, it may well have its rationales, may be responding to certain social needs, or may be consistent with social conditions. It therefore has a prima facie legitimacy or reasonableness within its social context, and as such deserves to be studied, understood, and even respected.[62]

On the basis of interviews with judges, Zhu concludes that the adjudication committee as an institution in the basic-level courts (he does not propound any thesis regarding adjudication committees in higher level courts) is not only not detrimental to justice or judicial independence but plays a positive role in five ways.[63] First, the adjudication committee can serve to check the abuse

59. Su Li, *Songfa xiaxiang* (N9) 20.

60. *Ibid.*, 88–145. This chapter was also published separately; see Su Li, "Investigations and Reflections on the System of Adjudication Committees in Basic-level Courts" (1998) 1:2 *Beida falu pinglun* [*Peking University Law Review*] 320 (in Chinese).

61. See generally Albert H.Y. Chen, *An Introduction to the Chinese Legal System* (Hong Kong: LexisNexis, 5th edition, 2019) 169–172.

62. Su Li, *Songfa xiaxiang* (N9) 90.

63. *Ibid.*, 106–123. See also the two cases discussed at 127–136 of the same work.

of power (particularly corruption affecting decision-making) of individual judges. Second, the adjudication committee can help to unify the differing interpretations and criteria of law-application used by individual judges. Third, given that many judges in the basic-level courts have low educational standards and limited judicial abilities, the adjudication committee can exercise a check upon the incompetence of individual judges. Fourth, in rural communities in which judges have close ties with the local community, judges sometimes prefer to shift the responsibility for the final decision to the adjudication committee so as to resist attempts at interference with their work by powerful people or friends and relatives, or to resist the pressure of local public opinion. Finally, reference of a case to the adjudication committee may enable the leaders of the court to take administrative measures to coordinate with other government departments so as to provide a more satisfactory solution to the problems raised by the case (problems which cannot be simply resolved by a paper judgment). In this regard, Zhu points out that the primary function of basic-level courts in rural areas is often dispute resolution and problem solving rather than the strict application of legal norms in rendering a judgment.

Despite his basic affirmation of the adjudication committee as an institution in the basic-level courts, Zhu does acknowledge that there are problems with it.[64] One of them is that the professional standards of the adjudication committee are often inadequate. As a remedy, Zhu proposes the administrative re-organisation of the courts, so that members of the adjudication committee would not necessarily be the holders of senior administrative positions in the court. His thesis regarding the separation of the administrative operations of the court from its judicial operations is further developed in another chapter of the book.

In that chapter,[65] Zhu points out that, in addition to judicial functions, Chinese courts have to discharge quite a lot of administrative functions, such as organising training programs for judges, organising income-generating activities, participating in local anti-poverty work, etc. The administrative system in the courts, consisting of office-holders such as presidents, vice-presidents, divisional heads, and vice-heads, was legitimately set up to perform such administrative functions. The problem as Zhu sees it is that the administrative system has infiltrated the judicial operations of the courts and

---

64. *Ibid.*, 124–127.

65. *Ibid.*, 61–87. This chapter was also published separately; see Su Li, "The Judicial Functions and Administrative Management of Courts" (1999) 5 *Zhongwai faxue* [*Peking University Law Journal*] 36 (in Chinese).

distorted their proper functioning in judicial decision-making. For example, although this practice is not required by law, a custom has developed in the court system whereby individual judges cannot render their judgment without prior approval of the judgment by their administrative superiors, such as the president, vice-president, or divisional head. Furthermore, since these administrative office-holders within the court also play an important role in the appointment and dismissal of judges of the court, they are able to exercise disproportionate influence in the judicial work of the court.[66] Thus, Zhu proposes the separation of the administrative functions of courts from their judicial function to reform the system.

Apart from distinguishing the courts' administrative function from their judicial function, Zhu also draws a distinction between the "dispute resolution" (or problem-solving in concrete and specific cases) function of the courts and their "rule application" function (or contributing to the Rule of Law as governance by general and abstract rules), and discusses the possible tension or conflict between the two functions and the apparent priority of the dispute resolution function in the work of the basic-level courts.[67] Zhu illustrates the thesis with a case in which a woman who had been battered by her son (because she refused to give him money) went to court seeking to terminate the mother-son relationship. There was no law that could be used to grant her such a remedy. Instead of dealing with the son under the criminal law (which would not solve the real problem in this case), the judge devised the ingenious solution of arranging for her divorce from her husband (who had deserted her more than 20 years ago and could not be found), so that she could find a new husband who could give her protection from her son. In another case,[68] the plaintiff was a peasant who lost a leg in an accident for which the defendant was responsible. However, the defendant had no means to pay the plaintiff. The court arranged for the plaintiff to be assigned a job as a watchman so that his livelihood could be guaranteed. It asked the township government to provide tax relief to the plaintiff. It also persuaded the bank to lend money to the defendant so as to pay for the cost of a prosthetic leg for the plaintiff as well as some compensation to him. Finally, the court arranged for

66. Su Li, *Songfa xiaxiang* (N9) 73–78.

67. *Ibid.*, 176–196. See also Su Li (N22).

68. Su Li, *Songfa xiaxiang* (N9) 131–132.

an additional sum to be paid as "social welfare benefits" to the plaintiff by the farm for which the defendant worked. Commenting on this case, Zhu writes:

> If the court simply decides the case according to law and only emphasizes its judicial function, the problem cannot be solved. This might not only lead to serious social consequences ... but the court's authority would be completely lost because its judgment cannot be enforced.[69]

The case also illustrates another special feature of basic-level courts in rural China: rather than serving as an impartial arbiter of disputes who is distanced from the parties to the case, the judge sometimes plays the role of a lawyer in helping a party to solve the issue.[70] This is a result of there being few lawyers in China's rural areas who can cater for the people's need for legal services. In these circumstances, the judge in rural China may have to play a role quite different from a judge in a commercial or industrial urban society. Zhu states: "Perhaps we should review afresh the rich content of the concept of the judge."[71]

A third feature of the work of the basic-level courts in rural China is that the courts often have to apply Western legal concepts enshrined in contemporary Chinese law to indigenous practices that may not fit well into Western legal categories. Zhu describes this as a tension between law and fact, or between the "standardised" nature of modern judicial thinking and the "non-standardised" nature of social reality in rural China.[72] He cites a case in which A was the owner of a cow. He bought the cow by partly using his own means and by borrowing from his fellow villager B. Subsequently B's own cow died, and B entered into a *dahuo* (which can be translated as "joining together"[73]) agreement with A, whereby B waived his right to repayment of the loan, and A and B would share the use of A's cow for farming purpose. After a few years a dispute arose regarding the distribution of the sale proceeds of cows bought with the sale proceeds of A's original cow. The problem in this case was that the concept of *dahuo* is an indigenous one which is not recognised in Chinese civil law, which only provides for the concept of partnership. The Court of First

69. *Ibid.*, 132.
70. *Ibid.*, 316–317.
71. *Ibid.*, 321.
72. *Ibid.*, 197–237. See also Su Li, "Intertwined with Facts and Law" (2000) 3 *Falu kexue* [*Legal Science*] 3 (in Chinese).
73. The Chinese legal term for "partnership" is *hehuo*, which is similar to but not exactly the same as *dahuo*.

Instance decided the case on the basis of partnership principles. The decision was overturned on appeal and a re-trial was ordered. Finally, the court decided the case on the basis of the concept of common ownership. Zhu writes:

> The problem is that in Chinese basic-level and rural society, it is difficult to fit many disputes into the framework of legal concepts that has largely been transplanted from abroad.[74] ... The enacted law has always been more concerned with commercial life or the urban area, even though it carries with it the flag of universal civil rights. ... In every society, areas of the traditional rural economy are to some extent "land not reached by the modern law".[75]

However, Zhu accepts that change will occur as modern legal discourse penetrates into rural life. The application of legal concepts such as "partnership" or "common ownership" by the local court in this case exemplifies this process, whereby "a change in the conceptual world ... will bring about a change in human behaviour".[76] The rural population may then rely more on lawyers and express their interests and expectations in modern legal language.[77] Zhu goes on:

> As legal discourse continuously reproduces itself and continuously conquers new territories and bodies, the world will become standardized or re-standardized. ... There will occur the process of continuous rationalization that Weber described, particularly as the market economy develops. ... Confronted with such a picture, people will form their own judgment. Some will see the beauty of the colour of roses — the modernization of the Rule of Law. But, I believe, there will be some (such as Weber and Foucault) who see in the roses the colour of blood. I do not want to make any evaluation of my own.[78]

Another important thesis that Zhu develops regarding the basic-level courts is that there is a division of labour in terms of comparative advantage in the possession and use of different kinds of knowledge and techniques as between the basic-level courts and the higher courts.[79] As mentioned above, the more

74. Su Li, *Songfa xiaxiang* (N9) 216.
75. *Ibid.*, 227.
76. *Ibid.*, 235.
77. *Ibid.*, 233–234.
78. *Ibid.*, 236–237.
79. *Ibid.*, 264–295. See also Su Li, "Revelations about the Judicial Knowledge of Basic-level Judges" (2000) 3 *Xiandai faxue* [*Modern Legal Science*] 9 (pt. I), and (2000) 4 *Xiandai faxue* [*Modern Legal Science*] 12 (pt. II) (in Chinese).

pressing task of the basic-level courts is dispute resolution and problem solving, while rule-application in the sense of developing the Rule of Law on a national scale is left to the higher courts. This does not, however, mean that the basic-level courts can afford to ignore the written norms in Chinese legislation. Zhu suggests that while their uppermost concern would be to ensure a fair outcome in a case that would be acceptable to the parties and to public opinion and that they will also not be troubled by procedural niceties, they will still take care to use legal concepts and norms in the "packaging" of their judgment and use law to legitimise their decisions. They will decide the outcome of the case first by relying mainly on their intuitions, and only then find the relevant law to justify their decision. They will also exploit the uncertainty in legal language so as to secure the desired outcome. They will select from the facts of the case those that can fit into the official legal framework. Before they give their judgment, they will try to secure a settlement by mediation. They will try to avoid the escalation of conflict. They will also pay special attention to the enforceability of the judgment and, if necessary, secure the cooperation of other local government departments in this regard. These, according to Zhu, are some of the characteristics of the specific kind of knowledge and specific set of techniques developed by China's basic-level courts in the course of their problem-solving work.

Finally, Zhu attempts to offer a socio-political explanation of the practice, developed since the early period of Chinese communism, whereby sometimes judges will, instead of summoning parties to the court, visit the locality of the case and try the case there and then.[80] Zhu suggests that orthodox explanations in terms of the ideology of the "mass line" or the force of tradition are inadequate because they fail to consider the underlying social, economic, and institutional context of this practice of "bringing the law to the villages" (which is also the title of Zhu's book). In his chapter on this topic,[81] Zhu cites a case in which a rural credit association tried to recover a debt from a peasant. The judge, together with the representatives of the credit association, went to the village in which the peasant lived. They visited his home together with the village cadre, where the trial was held. In the end, the peasant accepted a set of terms regarding repayment proposed by the village cadre. Zhu interprets this practice of the judge

80. Su Li, *Zhidu shi ruhe xingcheng de* (N9) 56–82.

81. Su Li, *Songfa xiaxiang* (N9) 27–53. This chapter is a re-print of Su Li (N79).

visiting the locality and holding a trial there as a "strategy of power":[82] since State power is weak in and does not effectively penetrate some rural areas which can be described as the "peripheral zone"[83] of State power, it needs to assert its authority and establish its relationship with the subject. The visit to the village and the trial in the peasant's home can thus be seen as a "reconstruction of a power relationship".[84]

## CONCLUSION

Zhu's penetrating and insightful analysis of some of the most important issues arising from legal developments in contemporary China makes him one of present-day China's most outstanding legal sociologists, or even perhaps the most outstanding among them. He is also by far the most controversial among them. As he himself acknowledges in one of his articles, some people label his thinking as "conservatism, postmodernism or dangerous thoughts".[85] His approach to legal scholarship as well as the substantive views he holds on a number of key issues clearly place him quite far apart from the mainstream position of most scholars of legal theory and of substantive law in contemporary China, who generally endorse the Western concept of rights, adopt a universalistic and Enlightenment-based discourse of legal modernisation and legal progress, and advocate the reform of Chinese legal and judicial institutions in accordance with internationally accepted norms regarding the Rule of Law.[86]

Zhu's dissent from this mainstream paradigm is by itself an important contribution to the jurisprudential debate in contemporary China. It enables us to have a more balanced view of the whole picture. While most Chinese

82. Su Li, *Zhidu shi ruhe xingcheng de* (N9) 63.

83. *Ibid.*, 59.

84. *Ibid.*, 67, 72.

85. Su Li (N22) 90.

86. For general surveys of the field, see Albert H.Y. Chen, "Developing Theories of Rights and Human Rights in China" in Raymond Wacks (ed.), *Hong Kong, China and 1997: Essays in Legal Theory* (Hong Kong: Hong Kong University Press, 1993) 123–149; Albert H.Y. Chen, "The Developing Theory of Law and Market Economy in Contemporary China" in Wang Guiguo and Wei Zhenying (eds.), *Legal Developments in China: Market Economy and Law* (Hong Kong: Sweet & Maxwell, 1996) 3–20; Albert H.Y. Chen, "Confucian Legal Culture and its Modern Fate" in Raymond Wacks (ed.), *The New Legal Order in Hong Kong* (Hong Kong: Hong Kong University Press, 1999) 505–533 (Chapter 6 of the present volume); Albert H.Y. Chen, "Toward a Legal Enlightenment: Discussions in Contemporary China on the Rule of Law" (1999) 17 *UCLA Pacific Basin Law Journal* 125.

jurists assume that legal modernisation is legal Westernisation, Zhu cautions that Western norms and practices are not necessarily universally valid and applicable. While most Chinese jurists believe in the use of legislation to promote social and economic transformation, Zhu points out that the spontaneous order and customary practices that emerge from the rational choice of countless individuals cannot be easily dictated by the State's legislative decrees. While most Chinese jurists advocate the Rule of Law, judicial independence, and the protection of people's rights on an abstract and philosophical level, Zhu calls attention to the social reality of the people. While most Chinese jurists presuppose that enlightened legal ideas constitute one of the most powerful forces behind legal and institutional progress, Zhu relies on Marxist historical materialism in arguing that what ultimately matters are the material and social conditions in which people live, and that the "modern" Rule of Law is a response to the commercialisation, industrialisation, and urbanisation of society rather than a liberation from despotism and authoritarianism. He even reminds colleagues that "law talk" might degenerate into an instrument of the power and privilege of the legal elite.

Zhu's empirical work on the basic-level courts in rural China and his theoretical reflections on the outcome of his study also constitute a very important contribution to legal sociology in contemporary China. There is a dearth of such empirical work in China today. Most Chinese legal sociologists engage in theoretical and philosophical study rather than fieldwork. Zhu's work is therefore exemplary and ground-breaking in this regard. For example, his analysis of the adjudication committee in the basic-level court demonstrates how theoretical critique without an empathic understanding of the actual facts and practices as well as their rationales may well be inadequate and misguided. His study of the primacy of the dispute resolution and problem solving function of the basic-level courts demonstrates that the words "court" or "judge" can mean very different things in different contexts.

Although Zhu's contribution to jurisprudence and socio-legal scholarship in contemporary China is highly significant, his work to date is not without limitations and problems. First, his deliberate under-emphasis of the role and significance of legal ideas and ideals may be questioned. He affirms Marxist historical materialism as self-evident truth (note that it is still not permissible in contemporary China to openly reject Marxist historical materialism in published writings, and it is still considered "politically correct" for a scholar to pay lip service to historical materialism even if one does not genuinely believe in it — but in Zhu's case he is a genuine and fervent believer in historical materialism) and has taken for granted theoretical presuppositions not grounded on an objective study of the relative significance of ideas or of changes in material and social conditions in the legal history of humankind.[87] This issue regarding the role of ideas in legal development is not merely academic. For example, if Zhu is right, then scholars who spend most of their time developing theories of the Rule of Law or human rights and propagating them among China's huge populace are largely wasting their time.

Second, Zhu is apparently too quick and ready to accept that because long-standing practices and spontaneously evolving customs must have their rationales in social and material conditions (and the discovery of such rationales is, for Zhu, one of the most important tasks of the jurist in their attempt to explain such practices and customs), they must be prima facie reasonable and legitimate. Zhu's framework of thought apparently allows little room for independent moral criticism. The only kind of criticism he envisages is that because of a change in the social and material conditions, the existing customs and practices may no longer be appropriate on the basis of a cost-benefit analysis. The heart of the problem goes to Zhu's view of morality,[88] which he believes is based on the self-interest of individuals living and acting under social constraints and as largely explicable from the sociobiological perspective. Just as Zhu does not believe in the possibility of legal development being promoted by enlightened legal ideas, he also does not believe in the possibility of legal reform of traditional practices on the basis of a critical and humanistic moral evaluation that transcends materialistic and utilitarian considerations. This view is difficult to accept by many who believe in human dignity and the possibility of the moral progress of humankind.

Take the issue of corruption, which is probably the most endemic and serious problem in contemporary China. Corrupt practices can be interpreted as a spontaneously developing customary practice resulting from officials promoting their self-interest under a certain set of institutional conditions. Extrapolating from Zhu's theoretical presuppositions, corruption as a practice emerging during China's transition from the planned economy to the market economy can probably be regarded as prima facie legitimate and reasonable, just as Zhu considers some practices of "avoidance" of the law by the rural

87. This does not mean that Zhu has not written insightfully on aspects of legal history. See, for example, Su Li, *Zhidu shi ruhe xingcheng de* (N9) 83–99 (on the history of *Marbury v Madison*), 127–151 (on the origin of the character *fa* — the Chinese character for the word "law"); Su Li, *Yuedu zhixu* (N9) 232–274 (on the history of social contract theory).

88. See, for example, Su Li, *Yuedu zhixu* (N9) 49–60; Su Li, *Zhidu shi ruhe xingcheng de* (N9) 15–43.

population as legitimate and reasonable. Since Zhu has not so far investigated into the problem of corruption in his writings, it is difficult to say that this would be his conclusion, and I suspect that if pressed he would not defend corruption. However, the fact that his ambitious theory of socio-legal study has not yielded any result so far on one of the most serious law-related socio-political problems confronting China today speaks something about the limits of the theory.[89]

Third, although Zhu cites Foucault fairly frequently in his writings and directly employs the Foucauldian conceptions of power and power/knowledge in some of his articles, he has never applied the Foucauldian critique of power to the CCP and the ruling apparatus in China today. It is true that Chinese scholars are not yet free to directly criticise the CCP or the regime. However, many Chinese scholars of jurisprudence have in fact severely criticised the abuse of power on the part of officials and judges, and advocated the Rule of Law as a solution to the problems of the abuse of power. Zhu has never joined in this "chorus". On the contrary, he seems to suggest that this kind of talk about the Rule of Law is too metaphysical, abstract, and conceptual to have any real intellectual value. The abuse of power does not appear in Zhu's writings as a serious problem in contemporary China, neither does he provide any remedy for it. At a time when increasing criticisms of judicial corruption are voiced, Zhu defends the record of performance of the basic-level courts by pointing to the declining rate of appeals to higher courts over the years.[90] On the whole, Zhu appears to be more critical of the critics of the existing legal system than of the existing legal system itself. That is why some consider him a defender of the status quo or a neo-conservative.[91]

Thus, in Zhu's socio-legal thought, we find a curious mix of conservatism, pragmatism, economic analysis of law, post-modernism,[92] nationalism, anti-

---

89. In a conversation with the author in 2002, Su Li pointed out that officials' abuse of power and corruption are political issues, including issues of supervision, rather than legal issues.

90. Su Li, *Songfa xiaxiang* (N9) 393–421.

91. This is not to suggest that Zhu's scholarly views were consciously influenced by politics. Indeed, unlike many Chinese legal theorists in the 1980s and 1990s whose research agendas have been shaped by changing political slogans of the CCP, Zhu's scholarship has not apparently been influenced by the winds or atmosphere of Chinese politics. There is no question that Zhu is an independent scholar rather than a spokesman for the regime.

92. See, for example, Zhu Suli's chapter on post-modern jurisprudence, titled "Kebie chengle 'dengdai Geduo'" [Let It Not Be "Waiting for Godot"] in Zhu Jingwen (ed.), *Dangdai xifang houxiandai faxue* [*Contemporary Western Postmodern Jurisprudence*] (Beijing: Law Press, 2002) 41–50; Su Li, *Fazhi ji qi bentu ziyuan* (N9) 268–291.

"Western ethnocentrism",[93] and Marxist materialism. It seems that what distinguishes Zhu from his colleagues in Chinese jurisprudence is that while most contemporary Chinese jurists have come to subscribe to liberalism[94] and its legal values as a faith, and are explicitly or implicitly promoting liberal values as the guiding principles for the reform and modernisation of Chinese law and legal institutions, Zhu has remained a sceptic as to such faith or ideology. The defining characteristic of Zhu's jurisprudence is a healthy dose of scepticism — inspired by diverse intellectual traditions such as Marxism, Foucauldianism, American legal realism, and economic analysis of law — regarding the Rule of Law as a liberal ideology.

Liberalism and the liberal version of the Rule of Law[95] are still distant ideals for China, but they have already become the living reality of the Western world. The question for China is whether it can or ought to come closer to the liberal world and ultimately become part of it. This is the most interesting question raised by the contrast between Zhu Suli's thoughts and those of his adversaries. If Zhu Suli is right, then it is a question that legal sociology cannot and should not answer — it is a question that only the hundreds of millions of people of China can answer in the course of time.

## Acknowledgement

This chapter was first published as "Socio-legal Thought and Legal Modernization in Contemporary China: A Case Study of the Jurisprudence of Zhu Suli" in Guenther Doeker-Mach and Klaus A. Ziegert (eds.), *Law, Legal Culture and Politics in the Twenty-First Century* (2004), pp. 227–249. This edited version is reprinted with permission from the publisher, Franz Steiner Verlag Stuttgart.

93. This is not to suggest that Zhu is anti-Western. As can be seen in this chapter, most of the analytical tools in Zhu's intellectual apparatus have been borrowed from the West.

94. By "liberalism" I mean the political and legal thought founded in the seventeenth and eighteenth centuries by thinkers such as Locke, Montesquieu, and Kant as well as the founding fathers of the American Constitution, as propounded in the late twentieth century by political and legal philosophers such as John Rawls and Ronald Dworkin. Liberalism privileges individuals' rights and advocates the Rule of Law and constitutionalism as means for the control of political power, the abuse of which constitutes one of the gravest threats to the rights of individuals.

95. For liberal and non-liberal versions of the Rule of Law and their relevance to China, see Randall Peerenboom, *China's Long March Toward Rule of Law* (Cambridge: Cambridge University Press, 2002).

# Part III

## Constitutionalism in Asia

# 13

# Constitutions, Constitutional Practice, and Constitutionalism in East Asia

## INTRODUCTION

The constitutions and constitutional practices in East and Southeast Asia (hereafter called "East Asia") provide worthwhile case studies for scholars of comparative constitutional law, constitutional theory, and politics. This chapter seeks to provide a conceptual framework for such comparative studies and briefly discusses some key components of selected existing literature on this subject in particular countries.

East Asia is a region characterised by great ethnic, cultural, religious, and linguistic diversities, different levels of economic development, and large variations in the types of political regimes that have existed or are now prevalent. This is highly relevant to the study of Asian constitutionalism, as constitutional law is bound up with history and politics. All East Asian countries have adopted written constitutions in modern times, but the nature, purposes, and functions of these constitutions vary according to the nature and character of the political regime in which they exist.

## GENERAL TYPES OF REGIMES IN MODERN EAST ASIA

Political regimes in the contemporary world may be classified as democratic, non-democratic (or authoritarian), and hybrid regimes (which have both democratic and authoritarian elements). It is easy to recognise political systems in East Asia that resemble Western liberal democracies as democratic regimes. Such cases include post-War Japan as well as South Korea and Taiwan after they embarked on democratisation in the 1980s. Non-democratic regimes in the modern world[1] and in contemporary Asia are those in which political power is concentrated in one single party (as in the People's Republic of China and Vietnam), one single strongman (as in North Korea), or the military (as in Thailand for various periods since royal absolutism was replaced with constitutional monarchy in 1932, and in Myanmar for significant periods). Hybrid regimes[2] constitute a more complex category.

1. P. Brooker, *Non-Democratic Regimes* (London: Macmillan, 2000).
2. L. Diamond, "Thinking about Hybrid Regimes" (2002) 13:2 *Journal of Democracy* 21.

Political scientists have pointed out that the boundary between democratic and non-democratic political systems is often "blurred and imperfect".[3] There exist regimes which may be described as a "half-way house" between democracy and authoritarianism;[4] they inhabit the "vast gray zone that occupies the space between authoritarianism … and consolidated democracy".[5] These are what may be called hybrid regimes,[6] alternatively known as semi-democratic[7] or semi-authoritarian regimes, and scholars have spent much time researching the "grades of distinction among less than democratic systems".[8] For example, in their authoritative work on politics in developing countries, Diamond, Linz, and Lipset[9] identified several species of hybrid regimes: semi-democracy, a hegemonic party system, and pseudo-democracy.

In a semi-democracy, competing political parties and elections exist, but the elections held are not completely free or fair, restrictions exist on political parties' activities, and civil and political liberties are limited. As a result, the "electoral outcomes, while competitive, still deviate significantly from popular preferences". "[S]ome political orientations and interests are unable to organize and express themselves." Furthermore, in a semi-democracy, the "effective power of elected officials" may be "limited".

Similarly, in a hegemonic party system, opposition political parties are allowed to exist and elections are held. However, there are "pervasive electoral malpractices" and "frequent state coercion" against the opposition. As a result, the opposition is "denied … any real chance to compete for power". This means that the existing power-holders are able to perpetuate their monopoly of political power and pass it to others within the same "hegemonic party system".

In this classification scheme, a pseudo-democracy is a "subset of authoritarian regimes". Authoritarian regimes are those in which little "pluralism" is permitted, there are few or no civil or political freedoms, and "most forms of political organization and competition" are banned. It is

3. L. Diamond, J.J. Linz, and S.M. Lipset (eds.), *Politics in Developing Countries* (Boulder: Lynne Rienner, 1990) 7.
4. W.F. Case, "Can the 'Halfway House' Stand? Semidemocracy and Elite Theory in Three Southeast Asian Countries" (1996) 28:4 *Comparative Politics* 437.
5. M. Ottaway, *Democracy Challenged: The Rise of Semi-Authoritarianism* (Washington D.C.: Carnegie Endowment for International Peace, 2003) 6.
6. Diamond (N2).
7. Case (N4).
8. Diamond, Linz, and Lipset (N3) 7.
9. *Ibid.*, 7–8. The quotations in the next three paragraphs are all from these pages.

recognised that authoritarian regimes vary in terms of the space available for "independent and critical political expression and organization", whereas in the "totalitarian" regime, there is no such space at all. In a pseudo-democracy, "the existence of formally democratic political institutions, such as multiparty electoral competition, masks ... the reality of authoritarian domination". In this theory, the difference between a pseudo-democracy and a hegemonic party system seems to be a matter of degree. The former is "less institutionalized", "more personalized, coercive, and unstable".[10]

The concepts of semi-democracy and hegemonic party system may be usefully compared with that of "semi-authoritarianism" as formulated by Ottaway[11] (who considered Egypt under Mubarak and Venezuela under Chávez as typical examples of this type of regime) and that of "semi-democracy" as formulated by Case[12] (who applied it to the study of politics in Singapore and Malaysia). According to Ottaway, the key feature of semi-authoritarianism is that although there exist opposition political parties and elections, there is "little real competition for power",[13] because there are "mechanisms that effectively prevent the transfer of power through elections from the hands of the incumbent leaders or party to a new political elite or organization".[14] Ottaway points out that semi-authoritarianism usually relies on "power networks independent of the formal democratic processes and institutions".[15] The latter are often weak and manipulated by the rulers.[16] There is thus a "discrepancy between the way in which power is generated and allocated in practice and the way in which it ought to be generated and allocated according to the formal institutional framework".[17]

Ottaway stresses that the semi-authoritarian systems which she describes in her book are not "imperfect democracies struggling toward improvement and consolidation".[18] The countries concerned are "semi-authoritarian by design, not by default, they are successful semi-authoritarian regimes rather than failed

10. *Ibid.*, 8.
11. Ottaway (N5).
12. Case (N4); W.F. Case, *Politics in Southeast Asia* (Richmond: Curzon, 2002).
13. Ottaway (N5) 3.
14. *Ibid.*, 15.
15. *Ibid.*, 134.
16. *Ibid.*, 16–17.
17. *Ibid.*, 16.
18. *Ibid.*, 3.

democracies".[19] This converges with Case's assessment of what he calls "semi-democracy", where the rulers "borrow cunningly some features of democracy in order substantially to avoid it".[20] According to Case, semi-democracy is characterised by "electoral contestation" without "liberal participation".[21] Restrictions on civil liberties and on the opposition's activities are such that the opposition would not be able to win power in an election, which is no more than a "visible outlet for social grievances".[22] Case argues that as a "distinct regime form",[23] semi-democracy can be stable. Developing this theory of semi-democracy in the mid-1990s, Case considered Singapore and Malaysia to be typical examples, as contrasted with the Philippines and Thailand, which in his view[24] were unstable, low quality, or unconsolidated democracies (which are more democratic than semi-democracy), although he classified Thailand in the 1980s as a semi-democracy.

On the basis of the above, the key distinction between a hybrid regime and a full democracy is that in the former although different political parties are allowed to exist and regular elections are held, the possibility of different political parties taking turns to form the government after winning a general election is largely or completely ruled out in practice. The monopoly of power by the ruling elite, or the practical impossibility of transfer of power to a different political party or group, is secured by restrictions on civil and political liberties, persecution of and coercion against opposition politicians (for example, by means of repressive laws or selective enforcement of the law), informal power networks (including those based on a culture of patrimonialism, patronage, and clientalism), practices inconsistent with free and fair elections (including vote-buying, rigging the election), etc. On the other hand, the difference between a hybrid regime and a completely authoritarian one is that in the latter case, there exist minimal or no civil and political liberties (including freedom of the press), little or no space for political and social pluralism such as political parties other than the ruling party and civil society organisations outside the control of the regime, and elections (if they exist) include no candidates who are not from or approved by the ruling party.

---

19. *Ibid.*, 9.
20. Case (N4) 438.
21. *Ibid.*, 439.
22. *Ibid.*
23. *Ibid.*, 437.
24. *Ibid.*, 437; Case (N12) 26–28.

## EXISTING CLASSIFICATIONS OF CONSTITUTIONS

The differences between democratic, authoritarian, and hybrid regimes have important implications for their constitutions, constitutional practice, and constitutionalism. Two schemes of classification of constitutions will be considered here: that developed by Loewenstein, and that by Sartori.

Loewenstein proposes an "ontological" approach to the classification of constitutions,[25] which focuses on the degree to which political practice conforms to or relates to the norms set out in the constitution. In his theory, there are three types of constitutions: normative, nominal, and semantic. A constitution is normative if it is "faithfully observed by all concerned" and is effective in "governing the dynamics of the power process".[26] A constitution is said to be nominal if it is "not lived up to in practice" — because of, for example, unfavourable "socio-economic conditions" — but it serves an "educational" purpose and function, "with the goal, in the near or distant future, of becoming fully normative".[27] According to Loewenstein, this type of constitutions is often found in "states where Western democratic constitutionalism has been implanted into a colonial or feudal-agrarian social order".[28] The semantic constitution, which in Lowenstein's view was exemplified by that of the former Soviet Union (or USSR), does provide information about the political and legal systems, but is no more than an instrument of political control and "the formalization of the existing location of political power". "The peaceful, non-revolutionary change in the location of political power is impossible."[29]

Sartori[30] also developed a three-fold classification of constitutions, but the terms he used and their meaning are slightly different from Loewenstein's. In Sartori's theory, the three types of constitution are the "garantiste constitution", the "nominal constitution", and the "façade constitution (or fake constitution)". The garantiste constitution secures civil liberties, restricts arbitrary power, and

---

25. K. Loewenstein, *Political Power and the Governmental Process* (Chicago: The University of Chicago Press, 1957).
26. *Ibid.*, 148–149.
27. *Ibid.*
28. *Ibid.*
29. *Ibid.*, 149–150.
30. G. Sartori, "Constitutionalism: A Preliminary Discussion" (1962) 56:4 *American Political Science Review* 853.

ensures a limited government.[31] It is, therefore, equivalent to Loewenstein's normative constitution. Satori's nominal constitution is, as Satori himself acknowledges, the same as Loewenstein's semantic constitution. It is a "collection of rules which organize but do not restrain the exercise of political power".[32] The main discrepancy between Satori's scheme and Loewenstein's lies in Sartori's concept of the façade constitution, which "give[s] us no reliable information about the real governmental process" and is "basically a disguise".[33] Façade constitutions "take the appearance of 'true constitutions'", but "are disregarded (at least in their essential *garantiste* features)". Sartori goes on to say that "[a]s far as the techniques of liberty and the rights of the power addressees are concerned, they are a dead letter."[34] He considered his concept of the façade constitution to be different from Loewenstein's nominal constitution, which (in Loewenstein's view) is intended to become fully normative at some future point in time. Sartori also pointed out that there is "often a considerable overlapping between nominal and façade constitutions", thus giving rise to "a 'mixed type' (partly nominal and partly fake) of pseudo constitution".[35]

## MAPPING CONSTITUTIONS AND REGIMES

We can now map the types of constitutions on to the types of regimes as shown in Table 13.1. Democratic regimes that are governed by liberal-democratic constitutions have normative or garantiste constitutions. Such constitutions may also operate to varying degrees in democracies that are fragile, unstable, unconsolidated, or of poor quality. On the other hand, transitional or new democratic regimes, which have enacted liberal-democratic constitutions and are aspiring towards the full practice of democracy, may have nominal constitutions in Loewenstein's sense. Authoritarian and hybrid regimes, which have constitutions that are textually liberal-democratic, are likely to have what Sartori calls a façade constitution or pseudo-constitution. Authoritarian or totalitarian regimes of the Marxist-Leninist type, in which the leadership of the communist party is prescribed by the constitution which also rejects multi-

31. *Ibid.*, 854–855.

32. *Ibid.*, 861.

33. *Ibid.*

34. *Ibid.*

35. *Ibid.*

**Table 13.1: Mapped regimes and constitutions**

| Types of regimes | Types of constitutions |
|---|---|
| Democratic | Normative (Loewenstein) or Garantiste (Sartori) |
| Transitional (towards democracy) | Nominal (Loewenstein) |
| Hybrid | Façade (Sartori) or Pseudo-constitution (Sartori) |
| Authoritarian | Façade (Sartori) or Pseudo-constitution (Sartori) |
| Authoritarian (communist) | Semantic (Loewenstein) or Nominal (Sartori) |
| Totalitarian (communist) | Semantic (Loewenstein) or Nominal (Sartori) |

party competitive elections, may be said to have semantic constitutions (in Loewenstein's sense) or nominal constitutions (in Sartori's sense).

We now turn to examine the constitutional practices of different types of regimes in East Asia. The survey here is by no means comprehensive or exhaustive; we will consider countries whose constitutionalism has figured more prominently in the existing literature. The following four groups and the species of constitutionalism practiced by each will be discussed: (a) the relatively well-developed democracies of Japan, South Korea, and Taiwan (Category I Cases), which, together with Singapore and Hong Kong, represent the East Asian political entities with the highest level of economic development; (b) the new, fragile, unstable, or low-quality democracies of the Philippines, Thailand, and Indonesia (Category II Cases); (c) the semi-democracies of Singapore and Malaysia (Category III Cases); and (d) the authoritarian regimes of the People's Republic of China (PRC) and Vietnam (Category IV Cases), which may be distinguished from the totalitarian regime of North Korea.

## Category I: Japan, South Korea, Taiwan

Japan was the first East Asian country to adopt a Western-style constitution — the Meiji Constitution of 1889. Since the end of Second World War, Japan has developed into the wealthiest nation in East Asia and a stronghold of liberal democracy in the region. In the post-War era, Taiwan and South Korea, together with Hong Kong and Singapore, achieved rapid economic growth as the "Four Little Dragons" of East Asia. Whereas both South Korea and Taiwan had experienced authoritarian strongman rule under Park and the Chiangs, respectively, democratisation in both has made good progress since the late 1980s, and both South Korea and Taiwan today may be regarded as reasonably consolidated democracies. Indeed, if the turnover of ruling parties is to be used as an important measure of democracy, South Korea and Taiwan in their relatively short lives as democracies thus far have perhaps surpassed Japan, where the Liberal Democratic Party has been long dominant.

The constitutions and constitutional practice of these Category I Cases have been studied systematically by Yeh and Chang[36] in their definitive article on "The Emergence of East Asian Constitutionalism". Yeh and Chang point out that Japan, South Korea, and Taiwan are "vibrant constitutional democracies" today.[37] They discuss the historical and social contexts in which liberal democracy has evolved in the post-War period, including rapid economic growth, political pluralism and development of civil society, modernising social changes, and relative ethnic homogeneity. They then identify what they believe to be four features common to the constitutional practice of these states: (a) an "instrumental approach" to constitutions as part of the project of modernisation and state-building; (b) "continuity" in terms of the text and institutions of the constitution which has been maintained as "incremental" constitutional changes took place; (c) "a reactive and cautious style of judicial review"; and (d) the recognition of "a wide range of rights responsive to social and political progress", including both civil and political rights and social and economic rights.[38] Yeh and Chang then argue that these four features define what they call "East Asian constitutionalism",[39] which they consider to be a "distinctive form"[40] of constitutionalism or "a distinct constitutional model"[41] that can be compared and contrasted with Western constitutionalism, "transitional constitutionalism" as in Eastern Europe, and "Asian values" constitutionalism.[42]

"East Asian constitutionalism" is indeed a useful term that can conveniently be used to refer to the collective and similar constitutional experience of Japan, South Korea, and Taiwan, which can be distinguished from that of the Category II, III, and IV Cases discussed below. However, what justifies the

36. J.R. Yeh and W.C Chang, "The Emergence of East Asian Constitutionalism: Features in Comparison" (2011) 59 *American Journal of Comparative Law* 805–839.

37. *Ibid.*, 805.

38. *Ibid.*, 816–833.

39. *Ibid.*, 833.

40. *Ibid.*, 805.

41. *Ibid.*, 834.

42. *Ibid.*, 834–838.

grouping of these three states within one category is that, compared to the other three categories, Category I Cases are more successful and mature in their practice of the normative constitution (in Loewenstein's sense) or the garantiste constitution (in Sartori's sense), which may be correlated with the fact that unlike the other three categories, Category I Cases are well-developed, consolidated, and relatively mature liberal democracies — a fact noted by Yeh and Chang when they describe the socio-political context of the emergence of East Asian constitutionalism. In these Category I Cases, the liberal-democratic constitutions are fully effective and regulate the behaviour of political actors. Free elections are regularly held in which there is fair competition for political power among political parties with different platforms. There exist healthy legal systems which afford protection for human rights and civil liberties. The Rule of Law both empowers and constrains administrative authorities, which are capable of enforcing the law efficiently and are largely free of corruption. Separation of powers and judicial independence are well-established, and the constitutionality and legality of legislative and executive actions are often subject to judicial review. Freedom of the press and civil society flourish. The practice of democracy is stable, and competition for power in accordance with constitutional and electoral law is "the only game in town". These are all features of a normative constitution that is successfully at work.

Regarding the four features of East Asian constitutionalism identified by Yeh and Chang, it is doubtful as to whether any of them or their combination together is unique to these three East Asian countries and thus contribute to constitute a distinctive form of constitutionalism. First, Yeh and Chang stress that East Asian constitutionalism is characterised by an instrumental approach to the constitution in the sense that the constitution was adopted by modernising elites for purposes such as nation-building rather than an act of "We the People" in a revolutionary or constitutional moment for the protection of their rights and limitation of state power. However, a broader view of the emergence of constitutions in the non-Western world would suggest that the phenomenon identified by Yeh and Chang is in fact common among non-Western states in the late nineteenth and early twentieth centuries whose survival were threatened by the expansion of the West.[43] This is also true for states that emerged towards the end of the age of colonialism and imperialism which used

43. Albert H.Y. Chen, "The Achievement of Constitutionalism in Asia: Moving beyond 'Constitutions without Constitutionalism' " in Albert H.Y. Chen (ed.) *Constitutionalism in Asia in the Early Twenty-First Century* (Cambridge: Cambridge University Press, 2014) ch. 1.

their newly promulgated constitutions to assert their newfound national identity and to legitimise their newly established political systems. Such constitutions are often "politically enabling documents".[44] Referring to the invention of the modern constitution in the West and the subsequent widespread adoption of constitutions all over the world, Grimm has pointed out that "once invented the constitution could be instrumentalized for purposes other than the original ones, adopted only in part or even as a mere form".[45]

Second, it seems that the constitutional continuity discussed by Yeh and Chang is only a question of degree. The constitutional histories of different countries display varying degrees of constitutional continuity or discontinuity, and it is by no means clear or obvious that those in East Asian exhibit a high degree of continuity in this regard that distinguishes them from other countries in the world. For example, the degree of constitutional continuity in East Asia cannot be said to be high when compared to older democracies in the West, such as Britain, the United States, Canada, and Australia, or some other countries in Asia, such as India, Malaysia, and Singapore. Even among the three East Asian states themselves, it would appear that Japan differs considerably from South Korea and Taiwan. As Yeh and Chang point out in their work, the Japanese Constitution of 1946 has not experienced even a single amendment (though there have been calls to amend it, particularly article 9 on pacifism), though constitutional reforms (such as electoral reforms) have been introduced by statute. On the other hand, South Korea's first constitution of 1948 has been amended eight times in the course of a fairly tumultuous constitutional history,[46] culminating in the 1987 Constitution of the "Sixth Republic" which established the subsequently famous and successful Constitutional Court. Since democratisation began in the late 1980s, the Constitution of the Republic of China (ROC) that has been in force in Taiwan has undergone seven major amendments (the last one being in 2005), in addition to the repeal in 1991 of its "Temporary Provisions" of 1948.

---

44. N.J. Brown, "Regimes Reinventing Themselves: Constitutional Development in the Arab World" in S.A. Arjomand (ed.) *Constitutionalism and Political Reconstruction* (Leiden: Brill, 2009) 49, 67.

45. D. Grimm, "Types of Constitutions" in M. Rosenfeld and A. Sajó (eds.) *Oxford Handbook of Comparative Constitutional Law* (Oxford: Oxford University Press, 2012) 104.

46. Albert H.Y. Chen, "Pathways of Western Liberal Constitutional Development in Asia: A Comparative Study of Five Major Nations " (2010) 8:4 *International Journal of Constitutional Law* 867–871.

The third feature is what Yeh and Chang describe as the "reactive and cautious style" of constitutional adjudication in East Asia. Their work provides useful data on the records of constitutional review by the Supreme Court of Japan and the constitutional courts of South Korea and Taiwan. It is well-known that the Japanese Supreme Court is conservative and has only made rulings of unconstitutionality in eight cases over six decades. On the other hand, as Yeh and Chang point out, the constitutional courts in both South Korea and Taiwan have ruled against legislative or governmental acts in roughly one-third of cases in the last two decades. Indeed, these constitutional courts have established themselves as respectable guardians of constitutional rights and have made a significant contribution to reforming the repressive laws of the previous authoritarian eras in the two states and to adjudicating difficult issues of political and social conflicts that emerged in the course of democratisation.

Yeh and Chang argue that the three courts of Japan, South Korea, and Taiwan "share an underlying attitude: they are reactive and cautious".[47] They are "reactive — rather than proactive — to social and political demands and constrained largely by social and political circumstances" as well as "'cautious' because they did not rule directly against the majoritarian preferences of the public".[48] They seek to provide "more space for political dialogue and deliberation". Being reactive and cautious (and politically prudent) can be considered traits of successful constitutional or supreme courts engaged in constitutional adjudication all over the world. Furthermore, the constitutional court of South Korea and the post-1987 constitutional court of Taiwan (which dated back to the 1946 Constitution) can be said to have engaged in a significant degree of judicial activism, as contrasted with the judicial restraint of the Japanese Supreme Court. It is therefore doubtful whether all three courts should fall under the same rubric of being "reactive and cautious" in their approach to constitutional adjudication.

Finally, with regard to their willingness to recognise a wide range of rights, including civil and political rights as well as social and economic rights, this again can hardly be said to be a defining feature of constitutional adjudication in East Asia. Indeed, progressive constitutional and supreme courts all over the world share such willingness; hence the trends of the globalisation

47. Yeh and Chang (N36) 823.

48. *Ibid.*, 836.

of constitutional law[49] and the increasing judicialisation of constitutional rights and of governance as a global phenomenon.[50] However, Yeh and Chang[51] do have a good point in drawing a distinction between East Asian constitutionalism and what they call "Asian values" constitutionalism, in the sense that the former is more liberal in prioritising individuals' rights whereas the latter emphasises collective or communitarian values. We shall visit "communitarian constitutionalism" in a later section of this chapter.

## Category II: The Philippines, Thailand, and Indonesia

In the Category II Cases, democracy exists but is young, unconsolidated, fragile, unstable, or otherwise of poor quality. These states operate a normative constitution to varying degrees, but the normative constitution may break down from time to time as a result of coups (as in Thailand frequently and most recently in 2014), states of emergency or martial law, popular uprisings (including what has been known in the Philippines as "People Power" events, which occurred in 1986 when Marcos was ousted and again in 1998 when Estrada was ousted, and also occurred in Indonesia in 1998 leading to Suharto's downfall), and civil unrest or serious confrontations (as in Thailand since 2006). The operation of a normative constitution may also suffer from the "poor quality" of the democracy. As the "quality" of the democracy that exists today in the three Southeast Asian Category II states leaves much to be desired, the concept of the quality of democracy needs to be elaborated here.

According to Morlino, Dressel, and Pelizzo,[52] the quality of democracy in a particular country may be assessed by reference to a multi-dimensional framework, in which the three main dimensions are (a) procedural, (b) content-based, and (c) outcome-based. These can be further divided into sub-dimensions. The quality of democracy in each dimension or sub-dimension may be evaluated on the basis of a number of indicators. With regard to the procedural dimension of democracy, the sub-dimensions include the Rule of

49. M. Tushnet, "The Inevitable Globalization of Constitutional Law" (2009) 49 *Virginia Journal of International Law* 985.
50. T. Ginsburg and Albert H.Y Chen (eds.), *Administrative Law and Governance in Asia* (Abingdon: Routledge, 2009).
51. Yeh and Chang (N36) 838.
52. L. Morlino, B. Dressel, and R. Pelizzo, "The Quality of Democracy in Asia-Pacific: Issues and Findings" (2011) 32:5 *International Political Science Review* 491. For more details, see L. Morlino, *Changes for Democracy: Actors, Structures, Processes* (Oxford: Oxford University Press, 2011).

Law (the indicators of which include respect for physical integrity, government effectiveness, and level of corruption), electoral accountability (indicators of which include press freedom and voters' electoral self-determination), inter-institutional accountability (the indicators of which include the parliament's oversight capacity and effectiveness of constraints on executive powers), political participation (an indicator of which is the voter turnout rate), and political competition (the indicators of which include the number of political parties and the difference in the numbers of parliamentary seats held by the largest and second largest parties). Morlino's content-based dimension of democracy is an assessment of the degree of freedom and of equality that exists in the country concerned. The outcome-based dimension mainly addresses the perceived legitimacy of, or degree of popular satisfaction with, the regime.

Whereas some of the dimensions and sub-dimensions of democracy relate directly to democracy (e.g., political participation and electoral competition), some are more relevant to constitutionalism (e.g., the Rule of Law, separation of powers, checks and balances, and constitutional protection of human rights). The inclusion of elements of constitutionalism in the assessment of the quality of democracy shows that there is a close relationship between constitutionalism — particularly the practice of the "normative constitution" in Loewenstein's sense — and democracy, and that a democracy of low quality is likely to be a country where the constitution is not fully normative, or is a nominal constitution in Loewenstein's sense.

Compared to the Category I Cases above, Category II Cases are less wealthy economically and less well-developed or well-established in terms of their democracy, and thus have democracy of a weaker quality. While democratisation in South Korea and Taiwan may be understood as a "negotiated trans-placement" or "state-modulated transformation"[53] characterised by negotiation between government and opposition (in South Korea in 1987) or liberalisation initiated by the regime itself (in Taiwan in 1987), the "modal form of transition" and of democratisation in Southeast Asia seems to be a kind of "opposition-led replacement" that was more of a bottom-up process led by civil society protests[54] (as in the Philippines in 1986, Thailand in 1973 and 1992, and Indonesia in 1998). In these three Category II Cases, either new constitutions were drafted or the existing constitution was substantially

53. Case (N12) 25, 247, 250.

54. *Ibid.*

amended to mark the transition from authoritarianism or hybrid regime to democracy, with strenuous efforts in constitutional engineering for the purpose of constructing a more perfect democratic political system with strong constitutional guarantees of citizens' rights and high aspirations towards social justice, elaborate mechanisms of separation of powers and checks and balances, and a powerful judicial machinery to safeguard the integrity and supremacy of the constitution. This is apparent in the empowerment of the Supreme Court of the Philippines by the 1987 Constitution[55] and the establishment of new constitutional courts in Thailand and Indonesia by Thailand's 1997 Constitution and Indonesia's constitutional amendment of 2001, respectively.[56] This in turn gave rise to the phenomenon of the judicialisation of politics,[57] and, in the cases of the Philippines and Thailand, even the politicisation of the judiciary, as discussed below.

During Indonesia's transition from Suharto's strongman rule to democracy, the constitutional foundation for which was laid by a series of constitutional amendments adopted by Indonesia's People's Consultative Assembly in 1999–2002. Given the country's complex ethnic and cultural cleavages, the sudden collapse of Suharto's regime in 1998 amidst the Asian financial crisis and mass protests, the fragmented political configuration of the country at the time, the long-standing role of the military in Indonesia's politics, the weakness of the legal system, and the political subordination and corruption of the judiciary, Indonesia was not, as of the turn of the century, a likely candidate for successful transition to constitutional democracy. Yet this most populous and Muslim nation of Southeast Asia succeeded against the odds and achieved a democratising transition whose relative smoothness went beyond expectations. Horowitz[58] points out that the process of constitutional renovation that took place in Indonesia was unconventional in the sense that it did not follow the "standard operating procedures" or "rules … of democratic constitution making" usually advocated by international experts. Instead, the process was

55. A.N. Ciencia, Jr., "From Judicialization of Politicization of the Judiciary: The Philippine Case" in B. Dressel (ed.), *The Judicialization of Politics in Asia* (Abingdon: Routledge, 2012) ch. 7.

56. A. Harding and P. Leyland, "The Constitutional Courts of Thailand and Indonesia: Two Case Studies from South East Asia" (2008) 3:2 *Journal of Comparative Law* 118; A. Harding and P. Nicholson, *New Courts in Asia* (London: Routledge, 2010).

57. B. Dressel, "The Judicialization of Politics in Asia: Towards a Framework of Analysis" in Dressel (N55) ch. 1.

58. D.L. Horowitz, *Constitutional Change and Democracy in Indonesia* (New York: Cambridge University Press, 2013) 8–10.

managed by the political elites and involved minimal public participation; a national election was conducted before constitutional reform took place; there was no constituent assembly specially elected for the purpose of constitution-making; and the constitutional reform was achieved in an "incremental" and "gradualist" manner in the course of four years. Yet, according to Horowitz, the success of Indonesia's democratisation was largely attributable to this particular process chosen by the political elites at the time.

Another interesting feature of Indonesia's constitutional reform was the creation of a constitutional court, which in some respects (particularly with regard to the manner of selection of its justices) was closely modelled on the reputable and successful Constitutional Court of South Korea.[59] It seems that the historically contingent and politicised event of the impeachment of President Wahid in 2001 contributed to the Assembly's decision to establish a constitutional court in Indonesia that can render a fair and impartial decision in any future case of impeachment.[60] Starting to function in 2003, the Indonesian Constitutional Court has since established a good record in independent and active review of laws that were challenged before it and in the performance of other functions such as adjudication of disputes arising from elections.[61]

Compared to other Southeast Asian states, the Philippines has had a longer experience of the practice of constitutional democracy, as one of the expressed aims of American colonial rule in the Philippines had been to prepare the Filipinos for democracy and self-government.[62] Democracy was practiced in the Philippines after it acquired its independence in 1946, until Marcos declared martial law in 1972. The "People Power" revolution of 1986 that toppled Marcos was a watershed event in Southeast Asian democratisation and ushered in the 1987 Constitution which was carefully designed to guard

---

59. Hendrianto, "Institutional Choice and the New Indonesian Constitutional Court " in Harding and Nicholson (N56) ch. 8. For the Korean Constitutional Court, see T. Ginsburg, "The Constitutional Court and Judicialization of Korean Politics" in Harding and Nicholson (N56) ch. 7. For a discussion of Asian constitutional courts generally, see T. Ginsburg, "Constitutional Courts in East Asia: Understanding Variation" (2008) 3:2 *Journal of Comparative Law* 80–99.

60. Hendrianto (N59) 162; Harding and Leyland (N56) 125. See generally Ginsburg's "insurance theory" which seeks to understand and explain political elites' decisions, at the time a constitutional settlement is made by opposing camps, to establish a constitutional court, with reference to what might happen if they lose power in future, and how a constitutional court might offer protection in such circumstances; T. Ginsburg, *Judicial Review in New Democracies: Constitutional Courts in Asian Cases* (Cambridge: Cambridge University Press, 2003).

61. Harding and Leyland (N56); Hendrianto (N59).

62. K.M. Nadeau, *The History of the Philippines* (Westport: Greenwood, 2008).

against any recurrence of authoritarianism, dictatorship, or abuse of human rights, and to stipulate social and economic policies that were considered just and progressive. The power of the judiciary led by the Supreme Court as the constitutional guardian was considerably strengthened by the new constitution.[63]

It has been argued that the enhancement of court's authority by the 1987 Constitution actually contributed to the judicialisation of politics in the Philippines, which was a gradual process that reached a climax during the presidency of Arroyo in the first decade of the twenty-first century.[64] Such judicialisation was largely a result of the operation of a normative constitution in circumstances of fierce political struggles, in which political and social actors used litigation as a means of advancing their interests and claims. East Asian countries with constitutional courts or tribunals (e.g., Taiwan, South Korea, Mongolia, Cambodia, Thailand, Indonesia, and Myanmar) or supreme courts actively involved in constitutional adjudication of political controversies (e.g., the Philippines) provide interesting case studies of the judicialisation of politics and politicisation of the judiciary.[65]

The judicialisation of politics may be understood as the increasingly active role of the constitutional or supreme court in making crucial decisions in the domain of what Hirschl[66] calls "mega-politics" (including fundamental moral and policy issues, electoral outcomes and issues of regime change, collective identity, and nation-building). Regarding the politicisation of the judiciary,[67] this would occur when public perceptions of the judiciary (particularly the constitutional or supreme court) are such that it is not considered to be fair and impartial in its decision-making, but is partisan and has been co-opted or captured by one among several competing political forces or groups. The judicialisation of politics may or may not be accompanied by the politicisation of the judiciary.[68] However, the more powerful the court is and the greater the

63. Ciencia (N55).

64. *Ibid*.

65. Dressel (N57).

66. R. Hirschl, "The Judicialization of Mega-Politics and the Rise of Political Courts" (2008) 11 *Annual Review of Political Science* 93.

67. Ciencia (N55) 118, 128–129.

68. See in this regard Dressel's 4-category typology of judicial politics: "Working from the two dimensions of de facto judicial independence and engagement in mega-politics, we can build a matrix that illustrates a typology of ideal judicial pattern types, ranging from judicial restraint and judicial muteness to judicial activism and politicization of the judiciary." See Dressel (N57) 6–7.

degree of judicialisation of politics, the greater the incentive will be on the part of political actors to "capture" the court by ensuring that it is staffed by their allies.

The politicisation of the judiciary in the Philippines is evident from the fact that by 2009, the number of Supreme Court justices appointed by President Arroyo was so significant that it was perceived as an "Arroyo Court".[69] This court decided in favour of Arroyo and her government in "the most politically sensitive cases".[70] Arroyo's "midnight" appointment of Corona as chief justice just before she was due to vacate her presidency, which was upheld by the Supreme Court although it was apparently in violation of a constitutional prohibition against the President's exercise of general powers of appointment near the time of a presidential election, also highlights politicisation of the judiciary.[71] The subsequent impeachment of Corona by the Senate in 2012[72] was partly a reaction against such a politicised appointment.

Compared to Indonesia and the Philippines, Thailand has been the most constitutionally unstable state in East Asia since the first decade of the twenty-first century, and it is also a place where constitutionalism and constitutional adjudication is put to the most severe test. After experiencing many cycles of constitution-making, election, conflict, coup, and constitutional reordering in the six decades since royal absolutism was replaced by constitutional monarchy in 1932 (during which a total of fourteen constitutions had come and gone), Thailand in the mid-1990s experienced democratic participation on the making of a new constitution — the "People's Constitution"[73] — that was intended to put an end to the vicious cycles of the past and to introduce in Thailand once and for all a genuine constitutional order that is democratic and progressive, and that would minimise bureaucratic domination, politicians' corruption, and the instability of coalition governments. The 1997 Constitution, in its broad declaration of rights and its elaborate design of electoral systems and mechanisms of checks and balances such as the new "watchdog"[74] or

69. Ciencia (N55) 129.

70. *Ibid.*, 130.

71. *Ibid.*

72. C. Bonaan, A. Ciencia, and B. Dressel, "Thrilla' in Manila: The Impeachment of a Chief Justice" (10 March 2012) *Blog of the International Journal of Constitutional Law*, available at: www.iconnectblog.com/2012/03/thrilla-in-manila-the-impeachment-of-a-chief-justice/.

73. E.M. Kuhonta, "The Paradox of Thailand's 1997 'People's Constitution': Be Careful What You Wish For" (2008) 48:3 *Asian Survey* 373.

74. Harding and Leyland (N56) 132, 136.

"guardian"[75] agencies of the Constitutional Court, Administrative Court, and independent commissions on elections and anti-corruption, was a codification of the world's most advanced constitutional jurisprudence and has been described as a "post-political" constitution.[76] The tragedy is that it was one of the instances in the world's modern constitutional history in which the ambitions, hopes, and ideals of constitution-makers were particularly high and yet the consequences and end results were particularly disappointing and disastrous.

It has been argued that the text and institutions of the 1997 Constitution actually contributed to Thaksin Shinawatra's autocratic rule which ended in a coup in 2006.[77] However, there is insufficient evidence in support of this thesis, and the 1997 Constitution could have worked well if the person elected to power under it had been a different person. In other words, the fateful path taken by Thailand was more a result of the individual's agency than a result of institutional design and constitutional rules. On the other hand, the establishment of a constitutional court by the 1997 constitution, which lives an "afterlife"[78] in the current 2007 Constitution, did inaugurate a new era of judicialisation of politics in Thailand. Such judicialisation was subsequently accompanied by politicisation of the judiciary; indeed, the degree of judicialisation of politics in Thailand since 2006 has become extremely high by world standards.

The constitutional court under the 1997 Constitution, the constitutional tribunal under the interim 2006 constitution promulgated after the coup, and the new constitutional court established by the 2007 constitution, have each rendered the boldest decisions at the highest level of "mega-politics", including decisions on the survival of an existing government or political party and the validity of national electoral outcomes and of constitutional amendments. In May 2006, in the midst of popular protests against Thaksin and shortly after King Bhumibol intervened (in exercise of a residual power which, according to Ginsburg's study,[79] exists under Thailand's unwritten constitution which operates side by side with, and is even more enduring than, the formal written constitution) by meeting the judges of the Constitutional, Supreme, and

75. T. Ginsburg, "Constitutional Afterlife: The Continuing Impact of Thailand's Post-Political Constitution" (2009) 7 *International Journal of Constitutional Law* 83–84; reprinted in Albert H.Y. Chen and T. Ginsburg (eds.), *Public Law in East Asia* (Farnham: Ashgate, 2013) ch. 10.

76. *Ibid*.

77. Kuhonta (N73).

78. Ginsburg (N75).

79. *Ibid*.

Administrative Courts and encouraging them to take action to resolve the current constitutional crisis,[80] the Constitutional Court invalidated the result of the general election held on 2 April 2006 — the "snap election"[81] that was called (and won) by Thaksin and boycotted by the opposition.

After the coup on 19 September 2006, the constitutional tribunal that replaced the constitutional court decided in May 2007, on the basis of findings of electoral misconduct, to dissolve Thaksin's political party (the Thai Rak Thai) and to ban its leaders from running in elections in the next five years.[82] In December 2007, the first general election was held under the 2007 Constitution (adopted by a referendum in August 2007 and retaining most of the institutional innovations of the 1997 Constitution), and was won by pro-Thaksin forces. In September 2008, the new Constitutional Court held that Prime Minister Samak had violated the law by hosting a cooking program on TV; he was thus forced to resign. In December 2008, in the midst of large-scale demonstrations against the pro-Thaksin government, the court disbanded the ruling pro-Thaksin coalition on the ground of electoral fraud; Prime Minister Somchai, Samak's successor, was forced to step down.[83] A new government led by the anti-Thaksin Democratic Party then came to power. In May 2010, a violent crackdown on pro-Thaksin demonstrators occurred.

In July 2011, the second general election held under the 2007 Constitution again resulted in the victory of pro-Thaksin forces, and Thaksin's sister, Yingluck Shinawatra, became prime minister. Under the new government, Thai society continued to be polarised between pro- and anti-Thaksin forces, culminating in anti-government protests which engulfed Bangkok in late 2013 and early 2014. In the meantime, the Constitutional Court made several controversial decisions on issues of mega-politics.[84] In July 2012, it held that in the absence of a referendum, the government and National Assembly could not proceed to enact an entirely new constitution and could only amend the existing

80. *Ibid.*, 98; A. Harding, "The Constitutional Court of Thailand, 1998–2006: A Turbulent Innovation" in Harding and Nicholson (N56) 121.

81. Harding (N80) 121.

82. Harding and Leyland (N56) 122; Ginsburg (N75) 100.

83. Harding and Leyland (N56) 133.

84. A. Harding, L. Rawin, and T. Khemthong, "Thailand Update: the Search for Perfect Paper Continues" (2 December 2013) *Blog of the International Journal of Constitutional Law*, available at: www.iconnectblog.com/2013/12/thailand-update-the-search-for-perfect-paper-continues/.

constitution piecemeal article by article.[85] In November 2013, a bill introduced by the government to amend the constitutional provisions on the composition of the Senate (by providing for a wholly elected Senate to replace the existing one which was half-elected) and passed by the National Assembly was struck down by the court as unconstitutional.[86] After Yingluck called the national election of 2 February 2014 in order to resolve the political crisis caused by large-scale demonstrations — an election that was boycotted by the opposition which also obstructed the conduct of the election — the court annulled the election result on technical grounds.[87] Finally, on 7 May 2014, the court found Yingluck and nine Cabinet ministers guilty of abuse of power in the making of a personnel decision and dismissed them from their offices with immediate effect. Yingluck thus became the third Prime Minister dismissed by the Constitutional Court since 2008. The caretaker government established after Yingluck's fall from power was toppled by a military coup on 22 May 2014, once again suspending Thailand's fragile constitutional democracy. On 24 March 2019, a general election was held under the new Constitution of 2017, resulting in General Prayut Chan-o-cha, leader of the coup in 2014 and prime minister since then, being elected by the new Parliament as prime minister on 5 June 2019.[88]

---

85. Section 291 of Thailand's 2007 Constitution, which governs constitutional amendment, does not provide for a referendum, and allows the Constitution to be amended by a simple majority of the National Assembly (i.e., the collective membership of the its two Houses, the House of Representatives and the Senate). However, the section prohibits any amendment "which has the effect of changing the democratic regime of government with the King as Head of State or changing the form of State".
86. The main legal basis for the court's decision was section 68 of the 2007 Constitution, which prohibits any act "to overthrow the democratic regime of government with the King as Head of State under this Constitution or to acquire the power to rule the country by any means which is not in accordance with the modes provided in this Constitution".
87. T. Ginsburg, "Preserve Ruling from Thai Constitutional Court Extends Political Crisis" (21 March 2014) *Blog of the International Journal of Constitutional Law*, available at: www.iconnectblog.com/2014/03/perverse-ruling-from-thai-constitutional-court-extends-political-crisis/.
88. See, for example, "Thai Parliament Elects Prayuth Chan-ocha as Prime Minister" (5 June 2019) *DW*, available at: www.dw.com/en/thai-parliament-elects-prayuth-chan-ocha-as-prime-minister/a-49071811, last accessed 26 February 2020; Toru Takahashi, "Prayuth's Return as Prime Minister Takes Thailand Back to 1980s" (8 June 2019) *NikkeiAsia*, available at: https://asia.nikkei.com/Spotlight/Comment/Prayuth-s-return-as-prime-minister-takes-Thailand-back-to-1980s, last accessed 26 February 2020.

It is clear from the above that Thailand has, since 2006, become an extreme example of the judicialisation of politics, and, given that the major judicial decisions documented above were all against Thaksin and his allies or supporters, the perception of the politicisation of the judiciary cannot be avoided. In fact, the 2007 Constitution has aggravated these trends by giving the judiciary prominent roles in the selection of the appointed (e.g., not popularly elected) half of Senate members and of members of the independent "watchdog" agencies. In modern Thai history, the Thai judiciary has generally been respected and trusted by the people.[89] The recent trend of its politicisation is therefore regrettable and sad.

The judicialisation of politics in Thailand was the inevitable and combined result of the constitutionalisation of politics by the 1997 Constitution and its successors (which charged the Constitutional Court with policing and enforcing constitutional rules governing matters such as elections, political behaviour, and constitutional change), and the intensity and continuity of the political conflict between pro- and anti-Thaksin factions. Had Thai society been less divided between two strongly opposing camps, the position of the constitutional court as the guardian of the constitution would not have been so difficult. Thailand thus illustrates the inherent limitations of constitutional democracy in socio-political circumstances where the key institutions of constitutional democracy, such as free and fair elections, civil and political liberties, and a constitutional court intended to be independent and impartial, are inadequate in coping with, regulating, and containing the deep divisions in a society torn by conflicting values, interests, and political convictions.

## Category III: Singapore and Malaysia

With no turnover in the ruling party or ruling coalition despite periodic elections in more than half a century, considerable restrictions on civil liberties — sometimes justified by the discourse of "Asian values" — for the purpose of upholding political stability and social harmony in a multi-ethnic society in pursuit of rapid economic development, strict national security and public order laws, and a very limited judicial role in constitutional adjudication, Singapore and Malaysia are often regarded as semi-democracies rather than full democracies. Despite the gains made by the opposition in Malaysia in the 2008 election and the opposition winning half of the votes (though not

89. Harding and Leyland (N56) 126.

a parliamentary majority) in the 2013 election, which seem to suggest that Malaysia is probably reaching what Ramraj calls a "constitutional tipping point",[90] both Malaysia and Singapore are classified as Category III, with particular reference to Thio's concept of communitarian constitutionalism.

Thio points out that insofar as constitutionalism means restraint on arbitrary power and government limited by the Rule of Law, it embraces varieties and trajectories other than liberal constitutionalism, and can be found in "illiberal polities".[91] Thio discusses two species of non-liberal constitutionalism in particular — "theocratic constitutionalism" (such as "Islamic constitutionalism" in Iran) and "communitarian constitutionalism" (as exemplified in Southeast Asia by Singapore and Malaysia). Unlike liberal constitutionalism which requires the state to be morally neutral and privileges the individual's autonomy and the judicial enforcement of individuals' rights, communitarian constitutionalism allows the state to be paternalistic, to uphold communitarian and cultural values, and to take actions to promote the common good, including the pursuit of economic growth and the maintenance of public order and religious harmony in a multiracial and multicultural society. Thus, in Singapore and Malaysia, free speech may be restricted to a greater extent than in Western liberal democracies.[92] In the case of Malaysia where the constitution itself defines Malays as Muslims, the judicial enforcement (in the famous *Lina Joy* case) of restrictions on the freedom of religious conversion and on apostasy on the part of Malays is considered to be justified.[93]

Communitarian constitutionalism, at least in the context of Southeast Asia, seems to be associated with the "Asian values" discourse which asserts that liberal Western notions of human rights are not necessarily universally valid

90. V.V. Ramraj, "Constitutional Tipping Points: Sustainable Constitutionalism in Theory and Practice" (2010) 1:2 *Transnational Legal Theory* 191. Notably, in Singapore's general election in 2011, the ruling party (the People's Action Party) won only 60 percent of the popular votes, though this also meant that it won the overwhelming majority of parliamentary seats.

91. Li-ann Thio, "Constitutionalism in Illiberal Polities" in Rosenfeld and Sajó (N45) ch. 5.

92. *Ibid.*, 138, 147.

93. *Ibid.*, 141–142. The full name of the *Lina Joy* case is *Lina Joy v Majlis Agama Islam Wilayah Persekutuan* [2004] 2 MLJ 119, [2007] 3 CLJ 557. Lina Joy is a Malay Muslim woman who converted to Christianity. She applied to the court to delete the reference to Islam as her religion from her identity card. She wanted to marry a Christian man, but under Malaysian law she could not do so if she was Muslim. The Federal Court rejected her application on the ground that such a change to her identity card could not be made in the absence of a certificate or declaration from the Syariah court that she had apostatised.

and applicable, and that Asian culture does not balance individuals' liberties and the collective interest in exactly the same manner as in the West.[94] Such an "Asian values" thesis was probably more persuasive in the 1970s than in the 2010s, given the spectacular advance of liberal constitutionalism in the last three decades in Taiwan, South Korea, the Philippines, Thailand, and Indonesia. Today, the sphere of influence of communitarian constitutionalism seems to be shrinking in Asia, except that this species of constitutionalism has an affinity with the emerging constitutionalism in the communist party-dominated polities of China and Vietnam.

## Category IV: China and Vietnam

One of the distinctive features of East Asia from the perspective of comparative constitutional law is that despite the global decline of communism after the collapse of the former Soviet Union, significant parts of East Asia today — China, North Korea, Vietnam, and Laos — are still ruled by communist parties that monopolise political power and do not permit the multi-party elections that take place in the Category I, II, and III Cases discussed above. Among these four states, China and Vietnam may be regarded as belonging to one sub-category, as both have successfully pursued market-oriented economic reforms since the 1980s, opened up their societies to Western influences, and moved from totalitarianism to some form of authoritarianism. It is particularly noteworthy that both China and Vietnam have in recent decades introduced rather similar constitutional revisions and legal reforms, including constitutional recognition of socialist legality or Rule of Law, human rights and private property rights, and the construction of a socialist legal system in which detailed laws govern all domains of economic and social activities, state organs and officials are required to exercise their powers in accordance with the law, and systems of courts, procuratorates, lawyers, and legal education have been built up for the purpose of operating the legal system effectively.[95]

Despite bold calls for liberal-democratic constitutional reforms by small numbers of intellectuals, such as the "Charter 08" of 2008 in China (led

94. Albert H.Y. Chen, "Conclusion: Comparative Reflections on Human Rights in Asia" in R. Peerenboom, C.J. Petersen, and Albert H.Y. Chen (eds.) *Human Rights in Asia* (London: Routledge, 2006) 492, 507–511.

95. J. Gillespie and Albert H.Y. Chen (eds.), *Legal Reforms in China and Vietnam* (London: Routledge, 2010).

by Liu Xiaobo, who was convicted and jailed as a result but also awarded a Nobel Peace Prize in 2010)[96] and "Petition 72" in Vietnam in 2013,[97] the regimes in both countries have firmly resisted any political reform that might weaken or threaten the Communist Party's monopoly of State power. Although human rights are now enshrined in the constitutions of both countries (and Vietnam's new Constitution of 2013 has placed increased emphasis on human rights and on the role of the courts in securing justice and human rights), the courts have no role to play in constitutional adjudication in their legal systems (and although a provision on the establishment of a constitutional tribunal was included in an earlier draft of the constitution, the final version of the Vietnamese Constitution adopted on 28 November 2013 does not include this provision.[98] According to the classification schemes developed by Loewenstein and Sartori discussed above, the constitutions of the PRC and Vietnam are "semantic constitutions" (Loewenstein's term) or "nominal constitutions" (Sartori's term) in the sense that they reflect the allocation of power (including the supreme leadership of the Communist Party) but do not effectively constrain its exercise. However, given the two regimes' normative commitment to the Rule of Law and reasonable records in making laws and developing legal institutions in the last three decades,[99] it may be doubted whether the concepts of "semantic" or "nominal" constitutions are completely adequate in describing and analysing the nature and character of constitutional practice or constitutionalism (if any) in contemporary China and Vietnam. In this regard, Backer's theory of "party-state constitutionalism",[100] which was developed in the course of his study of PRC constitutional practice but is

---

96. J.P. Béja, H.L. Fu, and E. Pils (eds.), *Liu Xiaobo, Charter 08, and the Challenges of Political Reform in China* (Hong Kong: Hong Kong University Press, 2012).

97. N.S. Bui, "Petition 72: The Struggle for Constitutional Reforms in Vietnam" (28 March 2013) *Blog of the International Journal of Constitutional Law*, available at: www.iconnectblog.com/2013/03/petition-72-the-struggle-for-constitutional-reforms-in-vietnam/.

98. N.S. Bui, "Vietnam's New Constitution: A Charter for Comprehensive Renovation?" (12 December 2013) *ConstitutionNet*, available at: www.constitutionnet.org/news/vietnams-new-constitution-charter-comprehensive-renovation, last accessed on 21 April 2014.

99. See particularly Peerenboom's discussion on "specifying the minimum conditions for rule of law" and how to distinguish between Rule of Law and mere Rule *by* Law; R. Peerenboom, *China's Long March Toward Rule of Law* (Cambridge: Cambridge University Press, 2002) 130–141.

100. L.C. Backer, "The Party As Polity, the Communist Party, and the Chinese Constitutional State: A Theory of State-Party Constitutionalism" (2009) 16:1 *Journal of Chinese and Comparative Law* 101.

equally applicable to Vietnam given the similar political-legal trends in the two countries, deserves to be considered here.

As in the case of Thio's theory mentioned above, Backer adopts a broad understanding of constitutionalism which is not limited to liberal constitutionalism. He states that "[c]onstitutionalism is grounded on the fundamental postulate of rule of law", which "avoid[s] tyranny or despotism by grounding state action in law and by limiting the reach of such lawful state action on the basis of values reflecting the values of the political collective".[101] Depending on the content of the "legitimating value system" in the state concerned, constitutionalism may take the form of "nationalist constitutionalism", "transnational constitutionalism", "theocratic constitutionalism", "natural law constitutionalism", etc. Backer goes on to say that "they all share equally in the commitment to the fundamental values of a constitutional order — a rule of law based governance structure grounded in limits on state power and popular accountability based on law."[102]

In studying the constitution and constitutional practice of the PRC, Backer takes as his point of departure the idea that the Chinese Communist Party (CCP) is constitutionally entrenched as the "party in power".[103] Thus, unlike political parties in liberal-democratic systems, the CCP is not merely one among several political parties, but is an integral and vital part of the State's constitutional, political, and legal systems. In Backer's view, the real constitution of the PRC includes not only the Constitution of the PRC State, but also the constitution of the CCP.[104] Insofar as the CCP promotes the Rule of Law, subordinates itself to the Rule of Law, and engages in "self-discipline" for this purpose,[105] and insofar as there is some form of "separation of powers"[106] between the CCP (which Backer considers to be the source of the values and fundamental policies that guide the government[107])

101. *Ibid.*, 103.

102. *Ibid.*, 104–105.

103. *Ibid.*, 108.

104. See Shigong Jiang, "Written and Unwritten Constitutions: A New Approach to the Study of Constitutional Government in China" (2010) 36:1 *Modern China* 12; Shigong Jiang, "Chinese-style Constitutionalism: On Backer's Chinese Party-State Constitutionalism" (2014) 40:2 *Modern China* 133; Shigong Jiang, "How to Explore the Chinese Path to Constitutionalism? A Response to Larry Catá Backer" (2014) 40:2 *Modern China* 196.

105. Backer (N100) 152.

106. *Ibid.*, 141.

107. *Ibid.*, 148.

and the State organs (which engage in concrete administrative tasks), constitutionalism can be said to be practiced in China. This may be called "state-party constitutionalism", a kind of "constitutionalism with Chinese characteristics".[108] Backer[109] admits that in this kind of constitutionalism, not all citizens have "political citizenship" and exercise political rights, although all of them have "economic and social citizenship" and exercise economic and social rights. Political citizenship in China, according to Backer's theory, is confined to members of the CCP, whose membership is open to everyone who subscribes to its values and vision.[110] The CCP as an updated version of the Leninist "vanguard" party[111] represents the interest of the Chinese people, acts as their "proxy" and in a "fiduciary capacity",[112] and discharges "pedagogical and tutelage responsibilities".[113]

Backer's analysis is useful for the purpose of studying the evolution of a Communist Party-dominated political system that abandons totalitarianism, withdraws itself from the control of many sectors of the economy and society, concedes a large space for private life and private pursuits, seeks to regulate itself by the Rule of Law, and recognises that citizens' rights should be afforded legal protection. The state-party constitutionalism theorised by Backer shares some of the features of the communitarian constitutionalism discussed above, particularly the adherence to the Rule of Law and legal restrictions on civil liberties, but differs from communitarian constitutionalism in that it does not permit any space for opposition political parties or multi-party elections. Without such space, it may be questioned whether Backer's portrayal of the role of the "party in power" under "state-party constitutionalism" is too idealised and too distant from the reality that despite the CCP having 90 million members today, its power is actually exercised by a small elite of Party leaders who are subject to little electoral accountability. The de facto lack of political citizenship on the part of the great majority of Chinese citizens as recognised by Backer also contradicts the text of the PRC Constitution itself, according to which all citizens have equal political rights. It is therefore doubtful whether this theory of party-state constitutionalism can fully legitimise the party-state itself.

---

108. *Ibid.*, 111.

109. *Ibid.*, 110.

110. *Ibid.*, 151.

111. *Ibid.*, 143, 150.

112. *Ibid.*, 109.

113. *Ibid.*, 150.

## CONCLUSION

East Asia has been and is a great laboratory for diverse constitutional projects. The study in this chapter is based on the premise that there is a close relationship between regime types and the nature and character of constitutional practice in the states concerned. It has discussed four categories of East Asian cases, which differ from one another in terms of the political systems and constitutional practices that exist today. It should be borne in mind that the present-day constitutional situations in these countries can only be fully understood and explained in the light of their constitutional history and the dynamics of their constitutional development, which are not covered in this chapter. Such a historical study would reveal that the constitutional landscape of most of these countries has changed beyond recognition in the last three decades, with most of the originally authoritarian or hybrid regimes being transformed into constitutional democracies. This has been the case in Taiwan, South Korea, the Philippines, and Indonesia, and also to some extent in Thailand. Even in communist China and Vietnam, legal reforms have made such progress in the last three decades that previous theorisations of constitutions and of the lack of constitutionalism in communist one-party states may have become out-of-date. Constitutions and constitutionalism, though originating from Western modernity, have thus been transplanted to Asian soils and have grown up considerably. The constitutional future of this part of the world promises to be an exciting and challenging one.

## Acknowledgement

This chapter was first published as "Constitutions, Constitutional Practice and Constitutionalism in East Asia" in Christoph Antons (ed.), *Routledge Handbook of Asian Law* (2017), chapter 5, pp. 75–93. This edited version is published with permission from the original publisher, Routledge.

# 14

# Five Decades of Constitutional Change in Hong Kong and East Asia

## INTRODUCTION

It is my great honour and pleasure to deliver this lecture[1] which forms part of the lecture series organised by our Faculty to commemorate the fiftieth anniversary of our law school which was founded in 1969. The title of this lecture was inspired by the title of a book edited by Professor Raymond Wacks, then Head of our Department of Law. The book is titled *The Law in Hong Kong: 1969 to 1989* and consists of chapters written by colleagues in our law school. It was published in celebration of the twentieth anniversary of the school in 1989. Another inspiration for the title of this lecture is a book published in Singapore to celebrate the fiftieth anniversary of the Republic of Singapore. The book is titled *Singapore: 50 Constitutional Moments that Defined a Nation*. It provides an overview of Singaporean constitutional history in fifty chapters. The lecture this evening is also about constitutional moments and constitutional history. As I specialise in constitutional law, I think the best way in which I can contribute to our school's fiftieth anniversary is to talk about constitutional history in the last fifty years.

On this occasion, I would like to begin by paying a special tribute to and expressing my great gratitude to Professor Peter Wesley-Smith, my teacher of constitutional law in this law school more than forty years ago. He retired about twenty years ago and now lives in Australia. It was Professor Wesley-Smith who first introduced me as a first-year law student to the world of constitutional jurisprudence. It was in the LL.B. subject called "Elements of Public Law and Legal System" that I first began to learn about the concept of the Rule of Law and other constitutional values. I still vividly remember Professor Wesley-Smith telling us in class that constitutional law is a particularly interesting area of law, because it is so closely connected with the history, politics, culture,

1. This is the text of a public lecture delivered by the author at the University of Hong Kong on 15 March 2019. It was part of a lecture series organised by the Faculty of Law, University of Hong Kong, in celebration of the fiftieth anniversary of the founding of the law school in 1969. This lecture draws on the following works of the author: "Pathways of Western Liberal Constitutional Developments in Asia: A Comparative Study of Five Major Nations" (2010) 8 *I-CON* 849; "Introduction: Constitutionalism and Constitutional Change in East and Southeast Asia" in Albert H.Y. Chen and Tom Ginsburg (eds.), *Public Law in Asia* (London: Ashgate 2013) 15–47; "The Achievement of Constitutionalism in Asia" in Albert H.Y. Chen (ed.), *Constitutionalism in Asia in the Early Twenty-first Century* (Cambridge: Cambridge University Press, 2014) 1–31. As the transcribed lecture contains few footnotes, readers may consult the above works for references to relevant sources. Section headings have been added to aid flow.

and traditions of the country or jurisdiction whose constitutional law we are studying. So it was the teachings of Professor Peter Wesley-Smith that initiated my interest in constitutional history.

In 1989, another book edited by Professor Raymond Wacks and published to celebrate the twentieth anniversary of our law school was on *The Future of the Law in Hong Kong*. I contributed a chapter on "Hong Kong's Constitutional Journey: From Colony to Special Administrative Region". In recent years, my research in constitutional law has broadened beyond Hong Kong and mainland China to include countries and jurisdictions in East Asia and Southeast Asia. That is why I decided that in this lecture, I will only briefly talk about Hong Kong and will devote the greater part of my lecture to several of Hong Kong's neighbouring jurisdictions in East and Southeast Asia — namely, Taiwan, South Korea, Indonesia, and Thailand, where the constitutional landscape has changed beyond recognition in the last five decades.

Let us turn our minds to Hong Kong and these four other jurisdictions fifty years ago, in 1969. Hong Kong had just gone through the trauma of the 1967 riots during which the law and courts were used to suppress political dissent and violence. At that time, Hong Kong had a political system which Peter Wesley-Smith called "gubernatorial government", meaning an authoritarian system with few checks and balances, and with a high degree of concentration of power in the hands of the colonial governor, who was Sir David Trench at the time. Taiwan in 1969 was under the authoritarian one-party rule of the Kuomintang (KMT) leader Chiang kai-shek. South Korea was under the strongman rule of President Park Chung-hee, who in the 1970s turned the regime into a military dictatorship. Indonesia was under the rule of another military strongman, Soeharto, who came into power by a coup in 1965 in the midst of a massacre of an estimated half a million people. In 1969, Thailand was under the rule of army general Thanom, who imposed a military dictatorship in 1971.

Now if we look at the political and constitutional system in each of these five jurisdictions today, we can appreciate the extensive and far-reaching political, constitutional, and legal changes that have taken place in these five jurisdictions in the last fifty years. Through the lens of constitutionalism, we can indeed observe an overall trend of progress in the building or development of constitutionalism in these five jurisdictions in the last five decades. Such progress is remarkable precisely because progress is not inevitable. If we look at the constitutional history of many states in the modern world, we will see that possibilities of progress as well as degeneration, decline, or retrogression existed at almost every moment. Think about Germany in 1905 which was a constitutional monarchy, and compare it with Germany thirty years later in 1935 when it had become a completely totalitarian regime. Or think about China in 1956 when a national congress of the Chinese Communist Party (CCP) decided to embark upon the development of socialist legality, and compare this with the situation twenty years later, in 1976, when China's legal system had been almost completely destroyed by the "Cultural Revolution". So we can see that there can be periods of history when not only no constitutional progress occurred, but there was serious deterioration in the level of legality, or what is more appropriately described as a descent from civilisation into barbarism. Thus, the notions of constitutions and constitutionalism, including the concepts of liberal constitutionalism and hybrid constitutionalism, which are implicit in the constitutional developments of these five jurisdictions in the last fifty years, are highly significant, particularly from the perspective of the "long-term rationality of history".[2]

## CONSTITUTIONS AND CONSTITUTIONALISM

The modern idea of a system of government being constituted by a written constitution was born in the Age of Enlightenment, particularly in the course of the American and French Revolutions of the late eighteenth century. The constitution was conceived as a fundamental written law which simultaneously establishes the governmental system of a state, and controls and regulates the exercise its political power. The constitution constitutes the state and its government; the government derives its legitimacy and authority from the constitution. The people of the nation-state are the makers of the constitution, acting directly or through their representatives in a constituent assembly. The exercise of such constituent power by the people is a manifestation of the sovereignty of the people, a fundamental concept that underlies most constitutions all over the world.

Modern constitutions represent attempts by their draftsmen to rationally design a form of government that can best serve the objectives of the nation-state. Influenced by liberalism, social contract theory, and Enlightenment thought, and determined to put an end to the absolutism of the post-feudal

2. Ray Huang, *China: A Macro History* (Armonk, N.Y.: M.E. Sharpe, 2nd edition, 1996).

state of the early modern era, the draftsmen of the first modern constitutions devised schemes of government for the purpose of minimising the possibility of abuse of political power, tyranny, or oppression, and maximising the protection of political freedom and the individual's rights to life, liberty, and property.

After the birth of the first modern constitutions in the United States and France, the practice of constitution-making quickly spread throughout Europe in the course of the nineteenth century, and then all over the world in the course of the twentieth century. In today's world, the possession of a constitution seems to have been accepted by all as a hallmark of the legitimacy of a regime for both domestic and external purposes. Unlike the earlier Western constitutions, the first constitutions adopted by regimes in the non-Western world were not enacted after a revolution in order to constitute a new state and a new political order, nor inspired by the liberal doctrine of the protection of individuals' rights. Instead, such constitutions were designed to bolster the legitimacy of regimes threatened by Western powers and to enhance the effectiveness of the regime's rule. An East Asian example is the constitution promulgated by the Meiji Emperor of Japan in 1889.

The end of the Second World War and the decolonisation of Asia and Africa that followed gave rise to many new states in the international community. The exercise of constitution-making proved to be useful for the founders of the new states. Constitutions served not only as declarations of sovereignty and independence, but also as symbols of nationhood and the unity and collective identity of the people of the new states. The widespread adoption of the Western practice of constitution-making by newly independent states in Asia and Africa does not necessarily mean that the new constitutions have served the goal of constitutionalism, a term that began to be used in the early nineteenth century to encapsulate the classical liberal conception of constitutions in the Western world. For significant periods, the constitutional circumstances of many non-Western countries may be aptly summarised by the term "constitutions without constitutionalism". Just as in the daily life of individuals, it is relatively easy to say something or make a promise, but more difficult to translate what is said or promised into action and reality, so in the political and legal life of nations, it is relatively easy to make a constitution, but more difficult to put it into practice, to implement it, and be governed by it — which is what "constitutionalism" is about. The distinguished German jurist Dieter Grimm has described constitutionalism as an "achievement". He writes:

> Constitutionalism ... deserves to be called an achievement, because it rules out any absolute or arbitrary power of men over men. By submitting all government

> action to rules, it makes the use of public power predictable … It provides a consensual basis for persons and groups with different ideas and interests to resolve their disputes in a civilized manner. And it enables a peaceful transition of power to be made. … [C]onstitutionalism … is not an ideal type … [that] can never be completely reached. It is a historical reality that was in principle already fully developed by the first constitutions in North America and France and fulfilled its promise in a number of countries that had adopted constitutions in this sense.[3]

In his famous book on *The Morality of Law*,[4] the American legal philosopher Lon Fuller describes the morality of law as a kind of "morality of aspiration".[5] Such a morality is concerned with striving to achieve a particular good that can be realised in different degrees. The higher the degree to which the good is achieved, the more successful and excellent the moral project concerned will be. The project of law, as Fuller understands it, is the project of subjecting human conduct to the governance of legal rules. Fuller develops eight principles, which he calls the principles of the internal morality of law, as criteria for evaluating the success of this project.

Fuller's concept of the morality of law as a morality of aspiration may be usefully applied to understand constitutionalism. Whereas Fuller conceives of the project of the Rule of Law as one to regulate human behaviour by legal norms or to subject human beings to the governance of rules, the project of constitutionalism seeks to subject rulers or government to the governance of constitutional and legal rules and to regulate the exercise of political power by means of such rules. As in the case of the Rule of Law, constitutionalism may also be achieved to varying extents. This is consistent with Grimm's view of constitutionalism as an achievement.

The degree to which constitutionalism is realised in a particular country or jurisdiction depends on the relevant historical and ideological contexts, the nature of the political and legal tradition concerned, and the culture, economic, and social circumstances and needs of the state and society concerned. There is also a distinction between liberal constitutionalism and hybrid constitutionalism. Liberal constitutionalism is the original or classical

---

3. Dieter Grimm, "The Achievement of Constitutionalism and Its Prospects in a Changed World" in Petra Dobner and Martin Loughlin (eds.), *The Twilight of Constitutionalism* (Oxford: Oxford University Press, 2010) 3, at 10.
4. Lon L. Fuller, *The Morality of Law* (London: Yale Uuniversity Press, revised edition, 1969).
5. *Ibid.*, 4.

form of constitutionalism as it first emerged in modern Western history.[6] This includes elements such as (1) the Rule of Law, (2) the separation of powers and judicial independence, (3) political checks and balances, (4) the legal protection of civil liberties and human rights, (5) a written constitution which is effective in regulating the exercise of political power, (6) judicial review of the constitutionality of governmental and legislative acts, and (7) peaceful transfer of political power in accordance with constitutional norms. In the contemporary world, this kind of constitutionalism is basically co-extensive with liberal democracy, although the first constitutional states in Western history were not yet fully democratic as the right to vote was the privilege of upper classes in society and there was no universal suffrage.

Hybrid constitutionalism is a concept analogous to that of "hybrid regimes" in political science. It is found in states that possess constitutions that are liberal-democratic on paper, in which there exist authoritarian practices that are inconsistent with liberal constitutionalism. Such practices may be derived from traditional or indigenous notions, norms, institutions, and practices of politics, culture, and religion (as in theocracy), or constitute deliberate attempts by rulers or ruling elites (such as a one-man dictatorship, one-party hegemony, military regime, or theocracy) to practise authoritarian rule behind a façade of liberal-democratic constitutional forms. They may do so, for example, by determining who may participate in elections, manipulating or rigging electoral and other constitutional processes, violating human rights guaranteed by the constitution, or otherwise denying opposition forces fair opportunities to compete for political power on a level playing ground in accordance with the constitution.

In the last five decades, some Asian countries have undergone a transition from hybrid constitutionalism to liberal constitutionalism, while other Asian jurisdictions have made progress towards liberal constitutionalism though the transition has not been completed. This is the most remarkable macro-historical trend in East Asia in the last five decades as far as the project or achievement of constitutionalism is concerned. Of particular interest are Hong Kong, Taiwan, South Korea, Indonesia, and Thailand.

---

6. See generally Carlos Santiago Nino, *The Constitution of Deliberative Democracy* (London: Yale University Press, 1996).

## HONG KONG[7]

Colonial Hong Kong was ruled by the British on the basis of a rudimentary constitution contained in the Letters Patent and Royal Instructions. Power was concentrated in the hands of the Governor, who ruled with the assistance of an Executive Council (ExCo) and a Legislative Council (LegCo) in which all the members were appointed by him. As of 1969, there was no election except to a portion of seats in the Urban Council (with responsibilities in the domains of public health, environmental hygiene, and recreational facilities) on the basis of a limited franchise. The number of eligible voters in 1969 was approximately 200,000 people out of a population of approximately 4 million. The English legal system based on the common law, the Rule of Law, and judicial independence was transplanted to Hong Kong. There was no Bill of Rights in the colonial constitution, and laws enacted by the colonial regime placed considerable restrictions on civil liberties, which were undoubtedly more restrictive than the law in Britain itself. Corruption was rampant in the police and some other government departments until the enactment of new anti-corruption laws and the establishment of the Independent Commission Against Corruption (ICAC) in the 1970s. The Chinese language was not recognised as an official language until a movement led by students and civil society pressurised the government to introduce the Official Languages Ordinance in 1974.

The prospects of Hong Kong's return to China and the Sino-British Joint Declaration of 1984 were the main impetus of constitutional change in the last one and a half decades of colonial rule in Hong Kong, which included the introduction of increasing numbers of elected members in LegCo and an improved system for the protection of civil liberties and human rights. In 1982, the District Boards — advisory bodies at local levels — were established consisting of members appointed by the government as well members elected by universal suffrage. At the same time, the franchise for the elected seats

---

7. See generally Albert H.Y. Chen, "From Colony to Special Administrative Region: Hong Kong's Constitutional Journey" in Raymond Wacks (ed.), *The Future of the Law in Hong Kong* (Hong Kong: Oxford University Press, 1989) 76–126; Albert H.Y. Chen, "A Tale of Two Islands: Comparative Reflections on Constitutionalism in Hong Kong and Taiwan" (2007) 37 *Hong Kong Law Journal* 647; Albert H.Y. Chen, "Development of Representative Government" in Johannes Chan and C.L. Lim (eds.), *Law of the Hong Kong Constitution* (Hong Kong: Sweet & Maxwell, 2nd edition, 2015) ch. 8.

in the Urban Council was broadened. In 1985, some of the seats in LegCo were opened up for election for the first time in the colony's history. Some members were elected by newly created functional constituencies, and others by electoral colleges comprising the District Boards, the Urban Council, and the newly created Regional Council.

After the Tiananmen Incident on 4 June 1989, there was an upsurge in demands for democratisation in Hong Kong. In 1990, the Basic Law of the Hong Kong Special Administrative Region (HKSAR) of the PRC was enacted by the National People's Congress (NPC). The Basic Law is a constitutional instrument enacted by the NPC in 1990 to provide for the legal and political system of the HKSAR and its relationship with Beijing. It contains provisions for the gradual democratisation of the HKSAR and the introduction of universal suffrage. In 1991, 18 of the seats in LegCo were opened to direct election by universal suffrage for the first time. In the same year, the Hong Kong Bill of Rights Ordinance (BORO) was enacted by LegCo. This legislative measure was part of the British Hong Kong Government's response to the crisis of confidence in Hong Kong arising from the 4 June incident in 1989. The Ordinance translated the provisions of the International Covenant on Civil and Political Rights (ICCPR), which Britain had already applied to Hong Kong in 1976, into domestic law. Corresponding amendments were made to the Letters Patent, Hong Kong's constitutional instrument. Under the new constitutional regime, Hong Kong courts were empowered to review and to strike down laws and administrative actions that the courts determined to be inconsistent with the human rights guarantees in the Hong Kong Bill of Rights or the ICCPR. Since 1991, a body of case law has developed in which the Hong Kong courts have exercised this power of constitutional review and applied principles of "proportionality" to check whether a restriction on a relevant right is constitutional. This system of constitutional judicial review of legislation and executive action has continued to operate after 1997, though its constitutional basis is no longer the colonial constitution but is the Basic Law.

Over the last five decades, Hong Kong has undergone a transition from a kind of non-democratic constitutionalism that was quite typical of the authoritarian mode of British colonial rule in Asia and Africa to some form of liberal constitutionalism. Although Hong Kong has not yet achieved full democratisation in the sense of the election of its Chief Executive and of all its LegCo members by universal suffrage, its constitutional and political practices since the 1990s and after the handover in 1997 have included elements of liberal constitutionalism, such as the Rule of Law, judicial independence, civil liberties, separation of powers, political checks and balances, judicial review of the constitutionality of legislative and administrative actions, and a free press and vibrant civil society.

Although Hong Kong is not a liberal constitutional democracy, there exists in Hong Kong an open and pluralistic society. As the Hong Kong Court of Final Appeal (CFA) has repeatedly said in its judgments,[8] the civil and political rights that receive constitutional protection in Hong Kong stand at the heart of Hong Kong's separate system under the "One Country, Two Systems" (OCTS) model. Taken together, the values and ideals of constitutionalism undoubtedly lie at the heart of Hong Kong's separate system.

## TAIWAN[9]

During the last decade of its dynastic rule in China, the Qing court began to move towards a constitutional monarchy. An "Imperial Constitutional Outline" was promulgated in 1908, and provincial assemblies were elected. The 1911 Revolution overthrew the Qing Empire, and the Republic of China (ROC) was established in 1912 with a liberal-democratic provisional constitution. In the first one and a half decades of the republican era, several constitutions were promulgated or drafted by successive governments in Beijing, but none was effective as China was beset with warlordism and civil strife. In 1928, the KMT (or Chinese Nationalist Party) under Chiang Kai-shek's leadership succeeded to unify large parts of China (but not areas under the control of the CCP) and established a new ROC Government in Nanjing. The KMT adhered to the strategy of constitutional development advocated by its founder, Dr Sun Yat-sen, which involved a three-stage process of military government, political tutelage (under one-party rule in preparation for the third stage), and constitutional government. This may be understood as a theory about establishing hybrid constitutionalism first and then moving towards liberal constitutionalism. A provisional constitution for the period of political tutelage was promulgated in 1931 which expressly vested power in the KMT. After the end of the Sino-Japanese War in 1945, a new Constitution of the ROC,

---

8. See, for example, *Ng Ka Ling v Director of Immigration* (1999) 2 HKCFAR 4; *HKSAR v Ng Kung Siu* (1999) 2 HKCFAR 442; *Gurung Kesh Bahadur v Director of Immigration* (2002) 5 HKCFAR 480; *Yeung May-wan v HKSAR* (2005) 8 HKCFAR 137.
9. See generally Chen, "A Tale of Two Islands" (N7).

containing all the key ingredients of a liberal constitutional democracy was adopted by a constituent assembly in 1946.

This new constitution was not accepted by the CCP, and a civil war between the CCP and the KMT raged for several years, ending in the KMT's defeat and their retreat to Taiwan, which had been ceded by the Qing Empire to Japan in 1895 and liberated from Japanese rule in 1945. During the civil war, the KMT regime introduced a constitutional amendment known as the "Temporary Provisions for the Period of National Mobilisation to Suppress the Communist Rebellion", which expanded the emergency powers of the President. Martial law was decreed by the KMT Government, first in the mainland and then in Taiwan. The civil liberties and democratic elections promised by the 1946 Constitution were suspended by the KMT regime in Taiwan for nearly four decades, during which Taiwan under the rule of Chiang Kai-shek and then his son Chiang Ching-kuo underwent rapid economic development and rose to become one of the "Four Little Dragons" of East Asia, together with South Korea, Hong Kong, and Singapore. As time progressed, there was a considerable degree of social and even political pluralism, and elections took place at the municipal and county levels, as well as elections to a minority of seats in the parliamentary institutions. The constitutional and political practices of this period may be understood as falling within the concept of hybrid constitutionalism.

Taiwan's transition from hybrid constitutionalism to liberal constitutionalism began with the lifting of the martial law decree by President Chiang Ching-kuo in 1987. In the late 1980s and the early 1990s, Taiwan underwent rapid liberalisation and democratisation. The Temporary Provisions were repealed in 1991. Seven exercises of constitutional revision in 1991–2005 substantially changed the nature and structure of the government. A "silent revolution"[10] was achieved in Taiwan. Multi-party elections were periodically held, leading to changes in government and transfers of power between political parties (the KMT and the Democratic Progressive Party) in 2000, 2008, and 2016. It is clear that the processes of liberalisation and democratisation that started in Taiwan in the late 1980s have resulted in democratic consolidation in the course of the last three decades.

The ROC Constitution of 1946 has established a constitutional court known as the Council of Grand Justices (CGJ) of the Judicial Yuan, charged with the task of issuing authoritative interpretations of the Constitution. After the

10. Lee Teng-hui, *Taiwan de zhuzhang* [*The Views of Taiwan*] (Taipei: Yuanliu, 1999) 162–163.

regime's retreat to Taiwan, the CGJ has gradually built up a record of judicial interpretations and thus also its institutional capacity and judicial authority. Most of the early judicial interpretations dealt with technical jurisdictional issues of separation of powers rather than citizens' rights. Although the CGJ had the power of constitutional review of laws, regulations, and decrees, it did not exercise this power in practice until 1980. Before the late 1980s, the CGJ, because of its unimpressive record in dealing with several politically sensitive cases, was not perceived as a strong and independent guardian of constitutional norms and rights, but was regarded by some as an accomplice of the authoritarian regime merely adding constitutional legitimacy to it.

The image of the CGJ began to change for the better in the second half of the 1980s. The CGJ became more activist and more ready and willing to exercise its power of constitutional review of legislative and administrative acts. In 1990, the CGJ had the opportunity to prove its importance and establish its authority when the question of the re-election of the parliamentary institutions[11] (the majority of whose members were still those elected in mainland China in the late 1940s, whose seats had not been subject to periodic elections because in theory the parliamentary institutions still represented the whole of China and yet it had not been possible to hold elections in the mainland since 1949) came before it. In the celebrated Interpretation No. 261 issued in 1990, the CGJ in effect ordered fresh elections in Taiwan for all seats in the parliamentary institutions. After this interpretation, the CGJ has issued many more interpretations on questions of citizens' rights and separation of powers that have collectively established the CGJ's reputation as a credible, respected, and activist constitutional court.

Since the late 1980s, the constitutional court has played an active role in declaring the laws and regulations of the previous authoritarian regime unconstitutional. The Constitutional Amendment of 1999 was even declared unconstitutional and invalid by the constitutional court,[12] invoking the jurisprudence that certain fundamental principles of the liberal-democratic constitutional order ought to be protected against amendment or violation. In the first decade of this century, the constitutional court has played a more crucial role than ever before in adjudicating political conflicts arising from

11. The major parliamentary institutions included the National Assembly and the Legislative Yuan. The National Assembly has since been abolished by the constitutional amendment of 2005.

12. Interpretation No. 499 (March 2000). See generally www.judicial.gov.tw/constitutionalcourt.

the circumstances of a "divided government" in which the presidency and government on the one hand and the Legislative Yuan on the other hand were controlled by different political parties (the Democratic Progressive Party and the KMT, respectively). The constitutional court has also been active in rights adjudication. In 2017, it became the first constitutional or supreme court in Asia to declare, in its Interpretation No. 748, that it is unconstitutional not to recognise the legality of same-sex marriage.

## SOUTH KOREA

In Korea, once a tributary state of China's, the Chosen dynasty (1392–1910) came to an end in 1910 with the Japanese annexation of Korea after Japan's victories in its wars with China (1895) and Russia (1905). The Korean people experienced colonial Japanese rule of a highly authoritarian nature until the end of Second World War, when Korea became divided into the Republic of Korea in the South and the Democratic People's Republic of Korea in the North. North Korea has been under one-man rule through a communist party — the Korean Workers' Party — up to this day.

South Korea, which adopted a liberal-democratic constitution in 1948, experienced four tumultuous decades and nine major constitutional revisions in its history, the last of which resulted in the 1987 Constitution of the "Sixth Republic" which is currently in force. The varying patterns of constitutional and political practices over these four decades fall under the rubric of hybrid constitutionalism, with different mixes of democracy, constitutionalism, and authoritarianism at different points in time. South Korea achieved rapid economic development under the rule of President Park Chung-hee (1961–1979), who steered Korea's rise as one of the "Four Little Dragons" of East Asia. In 1972, he proclaimed martial law and pushed through the Yushin Constitution. The *Yushin* (meaning "revitalising reforms")[13] Constitution purported to introduce a "Korean-style democracy".[14] Critics described it as "a constitution which legalized authoritarian rule",[15] inaugurating a "'dark age' of

13. "Yushin" is the Korean equivalent of the Japanese term "issin" which was the slogan of the Meiji Reform of 1868.
14. Bruce Cumings, *Korea's Place in the Sun: A Modern History* (New York: W.W. Norton, 1991) 156.
15. Jürgen Kleiner, *Korea: A Century of Change* (Singapore: World Scientific, 2001) 156.

constitutionalism".[16] The 1972 Constitution expanded the emergency powers of the President, and expressly authorised the suspension of constitutional rights by emergency measures. These powers were used extensively to introduce draconian measures to suppress movements for amendment of the Constitution, liberalisation, and democratisation.

In October 1979, "the most serious student uprising since 1960"[17] developed after the expulsion of Kim Young-sam, a leading opposition politician, from the National Assembly. On 26 October, President Park was assassinated. Martial law was immediately proclaimed throughout South Korea. In December 1979, General Chun Doo-hwan seized power within the military. In May 1980, demonstrations erupted all over the country demanding the termination of martial law and democratisation. Chun opted for repression. In protest, what became known as the "Kwangju Uprising" occurred on 18–27 May 1980, which only ended when, "[i]n the early hours of 27 May 1980, Kwangju was conquered by troops in an assault like in times of war".[18] The event was "Korea's Tiananmen nightmare in which students and young people were slaughtered on a scale the same as or greater than that in 'People's' China in June 1989".[19]

In August 1980, the electoral college known as the National Conference for Unification (NCU) elected Chun as President. A new constitution, which, unlike the *Yushin* Constitution, was relatively liberal-democratic in orientation, was approved by a referendum on in October 1980. In February 1981, Chun was elected President of the new Fifth Republic by an electoral college in accordance with the new Constitution. During Chun's rule, the democracy movement in South Korea continued to demand the direct election of the President by citizens themselves. The movement escalated into large-scale demonstrations in 1987. On 29 June that year, Roh Tae-woo, Chun's designated successor, opted for conciliation rather than repression, and by consensus between the government and the opposition a new Constitution was produced and approved by the National Assembly on 12 October and in a referendum on 25 October 1987. This Constitution provides for direct popular

16. Kim Tscholsu and Lee Sang Dong, "The Influence of U.S. Constitutional Law Doctrines in Korea" in Lawrence W. Beer (ed.), *Constitutional Systems in Late Twentieth Century Asia* (Seattle, Wash.: University of Washington Press, 1992) 303–330, at 318.

17. Andrew C. Nahm, *Korea: Tradition and Transformation* (Carlsbad, Cali.:Hollym International, 2nd edition, 1996) 431.

18. Cumings (N14) 177.

19. *Ibid.*, 338.

election of the President and the establishment of a Constitutional Court. This Constitution is still in force today.

Roh Tae-woo won the presidential election in December 1987. In December 1992, Kim Young-sam won the election and became South Korea's first civilian President in 32 years. Then, with the election of Kim Dae-jung as President in 1997, the first peaceful transfer of power from a ruling party to an opposition party occurred. The consolidation of constitutional democracy in South Korea has clearly taken place, and regression back to authoritarianism or military rule has become inconceivable. "Transitional justice" has been achieved to some extent by the prosecution and conviction in 1995 of two former presidents, Chun and Roh, for treason and corruption. Since its establishment in 1988, the Korean Constitutional Court[20] has built up a strong reputation as custodian of the Constitution and defender of human rights, has declared statutory provisions and governmental actions unconstitutional in hundreds of cases, and has adjudicated on critical political issues such as those arising from the criminal trials of the two former presidents and the National Assembly's impeachment of President Roh Moo-hyun in 2004 and President Park Geun-hye in 2017. Indeed, "[t]hrough the activities of the Constitutional Court, the Constitution has become a normative document regulating the lives of the people and the operation of the government".[21] South Korea today, one of Asia's major economic powers, has thus become one of the strongholds of liberal constitutionalism in Asia. As one historian of modern Korea writes:

> [D]emocracy is not a gift or a political regime that one is born with but something that must be fought for every inch of the way, in every society. In this sense, the Korean struggle has been so enduring that there may be no country more deserving of democracy in our time than the Republic of Korea.[22]

## INDONESIA

The case of Indonesia is important because it is the most populous nation and largest economy in Southeast Asia, and provides the latest example in

---

20. See generally Albert H.Y. Chen and Andrew Harding (eds.), *Constitutional Courts in Asia* (Cambridge: Cambridge University Press, 2018).
21. Chaihark Hahm, "Rule of Law in South Korea" in Randall Peerenboom (ed.), *Asian Discourses of Rule of Law* (New York: Routledge, 2003) 385–416, at 392.
22. Cumings (N14) 339.

East Asia of a successful transition from hybrid constitutionalism to liberal constitutionalism. Dutch colonisation of what is today Indonesia began in the mid-eighteenth century. After the Pacific War, the indigenous Indonesians fought against the Dutch for independence. The Dutch were defeated and at the Hague Conference of 1949, the independence of Indonesia as a republic was recognised. Earlier, in 1945, an independence constitution had been promulgated, which expressed Soekarno's "Pancasila" ideology and was also based on Soepomo's concept of the integralist or organic state (as opposed to individualism and liberalism).[23] The new 1950 Constitution established a parliamentary system, and the first general election was held in 1955 in which 16 political parties secured parliamentary seats. However, Soekarno declared martial law in 1957 and restored the 1945 Constitution. His authoritarian rule continued until 1965, when a coup occurred during which an estimated half a million people were massacred in an anti-communist drive. General Soeharto came to power and established a "New Order" regime with guaranteed participation of the military in the political system (*dwifungsi*). In the New Order regime only three political parties were allowed to participate in elections which were generally stage-managed. Soeharto's rule finally came to an end in 1998 when Indonesia was badly hurt by the Asian financial crisis and there was civil unrest.

When the Soeharto regime collapsed in 1998, many observers were not optimistic about the prospects for a successful transition in Indonesia from authoritarianism to democracy, or from hybrid constitutionalism to liberal constitutionalism. There existed several factors that were unfavourable to such a transition, including the country's complex ethnic and cultural cleavages, the sudden collapse of the existing regime of strongman rule amidst a financial crisis and mass protests, the fragmented political configuration of the country at the time, the long-standing role of the military in Indonesia's politics, the weakness of the legal system, and the political subordination and corruption of the judiciary. Yet this most populous and Muslim nation of Southeast Asia succeeded against all the odds and achieved a successful transition to liberal constitutionalism, the relative smoothness of which went beyond expectations.

After the collapse of the Soeharto regime, civil liberties were immediately restored, and in 1999 the first free election since 1955 was held in which 48 political parties participated. The newly elected national assembly enacted

23. See generally Chen, "Pathways of Western Liberal Constitutional Developments in Asia" (N1) 860–867.

a series of constitutional amendments in 1999–2002 which transformed Indonesia into a liberal-democratic constitutional state. The constitutional reform was achieved in an "incremental" and "gradualist" manner in the course of four years.

Since then, direct presidential elections have been successfully held in 2004, 2009, and 2014, with the elections in 2004 and 2014 resulting in peaceful transfers of power. The next election will be held in April 2019.[24] It seems that democratic consolidation has occurred in Indonesia in the last twenty years. A significant feature of Indonesia's constitutional reform was the creation of a constitutional court, which was in some respects (particularly regarding the manner of justice selection) closely modelled on the reputable and successful Constitutional Court of South Korea. It seems that the historically contingent and politicised event of the impeachment of President Wahid in 2001 contributed to the Assembly's decision to establish a constitutional court in Indonesia that could render a fair and impartial decision in any future case of impeachment. Since its establishment in 2003, the Indonesian Constitutional Court has maintained a good record in independent and active review of laws that were challenged before it, and in the performance of other functions, such as adjudication of disputes arising from elections. Human rights protection has been strengthened, and civil and political rights in Indonesia have been highly evaluated by international non-governmental organisations, such as Freedom House, relative to other Southeast Asian countries. Key political actors in Indonesia are apparently committed to resolving their disputes non-violently through constitutional processes. Indonesia as the most populous Muslim country in the contemporary world is now also one of the world's most populous constitutional democracy. Indonesia may be able to provide a model for other countries of the reconciliation of Islam with constitutional democracy.

## THAILAND[25]

Thailand is the only nation in Southeast Asia which was not colonised by Western powers. Its constitutional practice, which began with the

24. General elections were held on 17 April 2019, including the election of the President and the national assembly. Joko Widodo, the incumbent President, was re-elected.

25. See generally Chapter 13 of this volume.

establishment of a constitutional monarchy in 1932, is therefore an entirely indigenous enterprise. Thai constitutional history is characterised by frequent oscillations between military and civilian rule, with recurring cycles of constitution-making, general election, formation of and rule by a constitutional civilian government, and then military coup. Nineteen constitutions, some provisional and some intended to be more permanent, have come and gone. There existed critical moments of popular protests changing the course of Thai political history, such as the students' revolution of 1973, and the popular protests in Bangkok in 1992 which led to bloodshed and intervention by the highly respected King Bhumibol.

Thailand in the mid-1990s experienced democratic participation on the making of a new constitution that was intended to put an end to the vicious cycles of the past and to introduce in Thailand, once and for all, a genuine constitutional order that is democratic and progressive. The 1997 Constitution was hailed as the most liberal and democratic constitution in Thai history, and as a "people's constitution" enacted only after extensive public consultation. The ambitions, hopes and ideals of the 1997 Constitution were high, and yet it failed to secure a transition from hybrid constitutionalism to liberal constitutionalism in Thailand.

The great promises of the 1997 Constitution were dashed when a military coup in 2006 toppled Prime Minister Thaksin Shinawatra, who was elected in 2001 in the first election held under the 1997 Constitution but encountered massive protests in 2006. Although the military returned power to a civilian government elected under the new 2007 Constitution (which replaced the interim constitution of 2006) that was approved by the people in a referendum, the political situation soon deteriorated with the continuous and violent confrontation between the anti-Thaksin "Yellow Shirts" and the pro-Thaksin "Red Shirts". Political instability continued after the 2011 election by which Yingluck Shinawatra came to power, and she was eventually overthrown by a coup in 2014. The military government established after the coup is still in power today, although a new election will be held on 24 March 2019 in accordance with Thailand's 20th Constitution adopted in 2017.[26]

From the perspective of comparative constitutional studies, the political role played by Thailand's Constitutional Court since it was first established under

26. The general election was held on 24 March 2019, resulting in General Prayut Chan-o-cha, leader of the coup in 2014 and prime minister since then, being elected by the new Parliament as prime minister on 5 June 2019.

the 1997 Constitution is particularly worthy of attention. This Constitutional Court, the Constitutional Tribunal under the interim 2006 Constitution promulgated after the coup and the new Constitutional Court established by the 2007 Constitution have each rendered the boldest decisions at the highest level of "mega-politics",[27] including decisions on the survival of an existing government or political party, and the validity of national electoral outcomes and of constitutional amendments.[28]

Thailand has, since 2006, become an extreme case of what scholars have termed "the judicialisation of politics" or even "the politicisation of the judiciary". The division of Thai society between two strongly opposing camps made the position of the Constitutional Court as the guardian of the constitution particularly difficult. Thailand thus illustrates the inherent limitations of constitutional democracy in socio-political circumstances in which the key institutions of constitutional democracy (such as free and fair elections, civil and political liberties, and a constitutional court intended to be independent and impartial) are inadequate in coping with, regulating, and containing the deep divisions in a society torn by conflicting values, interests, and political convictions.

## CONCLUSION

In the 1960s and 1970s, when forms of hybrid constitutionalism and authoritarian rule were practised in South Korea, Taiwan, and many Southeast Asian states, it looked as if there did exist an Asian mode of constitutionalism or political-constitutional practice that was distinct from Western liberal constitutionalism. Such Asian political-constitutional practice seemed to be informed by Asian culture and values, including Confucianism and communitarian, and to consist of a mixture of Western constitutional forms and indigenous ideas and practices that inclined towards authoritarianism and personal, party, or military domination. The constitutions of the relevant states contained some features of constitutionalism and liberal democracy; yet constitutional institutions and processes were used by authoritarian rulers as a façade and as means to confer legitimacy on their regimes and to express their

27. See Ran Hirschl, "The Judicialization of Mega-politics and the Rise of Political Courts" (2008) 11 *Annual Review of Political Science* 93.

28. For details, see Chapter 13 of this volume.

national identity. These authoritarian strongmen included Park Chung-hee in South Korea, Chiang Kai-shek in Taiwan, Soeharto in Indonesia, and also Marcos in the Philippines and Lee Kuan Yew in Singapore, though these two cases have not been covered in this lecture. Rapid economic growth in South Korea under Park, in Taiwan under the Chiangs, in Singapore under Lee Kuan Yew, in Malaysia under Mahathir, and in Indonesia under Suharto, all contributed to the regimes' legitimacy as "developmental states".

However, with the democratic transition and consolidation of liberal constitutionalism in South Korea, Taiwan, and Indonesia, the idea that there exists a distinctly Asian form of constitutionalism or political-constitutional practice may be regarded as bankrupt. In retrospect, the hybrid constitutionalism once practised in these states that seemed to bear specifically Asian characteristics were no more than the earlier or transitional phase of a historical trajectory towards liberal constitutionalism — a phase in which political practices failed to conform to the promises of liberty and democracy in the constitutional texts. It is also noteworthy that in South Korea, Taiwan, and Indonesia, the transitions from hybrid constitutionalism to liberal constitutionalism have been largely peaceful (in the sense of the absence of violent revolutions, though large-scale demonstrations or even civil unrest were witnessed in South Korea and Indonesia). Furthermore, constitutional continuity has been maintained by the introduction of constitutional amendments or new constitutions by bodies that had legitimate authority under the existing constitutions. The case of Indonesia is particularly instructive, as the relative success in the establishment of constitutionalism in this relatively poor and ethnically heterogeneous country could not have been easily forecasted when the Soeharto regime collapsed twenty years ago. The cases of South Korea, Taiwan, and Indonesia suggest that constitutionalism can be compatible with Confucian and Muslim cultures and values and with different levels of economic development.

The development of constitutionalism in non-Western parts of the world such as Asia has been a process of legal transplant, as constitutionalism originated in the Western world. Given the inherent difficulties of transposing a Western plant to Asian soil, the phenomenon of "constitutions without constitutionalism" is by no means surprising. Again, the "achievement of constitutionalism" is a matter of degree, governed by what Fuller calls the morality of aspiration.

To conclude, the achievement of constitutionalism in Asia since the end of the Second World War, and particularly since the 1980s, has been considerable and significant. The historical evidence shows that constitutionalism has appealed to Asian peoples in their struggles for emancipation and justice, and has also been embraced by the political elite in a number of Asian countries as a political order that is both morally legitimate and practically appropriate for local conditions. Liberal constitutionalism, though originating in the Western world, seems to have an appeal beyond the West and addresses the fundamental problems of governance, government, and political power in a number of modern societies in Asia. A macro-historical perspective covering developments in East Asia in the last five decades would suggest that liberal constitutionalism has in fact broadened and deepened its reach in this period of time. As demonstrated in this lecture, South Korea, Taiwan, and Indonesia have witnessed spectacular transitions from hybrid constitutionalism to liberal constitutionalism. Significant progress in constitutionalism has been made in Hong Kong, while Thailand has made genuine attempts to establish liberal constitutionalism, though success has not yet been achieved to date.

If progress is at all possible in human history, then the achievement of constitutionalism in the governance of human societies may be regarded as a significant element and sign of such progress. Van Caenegem, a historian of Western constitutional law, reflected on history as follows:

> So many forms of government have been tried and discarded, and so often statesmen have stumbled or blundered from one experiment to another that a certain pessimism seems justified. Nevertheless they have from time to time hit upon a formula that has proved valuable and a lasting gain: the constitutional and parliamentary form of government appears a case in point.[29]

The Japanese constitutional law scholar Yasuo Sugihara commented that "[t]he history of constitutions is filled with wisdom and insight derived from human suffering in various stages of history".[30] The Hungarian jurist András Sajó pointed out that "[c]onstitutions that serve constitutionalism … reflect the fears originating in, and related to, the previous political regime. If a constitution has a vision, it should concern a different exercise of power than

29. R.C. van Caenegem, *An Historical Introduction to Western Constitutional Law* (Cambridge: Cambridge University Press, 1995) 32.

30. Yasuo Sugihara (杉原泰雄), 《憲法的歷史——比較憲法學新論》 [*The History of Constitutions: A New Perspective on Comparative Constitutional Law*], translated from Japanese into Chinese by Lü Chang and Qu Tao (Beijing: Shehui kexue wenxian chubanshe, 2000) 7.

the past one, which is to be avoided."[31] As I wrote in my chapter for the book on *Constitutionalism in Asia in the Early Twenty-first Century*:

> [C]onstitutionalism is still very much a work in progress in many parts of Asia, a goal, an ideal and an aspiration for and towards which many people, famous or anonymous, high or low, are working, toiling struggling or suffering. The "end of history"[32] is not yet in sight.[33]

## Acknowledgement

The author thanks the lecture series organisers at the Faculty of Law, University of Hong Kong, for inviting the presentation of the above text at the fiftieth anniversary celebration of the founding of the law school.

---

31. András Sajó, *Limiting Government: An Introduction to Constitutionalism* (Budapest: Central European University Press, 1999) 2.
32. Francis Fukuyama, *The End of History and the Last Man* (New York: The Free Press, 1992).
33. Chen, "The Achievement of Constitutionalism in Asia" (N1) 31.

# Epilogue

## INTRODUCTION

This epilogue was written during and after the Anti-Extradition Bill Movement of 2019 and incorporates some of my work reflecting on recent developments. Here, I will share with readers some of my thoughts about the implications of this movement and its aftermath for the future of "One Country, Two Systems" (OCTS) and about the future of the Rule of Law and constitutionalism in mainland China in the aftermath of its Constitutional Amendment of 2018.

## THE ANTI-EXTRADITION BILL MOVEMENT AND THE CONTRADICTIONS OF OCTS[1]

Until recently, the practice of the policy of OCTS as enshrined in the Sino-British Joint Declaration of 1984 and the Hong Kong Basic Law was apparently largely successful, and cautious optimism regarding its future seemed to be justified. The post-1997 journey of Hong Kong as a Special Administrative Region (SAR) was not entirely smooth sailing. Hong Kong experienced some moments of stress and tension, but the government and the people of Hong Kong rose to the challenge and withstood the tests reasonably well. The protest on 1 July 2003 of an estimated half a million demonstrators against the proposed National Security (Legislative Provisions) Bill to implement article 23 of the Basic Law led to a change of mind of a pro-government political party and the bill was shelved indefinitely. The Occupy Central Movement in 2014 that resulted in key government and business districts in Hong Kong being occupied for more than two months was largely peaceful. By contrast, in the second half of 2019, Hong Kong experienced prolonged civil unrest and the most serious riots since the riots against the colonial government in 1967. Chapter 5 of this volume explains how this happened. This epilogue goes further to ask: What does this portend for the future of the OCTS model in Hong Kong?

1. This section draws on the author's article, "Hong Kong's Internal Contradiction of 'One Country, Two Systems' " (11 October 2019) *The Economist*, available at: www.economist.com/open-future/2019/10/11/hong-kongs-internal-contradiction-of-one-country-two-systems.

In an internal speech which was leaked to Reuters,[2] Chief Executive Carrie Lam pointed out that the Central Government considered the Anti-Extradition Bill Movement in Hong Kong a matter involving national "sovereignty and security". The Central Government's position on the matter was revealed by the spokesmen of the Hong Kong and Macau Affairs Office at several press conferences, and also by the publicised speeches of the heads of the State Council's Hong Kong and Macau Office and the Liaison Office of the Central Government in Hong Kong.

The Chinese Government believed that the movement was at least partly fuelled by foreign and local political forces hostile to the Chinese Government, and was "designed to create chaos and disorder in Hong Kong, paralyse the HKSAR Government, enable opposition forces to seize political control of Hong Kong, and turn Hong Kong into an independent or semi-independent political entity".[3] It was also said that characteristics of "colour revolutions" elsewhere were evident in this movement. There would be no compromise by the Central Government.

The Anti-Extradition Bill Movement has revealed that many people in Hong Kong, particularly young people, are dissatisfied with the policy of OCTS as practised in recent years, do not have trust in either the HKSAR Government or the Central Government, identify themselves as Hongkongers rather than Chinese citizens, and even consider the People's Republic of China (PRC) and mainland Chinese to be an alien "Other". The political polarisation and socio-economic problems of Hong Kong society, and the contradictions between the "two systems" in OCTS revealed by the Anti-Extradition Bill Movement, are doomed to continue to plague Hong Kong.

The basic contradiction is that between the aspirations for liberty and democracy on the part of many Hong Kong people and the Central Government's imperative of maintaining sovereign control. The paradox of OCTS is such that it simultaneously generates aspirations for "Western-style"

2. "Exclusive: 'If I have a choice, the first thing is to quit' — Hong Kong Leader Carrie Lam — Transcript" (3 September 2019) *Reuters*, available at: www.reuters.com/article/us-hongkong-protests-carrielam-transcrip/exclusive-if-i-have-a-choice-the-first-thing-is-to-quit-hong-kong-leader-carrie-lam-transcript-idUSKCN1VO0KK, last accessed 25 March 2020.

3. "港澳辦就香港局勢答記者問" [Hong Kong and Macau Affairs Office Speaks to Press on Hong Kong Situation] (3 September 2019) 中國評論新聞網 [*China Review News*], available at: http://hk.crntt.com/doc/1055/3/1/0/105531031.html?coluid=93&kindid=10095&docid=105531031, last accessed 25 March 2020.

liberal democracy along with limits on the realisation of such aspirations. The former aspirations are nurtured by the Rule of Law, judicial independence, constitutional protection of human rights, free press, and the vibrant civil society in Hong Kong. The latter limits are dictated by the nature of the PRC's political system and its ideology, and the developing tension between China and the United States.[4] In May 2020, the PRC took a decisive step to turn these limits into enforceable legal norms via the Law of the PRC on Safeguarding National Security in the HKSAR, or the National Security Law (NSL).

## THE DECISION OF 28 MAY 2020 AND THE NATIONAL SECURITY LAW[5]

The Hong Kong and international community was taken by surprise when the agenda released on the evening of 21 May 2020 for the Natioanl People's Congress (NPC) meeting that was to commence on 22 May showed that one legislative item to be dealt with was a proposed Decision on Establishing and Improving the Legal System and Enforcement Mechanisms for the HKSAR to Safeguard National Security.

In his speech[6] on 22 May at the NPC Standing Committee (NPCSC) meeting on the bill for the Decision, Wang Chen, one of the vice-chairmen, explained that the arrangements proposed in the bill were designed to plug the loophole in existing Hong Kong laws which allowed the riots in the Anti-Extradition Bill Movement of 2019. He pointed out that the HKSAR had a

4. See generally Johannes M.M, Chan, "A Shrinking Space: A Dynamic Relationship between the Judiciary in a Liberal Society of Hong Kong and a Socialist-Leninist Sovereign State" (2019) 72 *Current Legal Problems* 1–38; Benny Tai, Scott Veitch, Fu Hualing, and Richard Cullen, "Pursuing Democracy in an Authoritarian State: Protest and the Rule of Law in Hong Kong" (2019) 29:1 *Social & Legal Studies* 107–145; Han Zhu, "Beijing's 'Rule of Law' Strategy for Governing Hong Kong: Legalisation without Democratisation" (2019) 1 *China Perspectives* 23–33; Cora Chan, "Thirty Years from Tiananmen: China, Hong Kong, and the Ongoing Experiment to Preserve Liberal Values in an Authoritarian State" (2019) 17 *I-CON* 439–452.

5. This section draws on the author's article, "Constitutional Controversies in the Aftermath of the Anti-Extradition Movement of 2019" (2020) 50 *Hong Kong Law Journal* 609–632.

6. See "王晨作關於《全國人民代表大會關於建立健全香港特別行政區維護國家安全的法律制度和執行機制的決定(草案)》的説明" [Wang Chen Explains Bill for the Decision on Establishing and Improving the Legal System and Enforcement Mechanisms for the HKSAR to Safeguard National Security] (22 May 2020) 新華網 [*Xinhua News*], available at: www.xinhuanet.com/politics/2020-05/22/c_1126019468.htm.

constitutional duty to legislate to protect national security under article 23 of the Basic Law, but this legislative task had remained unfulfilled 23 years after the handover. He added that article 23 legislation had been demonised over the years by opposition politicians in Hong Kong, and it was difficult for the HKSAR Government to introduce article 23 legislation. It was therefore entirely legitimate for the Central Authorities to step in to make the proposed Decision. Wang also commented that the Decision was to be made in pursuance of the Decision of the Fourth Plenum of the Nineteenth Central Committee of the Chinese Communist Party (CCP) in late October 2019 which, *inter alia*, expressly called for the "establishment and improvement of the legal system and enforcement mechanisms for safeguarding national security in the SARs".[7]

In a press conference on the evening of 22 May, Carrie Lam, Chief Executive of the HKSAR, admitted that "Hong Kong society must recognise the reality that it would be difficult for the executive and legislative organs of the HKSAR to complete the task of legislating on national security within a period in the foreseeable future".[8] A press statement from a spokesman of the Hong Kong and Macau Office of the State Council on 22 May[9] explained that the power to legislate on national security is part and parcel of the legislative power of the Central Authorities of the State. Although the Central Authorities have, through article 23 of the Basic Law, authorised the HKSAR to exercise part of the legislative power on national security matters, this has not changed the fundamental principle that, by its very nature, national security legislation is the power and responsibility of the Central Authorities.

In his speech at the NPCSC meeting, Wang disclosed that the Central Authorities had considered several policy options for dealing with the loopholes Hong Kong's national security and finally decided to adopt a "two-step approach". This approach involves the NPCSC Decision followed by a law made by the NPCSC on the protection of national security in the HKSAR.

---

7. See "中共中央關於堅持和完善中國特色社會主義制度，推進國家治理體系和治理能力現代化若干重大問題的決定" [Decision of the CCP Central Committee on Several Important Questions relating to Insisting on and Improving the Chinese Socialist System and Promoting the Modernisation of the Governance System and Governance Capacity of the State], available at: www.xinhuanet.com/2019-11/05/c_1125195786.htm, last accessed 5 November 2019.
8. See transcript of Carrie Lam's Chinese speech at the press conference on 22 May 2020, available at: www.info.gov.hk/gia/general/202005/22/P2020052200858.htm.
9. See "國務院港澳辦發言人談全國人大會議涉港議程" [HKMAO Spokesman Speaks on Hong Kong-related NPC Agenda] (22 May 2020), available at: www.locpg.gov.cn/jsdt/2020-05/22/c_1210629407.htm.

The proposed Decision would set out the basic policies and principles as well as authorise the NPCSC to draft a law for the HKSAR. The law would then be inserted into Annex III to the Basic Law and applied to the HKSAR by direct promulgation in accordance with article 18 of the Basic Law.[10]

The proposed Decision would specify four areas of national security to be covered by the law to be enacted by the NPCSC. They are (1) secession, (2) subversion against the regime, (3) terrorism, and (4) foreign interference with Hong Kong affairs.[11] These topics overlap, but do not coincide completely, with those covered by article 23.[12] According to the proposed Decision, even after the NPCSC law has been made, the HKSAR still has to fulfil its constitutional duty of legislating on other areas of national security, such as the subjects of article 23 that are not covered by the NPCSC law. Presumably the four areas included in the NPCSC law were considered the most pressing matters that could not wait to be dealt with by the HKSAR itself.

The proposed Decision was passed by the NPC on 28 May.[13] Thereafter, a specially expedited procedure was adopted by the NPCSC to enable the new law to be enacted as soon as possible. Departing from its usual practice of having one session of meetings every two months, two sessions of the NPCSC were held in the second half of June 2020 in which the new law was — together with several other legislative items — put on the agenda. The bill was introduced into the NPCSC on the first day of the session on 18 June.

Although the PRC Law on Legislation provides for the publication of a bill for a law for public consultation as a usual procedure, it also permits departure from this practice where so authorised by the Council of Chairpersons of the

10. Art. 18(2) provides that a national law may be applied to the HKSAR either "by way of promulgation or legislation by the Region".
11. In the NSL that was enacted at the end of June 2020, the fourth subject of "foreign interference with Hong Kong affairs" was narrowed down to become "collusion with foreign countries or external elements to endanger national security".
12. Seven subjects are covered by art. 23: treason, secession, sedition, subversion against the Chinese Government, theft of State secrets, prohibition of foreign political organisations or bodies from conducting political activities in Hong Kong, and prohibition of local political organisations or bodies from establishing ties with foreign political organisations or bodies.
13. See the Decision of the NPC on Establishing and Improving the Legal System and Enforcement Mechanisms for the HKSAR to Safeguard National Security, *HKSAR Government Gazette*, LN 135 of 2020, p. B2335 (unofficial English translation; there is no English translation with official status or legal force).

NPCSC.[14] In the case of the NSL, the details were not published before its eventual enactment, and there was only consultation with selected individuals and institutions in Hong Kong and mainland China. The speech explaining the bill to the NPCSC was published by the Xinhua News Agency on 20 June, thus publicising the main features of the bill.

The bill was further considered by the NPCSC in its session on 28–30 June. On the morning of the last day of this session, the NPCSC enacted the NSL. On the afternoon of the same day, the NPCSC (after consultation with the HKSAR Government and the Hong Kong Basic Law Committee in accordance with article 18 of the Basic Law) decided to insert the NSL into Annex III to the Basic Law, and it was gazetted in Hong Kong on the evening of 30 June.[15] This controversial and internationally publicised legislative exercise was thus completed, and the NSL came into force shortly before midnight between 30 June and 1 July 2020 — the twenty-third anniversary of the establishment of the HKSAR.

The NPC Decision is the first and only legal instrument relating to Hong Kong promulgated by the NPC since it enacted the Basic Law of the HKSAR and made related decisions in 1990. The first paragraph of the Decision states that it was made pursuant to articles 31 and 62(2), (14), and (16) of the PRC Constitution as well as the Basic Law. Article 31 of the PRC Constitution provides for the establishment of SARs and authorises the NPC to make laws to provide for the systems to be practised in these SARs. Article 62(2) and (14) provide for the power of the NPC to supervise the implementation of the Constitution and to decide on the establishment of SARs and the systems to be practised there, respectively. Article 62(16) is a residual provision enabling the NPC to exercise other powers and functions. In light of these provisions, the NPC Decision on 28 May 2020 can be regarded as a major legislative step taken by the NPC to *supplement* the provisions of the Basic Law in response to changing circumstances in the HKSAR which were not anticipated when the Basic Law was made in 1990.

14. See art. 37 of the Law on Legislation (立法法).
15. See Promulgation of National Law 2000, *HKSAR Government Gazette*, LN 136 of 2020, p. B2345 (in Chinese); GN(E) 72 of 2020 (unofficial English translation of the Law of the PRC on Safeguarding National Security in the HKSAR; there is no English translation with official status or legal force).

The introduction of the NSL in the aftermath of the Anti-Extradition Bill Movement of 2019 exemplifies a "vicious cycle" and increasing degrees of mutual suspicion and distrust which have plagued the operation of OCTS since the Occupy Central Movement in 2014. Opposition and resistance to policies adopted by the Central Authorities towards Hong Kong increasingly took the form of actions which Beijing considered to have crossed the line. The Central Authorities responded by taking firm actions which were seen by many in Hong Kong to mean the tightening of the space for freedom in Hong Kong.

For example, the failure of the Occupy Central Movement to secure what its proponents considered to be "genuine universal suffrage" gave rise to calls for Hong Kong independence, as activists lost hope of achieving "genuine universal suffrage" in Hong Kong under Chinese sovereignty. Improper oath-taking by pro-independence legislators in 2016 led to the NPCSC making an interpretation in the course of the litigation related to their disqualification.[16] In the Anti-Extradition Bill Movement of 2019, activists were not satisfied with the indefinite suspension and subsequent withdrawal of the Extradition Bill, but continued to engage in protests to express their discontent.

Unfortunately or tragically, this social movement using both peaceful and violent actions to fight for liberty, governmental accountability, and democracy in Hong Kong[17] ultimately backfired and only had the effect of prompting the Central Authorities to impose even tighter control on Hong Kong by means of the NSL. The NSL may be regarded as stipulating, in the form of legal norms, the bottom line for the "one country" element in OCTS. The Central Authorities argue that the new legislative scheme of national security in Hong Kong will enable the OCTS policy to be more successfully practised in the future.[18] On the other hand, critics of the scheme accuse Beijing of abandoning the "Two Systems" aspect of OCTS.

---

16. See generally Johannes Chan, "A Storm of Unprecedented Ferocity" (2018) 16:2 *I-CON* 373.
17. See generally Z. Ibrahim and J. Lam (eds.), *Rebel City: Hong Kong's Year of Water and Fire* (Singapore: World Scientific, 2020).
18. See the speech given by Zhang Xiaoming (Deputy Director of the HKMAO) at a seminar to celebrate the thirtieth anniversary of the Basic Law of the HKSAR held on 8 June 2020, titled "國家安全底線愈牢，'一國兩制' 空間愈大" [The Firmer the Red Line for National Security, the Greater the Space for "One Country, Two Systems"], available at: www.basiclaw.gov.hk/gb/anniversary30/pdf/speeches_file2.pdf.

## THE CONSTITUTIONAL AMENDMENT OF 2018[19]

The first amendment to the PRC Constitution since 2004 was adopted by the NPC on 11 March 2018. This was the fifth amendment of the 1982 Constitution. The amendment gave constitutional recognition to "Xi Jinping's Thoughts on Socialism with Chinese Characteristics for a New Era" (習近平新時代中國特色社會主義思想) which, together with the "scientific concept of development",[20] was written into the Preamble of the Constitution.

"Xi Jinping Thought on Socialism with Chinese Characteristics for a New Era" refers to Xi's comprehensive platform, vision, and strategies for China's "socialist modernisation", which were first codified and given this title in his report as CCP General Secretary to the Nineteenth National Congress of the CCP in October 2017. Xi's vision is that China would become a "society of moderate prosperity" (*xiaokang*, 小康) by the year 2020; "socialist modernisation" would be realised by the year 2035; and by 2050 China would become a "modernised and strong socialist state that is wealthy, democratic, highly civilized, harmonious and beautiful".

One important element of the 2018 constitutional amendment is the incorporation of the doctrine of Party leadership into article 1 of the Constitution. Before the 2018 amendment to the 1982 Constitution, Party leadership was only touched upon in the Preamble of the Constitution.[21] The 2018 amendment states in the amended article 1 that CCP leadership "is the most essential characteristic of Socialism with Chinese Characteristics".[22] However, there is still no constitutional definition of the meaning, scope, or implications of CCP leadership in State affairs.

---

19. This section draws on the author's book, *An Introduction to the Chinese Legal System* (Hong Kong: LexisNexis, 5th edition, 2019) ch. 11.
20. The "scientific concept of development" was introduced by Hu Jintao, Party General Secretary, in 2002–2012. Hu succeeded Jiang Zeming (who developed the idea of the "three represents") and was in turn succeeded by Xi Jinping.
21. There is, however, no doubt that the principle of Party leadership is a core element of China's "living constitution". See, for instance, Xin He, "The Party's Leadership as a Living Constitution in China" (2012) 42 *Hong Kong Law Journal* 73–93; Jianfu Chen, "Out of the Shadows and Back to the Future: CCP and Law in China" (2016) 24:2 *Asia Pacific Law Review* 176–201.
22. Art. 1 may be regarded as the single most important article in the Constitution as it defines the nature of the PRC State. The principle of the sovereignty of the people is only mentioned in art. 2 of the 1982 Constitution, which states, *inter alia*, that "all power in the PRC belongs to the people".

Another major aspect of the 2018 Constitutional Amendment was the amendment of article 79, which removed the two-term limit on the offices of President (*zhuxi*, 主席) and Vice-President of the PRC State. Although under the PRC Constitution, the President enjoys few real powers relative to the Premier of the State Council, CCP General Secretary Xi Jinping and his two predecessors — Jiang Zemin and Hu Yaobang — all held the office of the President of the State. There is therefore an emerging constitutional convention that the General Secretary of the Party will occupy the office of President of the PRC State (as well as Chairman of the Central Military Commission of the Party and of the State). The official explanation[23] on the amendment of article 79 pointed out that the Charter of the CCP does not provide for any limit on the number of (five-year) terms that the General Secretary may serve;[24] it was therefore argued that similarly there should be no term limit on the President, so that a General Secretary who serves a third term may also serve a third term as President. From this perspective, the constitutional amendment brought the term limit rule (i.e., the absence thereof) on the President of the State in line with that on the CCP General Secretary. This amendment clearly paved the way for Xi Jinping to continue as both General Secretary and President after his second term expires in 2022 and 2023, respectively.

The constitutional amendment was expected to have the effect of further strengthening Xi's strongman rule in the foreseeable future, as there would be no need to prepare for a handover to a successor during Xi's second term of office (2017–2022) as CCP General Secretary. The advantage of this, as perceived by Xi's supporters, is that he would be able to tackle China's complex problems of corruption control, economic reform, and social development more effectively so as to realise the "Chinese dream" outlined by Xi in his report to the Nineteenth Party Congress in 2017. The price to be paid, however, is the potential imperilment of Deng Xiaoping's legacy of moving

23. Xuan Li (軒理), "保證黨和國家長治久安的重大制度安排" [An Important Institutional Arrangement to Secure the Long-term Stability of the Party and the State] (1 March 2018) *Renmin ribao* 3. See also Wang Chen's speech to the NPC on 5 March 2018 explaining the proposed constitutional amendments, titled "王晨作關於《中華人民共和國憲法修正案(草案)》的說明(摘要)", available at: www.xinhuanet.com/politics/2018lh/2018-03/06/c_1122496003.htm?ivk_sa=1023345p, last accessed 2 January 2021.

24. Hu Jintao served two terms, while Jiang Zemin served two terms in addition to the remainder of his predecessor's (Zhao Ziyang) term. Before the 2018 constitutional amendment, it was assumed that the CCP had adopted an "unwritten norm" or convention that the General Secretary would only serve two terms.

away from the Maoist era of strongman politics, personality cult, and strict ideological control, and of working towards collective leadership and greater institutionalisation of the CCP's operation so as to secure a more orderly leadership succession within the CCP. Thus, while it may be true that greater political stability and effectiveness in governance may be secured in the short-term, China's longer term future will become more unpredictable and risky, as the problems of leadership succession and possible political reform have merely been postponed and remain unresolved.[25]

It is also noteworthy that the 2018 constitutional amendment has added to the Constitution a new section 7 ("Supervisory Commissions"). This is a major reform of the structure of PRC State organs, which originally consisted of the NPC as the supreme organ of State power, under which there are the State Council, the Supreme People's Court, and the Supreme People's Procuratorate — the leading members of all three of which are appointed by and accountable to the NPC.[26] The 2018 amendment establishes a fourth State organ appointable by and responsible to the NPC, which is the National Supervisory Commission (NSC), with supervisory commissions under it at provincial and other local levels.[27] The principal rationale for the creation of this new organ was to combat and investigate corruption among Party cadres, public servants, and State employees more effectively, given that anti-corruption has been one of Xi Jinping's key policies.[28] The NSC merged and incorporated into itself several existing agencies engaged in anti-corruption work and supervision of State functionaries and Party cadres, including the anti-corruption unit of

---

25. See, for example, Cheng Li and Ryan McElveen, "China's Constitutional Conundrum" (28 February 2018) *Brookings*, available at: www.brookings.edu/blog/order-from-chaos/2018/02/28/chinas-constitutional-conundrum/; David Dollar, "Xi's Power Grab Gives a Short-term Boost with Long-term Ramifications" (26 February 2018) *The Hill*, available at: http://thehill.com/opinion/international/375608-xis-power-grab-a-short-term-boost-with-long-term-ramifications, last accessed 25 March 2020.
26. See the text of the 1982 Constitution.
27. At the same time as adopting the constitutional amendment, the NPC also enacted the Supervision Law (*Jiancha fa*, 監察法), which regulates the organisation, functions, and powers of the NSC and the local levels of supervisory commissions under it.
28. See Hualing Fu, "Wielding the Sword: President Xi's New Anti-corruption Campaign" in Susan Rose-Ackerman and Paul Lagunes (eds.), *Greed, Corruption, and the Modern State* (Cheltenham, UK: Edward Elgar, 2016) 134–160; Hualing Fu, "China's Striking Anticorruption Adventure: A Political Journey toward the Rule of Law?" in Weitseng Chen (ed.), *The Beijing Consensus? How China has Changed Western Ideas of Law and Economic Development* (Cambridge: Cambridge University Press, 2017) 249–274.

the Supreme People's Procuratorate, the Ministry of Supervision under the State Council, and the National Bureau of Corruption Prevention. The NSC engages in *heshu bangong* (合署辦公) with the CCP's Central Commission for Disciplinary Inspection (CCDI),[29] which means they work as "one work organ with two different names" ("一套工作機構，兩個機關名稱").[30]

Article 27 of the Constitution has been amended to require all State officials to swear an oath of allegiance to the Constitution upon assumption of office.[31] This new constitutional rule demonstrates that the PRC regime intends to further promote the authority of the Constitution, and to derive legitimacy from it.[32] Given the amendment to article 1 of the Constitution, allegiance to the Constitution implies loyalty to the CCP itself. The legitimacy of the principle of CCP leadership is thus reinforced by the authority of the Constitution.

The final feature of the Constitutional Amendment which is noteworthy is article 70, which has been amended to rename the existing Law Committee of the NPC as the "Constitution and Law Committee". The amendment was for the purpose of adding to the powers and functions of this Committee so that it can engage more actively in constitutional interpretation and the review of the constitutionality of legal norms, and to make recommendations to the NPC

29. See Ling Li, "The Rise of the Discipline and Inspection Commission, 1927–2012: Anticorruption Investigation and Decision-making in the Chinese Communist Party" (2016) 42:5 *Modern China* 447–482.

30. See www.ccdi.gov.cn/special/zmsjd/zm19da_zm19da/201802/t20180202_163176.html, last accessed 25 March 2020. The CCDI and NSC share a common website (with the CCDI being the first named institution: www.ccdi.gov.cn/. There is very substantial overlap between the leading members of the CCDI and the NSC: one of the Deputy Secretaries of the CCDI is the Director of the NSC; all the Deputy Directors of the NSC are also Deputy Secretaries of the CCDI; the Secretary (head) of the CCDI is Zhao Leji — one of the 7-member CCP Politburo Standing Committee. See also https://baike.baidu.com/item/中國共產黨中央紀律檢查委員會/5655314, last accessed 25 March 2020.

31. This constitutional amendment reinforces the NPCSC's Decision on the Implementation of the System of Constitutional Oath-taking (dated 1 July 2015), which was amended on 24 February 2018 with regard to the precise text of the oath and the application of the oath-taking requirement to the newly created supervisory commissions.

32. A related development in this regard was the designation of 4 December (4 December 1982 being the date of the adoption of the 1982 Constitution) as "National Constitution Day"; see the NPCSC's Decision on the Establishment of a National Constitution Day (dated 1 November 2014).

and NPCSC about these matters.[33] This reform is in line with Xi Jinping's report to the Nineteenth National Congress of the CCP in October 2017, which mentioned, *inter alia*, the need to "strengthen constitutional implementation and supervision and promote the work of constitutional review (*hexianxing shencha*, 合憲性審查)".

## RULE OF LAW IN CHINA?[34]

After Xi Jinping assumed office as CCP General Secretary at the Eighteenth National Congress of the CCP in November 2012, the new Party policy of "full devotion to four major tasks" (*sige quanmian*, 四個全面) gradually unfolded, the four major tasks being the construction of a society of moderate prosperity (*xiaokang shehui*, 小康社會), the deepening of reforms, ruling the country according to law, and governing the Party strictly.[35] It is noteworthy that "ruling the country according to law" has been included as one of the four tasks. The Fourth Plenum of the Eighteenth Central Committee of the CCP held in October 2014 adopted a "Decision on Several Important Questions relating to the Full Promotion of Ruling the Country According to Law".[36] This was the first time a plenary meeting of the CCP Central Committee was wholly devoted to the question of legal development. The Decision outlined the concept of "the system of socialist Rule of Law with Chinese characteristics" (中國特色社會主義法治體系) and proposed reform

33. Follow-up action was taken by the NPCSC on 22 June 2018 when it adopted a Decision on the Functions of the Constitution and Law Committee of the NPC.

34. This section draws on the author's article, "China's Long March Towards Rule of Law or China's Turn Against Law?" (2016) 4 *Chinese Journal of Comparative Law* 1–35.

35. See, for example, the communiqué of the Fifth Plenum of the 18th Central Committee of the CCP held in Beijing on 26–29 October 2015.

36. See "中共中央關於全面推進依法治國若干重大問題的決定" [CCP Central Committee Decision concerning Some Major Questions in Comprehensively Moving Governing the Country According to the law Forward] (28 October 2014) *China Copyrigh and Media*, English version available at: https://chinacopyrightandmedia.wordpress.com/2014/10/28/ccp-central-committee-decision-concerning-some-major-questions-in-comprehensively-moving-governing-the-country-according-to-the-law-forward/, last accessed 25 March 2020. For legal trends in the Xi Jinping era, see generally Taisu Zhang and Tom Ginsburg, "China's Turn Toward Law" (2019) 59:2 *Virginia Journal of International Law* 306–389; Jianfu Chen, "Chinese Law and Legal Reform: Where to from Here" (2020) 50 *Hong Kong Law Journal* 243–274.

measures in the four domains of (a) law-making; (b) implementation of the law, including "administration in accordance with law" (*yifa xingzheng*, 依法行政), no exercise of executive power (and no governmental action prejudicing citizens' interests) without legal authorisation, and control and supervision of executive power; (c) the judiciary; and (d) promotion of compliance with law. At the same time, the Decision emphasised the importance of Party leadership in legal reforms and the compatibility between Party leadership and ruling the country according to law — including "ruling the country in accordance with the Constitution" (*yixian zhiguo*, 依憲治國) as well as the Party "governing in accordance with the law" (*yifa zhizheng*, 依法執政) and "governing in accordance with the Constitution" (*yixian zhizheng*, 依憲執政).

Is China likely to succeed in realising its self-proclaimed project of "ruling the country according to law" and developing "a socialist Rule of Law with Chinese characteristics"? What degree of "Rule of Law" has been achieved by China more than four decades after Deng Xiaoping initiated the era of "reform and opening" in 1978 and launched the project of re-building the legal system of the PRC after the damages of the Cultural Revolution era?

Assuming that the "Rule of Law" is still a useful paradigm for the purpose of studying and evaluating contemporary Chinese law-related phenomena,[37] it is necessary to clarify what "Rule of Law" means. Peerenboom's well-known "thin theory" or "thin conception" of the Rule of Law[38] emphasises the formal characteristics and procedural aspects of the existence and operation of laws and legal institutions, while thick conceptions of the Rule of Law link it to the substantive content of the law and to particular forms of economic, social, and political systems that the law embodies. For example, the dominant thick

37. My colleague Professor He Xin has recently questioned this "Rule of Law" or legality paradigm and proposes an alternative paradigm of "governmentality" inspired by Foucault's work; see He Xin, "(Non)legality as Governmentality in China", University of Hong Kong Faculty of Law Research Paper No. 2020/035, available at: https://ssrn.com/abstract=3612483. He writes: "The paradigm of governmentality elicits another set of research questions. Instead of assuming that the rule of law, as practised in Western liberal democracies, is the terminus of China's legal evolution, it argues that China has a qualitatively different trajectory. Its course may never intersect with the rule of law. Even if it does intersect, it may have a different trajectory." See also Donald C. Clarke, "Anti Anti-Orientalism, or is Chinese Law Different?" (2020) 68 *American Journal of Comparative Law* 55; Thomas Coendet, "Critical Legal Orientalism: Rethinking the Comparative Discourse on Chinese Law" (2019) 67 *American Journal of Comparative Law* 775.

38. See generally Randall Peerenboom, *China's Long March Toward Rule of Law* (Cambridge: Cambridge University Press, 2002).

conception of the Rule of Law in the Western world today is the liberal-democratic version of the Rule of Law, which sees the recognition and protection of civil liberties, human rights (particularly civil and political rights), and democratic freedoms as essential ingredients of the Rule of Law.

The "thin" conception of the Rule of Law is reflected in Lon Fuller's famous account[39] of the eight principles of legality or the "internal morality of law",[40] which concern the formal and procedural aspects of the law and its enforcement rather than the substantive content of the law itself. Fuller himself characterises what he calls the "morality of law" as a kind of "morality of aspiration",[41] which means that it can be realised or achieved to different degrees. For instance, one of the eight requirements is "congruence between official action and declared rule".[42] This is one crucial domain in which even official documents in the PRC admit that there is much to be desired, as officials' non-compliance with legal norms is openly admitted to be a problem that has plagued China's legal system. As the White Paper on "China's Efforts and Achievements in Promoting the Rule of Law" (2008)[43] states in its concluding section:

> China's legal construction is still facing some problems: The development of democracy and the rule of law still falls short of the needs of economic and social development; the legal framework shows certain characteristics of the current stage and calls for further improvement; in some regions and departments, laws are not observed or strictly enforced, violators are not brought to justice; local

39. As Peerenboom summarises, it requires laws to be "general, public, prospective, clear, consistent, capable of being followed, stable, and enforced"; Randall Peerenboom, "The X-files: Past and Present Portrayals of China's Alien 'Legal System'" (2003) 2 *Washington University Global Studies Law Review* 37–95, at 57–58.
40. Lon L. Fuller, *The Morality of Law* (London: Yale University Press, revised edition, 1969).
41. *Ibid.*, ch. 1 ("The Two Moralities").
42. *Ibid.*, 81. Simmonds points out that this is a crucial element of the Rule of Law, and a "wicked regime" (i.e., one "wholly unmotivated by moral considerations") "would have no good reason for complying" with it; see Nigel E. Simmonds, *Central Issues in Jurisprudence* (London: Sweet & Maxwell, 4th edition, 2013) 260–261. On the other hand, Kramer argues that "there are many credibly possible societies in which wickedly self-interested rulers have strong reasons for complying with rule-of-law requirements at quite high levels"; see Matthew H. Kramer, "For the Record: A Final Reply to N.E. Simmonds" (2011) 56 *American Journal of Jurisprudence* 115–133, at 117.
43. This White Paper was published by the Information Office of the State Council on 28 February 2008, see http://en.pkulaw.cn/display.aspx?cgid=1090521218&lib=dbref, last accessed 25 March 2020.

> protectionism, departmental protectionism, and difficulties in law enforcement occur from time to time; some government functionaries take bribes and bend the law, abuse their power when executing the law, abuse their authority to override the law, and substitute their words for the law, thus bringing damage to the socialist rule of law; and the task still remains onerous to strengthen education in the rule of law, and enhance the awareness of law and the concept of the rule of law among the public.

If the question of the Rule of Law in China is largely a question of improving compliance with legal norms by both citizens and officials alike — as official discourse seems to suggest — then the problem is relatively simple, and the degree to which the Rule of Law is realised in China is largely an empirical question to be answered by monitoring and measuring the extents of compliance with or violations of legal norms. However, the problem of the Rule of Law in China is actually more complex than this, because many critics and sceptics argue that China is at most practising or moving towards "Rule *by* Law" rather than practising or moving towards genuine "Rule *of* Law",[44] as China is an authoritarian one-party state in which the supremacy of the CCP cannot be reconciled with or made compatible with genuine Rule *of* Law.

If the view is simply that there can be no Rule of Law in any authoritarian one-party state, then it is arguably another version of "legal orientalism".[45] As a matter of legal history, the Rule of Law emerged in the West even before modern liberal democracy came into existence. However, if a clearly reasoned argument can be developed that the nature and structural or systemic characteristics of the Party-State in the PRC are such that it cannot sustain or be compatible with any Rule of Law, then the argument cannot be dismissed as mere orientalism.

Indeed, Peerenboom deals with the argument about Rule *by* Law versus Rule *of* Law. For him, Rule *by* Law means that rulers use the law as an instrument of rule, but rulers are not subject to the law themselves, while Rule *of* Law imposes restraint on the state and its officials.[46] He points out that the

44. See generally the discussion in Peerenboom (N38) 130–141.
45. Teemu Ruskola, "Legal Orientalism" (2002) 101 *Michigan Law Review* 179–234; Teemu Ruskola, *Legal Orientalism: China, the United States, and Modern Law* (Cambridge, Mass.: Harvard University Press, 2013).
46. Peerenboom (N38) 131, 136, 139.

legal system in imperial China can be characterised as Rule *by* Law,[47] but the contemporary Chinese legal system is at least transitioning towards Rule *of* Law",[48] even if it has not yet reached this goal. However, he also acknowledges that many critics and sceptics believe that there is no Rule of Law in China if senior officials and Party leaders who violate the law will not be brought to justice, and dissidents and others opposed to the regime are punished without fair trials or due process.[49]

Thus, the nature and structural or systemic characteristics of the Party-State are such that, despite all the legal developments to date, the Chinese legal system is *not* moving towards a system in which senior officials and top Party leaders who violate the law would be equally treated by the law and before the courts as others, and dissidents and others targeted by the regime would be accorded the same fair trials and due process that are accorded to others. In other words, even if China is making progress in extending some form of governance by law and adjudication in accordance with law in some domains of social and economic life, unless and until the Rule of Law is extended to "politically sensitive" domains in which the Party's important interests are at stake and the Party would have intervened but for the restraint of law, the system cannot be regarded or described as "Rule of Law".

This line of thinking is reflected in the debate between Peerenboom and Eva Pils in the context of Pils' comment[50] on Peerenboom's article[51] on the Fourth Plenum in 2014 on "ruling the country according to law". Whereas

---

47. *Ibid.*, 140.

48. *Ibid.* Peerenboom elaborates as follows: "Perhaps the biggest objection to the low-threshold, sliding-scale approach is that rule of law is an honorific term used to praise or criticize a legal system. Thus rule of law in ordinary usage implies a certain degree of achievement. ... In light of the many shortcomings of the legal system detailed throughout this work and the ordinary use of rule of law as an honorific term signaling a certain standard of achievement, I have described China's legal system as in transition toward rule of law but still falling short of the minimal standard of achievement required to be considered rule of law"; *ibid.*, 140.

49. *Ibid.*, 131, 134, 137.

50. Eva Pils, "China, the Rule of Law, and the Question of Obedience: A Comment on Professor Peerenboom" (2015) 7 *Hague Journal on the Rule of Law* 83–90.

51. Randall Peerenboom, "Fly High the Banner of Socialist Rule of Law with Chinese Characteristics! What Does the 4th Plenum Decision Mean for Legal Reforms in China?" (2015) 7 *Hague Journal on the Rule of Law* 49–74. See also Randall Peerenboom, "The Battle Over Legal Reforms in China: Has There Been a Turn Against Law?" (2014) 2 *Chinese Journal of Comparative Law* 188–212.

Peerenboom's article provides a rather positive evaluation of the Plenum's Decision, Pils casts doubt on Peerenboom's "optimistic"[52] assessment, pointing in particular to the persecution of activist lawyers, such as Xu Zhiyong, Tang Jingling, and Pu Zhiqiang,[53] and the existence of the Party's "unlawful detention system"[54] of *shuanggui* (雙規, involving detention for investigation of cadres and officials suspected of corruption or other violations of Party rules and State laws, such detention being authorised by Party regulations instead of State laws).[55] Peerenboom has replied by stating that he agrees that "the political and legal environment has become even more restrictive under Xi Jinping" and "that the [Fourth Plenum] Decision is not likely to improve the lot of liberals or better protect the exercise of civil and political rights when the exercise of such rights is deemed threatening to the government".[56] On the other hand, he points out that Pils "focuses almost exclusively on human rights issues", "assessing the Chinese legal system from the globally dominant liberal democratic rule of law perspective",[57] and "fails to appreciate or at least give adequate weight to how the reform agenda set out in the Decision would greatly improve the lives of most Chinese citizens".[58] He concludes as follows: "I do believe that rule of law, even socialist rule of law with Chinese characteristics, is better than socialism with no rule of law at all, and, for the moment at least, the only type of rule on offer in China is socialist rule of law".[59]

The Rule of Law — in the "thin" sense of compliance with Fuller's principles of legality — is, however, a matter of degree, and it can be realised or complied with in varying degrees in different domains of socio-economic and socio-

52. Pils (N50) 84.

53. See generally Eva Pils, *China's Human Rights Lawyers: Advocacy and Resistance* (New York: Routledge, 2015).

54. Pils (N50) 86.

55. For a more sympathetic view of *shuanggui*, see Larry Catá Backer and Keren Wang, "The Emerging Structures of Socialist Constitutionalism with Chinese Characteristics: Extra-Judicial Detention and the Chinese Constitutional Order" (2014) 23 *Pacific Rim Law and Policy Journal* 251–342. The debate about the legality/illegality of *shuanggui* has now been superseded by the establishment of the supervisory commissions by the 2018 Constitutional Amendment and the enactment of the Supervision Law; see N13 and accompanying text.

56. Peerenboom, "Fly High the Banner" (N51) 92.

57. *Ibid.*

58. *Ibid.*, 93.

59. *Ibid.*, 95.

political life. The nature and the structural or systemic characteristics of the contemporary Chinese Party-State are such that there are certain domains in which the Rule of Law is particularly weak, fragile, vulnerable, or even non-existent, while at the same time there exist other domains in which the Rule of Law has been making progress or expanding in recent decades. Similarly, there are certain types of court cases in which judicial professionalism, autonomy and independence has developed considerably, while there are also "politically sensitive" cases in which the courts would defer to relevant Party authorities. Thus, the concept of differential degrees of compliance with the Rule of Law in different domains and contexts of the Chinese State and society should be introduced for the purpose of scholarly discourse and research on the Rule of Law.

It is noteworthy in this regard that the concept of "partial Rule of Law" has been used by Wang Yuhua to describe the legal and judicial systems of contemporary China.[60] On the basis of empirical research, he suggests that there are regions in China in which the Rule of Law (particularly in the sense of the existence of courts that are fair, efficient, and free of corruption) in the commercial domain is much better realised than in other regions. In this sense a "partial" Rule of Law exists in China — it is "partial" because, in his view, it is limited to civil and commercial cases and has not been extended to domains in which citizens seek to challenge government actions in court. According to Wang, the regions in which the Rule of Law is better realised are those in which foreign investors play a considerable role in their economic development.[61] His thesis is that unlike domestic enterprises and ethnically Chinese investors from Hong Kong, Macau, and overseas, foreign investors have few connections in Chinese society and with officials and therefore demand the Rule of Law

---

60. Wang Yuhua, *Tying the Autocrat's Hands: The Rise of the Rule of Law in China* (Cambridge: Cambridge University Press, 2015), especially at 3–4. Wang argues that the Rule of Law in authoritarian regimes like China is a "partial form of the rule of law", in the sense that "judicial fairness is usually respected in the commercial realm but not in the political realm"; the authoritarian state "respect[s] the rule of law to make a credible commitment to investors, whose assets are urgently needed" but "discourage[s] citizens from utilizing the judiciary to sue the government".

61. Wang found that in China there has been "better enforcement of the rule of law in regions with a large number of foreign investors but a higher level of judicial corruption and inefficiency in regions with heavy investments from domestic and ethnic Chinese investors"; *ibid.*, 22.

as an essential element of a business environment acceptable to them.[62] Local governments respond positively to such demands because they need the foreign investment and the taxation revenues generated therefrom.[63]

The works of another scholar, my colleague Fu Hualing, also support the idea of differential degrees of Rule of Law in different domains of Chinese society. Fu identifies three kinds of official practices in the Chinese Party-State: practices based on law, those based on "extra-law", and those based on "extra-extra law".[64] Whereas "law" refers to the formally enacted legal norms of the legal system, "extra-law"[65] is not formally law but has some legitimacy, for example, because it is based on the Party's internal rules (e.g., *shuanggui*). Practices (e.g., "black jails" in which targets of persecution are detained, or the use of extra-legal violence by officials or even local gangsters recruited by officials) of what Fu calls "extra-extra law"[66] are completely illegal and illegitimate from the point of view of members of the public and of the legal

---

62. Wang suggests that "politically connected groups and individuals do not favor the rule of law, which creates a level playing field for all asset holders", whereas "those who are not politically connected will advocate the rule of law, under which everyone is treated equally"; *ibid.*, 6.

63. Wang considers the Chinese State "a revenue maximizer" which "cooperates with economic elites who pay taxes and generate rent"; *ibid.*, 7. His thesis is that "authoritarian rulers will respect the rule of law when they need the cooperation of organized interest groups that control valuable and mobile assets but are not politically connected"; *ibid.*, 3.

64. Hualing Fu, "Politicized Challenges, Depoliticized Responses: Political Monitoring in China's Transition" in Fergal Davis, Nicola McGarrity, and George Williams (eds.), *Surveillance, Counter-Terrorism and Comparative Constitutionalism* (New York: Routledge, 2014) ch. 17, 296–312, at 308 and note 36 thereon.

65. Fu defines what he calls "extra-law" as "an official system in which power is neither directly derived from properly constituted authorities nor subject to independent oversight (judicial or otherwise). It has a strong political or policy orientation and the whole system is largely geared to political expediency or convenience"; *ibid.*, 312. For further details, see Fu Hualing, "The Varieties of Law in China" (18 July 2011) *Human Rights in China*, available at: www.hrichina.org/en/crf/article/5422, last accessed 25 March 2020.

66. Fu points out that "[e]xtra-extra law comprises government measures that exist in some dark space, seemingly unrelated to any legal framework and devoid of any legal authority. It is an informal political institution characterized by a total lack of legality. It is used to advance some predatory and repressive government policies that cannot be justified by any law or extra-law. As such, extra-extra law is covered in secrecy and operates with no legal accountability. … [I]t survives and thrives because it is effective in achieving certain policy goals which cannot otherwise be achieved through law or extra-law. The legal or even the extra-legal system is regarded as weak and ineffective when it comes to sensitive issues. In these situations, intimidation through extra-extra law becomes expedient and even indispensable"; Fu (N65) 308.

system, but they are sometimes resorted to as extraordinary measures to deal with special circumstances. Fu observes that in the course of the development of the Chinese legal system over the years, the space governed by "law" has expanded while that governed by "extra-law" has decreased.[67] This is a form of progress in the movement towards Rule of Law in China, provided that practices of "extra-extra law" become strictly forbidden by the Party-State as it promotes the principle of "ruling the country according to law".

Commenting on the intense anti-corruption campaign engineered by Xi Jinping, Fu points out that the Party's disciplinary inspection system has played a primary role in this campaign, eclipsing and "marginalising" that of the procuratorates as the relevant institutions of the State's legal system that deal with corruption.[68] This was partly because only the Party institutions (as distinguished from State institutions) are powerful enough to deal with the "tigers" (senior officials, including very senior Party leaders such as Bo Xilai and Zhou Yongkang) who were the principal targets of the campaign. Also, because of the political and instrumental nature of the campaign, the top Party leadership considered it necessary to take charge of it directly. Officials under investigation by the Party disciplinary system cannot enjoy the legal protection afforded by the State's legal system (e.g., access to counsel),[69] until they are handed over for processing by the State's procuratorates and courts. Thus, the anti-corruption campaign launched by Xi Jinping has been a domain in which the Rule of Law has given way to the Party's prerogatives.[70]

Fu describes China's anti-corruption machinery as a "dual system" consisting of the disciplinary system operated by Party organs existing side by

---

67. Fu Hualing, "China's Striking Anticorruption Adventure: A Political Journey Toward the Rule of Law" in Weitseng Chen (ed.), *The Beijing Consensus?* (Cambridge: Cambridge University Press, 2017) ch. 10, 249–274. In Fu's view, "China's legal reform in the past 30 years is characterized by a slow transition from extra-law to law. Yet, after 30 years of law reform and improved legality, the size of extra-law still looms large, especially in core policy areas, such as criminal law and public law"; Fu (N65).

68. Fu Hualing, "Wielding the Sword" (N28).

69. *Ibid.*, 150.

70. Another episode of Party prerogatives overriding the Rule of Law was the campaign (commonly known as "Striking at the Black in Chongqing (重慶打黑)") against alleged criminal syndicates (or the underworld) launched by Bo Xilai when he was municipal Party chief of Chongqing in 2007–2012. Professor Tong Zhiwei, a leading scholar of constitutional law (and a leading advocate of "socialist constitutionalism"), was a vocal critic of the violations of legality committed during this campaign.

side with the legal system and its institutions. He states that they "are distinct institutions with different historical origins and political ideology. A dual system posits that regular and routine issues will be handled by the 'ordinary' system while exceptional, and largely political, matters will be handled by the 'extraordinary' system".[71] Although the latter system has been predominant in Xi's anti-corruption campaign, Fu believes that the legal system might become more important in the future and that there is "the possibility that, with some exceptions, China has the potential to develop a fully legal-centric anticorruption regime in the long run".[72]

Fu has also applied the concept of "dualism" or "duality" to the operation of the legal system generally. In his view, China is moving towards a judicial system in which the great majority of cases — "ordinary cases" — will be handled by the courts independently and professionally in accordance with the law, while the Party-State (which exercises "self-restraint" in the great majority of cases) reserves the power to intervene in what it considers "politically sensitive" cases, such as corruption cases involving the higher levels of the political elite or cases in which dissidents are prosecuted.[73] Thus, a "normal legal system" — in which there is "semi-autonomy of private law" — exists side by side with a "prerogative state" or "exceptional state" unconstrained by law.[74] He went on to state:

> Like the proverbial elephant that was touched by a blind man, Chinese law, reflecting Chinese political and socio-economic realities, takes different shapes. It is highly compartmentalised, and depending on where it is touched, one finds expanding gaps where law is largely irrelevant; legal traps where a thin legal veil tries to cover political repression; and legal practices of varying levels of institutionalisation but largely compatible with counterparts in any mature legal system.[75]

If we adopt the concept of differential degrees of realisation of the Rule of Law in different domains of the Chinese State and society, then the next

71. Fu (N67) 259–260.
72. *Ibid.*, 273.
73. Fu Hualing, "Building Judicial Integrity in China" (2016) 39 *Hastings International and Comparative Law Review* 167–181.
74. Fu Hualing, "Duality and China's Struggle for Legal Autonomy" (2019) 1 *China Perspectives* 3.
75. *Ibid.*, 4.

question is whether it is possible (and likely), in the absence of any revolution or revolutionary change of the existing political system of the Party-State, for the Rule of Law to be gradually extended to cover all domains of the Chinese State and society. This is an important question, because it is arguable that insofar as the Party reserves the right to intervene selectively in any matter or case in which it considers it necessary, expedient, or desirable to intervene, there is no Rule of Law, because Rule of Law is the antithesis of arbitrary power.[76] This point is well illustrated by the following passage by Fu Hualing: "[W]hile China may have been taking steps towards a rule-based legal system, in times of extraordinary threats, real or perceived, the limited rule of law and legal constraint on political powers vanish quickly."[77] What kind of Rule of Law is it if it can easily "vanish" when put to the test?

The crux of the matter, which concerns the compatibility between the Rule of Law and the supremacy of CCP rule, has been elucidated in recent years by theorists or advocates of "socialist constitutionalism", "state-party constitutionalism", and "single-party constitutional state" such as Tong Zhiwei,[78] Jiang Shigong,[79] and Larry Backer.[80] Unlike liberal scholars in China who do not agree that the monopoly of political power by the CCP is legitimate or should be given constitutional and legal recognition, these scholars accept the political reality or even legitimacy of Party rule in China, and seek to render it consistent with the Rule of Law or constitutionalism.

---

76. See generally Brian Z. Tamanaha, *On the Rule of Law: History, Politics, Theory* (Cambridge: Cambridge University Press, 2004); Tom Bingham, *The Rule of Law* (London: Allen Lane, 2010); Martin Krygier, "Rule of Law" in Michel Rosenfeld and András Sajó (eds.), *Oxford Handbook of Comparative Constitutional Law* (Oxford: Oxford University Press, 2012) ch. 10, 233–249.

77. Fu (N65) 309.

78. Tong Zhiwei (童之偉), 《中國憲制之維新》 [*The Reform and Renewal of China's Constitutionalism System*] (Hong Kong: City University of Hong Kong Press, 2016).

79. Jiang Shigong, "Written and Unwritten Constitutions: A New Approach to the Study of Constitutional Government in China" (2010) 36:1 *Modern China* 12–46; Jiang Shigong, "Chinese-style Constitutionalism: On Backer's Chinese Party-State Constitutionalism" (2014) 40:2 *Modern China* 133–167; Jiang Shigong (強世功), "黨章與憲法：多元一體法治共和國的建構" [Party Charter and State Constitution: The Construction of a Pluralistic but Unified Rule of Law Republic] (2015) 4 *Wenhua zongheng* (文化縱橫) [*Across Cultures*] 18–29.

80. Larry Catá Backer, "The Party as Polity, the Communist Party, and the Chinese Constitutional State: A Theory of State-Party Constitutionalism" (2009) 16:1 *Journal of Chinese and Comparative Law* 101.

## CONSTITUTIONALISM IN CHINA?[81]

Take, for example, the thesis of "socialist constitutionalism" as advocated by Tong Zhiwei.[82] Given the political reality and *de facto* legitimacy of the CCP's monopoly of power in China, socialist constitutionalism should seek to render CCP rule consistent with the Rule of Law and constitutionalism. This should be done by introducing and implementing constitutional and legal norms that define in detail the scope of the power of Party organs and personnel (including the respective boundaries of the power of State institutions and Party organs), and subject such power to precise legal control, regulation, and supervision. The existing Constitution of the PRC refers to the principle of CCP leadership, but does not contain provisions elaborating the legal implications or operation of this principle. In PRC legislation, legal norms governing the operation of the Party are almost completely absent. Thus, socialist constitutionalism would require not only precise constitutional definition of the meaning and operation of CCP leadership, but also the enactment of a comprehensive set of laws to regulate the exercise of power by the Party, and their effective enforcement by the judicial system.

In China today, socialist constitutionalism as advocated by Tong and his supporters and allies is opposed by both liberals and conservatives. Liberals believe in Western-style liberal democracy, and strongly object to the proposition that the monopoly of political power by the CCP is legitimate or should be given constitutional and legal recognition. On the other hand, conservatives believe that the existing political system — as a component of the "China Model" — has served China well and has contributed to its rapid economic and social development in the last few decades, and that there is no need to subject the Party to the legal norms of the State.

As far as the Party-State regime is concerned, developments in the Xi Jinping era suggest that the Party-State is not receptive to advocates of socialist constitutionalism. For example, although the Decision of the Fourth Plenum of the Eighteenth CCP Central Committee in 2014 on "ruling

81. This section draws on the author's book review, "*The Reform and Renewal of China's Constitutional System* by Tong Zhiwei" (2018) 16 *International Journal of Constitutional Law* 728.

82. See Tong's Chinese book, *ibid*.

the country according to law"[83] advocated, *inter alia*, the strengthening of the system of rules and regulations governing the Party (i.e., "intra-Party regulations" enacted by Party organs in accordance with the Charter of the CCP), there was no suggestion or intention to turn such rules and regulations into the laws and regulations of China's legal system, which — unlike Party rules and regulations — are enacted in accordance with the norms and procedures prescribed by China's Constitution and laws, publicly promulgated and enforceable before the courts of law. Although Xi Jinping's report at the Nineteenth National Congress of the CCP in October 2017 and the 2018 Constitutional Amendment legitimise the idea of "constitutional review" (*hexianxing shencha*, 合憲性審查), there is no suggestion or intention to alter the existing relationship between the Party and the constitutional and legal systems of the State, or to revise the Constitution to provide concrete norms on how the principle of Party leadership should operate.

Putting aside the question of whether it is likely that Tong's "socialist constitutionalism" proposal would be seriously considered by the CCP regime for implementation in the foreseeable future, the question remains as to whether "socialist constitutionalism" (as advocated by Tong) is theoretically defensible as a genuine form of constitutionalism. This in turn depends on how we understand the term "constitutionalism", of which there is no universally agreed definition. Most definitions of constitutionalism would require, at the minimum, the existence of constitutional and legal norms and institutions (including institutional checks and balance) that secure enforceable or effective constitutional and legal limitations on the exercise of state power, so that the likelihood of such power being abused can be minimised. If this is our understanding of constitutionalism, then it is highly doubtful whether constitutionalism can exist in any political-legal system in which absolute power is vested in one person, such as the leader of one political party in a one-party system.

What if this one-party has developed a system of rules and institutions which operate in such a manner that the party leader does not exercise absolute power, but their power is effectively limited and constrained? For example,

83. See Peerenboom, "Fly High the Banner" (N51); Sanzhu Zhu, "Socialist Rule of Law in the 21st Century" (2015) 7 *Hague Journal on the Rule of Law* 75; Jianfu Chen, "The Transformation of Chinese Law: Mark II" (2015) 45 *Hong Kong Law Journal* 911.

what if there exist independent courts, either within the Party[84] or outside it but within the State, which can adjudicate effectively even in cases concerning Party leaders, including the top leader? It is arguable that this would amount to a version of constitutionalism, but only if the constitution (as suggested by Tong) effectively regulates one-party rule, and does not purport to give all citizens equal political rights[85] in terms of freedom to form and join political parties and the right to be candidates in (as well as to vote in) elections.[86] Moreover, if such a constitution is drafted, would it be adopted by "We, the People" in exercising their constituent power of making a constitution, such as by a referendum of all citizens? The PRC Constitution currently does not require a referendum for the purpose of its revision or of the making of a new constitution. However, by imagining the scenarios mentioned above and raising such questions, we may come to understand how difficult and unlikely it would be for socialist constitutionalism to be realised in China.

## CONCLUSION

This book is titled *The Changing Legal Orders in Hong Kong and Mainland China*, with the emphasis being on "changing". Change is inevitable in legal orders, as it is in all human affairs. This book seeks to explore such change in its historical, political, and social contexts, not only for the purpose of understanding the nature of such change and the reasons behind it, but also to situate the present circumstances within history and to ponder possible future trends.

**Part I** of this book reviews the major constitutional and legal developments in the HKSAR since it was established in 1997. These chapters show how difficult it has been to manage the constitutional and legal dimensions

84. As suggested by Larry C. Backer, "A Constitutional Court for China Within the Chinese Communist Party" (2010) 43 *Suffolk University Law Review* 593.

85. Citizens' lack of political rights under socialist constitutionalism is recognised by Larry Catá Backer (N80).

86. If the Constitution purports to give citizens equal political rights which are in practice denied to them, this would be a "sham constitution", which is necessarily contrary to constitutionalism. On the other hand, if the constitution of a one-party state honestly stipulates that one-party rule is to be practised, then the existence of one-party rule does not render it a sham constitution. See David S. Law and Mila Versteeg, "Sham Constitutions" (2013) 101 *California Law Review* 863.

of OCTS by using various crises and challenges as examples, such as the article 23 controversy in 2003, the Occupy Central Movement in 2014, and the Anti-Extradition Bill Movement in 2019. OCTS is an experiment in the practice of the Rule of Law and constitutionalism, with the autonomy of and the protection of civil liberties in the HKSAR being secured by the Basic Law of the HKSAR. The Rule of Law in the HKSAR is at least partially dependent on the Rule of Law in mainland China. Generally speaking, the Rule of Law and autonomy in the HKSAR have worked reasonably well in the first one and a half decades of its history, but increasing tensions and conflicts in recent years have thrown the viability of OCTS into doubt.

**Part II** of this book analyses the development of Rule of Law (or what some would say Rule *by* Law) in modern Chinese history. It begins with the story of Confucianism and Legalism in China's long legal and political tradition, and then demonstrates the challenges that modern China has faced in its quest for legal reform and modernisation. Considerable progress has been made, drawing from both the Soviet legal tradition and the Continental European legal tradition. However, as "law and society" studies reveal, there is still a considerable gap between "law in the books" and "law in action". Indeed, legal system building in the post-Mao era of "reform and opening" has resulted in legal norms and institutions that facilitate rapid economic development and effective governance by the Party-State. It has not, however, ushered in a liberal constitutional-legal order that secures civil and political rights that are well-protected in Western legal systems. This is an important factor that fuels Hong Kong people's lack of confidence in the Chinese legal system as well as in the maintenance of Hong Kong's own "system" under OCTS.

By exploring constitutional developments elsewhere in Asia, **Part III** of this book examines the possible grounds for optimism or hope regarding changing legal orders in the region. There appear to be more similarities than differences among societies, peoples, and nations in the contemporary world. Although each has its own historical trajectory, there are numerious political, economic, and social forces and dynamics that operate similarly almost everywhere in the world, just as there are universal aspirations of humankind that have found increasing degrees of expression and recognition through globalisation. Legal orders and the societies they serve are never stagnant; social and legal change will never cease. How and what changes will occur will depend on the operation of these forces, dynamics, and aspirations in the years to come.

# *Selected Bibliography*

The following is a list of Professor Chen's major publications related to the themes of this volume, other than those reprinted in the earlier chapters. The list is divided into four sections based on the four relevant fields of study.

## HONG KONG CONSTITUTIONAL LAW

### Books

*Hong Kong's Legal System and the Basic Law*《香港法制與基本法》(Hong Kong: Wide Angle Press, 1986) [in Chinese].

*Human Rights and the Rule of Law: The Challenges of Hong Kong's Transition*《人權與法治：香港過渡期的挑戰》(Hong Kong: Wide Angle Press, 1987) (co-authored with Johannes M.M. Chan) [in Chinese].

*The Basic Law and Hong Kong's Future* (Singapore: Butterworths, 1988) (co-edited with Peter Wesley-Smith).

*Law and Politics in Hong Kong* 《香港法律與香港政治》(Hong Kong: Wide Angle Press, 1990) [in Chinese].

*Hong Kong's Explorations in the Rule of Law Under One Country Two Systems*《一國兩制下香港的法治探索》(Hong Kong: Chung Hwa Bookstore, 2nd edition, 2014).

*Perspectives on the Hong Kong Basic Law*《香港基本法面面觀》(Hong Kong: Joint Publishing, 2015) (co-edited with Zou Pingxue) [in Chinese].

*General Principles of Hong Kong Law*《香港法概論》(Hong Kong: Joint Publishing, 3rd edition, 2015) (co-edited with Jonathan Cheung, Johannes Chan, and Alice Lee) [in Chinese].

*Democracy and Elections*《民主與選舉》(Hong Kong: Cosmos Books, 2017) (co-authored with Zhao Xinshu) [in Chinese].

### Articles/book chapters

"The Development of Immigration Law and Policy: The Hong Kong Experience" (1988) 33:4 *McGill Law Journal* 631–675.

"From Colony to Special Administrative Region: Hong Kong's Constitutional Journey" in Raymond Wacks (ed.), *The Future of the Law in Hong Kong* (Hong Kong: Oxford University Press, 1989), chapter 3, pp. 76–126.

"The Basic Law and the Protection of Property Rights" (1993) 23 *Hong Kong Law Journal* 31–78.

"Constitutional Crisis in Hong Kong: Congressional Supremacy and Judicial Review" (1999) 33 *The International Lawyer* 1025–1040.

"The Interpretation of the Basic Law: Common Law and Mainland Chinese Perspectives" (2000) 30 *Hong Kong Law Journal* 380–431.

"*Ng Ka-ling* and Article 158(3) of the Basic Law" (2001–2002) 5:2 *Journal of Chinese and Comparative Law* 222–247.

"Hong Kong's Legal System in the New Constitutional Order" in Jianfu Chen, Yuwen Li, and Jan Michiel Otto (eds.), *Implementation of Law in the People's Republic of China* (The Hague: Kluwer Law International, 2002), chapter 11, pp. 213–245.

"Debating Rule of Law in the Hong Kong Special Administrative Region, 1997–2002" in Randall Peerenboom (ed.), *Asian Discourses of Rule of Law* (London: Routledge, 2004), chapter 8, pp. 250–285 (co-authored with Anne Cheung).

"Constitutional Adjudication in Post-1997 Hong Kong" (2006) 15 *Pacific Rim Law and Policy Journal* 627–682.

"The Basic Law and the Development of the Political System in Hong Kong" (2007) 15 *Asia Pacific Law Review* 19–40.

"The Theory, Constitution and Practice of Autonomy: The Case of Hong Kong" in Jorge Oliveira and Paulo Cardinal (eds.), *One Country, Two Systems, Three Legal Orders — Perspectives of Evolution* (Berlin: Springer, 2009), pp. 751–767.

"International Human Rights Law and Domestic Constitutional Law: Internationalisation of Constitutional Law in Hong Kong" (2009) 4:3 *National Taiwan University Law Review* 237–333.

"The Basic Law Jurisprudence of the Court of Final Appeal" in Simon N.M. Young and Yash Ghai (eds.), *Hong Kong's Court of Final Appeal: The Development of the Law in China's Hong Kong* (Cambridge: Cambridge University Press, 2014), chapter 14, pp. 352–390 (co-authored with P.Y. Lo).

"Unity and Plurality: The Basic Laws of the Special Administrative Regions under 'One Country, Two Systems'" in Zhang Qianfan [張千帆] (ed.), *Constitutional Law*《憲法學》(Beijing: Law Press, 3rd edition, 2015), chapter 12, pp. 480–527 [in Chinese].

"Development of Representative Government" in Johannes Chan and C.L. Lim (eds.), *Law of the Hong Kong Constitution* (Hong Kong: Sweet & Maxwell, 2nd edition, 2015), chapter 8, pp. 245–289.

"The Law and Politics of the Struggle for Universal Suffrage in Hong Kong, 2013–15" (2016) 3 *Asian Journal of Law and Society* 189–207.

"Hong Kong's Legal System and Judiciary in the Colonial Era" [殖民地時代香港的法制與司法], in Wang Gungwu [王賡武] (ed.), *Hong Kong History: New Perspectives*《香港史新編》, volume 1 (Hong Kong: Joint Publishing, 2017), chapter 10, pp. 445–482 (co-authored with Michael Ng and Christopher Munn) [in Chinese].

"The Implementation of the Basic Law and 'One Country, Two Systems': Review and Reflections" [《基本法》與'一國兩制'實施的回顧與反思] (2017) 34:1 *Shenzhen University Journal (Humanities and Social Sciences)*《深圳大學學報（人民社會科學版）》31–36 [in Chinese].

"Hong Kong's Judiciary under 'One Country, Two Systems'" in H.P. Lee and Marilyn Pittard (eds.), *Asia-Pacific Judiciaries: Independence, Impartiality and Integrity* (Cambridge: Cambridge University Press, 2018), chapter 7, pp. 131–168 (co-authored with P.Y. Lo).

"The Constitutional Orders of 'One Country, Two Systems': A Comparative Study of the Visible and Invisible Bases of Constitutional Review and Proportionality Analysis in the Chinese Special Administrative Regions of Hong Kong and Macau" in Rosalind Dixon and Adrienne Stone (eds.), *The Invisible Constitution in Comparative Perspective* (Cambridge: Cambridge University Press, 2018), chapter 8, pp. 230–267 (co-authored with P.Y. Lo).

"The Judicial Perspective of 'Separation of Powers' in the Hong Kong Special Administrative Region of the People's Republic of China" (2018) 5:2 *Journal of International and Comparative Law* 337–362 (co-authored with P.Y. Lo).

"The Oath-taking Cases and the NPCSC Interpretation of 2016" (2019) *Hong Kong Law Journal* 381–415 (co-authored with Han Zhu).

"Hong Kong in China: The Project of 'One Country, Two Systems' and the Question of National Security" in Cora Chan and Fiona de Londras (eds.),

*China's National Security: Endangering Hong Kong's Rule of Law* (London: Bloomsbury Academic/Hart Publishing, 2020), chapter 2, pp. 19–39.

"Yash Ghai and the Constitutional Experiment of 'One Country, Two Systems' in Hong Kong" in Humphrey Sipalla (ed.), *Liber amicorum Yash Pal Ghai* (Nairobi: Strathmore University Press, forthcoming), available at: www.academia.edu/42353225/Yash_Ghai_and_the_Constitutional_Experiment_of_One_Country_Two_Systems_in_Hong_Kong (co-authored with Cora Chan).

"Hong Kong" in David S. Law, Holning Lau, and Alex Schwartz (eds.), *Oxford Handbook of Constitutional Law in Asia* (Oxford: Oxford University Press, forthcoming).

## CHINESE LAW

### Books

*Legal Reforms in China and Vietnam: A Comparison of Asian Communist Regimes* (London: Routledge, 2010) (co-edited with John Gillespie).

*An Introduction to the Chinese Legal System* (Hong Kong: LexisNexis, 5th edition, 2019).

### Articles/book chapters

"Human Rights in China: A Brief Historical Review" in Raymond Wacks (ed.), *Human Rights in Hong Kong* (Hong Kong: Oxford University Press, 1992), chapter 5, pp. 176–221.

"Developing Theories of Rights and Human Rights in China" in Raymond Wacks (ed.), *Hong Kong, China and 1997: Essays in Legal Theory* (Hong Kong: Hong Kong University Press, 1993), chapter 5, pp. 123–149.

"The Developing Theory of Law and Market Economy in Contemporary China" in Wang Guiguo and Wei Zhenying (eds.), *Legal Developments in China: Market Economy and Law* (Hong Kong: Sweet & Maxwell, 1996), pp. 3–20.

"The Developing Chinese Law and the Civil Law Tradition" in M. Brosseau, S. Pepper, and S.K. Tsang (eds.), *China Review 1996* (Hong Kong: Chinese University Press, 1996), pp. 29–59.

"Rational Law, Economic Development and the Case of China" (1999) 8 *Social and Legal Studies* 97–120.

"Toward a Legal Enlightenment: Discussions in Contemporary China on the Rule of Law" (1999) 17 *UCLA Pacific Basin Law Journal* 125–165.

"Constitutions and Values in Three Chinese Societies" in Dennis Davis, Alan Richter, and Cheryl Saunders (eds.), *An Inquiry into the Existence of Global Values: Through the Lens of Comparative Constitutional Law* (Oxford: Hart Publishing, 2015), chapter 5, pp. 119–154.

"China's Long March Towards Rule of Law or China's Turn against Law?" (2016) 4 *Chinese Journal of Comparative Law* 1–35.

"The Chinese Tradition of Administrative Law" in Peter Cane, Herwig Hofmann, Eric Ip, and Peter Lindseth (eds.), *Oxford Handbook of Comparative Administrative Law* (Oxford: Oxford University Press, 2020), chapter 4, pp. 79–95.

"Constitutions and Constitutionalism: China" in David S. Law (ed.), *Constitutionalism in Context* (Cambridge: Cambridge University Press, forthcoming).

## ASIAN PUBLIC LAW

### Books

*Human Rights in Asia* (London: Routledge, 2006) (co-edited with Randall Peerenboom and Carole J. Petersen).

*Administrative Law and Governance in Asia: Comparative Perspectives* (London: Routledge, 2009) (co-edited with Tom Ginsburg).

*Public Law in East Asia* (Farnham: Ashgate, 2013) (co-edited with Tom Ginsburg).

*Constitutionalism in Asia in the Early Twenty-First Century* (Cambridge: Cambridge University Press, 2014) (edited volume).

*Constitutional Courts in Asia: A Comparative Perspective* (Cambridge University Press, 2018) (co-edited with Andrew Harding).

### Articles/book chapters

"Comparative Reflections on Human Rights in Asia" in Randall Peerenboom, Carole J. Petersen, and Albert H.Y. Chen (eds.), *Human Rights in Asia* (London: Routledge, 2006), chapter 16, pp. 487–516.

"A Tale of Two Islands: Comparative Reflections on Constitutionalism in Hong Kong and Taiwan" (2007) 37 *Hong Kong Law Journal* 647–688.

"Reflections on Administrative Law and Judicialized Governance in East and Southeast Asia" in Tom Ginsburg and Albert H.Y. Chen (eds.), *Administrative Law and Governance in Asia: Comparative Perspectives* (London: Routledge, 2009), pp. 359–380.

"Emergency Powers, Constitutionalism and Legal Transplants: the East Asian Experience" in Victor V. Ramraj and Arun K. Thiruvengadam (eds.), *Emergency Powers in Asia: Exploring the Limits of Legality* (Cambridge: Cambridge University Press, 2010), chapter 3, pp. 56–88.

"Comparing Legal Development in China and Vietnam" in John Gillespie and Albert H.Y. Chen (eds.), *Legal Reforms in China and Vietnam: A Comparison of Asian Communist Regimes* (London: Routledge, 2010), chapter 1, pp. 1–25 (co-authored with John Gillespie).

"Pathways of Western Liberal Constitutional Development in Asia: A Comparative Study of Five Major Nations" (2010) 8 *International Journal of Constitutional Law* 849–884.

"The Judiciary, Constitutional Review and Constitutional Interpretation" in Mark Tushnet, Thomas Fleiner, and Cheryl Saunders (eds.), *Routledge Handbook of Constitutional Law* (Abingdon, Oxon.: Routledge, 2012), chapter 8, pp. 97–109 (co-authored with M.P. Maduro).

"Introduction: Constitutionalism and Constitutional Change in East and Southeast Asia: A Historical and Comparative Overview" in Albert H.Y. Chen and Tom Ginsburg (eds.), *Public Law in East Asia* (Farnham: Ashgate, 2013), pp xv–xlvii.

"The Achievement of Constitutionalism in Asia: Moving Beyond 'Constitutions Without Constitutionalism'" in Albert H.Y. Chen (ed.), *Constitutionalism in Asia in the Early Twenty-First Century* (Cambridge: Cambridge University Press, 2014), chapter 1, pp. 1–31.

"Western Constitutionalism in Southeast Asia: Some Historical and Comparative Observations" in Dirk Ehlers, Henning Glaser, and Kittisak Prokati (eds.), *Constitutionalism and Good Governance: Eastern and Western Perspectives* (Baden-Baden: Nomos, 2014), pp. 63–80.

"Constitutional Courts in Asia: Western Origins and Asian Practice" in Albert H.Y. Chen and Andrew Harding (eds.), *Constitutional Courts in Asia: A Comparative Perspective* (Cambridge: Cambridge University Press, 2018), chapter 1, pp. 1–31.

## LEGAL AND POLITICAL PHILOSOPHY

### Books

*Ideals of the Rule of Law, Human Rights and Constitutional Democracy* 《法治、人權與民主憲政的理想》(Hong Kong: Commercial Press, 2012) [in Chinese].

*The Rule of Law, Enlightenment and the Spirit of Modern Law* 《法治、啟蒙與現代法的精神》(Beijing: Chinese University of Politics and Law Press, 2nd edition, 2013) [in Chinese].

*The World of Jurisprudence* 《法理學的世界》(Beijing: Chinese University of Politics and Law Press, 2nd edition, 2013) [in Chinese].

*Rule of Law and Human Rights in Western Civilisation* 《西方文明中的法治和人權》(Hong Kong: Commercial Press, 2013) [in Chinese].

*Chinese Traditional Culture and Modern Constitutional Democracy* 《中國傳統文化與現代民主憲政》(Hong Kong: Commercial Press, 2013) [in Chinese].

*The World of Constitutionalism* 《憲法學的世界》(Beijing: Chinese University of Politics and Law Press, 2014) [in Chinese].

### Articles/book chapters

"The Philosophy of Language Rights" (1998) 20:1 *Language Sciences* 45–54.

"The Rise of Rights: Some Comparative Civilizational Reflections" (1998) 25 *Journal of Chinese Philosophy* 5–30.

"Law, Development and the Typology of Legal Systems" (1999–2000) 4:1–2 *Journal of Chinese and Comparative Law* 30–49.

"The Political Thought of Twenty-First Century China" in Joseph C.W. Chan and Leung Man-to (eds.), *Political Theory in China* 《政治理論在中國》(Hong Kong: Oxford University Press, 2001), chapter 2, pp. 12–25 [in Chinese].

"Mediation, Litigation, and Justice: Confucian Reflections in a Modern Liberal Society" in Daniel A. Bell and Hahm Chaibong (eds.), *Confucianism for the Modern World* (Cambridge: Cambridge University Press, 2003), chapter 11, pp. 257–287.

"Is Confucianism Compatible with Liberal Constitutional Democracy?" (2007) 34:2 *Journal of Chinese Philosophy* 195–216.

"The Concept of 'Datong' in Chinese Philosophy as an Expression of the Idea of the Common Good" in David Solomon and P.C. Lo (eds.), *The Common Good: Chinese and American Perspectives* (Dordrecht: Springer, 2014), chapter 5, pp. 85–102.

"Confucianism and Constitutionalism: The Life and Vocation of Zhang Junmai" (2014) 1 *China Law Review*《中國法律評論》127–137 [in Chinese].

"The Discourse of Political Constitutionalism in Contemporary China" (2014) 14:2 *China Review* 183–214.